# GOODWOOD

# GOODWOOD

## ART AND ARCHITECTURE, SPORT AND FAMILY

ROSEMARY BAIRD

F

FRANCES LINCOLN LIMITED
PUBLISHERS

Frances Lincoln Limited
4 Torriano Mews
Torriano Avenue
London NW5 2RZ
www.franceslincoln.com

*Goodwood: Art and Architecture, Sport and Family*

For copyright of illustrations see page 243



British Library Cataloguing in Publication Data
A catalogue record for this book is available from the British Library.

ISBN 978-0-7112-2769-9

Designed by Elizabeth McWilliams

Printed in China

9 8 7 6 5 4 3 2 1

## Note on Names

All the heirs to the Richmond dukedom were christened Charles. For this reason they have to be talked about by their number. The only Duke of Richmond not to have been called Charles was Frederick, the 9th Duke: this was because his elder brother Charles, Lord Settrington, predeceased him. From the 6th Duke onwards they were all christened Charles Henry, initially after the Waterloo hero Henry, Marquis of Anglesey, maternal grandfather of the 6th Duke.

The present holder of the title is the 10th Duke of Richmond and Lennox, 5th Duke of Gordon and Duke of Aubigny. For brevity the numbering usually refers only to the first dukedom.

It is incorrect to speak of duchesses by number in the way that is accepted for their husbands. However, in a family where confusion is especially created by the name repetition mentioned above, it is occasionally handy to refer in the text to the wives by inclusion of the duke's number in brackets.

## Note on Dates

Prior to the introduction of the Gregorian calendar in 1752, the period 1 January to 24 March was reckoned not as being the first months of the New Year, but as the last months of the old. This potentially confusing situation is sometimes simplified by the use of double dates, e.g. 24 March 1745/6, then followed chronologically at the change of year by 25 March 1746. In this book, dates have been modernised, as from 1738/9 to 1739. In Europe the calendar was eleven days behind that of Great Britain.

For Rory, Cressida and Leonie,

who have always tolerated my historical distractions
with generosity, jokes, and great good humour.

# CONTENTS

An extempore poem by Ld Chesterfield on the Dutchess of Richmond, Ao 1730

What do Schollars, and Bards, & Philosophers wise,
Mean by Stuffing ones head with such nonsense & lyes?
By telling one Venus must always appear
In a Car, or a Shell, or a twinkling Star
Drawn by Sparrows, or Swans, a Dolphin or Doves,
And attended in form by the Graces & Loves!
That Ambrosia and Nectar is all she will tast*(e)*,
And a passport to hearts is a belt round her waist!
Without all this trouble, I saw the bright dame,
To Supper last night to *Poultney's* she came,
In a good warm sedan; no fine open car,
Two Chairmen her doves, & a flambeau her Star:
No Nectar She drank, no Ambrosia she eat,
Her cup was plain Claret, and Chicken her meat.
Nor wanted she Cestus her bosom to grace,
For Richmond that night had lent her her face.

# FOREWORD

THE DUKE OF RICHMOND AND GORDON

I welcome this new book on the history of my home and family. The house is of course at the heart of everything that we do on the estate, and the art and architecture have never before been assessed within their wider Georgian context. Our objective at Goodwood is to enable the family to continue to live here happily whilst making it possible both for the people who work here and for the local community to enjoy it as well. I think the convivial way in which people enjoy Goodwood now is not necessarily so very different from the experiences of much earlier visitors, who always appreciated the glorious location and sunlit rooms.

All the horseracing, motor racing, golf, flying, shooting and cricket that take place on the estate have grown from the passions and enthusiasms of various members of the family over the last three hundred years. I am a firm believer that both art and sport lift the spirits, and I hope that this book will provide an insight into the way life has always been enjoyed at Goodwood, both then and now.

*Richmond*

# INTRODUCTION

'I am not just some hunting, shooting and fishing old buffer,' declared the present Duke of Richmond in 2003, quoted in the columns of *The Financial Times*. The Dukes of Richmond have often been radical, have usually been family-minded and have always loved Goodwood. With the exception of the 1st Duke, they have always been conscientious, responsible and hard working.

The Dukes of Richmond are directly descended from Charles II. Like the Dukes of Grafton, Buccleuch and St Albans, they are more closely related to the Merry Monarch than is the present Royal Family, which descends from his grandfather, James I. Theirs is the fourth creation of Dukes of Richmond, dating from 1675.

Their home at Goodwood is situated a couple of miles south of St Roche's Hill, known as the Trundle, which from the fifth to the first century BC was a fortified city lived in by Celts. The tribe descended to the coast, building the port which was taken over by the Romans to become Chichester. In the Middle Ages the Saxon Earl Godwin or Goduinus owned much of the area, and 'Goodwood' may derive from his name. The area was dominated by Boxgrove Priory, a large medieval monastery which was dissolved by Henry VIII, and by Halnaker or 'Halfnaked' House. In the later seventeenth century the Charlton Hunt was the catalyst for the development of both Goodwood and Uppark.

There are two main collector dukes in the history of Goodwood, and this book concentrates on them. Charles Lennox, 2nd Duke of Richmond, Lennox and Aubigny (1701–50), became one of the main proponents of the Palladian movement in architecture, commissioning Lord Burlington to build him a fabulous new house on the banks of the Thames at Whitehall and adding an important new wing to Goodwood. The 2nd Duke's life and achievements have never been properly appraised, although, as the major influence in the creation of the two great family homes, his

story accounts for a large part of the history of Goodwood. All the Dukes of Richmond are directly descended from this ancestor.

Pride of place is shared with his son, Charles Lennox, 3rd Duke of Richmond, Lennox and Aubigny (1735–1806), who succeeded to the titles in 1750. This Duke has taken the limelight in recent years. As ambassador, politican, soldier and courtier, he fulfilled many public roles, while also playing the largest part in the development of the Goodwood that we see today. As his political and military life has already been documented, and this is a story of a house, the chapters focus on his personal life and art collecting.

Although the 4th Duke of Richmond did not greatly influence the house, material evidence of his life history is much in evidence, with trophies of Waterloo. The history of the Georgian house is completed with the 5th Duke (1791–1860), who finished off his great-uncle's interiors and developed the racecourse that he had begun. The interiors were completed just as Queen Victoria came to the throne. Although the two Victorian Dukes (5th and 6th) were each head of the family for over forty years, and although they both worked hard to develop the estate, this, the tale of the house, is not so much their story. The history of how the 5th Duke ran the estate is told elsewhere, as is as the story of his military, political and racing life. The Edwardian era saw the heyday of Goodwood as a seat of hospitality and entertainment.

The Duchesses are by no means forgotten. Paintings and furniture acquired by Louise de Keroualle, Duchess of Portsmouth, and brought back from France to Goodwood after her death, form the earliest group of items in the collection. In 2001, an exhibition of the talents and interests of the Duchesses of Richmond was shown at the House. Ironically for an author with a particular interest in patronage by women in the Georgian period, at Goodwood the building and collecting was mostly done by the men. However, whenever the contribution of the ladies can be

The Card Room, with the 3rd Duke's collection of Sèvres porcelain.

found in the documents, it is shown. Especially to be noted are the holding together of a family by Anne Brudenell (1669–1722); the organisation of the household by Sarah Cadogan (1706–1751); and the bossy matchmaking of Charlotte Gordon (1768–1842).

In the twentieth and twenty-first centuries the Dukes of Richmond have continued to love Goodwood, first gaining professional qualifications and working in the wider world before bringing their talents to bear on the estate. Both the 9th and the 10th Dukes handed the running of the estate down a generation, so the present Duke and the Earl of March both took over at the age of about forty. This has resulted in a dynamic and constantly evolving way of running what is at heart a traditional venture. It also means that the house is lived in by a young family. One of the delights of Goodwood is that the family has not had to retreat from the rooms that it has used since 1750, the more formal State Apartments being a Regency expansion from its original core.

Many mysteries remain. Were there Jacobite meetings in Charlton? What is the story of the Hôtel Lenox in Paris? How near to the house were the 2nd Duke's wild animals kept? Will any

further details come to light of his influence on Canaletto's career? The 3rd Duke's papers are still missing, leaving many more gaps. Henrietta Le Clerc claimed to have handed all her father's papers over to the 4th Duke, but they have never come to light.[1] Where did George Stubbs stay while he was at Goodwood? How many rare breeds of animal did the 3rd Duke keep at Goodwood? Was Madame de Cambis, the aristocratic French mistress of the 3rd Duke, the mother of his natural daughter, Henrietta Le Clerc? How well did the 3rd Duke know Sir William Hamilton? Did he meet Nelson? To what extent did the 3rd Duke want the Tapestry Drawing Room to look like those of other houses by Robert Adam? What exactly did the original Egyptian Dining Room look like? What shape was James Wyatt's model for the house? The book tries to answer these questions, but they can only be finally solved on the production of new documentary material.

This is therefore primarily the story of two Dukes of Richmond, their families and their homes, spanning the greatest period of all in the history of English architecture, painting, furniture, porcelain, silver and collecting, that of the Georgians (1714–1830). At the heart of the enormous enterprise that is now Goodwood lies their creation, the great historic house, flinted and turreted, gleaming in the evening sun or stony in the snow.

# 1  THE BEGINNINGS

## CHARLES, 1ST DUKE OF RICHMOND, 1672–1723

On a summer's day in 1672, a dark-haired, rosy-cheeked young Frenchwoman gave birth to a son in her bedchamber at Whitehall Palace. She gave him his father's Christian name of Charles. His surname of Fitzroy reflected the fact that the baby was a bastard; but also that he was the son of a king.

When the twenty-two-year-old Louise René de Penancoët de Keroualle (1649–1734) bore the child of her lover Charles II, King of England, she was alone in a foreign land. Her parents, the Comte and Comtesse de Penancoët de Keroualle, lived at the remote Château de Keroual near Brest in Brittany. Aristocratic, religious and morally scrupulous, they thoroughly disapproved of their daughter's relationship with the King of England. They saw it as immoral, as unworthy of a well-educated convent girl. The fact that they had not had enough funds to provide their daughter with a dowry must have made it especially galling: had Louise been wealthy, she would have been courted by young men of her own social level. As it was, she was the kept mistress of a king, and one who amused himself with a bevy of mistresses.

After a happy English childhood, Prince Charles's teenage years had been very unstable. During the Civil War he had swerved between the courageous desire to help his father, Charles I, against Cromwell and the Parliamentary forces and the fear of capture, which would be a political disaster. The execution of his father in 1649 was a scar that he would bear for ever. Escaping from England two years later, he spent much time both in Holland and in Paris, bereft of any real purpose. His mother, Queen Henrietta Maria, was half French, half Italian: she was the daughter of Henri IV of France and his queen, Marie de Medici.[1] In her exile from England it was natural for her to live near Paris. Ever a risk-taker, both in exile in these European courts and after his Restoration in 1660, Charles pursued pleasure and the love of many beautiful women. Aged only nineteen, he had a son by Lucy

ABOVE *Charles II*, by Samuel Cooper, signed and dated 1665, watercolour on vellum, 20 × 16 cm / 8 × 6 in. In this very rare and direct image, the King is shown wearing the insignia of the Order of the Garter.

FACING PAGE  Lane at Goodwood.

ABOVE, LEFT    *Princess Henrietta, Duchess of Orléans*, by Sir Peter Lely, oil on canvas, 127 × 101 cm / 50 × 40 in. The freely painted costume in this signed portrait denotes the artist's hand throughout. Henrietta introduced Louise de Keroualle, her maid of honour, to her brother Charles II.

ABOVE, RIGHT    *Frances Teresa Stuart, Duchess of Richmond* (of the earlier creation), by Sir Peter Lely, oil on canvas, 244 × 127 cm / 96 × 50 in. Frances Teresa arrived in England from France in 1662 at the recommendation of Queen Henrietta Maria, who called her 'the most beautiful girl in the world'. Some of the four portraits of her at Goodwood may have come through the gift to Louise de Keroualle of the two Stuart châteaux at Aubigny.

FACING PAGE, LEFT    *Louise de Keroualle, Duchess of Portsmouth, as Venus, with her son Charles as Cupid*, by Henri Gascars, oil on canvas, 137 × 112 cm / 54 × 44 in. The King called her 'My dearest, dearest Fubbs'. The French painter was the protégé of Louise: there were twelve paintings by him in the 1st Duke's collection.

FACING PAGE, RIGHT    *Charles Lennox, 1st Duke of Richmond and Lennox, wearing the chain of the Order of the Garter*, by William Wissing, oil on canvas, 120 × 100 cm / 47¼ × 39½ in. When the King came to bestow the blue ribbon of the Order of the Garter (which was the less formal version, worn by day) on his nine-year-old son, it was too long to go round his neck, and was placed instead over his left shoulder. The ribbon has been worn this way ever since.

Walters. Despite his dynastic marriage in 1662 to the Portuguese princess Catherine of Braganza, whom he had never previously met, other women of the court bore him many more progeny, not least Barbara Villiers, Countess of Castlemaine, by whom he had six, of which he only admitted five. Nell Gwyn, the Cockney actress famous for her humour and her superb legs, bore him two. Catherine herself tragically proved unable to bear children

and, although he always treated her with public respect, by the time of the birth of Charles Fitzroy the King already had at least fifteen illegitimate children.

## THE MEETING AT THE TREATY OF DOVER

Charles met Louise at Dover Castle in 1670. She had spent all her childhood in Brittany but at the age of nineteen a family friend gained her a position at court, as a maid of honour to Princess Henrietta of England, Duchess of Orléans. Henrietta was the youngest sister of Charles II, and was married to Philippe, Duke of Orléans, the younger brother of Louis XIV, the autocratic Sun King of France. Louise was therefore employed at the heart of the French court. When Louis decided that Henrietta should be sent to England as a diplomat, to negotiate on his behalf a treaty with her brother the English King, Louise was sent in attendance.

This may have been a deliberate ploy by Louis, who knew that his cousin Charles had an eye for a pretty girl. Festivities took place at Dover Castle for the meeting of Charles and his much-loved but long-unseen sister. The Queen also travelled with him from London, in turn bringing her beautiful lady-in-waiting, Frances Teresa, Duchess of Richmond, who had herself once been wooed by the King. After five days of meetings and banquets, the King decided to extend the festivities to a fortnight. He could not bear to see his sister depart.

Finally Henrietta had to leave for France. She asked Louise to take her royal jewel box to the King, so that she could offer her brother some jewels as a parting gift. Instead, Charles turned to the pretty young maid of honour. Gesturing to Louise, he told his sister '*This* is the jewel that I covet.' Farewells were made. The King rowed out in the dinghy with the two young women to their boat or 'packet'. Charles never saw Henrietta again: three weeks later she died, probably of peritonitis.

## The Spy in the Bedchamber

Suddenly Louise de Keroualle had no friend, no mistress and no employment. Events conspired to send her to England. Everyone wanted her to go: Charles wrote personally to invite her to the English court; the Duke of Buckingham offered to send his yacht to collect her; and Louis certainly made no objection. All three had ulterior motives. Charles's enthusiasm for the plan sprang from simply love and lust. Buckingham wanted someone to supplant his own tiresome cousin, Barbara Villiers, in the King's affections. Louis, more politically, wanted Louise to spy on his cousin Charles, to check that he really would privately become a Roman Catholic, as he had secretly promised in the Treaty of Dover. He had also agreed not to hinder Louis in his aggression against Holland. In return for these favours, Louis would give Charles badly needed funds.

The only way that Louis could check on Charles's private devotions was by placing a spy in the bedchamber. This was to be Louise. However, he had reckoned without the girl's pious upbringing. Although Louise came to court at Whitehall in October 1670, and thereafter was visited twice daily by the King in her splendid apartments, it was one whole year before she yielded to his advances. Charles II finally seduced Louise de Keroualle at Euston Hall, near Newmarket, in late October 1671. The courtiers connived in his cause, staging a mock rustic drama, at the end of which Louise and the King were bedded, and a stocking was thrown out of the window to denote the anticipated loss of chastity. Nine months later, on 26 July, she bore him a son.

## The Birth of Charles, 1st Duke of Richmond

Fitzroy was the surname traditionally given to the illegitimate children of the King. Charles's offspring by Barbara Villiers already bore this patronym: the descendants of their second son, the Dukes of Grafton, hold the family name to this day. The baby Charles held the surname for three years. However, on 31 July 1675, when the King was about to create him Duke of Richmond, he wrote to Sir Joseph Williamson, Secretary of State: 'Upon better thoughts I do intende that the Duke of Richmonds name shall be Lenox . . .'[2] The surname is often spelt this way in early documents.

When he selected the surname of Len(n)ox for his son, Charles II was making him the heir to the old medieval dynasty of the Earls of Lennox, whose origins were back in the twelfth century. The King was himself the current senior representative of that line. Thus he deliberately made his youngest son heir to that family tradition and blood line, whose titles and honours had died out in the year of the boy's birth when Charles Stuart, Duke of Richmond and Lennox (Frances Teresa's husband) died in December 1672.

## THE TITLES

There was also a resonance in the use of the name, and later the titles, of Lennox that was particularly appropriate to the son of a Frenchwoman. The Stuart Dukes of Lennox had held family properties at Aubigny-sur-Nère in France for two hundred and fifty years. In this rural location, east of Orléans, a rapport had been formed in the Hundred Years War, when in 1421, by request of the Dauphin, John Stuart of Darnley took four thousand Scotsmen to aid the French in their wars against the English. For this, he was given lands and properties at Aubigny and Concressault by the grateful French. John Stuart was created the 1st Seigneur of Aubigny, from which a further eleven descended.[3] As his wife was the daughter and heiress of the Earl of Len(n)ox, his descendants were also created earls and then, from 1581, dukes of Lennox.

Granting the Lennox lineage to the King's natural son was therefore a clever way of emphasising the boy's royal Stuart and Scottish ancestry, as well as expressing pride in the French connection. Giving him the title as a surname was a way of creating a new dynasty. His coat of arms gave visual expression to his ancestry. The family motto, adopted first by Louise, became 'En La Rose Je Fleurie' (I flourish in the rose). The red Lennox rose has a single layer of petals, unlike the Tudor rose of England, which combined the red rose of Lancaster and the white rose of York in a double format.

The notion of a natural son of the King being Duke of Richmond had a distinguished precedent. Henry VII had originally been 2nd Earl of Richmond, the title emanating from the Yorkshire stronghold of the same name. The first dukedom of Richmond was created by Henry VIII for his natural son Henry Fitzroy, Duke of Somerset and Richmond, in 1525. The boy died aged seventeen, and the title with him.[4] The title of Duke of Richmond was then paired with that of Lennox, firstly in 1623 for Ludovic Stuart, Great Chamberlain of Scotland, with whom it died out the following year. It was re-created in 1641 for his nephew James Stuart, an heroic Royalist commander in the Civil War. The Lennox title was at this time placed first as being the older one. The granting to them of the Richmond dukedom shows how close the Stuart cousins, Dukes of Lennox, had become to the English throne. When James Stuart's nephew, Charles Stuart, 3rd Duke of Richmond, 6th Duke of Lennox and 12th Seigneur of Aubigny, died in 1672, the Richmond dukedom became extinct – and available – for the third time. It was the first time that the Lennox title, which had different rules of succession, had died out.

These different historical layers shows the very clever and appropriate way in which titles were given. In July 1675 the King bestowed the titles of Baron Settrington,[5] Earl of March,[6] and Duke of Richmond (of the fourth creation) on his natural son, Charles Lennox, instructing Lord Treasurer Danby on 8 August 1675. Determined that her son should be the senior duke of the King's children, Louise de Keroualle rushed the patent to Danby that very night. It was signed in the early hours of the morning, on 9 August, just before the Lord Treasurer went away for a few weeks, ensuring that the little Duke of Richmond was quite clearly senior to the progeny of her rival Barbara Villiers. The Scottish titles of Baron Torboulton, Earl of Darnley and Duke of Lennox – making clear the importance of the Lennox ancestry – were added on 9 September. As early as 1763 Louise had been granted Lennox estates at Aubigny, property that had never belonged to her own family. Thus a whole new lineage was created for the boy, with French lands accompanying English and Scottish dukedoms. The French title of Seigneur d'Aubigny reverted to the Crown of France for the time being.

The graduated timing of these announcements suggests that Charles II's thinking was cautious, and it may have been that Louise was partly feeding him the ideas. To cap this, in 1684, following requests to her royal lover, Louise was made Duchess of Aubigny by Louis XIV. Thus the Stuart legacy of estates in France was, on her death in 1734, inherited by the Dukes of Richmond and was held by the family for nearly 170 years, until 1842. The titles of Duke of Lennox and Duke of Aubigny are still two of the present Duke of Richmond's four dukedoms.

A few Stuart items eventually came to Goodwood from Aubigny in 1765, notably a large narrative painting by Livinus de Volgelaare known as *The Icon*. This is the second version of that commissioned in 1567 by the 4th Earl and Countess of Lennox, showing them together with their younger son Charles and their grandson, the future James VI of Scotland and James I of England, grieving at the catafalque of the murdered Lord Darnley, and beseeching revenge. Latin inscriptions angrily implicate Darnley's widow, Mary Queen of Scots, in the murder.

## LIFE AT COURT

Despite the glory of titles and lands, the wonderful jewellery, weighty silver and plethora of pictures, tapestries and furniture given to her by the King, Louise often felt insecure at court. Her first main rival was Barbara Villiers, now Duchess of Cleveland, a beautiful, tempestuous woman. Nell Gwyn was also in favour. Charles liked all his women to get on well with each other, and Louise even entertained the other mistresses in her rooms and owned portraits of Barbara and Nell.[7] Individually, the King constantly assured them of his love. Louise saw that bed was not the only way to his heart, and always ensured that she had marvellous French chefs who could create sumptuous dinners for him in the luxury of her apartments. She suffered a near defeat when he had a passionate affair with the Duchesse de Mazarin in 1676, at which time she also had a miscarriage, but she managed to recover her prime position. Thereafter Louise de Keroualle, Duchess of Portsmouth, Countess of Fareham and Baroness Petersfield, reigned supreme in the King's affections.

The effect of this intoxicating, glamorous, emotional court life was ultimately to make Louise's son wild and undisciplined. The King was devoted to all his natural children. On one occasion he took all his three youngest teenage sons together to a service at the Chapel of the Savoy. The young Duke of Richmond was known as Prince Charles Lenox, and was treated as such. At the age of five an eventual arranged marriage with the great heiress Elizabeth Percy was suggested for him; but her grandmother rejected the scheme. Charles II was a patron of the earliest racecourse in England, at Newmarket, and the Duke rode there as a

FACING PAGE, LEFT  Château of La Verrerie, Aubigny. Formerly the home of the Stuart Dukes of Lennox, and latterly of Richmond, this was granted to Louise de Keroualle in 1673, together with the château in the town. It belonged to the Lennox Dukes of Richmond until 1842.

FACING PAGE, RIGHT  Arms of Charles Lennox, Duke of Richmond and Lennox. The little Duke of Richmond was granted the Royal Arms of England, with a wide border to denote illegitimacy. The border was alternately red and white, with the Lennox red rose of the King's Stuart ancestors. The shield is circled by the Garter.

BELOW  *Frances Teresa, Duchess of Richmond, as Minerva*, by Henri Gascars, *c*.1675, oil on canvas, 248 × 138 cm / 97 × 54 in. The iconography of Minerva, the goddess of wisdom and of war, is close to that of Britannia, a role in which Frances Stuart had earlier been portrayed in a medal to commemorate the Peace of Breda. On her death in 1702 the Duke of Richmond gained possession of some Lennox estates in Scotland in which she had retained a life interest. These he immediately sold.

ABOVE  *Charles II at Court*, by Henri Gascars, oil on canvas, 107 × 122 cm / 42 × 48 in. Commissioned from Louise's favourite painter in the 1670s, this is the only portrait to show the King with one of his mistresses (beyond, with her own maid of honour). The sculptural background may be suggestive of the Stone Gallery which led to her apartments at Whitehall.

FACING PAGE  *Louise de Keroualle, Duchess of Portsmouth and Aubigny*, by Sir Godfrey Kneller, 1684, oil on canvas, 234 × 145 cm / 92 × 57 in. The buxom and beautiful Louise is shown with her exotic black page, and with her King Charles spaniel.

boy aged only ten and had 'a room' there.[8] The King not only named his royal yacht *Fubbs*, his nickname for the Duchess of Portsmouth, but also named one of his warships the *Lennox*.[9] At the time of the first treachery in 1683 of the King's eldest son, the Duke of Monmouth, Louise was even led to believe that Prince Charles Lenox, Duke of Richmond, might become the next King of England.

In 1685 everything changed. On Monday 2 February, the King suddenly became ill. Genuinely concerned for the state of his soul, Louise begged his brother James, Duke of York, to find him a priest. On Wednesday he was dead. Louise and her son had tried hard to be friendly with James, but the young Duke was immediately divested of the important ceremonial post of Master of the Horse, which he had held for four years. Despite a suggestion that Louise might go to Greenwich, she had decided by 10 February to return to France. Her debts were £30,000, but her estate was worth more than £100,000.[10] Louise set sail with two ships full of precious objects from her rooms at Whitehall.[11] From now on she made her homes both in Paris and at Aubigny.

## Paris

The first of Louise's homes in Paris was at 3 quai Malaquais, on the left bank of the Seine opposite the royal palace of the Louvre, of which Louis XIV had recently completed the Cour Carrée.[12] A house a few streets away, on the corner of rue de l'Université and rue Pré aux Clers, seems to indicate some earlier family history in the area. The Lennox arms with the St Andrew's cross interspersed by four red roses showing on the present-day hotel's printed material suggests a possible link. It may be one reason why Louise always lived in that corner of Paris, now known as the 7ième arrondissement, which was anyway very fashionable at the time. Later she had a house even nearer to the Hôtel Lenox, on the corner of rue des Saintes-Pères and rue de Verneuil (now demolished). Louise loved Parisian life, her only lament being the expense of it all.

## Return to England

In 1692 the Duke returned permanently to England. He made a respectable marriage in January 1693[13] to Anne Brudenell (1669–1722), the second daughter of Francis, Lord Brudenell, and granddaughter of Robert, 2nd Earl of Cardigan. Anne had thoroughly blue blood: her mother Frances was the eldest daughter of Thomas Savile, 1st Earl of Sussex. It is not known exactly how the marriage came about, but they must at some stage have met at court, where Anne's aunt, Anna Maria Brudenell, Countess of Shrewsbury, would have known Louise de Keroualle.

At the time of the marriage the Duke was only twenty and Anne was barely twenty-three. Like many brides, Anne was a young widow: her first husband had been Henry, 2nd Baron Bellasis of Worlaby. She had already borne a daughter, who died young. She had probably entered on her first marriage with a good dowry; that of her sister Frances, who became Countess of Newburgh, was a generous £12,000. It is said that Anne married the Duke of Richmond against the advice of her best friends, and that King William and Queen Mary did not approve of the match: they probably feared the various family Catholic connections. A daughter, Louisa, was born to the couple in 1694.

## Goodwood

The first record of any connection between Charles Lennox, 1st Duke of Richmond, and Goodwood in West Sussex dates from 1689, when 'a fatte bucke presented by the Duke of Richmond at Goodwoode' was sent to a group of diners belonging to an ancient society, the Corporation of St Pancras in Chichester.[14] He was either renting the house at the time or staying there as a guest.

Some eighty years old, Goodwood House had been built for Henry, the scholar or 'Wizard' (9th) Earl of Northumberland in 1616–17: the specifications had been carried out through his steward, as the Earl was at the time incarcerated in the Tower of

London. The Earl had wanted the house as a retreat from his large and imposing home at nearby Petworth, but there is no evidence that he ever came to live in it. When it was first built, it was a simple rectangle, but at some stage quite early in its history, gabled cross wings were added. The house changed hands at various times through the century, residents including John Caryll from Harting and the Earl of Middleton, from whom the Duke is said to have purchased it.[15] In about 1692 John Kempe, who subsequently moved to Slindon, was living there: his daughter Mary married Sir Henry Tichborne, 4th Baronet, from Hampshire. The Duke was certainly renting Goodwood House by 1695.

In 1697 the twenty-seven-year-old Duke of Richmond bought the house, acquiring it for one principal purpose. From there he could go hunting, setting out from the village of Charlton, only two miles north over the Downs. The Charlton

ABOVE, LEFT  *Charles, 1st Duke of Richmond*, by Sir Godfrey Kneller, c.1705, oil on canvas, 123 × 100 cm / 48 × 39½ in.

ABOVE, RIGHT  *Anne Brudenell, Duchess of Richmond*, by Sir Godfrey Kneller, oil on canvas, 125 × 99 cm / 49 × 39 in. Anne held the family together through all the vicissitudes of her husband's rackety lifestyle.

Hunt had become fashionable as one of the earliest fox hunts in England. It had been founded in 1675, and became so popular in the later 1670s that the Duke of Monmouth claimed arrogantly that, when he was king, he should have his court at Charlton.[16] Under the Duke's ownership Goodwood was therefore a hunting lodge. It was his only country seat. Duchess Anne had grown up at Deene Park in Northamptonshire, a fine medieval house which had been developed further through the Elizabethan period. To live in the old-fashioned Jacobean house at Goodwood would therefore not be difficult for her, though it was smaller than her own home.

Relations with William III were uneasy: he had stopped Louise de Keroualle's allowance, and refused to give her permission to come to England. After some negotiation Louise appeared in 1698. She arrived by boat at Rochester on 14 August, where she was met by a coach and six, sent by the Duke to collect her.[17] She subsequently visited her son at Goodwood.[18] Louise was still famous enough for her every move to arouse comment; from a contemporary pamphlet it is known that she returned to France early in 1699. Two years later her daughter-in-law, the Duchess Anne, achieved a longed-for son and heir: the Duke and Duchess were by now eight years into their marriage.

It would appear from a large group of household bills paid between 1701 and 1703 that the Duke and Duchess moved into Goodwood House in 1701, perhaps after the birth of their son. Indeed, the upholsterer made a quilted lining for the baby boy's cradle, with a fur base. The extensive bill for upholstery shows that they were fitting the house out to a high standard. Twelve tall-backed chairs had seats 'stuft with curled haire' and were covered with velvet, with red serge on the very back, presumably to go round the edge of a formal room, as was the fashion. Further seat furniture included two black Japanned chairs (also very fashionable); chairs covered with crimson damask; a 'Couch' with a set of round stools; ten walnut chairs covered in Spanish leather fixed with gilt nails; turned Dutch chairs and ten cane chairs. The drawing room was 'hung', presumably with textiles or tapestries, as was Lady Louisa's room. A bed was expensively embroidered, and there were damask canopies. The Duchess's dressing room had a damask curtain which drew upwards. The damask was specially dyed, as was some yellow silk for a window curtain and valance.[19]

Two 'large Japan Bowls with Covers' imported by the East India Company cost a vast £20[20]: in this the couple followed the new fashion for collecting porcelain or 'China' from the East, which had been given great impetus by the enthusiasm of the late Queen Mary, wife of William III. A surviving carved and gilded stool, with a Richmond lion at the top, was probably from a suite of grand furniture.[21] The Duke also had many 'chimney glasses' fitted, perhaps in an attempt to smarten up the Jacobean house.

At the same time, a bill for 28 December 1701 shows the acquisition of a vast batterie de cuisine. This long list of kitchen equipment includes four mobile 'spitts with iron wheels' as well as three large spits, suggesting the needs of a large household. Seventy copper drinking pots were bought, five iron candlestands, together with knives, pans, ladles, a copper lamp, a large bell, candlesticks and 'hand candlesticks' (with a handle for carrying), and five pairs of snuffers. In the kitchen, the fishmonger's bill was considerable, showing that they ate a large amount of herring, as well as salmon, cod, shrimps, oyster, whiting, carp and flounder. For the table twelve dozen napkins of various types were acquired, and twenty tablecloths. Even more impressive is the wine bill: in February 1702 the Duke bought thirty bottles of champagne and eighteen of burgundy, usually acquiring them six at a time, but then moving in March to a much larger amount. Outside, a French gardener was acquiring apple, peach, pear and apricot trees.

A bill from Andrew, who was probably a footman or valet, proves that Goodwood was their main residence by the end of 1701: he charged for when he was in attendance on the Duke, making it sound as if he was, in modern terms, self-employed. As he had his own room in the house, he was clearly given board and lodging, and was paid on top of that for special jobs. The bill gives a good idea of the Duke of Richmond's movements, for which Goodwood seems to have been the base: 'once more to London nine days' (there are several such trips); 'two days upon ye road to Charlton' (for hunting), and six days' board 'when your Grace was at Uppark'. This reveals that the Duke was friendly with Ford, Lord Grey, who had been one of the founders of the Charlton Hunt, and for whom Uppark had only recently been built. In London on another trip, Andrew cleaned the Duke's pistols, paid for the powdering of his wig and also paid for sedan chairs across London. The Duke lived smartly, according to his status: he bought one or two pairs of shoes every month and a livery was made for his groom.[22] There were inevitably many charges for saddlery and transport.

Apart from the newly acquired property, the fortunes of the Lennox family were not large. With the dukedoms the Duke had gained Richmond Castle in Yorkshire and £2,000 a year. Aged five he had been assigned by his father 'twelve pence or one shilling' on every cauldron of coal leaving Newcastle by sea.[23] The estate at Goodwood was still small. Fortunes were usually made at court,

making attendance compulsory for an impoverished nobleman. However, William III had never quite trusted the Duke of Richmond, and with good reason.

## CHANGING ALLEGIANCES: THE JACOBITES

Despite his professed loyalty to the Crown, the 1st Duke of Richmond may well have been an intermittent Jacobite. This was the cause supported by Roman Catholics loyal to James II who hoped to return him to the English crown, if needs be with French support. After the Glorious Revolution, by which William of Orange was offered the English throne with his wife, Princess Mary of England, James had left England at speed in December 1688, and was given hospitality near to Paris at St Germain by Louis XIV. However, the French King was somewhat embarrassed by the presence of James's extensive and expensive court. By the Peace Treaty of Ryswick that he was forced to make with William III in 1697, Louis XIV agreed that he would no longer support James's claim to the English throne. Nevertheless, after the death of James II in 1701, war with England again being imminent, Louis XIV declared for James's son, James Francis Edward Stuart.

As the natural son of a Stuart king (Charles II), the nephew of another (James II) and the first cousin of the 'pretender' Prince of Wales, it would hardly be surprising if the Duke of Richmond had Jacobite sympathies. Jacobites living in England were by definition extremely secretive: disloyalty to the Crown was treason, punishable by death. Even now it can be difficult to establish the true allegiance of some public figures, and some Whigs protested their loyalty too much. (The Whigs were a political grouping initially defined by their support of the constitutional monarchy of William and Mary; the rival group, the Tories, largely supported James II.) The Duke had been brought up an Anglican for cosmetic reasons but probably also attended Mass with his mother. In France in 1685 he had converted to Catholicism at the insistence of the newly crowned James II in London. After the King's escape to Paris in December 1688, the young Duke swore allegiance to him, on New Year's Day 1689. This was again at his uncle's request. The following year he served in the French army as ADC to the French Duke of Orléans, whose first wife, now deceased, had been his aunt, Princess Henrietta of England. All this did not look good in England.

The Duke converted back to Anglicanism on his return in 1692 in order to prove allegiance to William III. However, the Duke's marriage to Anne Brudenell early the next year may have awakened his latent Catholic sympathies for a second time. Her ancestors had originally been Catholic, despite their recent move to loyal Protestantism, and her father, Lord Brudenell, had been imprisoned in the Tower of London on suspicion of promoting 'Popery' back in the nervous days of 1678. Francis Brudenell was again imprisoned in the Tower in the 1690s, where he spent four years on suspicion of treason as a Jacobite. Anne's first husband had also been a member of an ancient Catholic family and her sister Frances was married to a Catholic, the Earl of Newburgh.

However, after the death of James II in exile in 1701, Richmond remained loyal at the time of William III's death in 1702, supporting the accession of his first cousin Queen Anne, who was generally seen as a legitimate heir. Jacobitism was mostly quiescent during her reign. Fidelity brought rewards. The Duke's position improved under Queen Anne. At her coronation the Duke bore for her the royal regalia of the Sceptre with the Dove. As befitted her rank, his Duchess was made a lady-in-waiting, which necessitated spending more time in London.

## London Life

Anne did not have an easy life as Duchess: the Duke was often away, hunting, travelling and gambling, and she could be lonely. When she was in London, they kept moving house, and their financial position was not comfortable. In 1705 they were in rented accommodation in the Haymarket, moving from there to Cardigan House in Lincoln's Inn Fields, the townhouse of her brother, George, 3rd Earl of Cardigan. This was temporary: from 1706 they had a home in Arlington Street, off Piccadilly. Anne carried on with normal female responsibilities, such as buying rugs and cushions for the house and organising Lady Louisa's French master, and later that of Lady Anne, born in 1703. Louisa also learnt dancing from a French oboe player.[24] The Duchess acquired fabrics for the family's clothes; crimson velvet and rich cherry-coloured satin for the Duke, sky-blue velvet for her son, and poplin, crepe and sarcenet for herself and her daughters.[25]

From about 1710 the Duke built a house in London, on the site of the kitchens of his mother's apartments at Whitehall. The family were obviously keen to make a good show at their London home. Sir Godfrey Kneller, portrait painter to each monarch from 1688 until his death in 1723, executed portraits of the Duke and Duchess, and of their son the Earl of March, aged about nine. Kneller had already worked for Anne's family, producing a fine portrait of her grandfather Robert, 2nd Earl of Cardigan, early in his career. His pupil Michael Dahl also painted the Duchess. Lady Louisa was painted as a child, by Charles d'Agar, in 1706, when she was only twelve. She sat again for her portrait, this time by Charles Jervas (who also painted her parents), soon after her marriage in February 1711 to James, 3rd Earl of Berkeley, a distinguished vice-admiral.[26]

The Duchess was often strapped for cash: when her husband generously sent her a gold box, she immediately had to pawn it, lamenting: 'in my life I never wanted money more . . .'[27] In order to save money, she dined daily in London with her sister, the widowed Countess of Newburgh. Her brother Lord Cardigan, who became a devoted mentor to their son, later wrote to him, 'Your father had been ruin'd, if your poor mother had not taken care of the whole household affairs.'[28]

## Loyalties

As Queen Anne became older and iller, and following the death of her only son and possible heir the Duke of Gloucester, Louise de Keroualle again became anxious about the loyalties of her son. She feared that the Duke would ally himself with the Jacobite cause rather than see the Hanoverian royal family take over. Despite her Roman Catholicism, Louise had herself always been extremely careful to sail with the wind. She was aware of the innate opposition to Catholicism in England, with all its political overtones of authority and foreign domination. The Duke of Richmond professed a studious loyalty to the English Crown, writing to his ever-suspicious mother in 1712, 'You know well that I have always been attached to the Whig Party and that for four years in succession in Parliament I have always obeyed the Queen's commands.'[29] He apologised too much: 'as I have the honour to be a King's son, and an English Duke, I cannot change with whatever wind may blow . . .'[30] However, he maintained his French interests, declaring 'I trust in a great king that has never done an injustice . . .'[31] In the summer of 1714 he visited France, at about the time of the Queen's death, possibly seeking to shore up Catholic alliances. He had indeed moved away from the Whig party, perhaps secretly anticipating a Tory revolt in favour of the Pretender. Indeed, his next-door neighbour in London, John Erskine 11th Earl of Mar (1675–1732), raised his flag to lead the Jacobites in Scotland the following year.

However, in his usual opportunistic manner the Duke returned to the Whigs in 1714 at the accession of George I, to whom he became a Lord of the Bedchamber. Early the next year, January 1715, he wrote to tell his mother that the new king gave permission for her to come to court. Louise did not receive quite the welcome she would have liked. She was greeted at court by a former royal mistress, the Countess of Dorchester (mistress of James II), who, seeing both Louise and another royal mistress, the Countess of Orkney (mistress of William III), commented sardonically, 'Who would have thought that we three whores should have met here!'[32]

The need to be seen to be Anglican while Catholicism had at least some emotional pull must have been something that the Duke and Duchess of Richmond, now in their forties, held in common. They were ever aware of any suspicion against them: Anne commented to Louise de Keroualle that she hoped that soon 'people may goe and coome from France upon theire own business without its being deemd a crime.'[33] The Duchess wrote charming letters to Louise, defending the wild and reckless traits in the Duke's character that were worrying his mother. These characteristics were hardly surprising when he was a young man in his twenties, but he had become erratic in his behaviour and he increasingly drank too much. Anne often turned a blind eye to his defects but, as the Duke got older, she did complain about his consumption of 'strong waters'.

RIGHT *Lady Louisa Berkeley* (1694–1717), by Charles Jervas, oil on canvas, 100 × 125 cm / 39 × 49 in. The elder daughter of the 1st Duke and Duchess, painted soon after her marriage in February 1711 to James, 3rd Earl of Berkeley, a vice-admiral (later First Lord of the Admiralty). Louisa died in her twenty-third year.

BELOW A silver cup bearing the arms of Charles, 1st Duke of Richmond and Lennox, by Louis Metailler, 1716, 30 cm / 12 in high. The Duchess sometimes had to pawn the family silver.

The Duchess concentrated on her children, commenting that both Louisa and Charles had large features, looking 'much of King Charleses and ye Royal Family!'[34] However, she felt that the younger daughter Anne was neater, with 'very preety litle features'.[35] Louisa produced a grandson for the Duke and Duchess in February 1716, but, to their sorrow, the young mother died less than a year later, in January 1717. Two portraits of her survive at Goodwood that were painted posthumously, in profile.

Louise de Keroualle's visit to England in 1715 was certainly a politic one, aiming principally at getting her pension restored, on which account her gentle daughter-in-law wrote begging letters. She also wanted the new king to be assured that, despite her French nationality, she and her son would be loyal to the Hanoverians. The King's reign had an uneasy start: George I spoke only German, and did not have a queen, having imprisoned his wife in a German castle because of her supposed adultery. In 1717 a row broke out between the King and his son, causing there to be two rival courts. During these years an interesting and potentially treasonable friendship may have developed in the vicinity of Goodwood. This was between the Duke of Richmond and Richard Boyle, 3rd Earl of Burlington (1694–1753).

From 1714, a crucial time in Jacobite history, Lord Burlington was hunting with the Charlton Hunt. This was also the year of his first Grand Tour to Italy. It is now widely believed

An imaginary drawing, by Paul Draper, of Lord Burlington's 'Great Room' for the Charlton Hunt; this was the first Fox Hall.

that the architecture-loving Lord Burlington had Jacobite affiliations, and that the initial impetus for his foreign trips was political rather than artistic.[36] While there is no doubt about his dedication to architecture, Burlington's artistic interests may have continued to act as a useful cover. Although the Duke was ostensibly loyal to George I, theirs was not an especially close relationship.

## The Hunt Club in Charlton

It is possible that up to about the time of the Duke's death in 1723, Jacobite meetings took place near Goodwood at Charlton, in a primitive room used by the hunt. Despite a temporary hiatus in the 1680s when the huntsman, Edward Roper, fled abroad with the Duke of Monmouth, the Charlton Hunt had continued to be popular and fashionable. It was still patronised by the aristocracy, encouraged principally by Charles Powlett, 2nd Duke of Bolton, from Hackwood Park in Hampshire, and his wife, Henrietta, an illegitimate daughter of the Duke of Monmouth. Their meeting place for hunt business, on the southern edge of the village, could easily have doubled as a secret site for any Jacobite enthusiasts at around the time of the 1715 uprising. Whenever he went hunting between 1714 and 1722, Lord Burlington may have been meeting men who had travelled from France to the south coast, landing just five or six miles away at Chichester or Itchenor.

In around 1722 Lord Burlington designed a new building on the site for the Charlton Hunt, referred to as the 'Great Room'. This was first described some years later, in a poem dedicated to the 2nd Duke, *The Historical Account of the Rise, and Progress, of the Charlton Congress*.[37] The Great Room was said in the poem to have been built by Lord Burlington on the site of an earlier 'small dark cell'. This is the only record of their first meeting place. The location was on the edge of the forest which, with the Charlton farm, at the time belonged to the Earl of Scarbrough, the owner of nearby Stansted Park. As Master of the Horse, Lord Scarbrough was completely loyal to the King, but he was rarely in Charlton and the southern woodside location would have lent itself to secret meetings. The location had the added emotive history of Charles II having supposedly hidden in Charlton Forest on his escape to the continent in 1651.[38]

The new Great Room designed by Lord Burlington was built by subscriptions from many wealthy hunting men. It is believed to have been a single-storey edifice with a dome. With his enthusiasm for the hunt, the Duke must have been among the subscribers.[39] He certainly used to take his family there: 'Harry Budd remembers when Fox Hall was first built, and the first Duke and Duchess of Richmond with Lord March, Lady Anne Lenox (afterwards Countess of Albemarle) and Miss Macartney coming to Charlton, and having Assemblies there . . .'[40] There is no evidence that the subscribers to the Great Room were aware of any Jacobite overtones, nor that the Duke of Richmond himself was disloyal to his sovereign at this stage of his life, but Jacobites necessarily covered their tracks extremely carefully. Although it would be interesting to work out how many of the hunt followers might have had such leanings, too many of them were, by the time that Lord Burlington came to build, too close to George I to be suspect. However, given the history of his meetings on the continent, the building work in Charlton could have been a useful cover for his own activities.

Loyalty to the new monarch was at the time increasing, and the dangers of treason were extreme. The 2nd Duke of Richmond, who inherited in 1723, was a loyal Whig. He did not yet own the site, but his local influence would be paramount. The social 'Assemblies' (as opposed to hunt meetings, breakfasts and dinners) were 'kept up for two or three years of the second Duke's time.'[41] The fact that, despite repeated requests, Burlington never came back to build anything else in Sussex, may be a pointer to his having had a covert reason for his building activities at Charlton. In 1730 the 2nd Duke built his own hunting lodge next to it. By 1740 the Great Room built by Lord Burlington was called Fox Hall, but by about 1785 it had been destroyed.

## At Home

At Goodwood, the Duke and Duchess mostly retained the old-fashioned look to the house, with Dutch gables at the end of each wing. The façade was altered around the turn of the eighteenth century, making the windows symmetrical and adding *oeil de boeuf* dormers to the attic, as shown in a drawing dating from after 1724 (see page 22). It is likely that these amendments were carried out before the 2nd Duke inherited in 1723, and may therefore have been for the 1st Duke, especially as *oeil de boeuf* windows were very popular in France. A portrait of the 1st Duke in about 1705 by Sir Godfrey Kneller (see page 8) shows a balustraded house sketched in behind, possibly an indication of how the Duke liked to think that Goodwood appeared.

Although the Duchess was nursing the Duke towards the end of his life, complaining that because of his 'Long sickness' she had 'so little sleepe',[42] she predeceased him. The gentle lady died in December 1722, only six months after the return of her son from his travels. The Duke is little mentioned in the letters of the time, because he had become an invalid, a drunkard and an embarrassment. For these reasons he was probably little involved in the building of the Great Room at Charlton. Certainly Lord Cadogan (see page 15) had become a more active influence on the Earl of March. When the Duke died in May 1723, Louise de Keroualle wrote to her grandson, 'I am sure you cannot doubt my being acutely distressed at the death of your Father . . . although I suffered from his lack of response.'[43]

The Earl of March insisted on burying his father in Westminster Abbey, against the advice both of his father-in-law Lord Cadogan and of his uncle James Brudenell, and with the full panoply of a duke. The cortège carrying the body on the two-day journey from Goodwood to London was decorated with seventeen plumes of black ostrich feathers and accompanied by four horsemen in mourning. The drunken, gambling, womanising Duke lay in state in the Jerusalem Chamber, south of the west doorway of the Abbey, which was 'hung deep in mourning', with an elaborate black velvet alcove created as a catafalque. At the funeral on 7 June, fifteen men were needed to carry his banners and standards, sword, shield and spurs. At both Richmond House and at Goodwood all the rooms were veiled in grey.[44]

CHARLES LENNOX
EARL OF MARCH
AND DARNLEY.
Born 18 May 1701

# 2   THE ARCHITECTURAL DUKE

## CHARLES, 2ND DUKE OF RICHMOND, 1701–1750

The future 2nd Duke of Richmond (1701–1750) was born, in the old-fashioned house at Goodwood, on 18 May 1701. Charles Lennox, Earl of March, was well brought up by a kind and loving mother. After he suffered a riding accident at the age of about twelve, the Duchess begged her mother-in-law, Louise de Keroualle, to support her plea to the Duke to prevent his son from riding any more 'fine Hunters', complaining, 'For indeed Madam as he is very young, weake, and extreamly ratle-headed, his liffe upon those horses will be in the greatest of dangers.' Hunting was not, she said, necessary 'to make a fine gentleman', and in giving himself up to the sport he was neglecting his 'Booke and Learning', which the Duchess felt to be far more important. She was conscious that he was 'an only Hire [heir] to so great titles and estate'. Because he was tall for his age, and had not yet filled out, he was very 'weake in his Limbs', or gangly.[1]

### Marriage

His father was more of a liability. In 1719 the Duke found himself embarrassed by a gambling debt for £5,000, which he owed to the Earl Cadogan, Ambassador to The Hague. Cadogan was himself an obsessive gambler, who had made much of his fortune by the unscrupulous means of betting on the outcome of sieges in the War of the Spanish Succession. However, the debt from the Duke had a happy outcome. To obviate payment, the Duke negotiated the marriage of his son to Cadogan's daughter. The Richmonds were delighted to augment the family coffers, a considerable dowry also being a requirement, and the ambitious and newly rich Cadogan would see his daughter become a duchess. The boy was eighteen when he first saw his bride at her home in The Hague: Sarah Cadogan was only thirteen, never a very good age for a girl. When he saw her the Earl of March is reported to have commented, 'Oh no, they're not going to marry me to that dowdy.'

Above *William, Earl Cadogan*, by Hans Huysing, 1725, oil on canvas, 150 × 133 cm / 59 × 52½ in. The 2nd Duke's father-in-law was a distinguished, if ambitious, army officer and ambassador.

Facing Page *Charles, Earl of March, later 2nd Duke of Richmond and Lennox*, by Charles d'Agar, c.1716, oil on canvas, 123 × 100 cm / 48 × 39½ in.

ABOVE *The 2nd Duke and Duchess of Richmond and Lennox*, by Jonathan Richardson, oil on canvas, 99 × 117 cm / 39 × 46 in. Louise de Keroualle begged her grandson for a portrait of himself with his Duchess. This was painted *c.*1726, showing him soon after he became a Knight of the Garter. The buckles of Aubigny adorn the ornate frame. In 1740, when they had been married for over twenty years, the Duchess wrote to her Duke: 'Of all the time that I have lov'd you I never felt more love & tenderness for you than I did yesterday. I haunted all the places where you had been last . . .'

FACING PAGE Paintings in the ballroom. *The Five Eldest Children of King Charles I* is an early version of a full-length picture by Sir Anthony Van Dyck in the Royal Collection. The little picture of St Michael by the fashionable painter Sebastiano Conca was one of two by the artist acquired by the 2nd Duke on his Grand Tour. To the right can be seen the Duke's great-grandmother, La Comtesse de Keroualle, the mother of Louise.

They did, but to spare him embarrassment the young man was immediately dispatched on the Grand Tour, while the girl was returned to her mother, to be schooled as a future duchess. The couple exchanged dutiful letters. Three years later, after much vacillation, Charles March returned to The Hague to claim his bride: but for the first evening he put off the encounter. Instead, he went to the theatre. There the young Earl saw a lively sixteen-year-old, surrounded by admirers. He enquired of a bystander who she was.

'Oh, that', came the reply, 'is the beautiful Countess of March, the toast of London.' It was his own wife: the two were swept into the idyll of an arranged marriage that was a profound passion. The Duke was so pleased with the outcome that he regaled listeners with the history of their romance throughout his life.

## GRAND TOUR

It was natural if far-sighted that Charles, Earl of March, should have been sent on the Grand Tour. Although the fashion for the Tour had not yet reached its peak, the tradition of sending young men abroad to gain an understanding of classical and European culture had been developing gently since the late seventeenth century. Despite their popularity in earlier times, in the early eighteenth century the universities, which mostly meant Oxford and Cambridge, were not regarded as a requirement for young aristocrats. A focused finishing-off was considered necessary as a finale to the years of study of the Classics.

Charles March set off on his Grand Tour from The Hague in December 1719. He was accompanied by Tom Hill, who had already been his tutor for seven years. There is little evidence for

where he spent most of the year 1720, but in July they were in Vienna, from where March wrote to his mother to ask her to send some specially beautiful fans 'for all the fine ladys of Vienna'.[2] It was probably after this visit that he made a long stay in Milan.[3] He may have been in Florence in August. It was here that, at some stage, he met Alessandro Galilei (1691–1737), a Florentine architect who had just returned from spending five years in England and had become one of a group of men who called themselves 'the new Junta for Architecture', wishing to have a more classical and less baroque style of building in England. The young Earl became so keen on classical architecture that he ambitiously asked Galilei to design a house for him.

In January 1721 March was in Padua, travelling on to Venice for the carnival, where he lodged near the Rialto bridge. By this time he had met up with another young traveller in the form of Lord Malpas, accompanied by his eccentric tutor Johnny Breval. In the glittering *Serenissima* March had an affair with a courtesan, Angela Polli, in the antechamber of whose establishment Breval was bitten on the leg by a puppy belonging to the Earl. A jovial letter from Breval mentions 'your dear Angeletta', 'the Divine Creature', exclaiming, 'What eyes, what teeth, how much wit; and

(the worst of the story is) how vast an affection for your Ldsp!'[4] Through Owen McSwiny, an Irish entrepreneur, the Duke arranged to have both Angeletta's portrait and his own drawn in pastel by Rosalba Carriera.[5] In the summer he left Venice for an intended two months, but in fact for more. Angela continued to write him letters that were affectionate and yearning but also mature and sensible.[6] She always sent best wishes to Signor 'Montalto', presumably a little joke on the name of Hill. Similarly McSwiny often signed as 'Eugenio'.

In April they were in Rome, 'retiring some leagues' in order to avoid 'any insults on account of their religion' and preparing to depart for Naples.[7] In June, August and September they were again in Rome, where March bought paintings, paying deposits to Gaspar van Vittel (Van Vitelli) and Henrico van Lindt respectively for views of the Colosseum and the Roman Forum, as well as to Sebastiano Conca, a particularly elegant classical painter.[8] He admired the library of Cardinal Albani with all its sculptures. More prosaically, his dog was again having puppies. He befriended the Princess Pamphili, later described by him as 'the ugliest woman in the world. Damn'd proud also, and stark staring mad . . .'[9] He found the grand Italian ladies snobbish and pretentious, but they amused him.

Angela was hoping to see him in Venice in October, and thanked him for sending her flowers and a fan; but he seems to have decided not to go. In October and November he was back in Florence, also staying in Siena, where one of his friends suggested that 'the agreeable company of Sienna & the Civillitys of the Princess have I durst swear bin the occasion of your long stay att that place.'[10] Perhaps this was a different and more charming princess. In December he was in Parma and in January 1722 in Milan. By February Angela had given up on him and had taken another lover, commenting that he, by flirting with a married woman, had been the one to turn away first.

While March's father seems to have paid him little attention, his father-in-law was ever vigilant, working to get him elected as MP for Chichester in 1722 and paying his bills on the Grand Tour. Cadogan suggested that he go to Lorraine on his way home: 'The Academy there is the best in Europe, The Court very polite, and the Duke of Lorrain infinitely civil to the English.'[11] He arrived in May, via Strasbourg. Meanwhile the little Countess continued to be educated at home. The best efforts were put into this: she is said to have spoken fluent French, Italian and Spanish.

There was much excitement when March's return home became imminent. The Duchess was worried about him going to the Cadogans' house at The Hague, as Sarah's sister, Margaret, to whom she was close, had been very ill with smallpox.[12] Their mother, Margaretta Cecilia Munter, herself a daughter of an aristocratic Councillor of the Court of Holland, was looking after her. By June the Earl of March had at last arrived at The Hague. Here he met his wife and the marriage was consummated. Cadogan urged him to London, as the King was going to review the Horse Guards. They should go to see relations at Amsterdam en route; once in England they should spend part of the summer at Goodwood and part at Cadogan's own country estate at Causham (now Caversham), near Reading.

## Inheritance

When Charles, Earl of March, succeeded his father as 2nd Duke of Richmond in May 1723, his patrimony in Sussex consisted of a smallish old brick house with gables, surrounded by a modest estate consisting of the immediate park and of farms in Boxgrove and Westhampnett. The situation was beautiful: the architect Colen Campbell described the 'Park, Gardens and Plantations which for the beautiful variety and extension of prospect, spacious lawns, sweetness of herbage, delicate venison, excellent fruit, thriving plantations, lofty and aweful trees, is inferior to none.'[13] Although the Duke had the coal income from Newcastle, the family was not particularly wealthy, and he inherited little but debt from his father. His marriage settlement would enable him to buy more land, increasing the estate to about 1100 acres in his lifetime.

Sorrow at the demise of both parents was mixed with happier events. On 21 February 1723 March's sister Lady Anne Lennox had married William Keppel, 2nd Earl of Albemarle, whose father, Arnold Joost van Keppel, had assisted William III at the time of his accession. This was to prove a happy and successful match. 'Aunt Anne' stayed close to her brother's family until her death in 1789, while her son George, the 3rd Earl, married the daughter of Sir John Miller, a local luminary in Chichester.[14]

The next occasion for celebration was the birth in April of a daughter to the Earl and Countess. Georgiana Caroline was named in honour both of the King and of Caroline, Princess of Wales, by whose name she was actually known. Louise de Keroualle sent 'a thousand kind messages to your wife from me' but insisted that her granddaughter-in-law 'be very careful of her health, so that next year she may give me a little son!'[15] She was still maintaining the tactless pressure for a male heir at Christmas: 'I am most impatient for a little son . . .'[16] Sarah, now a duchess, was very popular: some young girls announced that 'of their Mamma's acquaintance the Duchess of Richmond is their Favourite Lady.'[17]

The young Duke was also surrounded by family supporters. His uncle, the Hon. James Brudenell, was often at Goodwood, advising his nephew and carrying out business affairs on his behalf. Tom Hill was seen as part of the family, and was a regular house guest with their friends and relations, while Lord Cardigan also kept a watchful eye, reprimanding the Duke for his extravagance. He suggested that Richmond make every effort to pay off his father's debts, and that he should borrow £10,000 in order to carry this through over five years. The Duke was also instructed to assign amounts of 'pin-money' and 'housekeeping' to the Duchess, as well as 'pocket money' for himself. Another helpful relation was Robert Webber (or Weber), the natural son of the 1st Duke and therefore Richmond's half-brother, elder by about ten years. Webber became a minor canon of Winchester Cathedral, and as chaplain to the 2nd Duke helped with arrangements for his father's funeral in Westminster Abbey. He was well treated and highly regarded by the young Duke.

In October 1723 Lord Cadogan asked his son-in-law's opinion in respect of a marriage proposition made to his younger daughter, Margaret, who was known as 'Titie'. Now that his elder daughter was married at the highest level, he wanted to be sure only to expand his family in a way that was acceptable to his son-in-law. Titie was given the go-ahead to marry Count Bentinck. After his years of success, in 1725 Cadogan was, to his shock, dismissed as Master General of the Ordnance. Fortunes quickly made could be rapidly dispersed: the marriage settlement agreed by the Earl for Sarah had comprised a fortune of £60,000, enabling the eventual acquisition of new estates in Charlton, but the arrangement almost beggared his estate at his death in July 1726. The Duke and Duchess paid a visit to The Hague, to comfort her mother and assist with sorting out affairs.

France was never far from the Duke's heart, and in September 1723 he had been in Paris, no doubt visiting his grandmother. He may have met Voltaire at the same time, possibly being one of a group of 'English Persons of Quality then at Paris' who subsequently invited him to go to England.[18] Certainly they became friends in the 1720s. The Duke's French interests were maintained at Goodwood by Monsieur de Carné, a former retainer of Louise de Kerouaille, who had also helped him to be elected as an MP. Monsieur de Carné had lived in the house with the 1st Duke and Duchess, but was moved out to an old cottage at the top of the hill behind the house; at his death in 1730 the Duke paid for a distinguished funeral. The Duke's paperwork was done by his secretary Labbé, also a Frenchman: 'my wife assures me that even if we had the misfortune to lose you, all your accounts, bills, receipts etc. are so well arranged and in such good order that she would be in touch with everything in a single hour.'[19] Later his steward in the country was the equally efficient Robert Sedgewick, whose work related more specifically to Goodwood.

The young family grew slowly at the start. Although the Duchess had many pregnancies, they had to wait fourteen years for a healthy male heir. In June 1724 a son was born, who lived only a very short time: the Duke received letters of condolence.[20] The following winter, November 1725, came a second daughter. Little Louisa Margaret was named after both her grandmothers. In the winter of 1726 a third little girl was born, Anne, who did not survive.

## ARCHITECTURE

Above all while he was on his Grand Tour the young Duke had been impressed by classical architecture. When he returned a new craze for the style of the sixteenth-century Italian architect Andrea Palladio (1508–1580) was well under way. His work had first been promoted in England by Inigo Jones (1573–1652) in the early seventeenth century, and was given a new impetus by two major publications in 1715. The first volume of *Vitruvius Britannicus or The British Architect* came out that year, in which the architect Colen Campbell (1676–1729) published engravings of recent classical buildings by celebrated architects, with the suggestion that the works of Inigo Jones were an English challenge to those of the French and Italians. In subsequent volumes Campbell added his own designs to take the style closer to Palladio. A first instalment of Giacomo Leoni's edition of Palladio's *I Quattro Libri dell'Architettura* was also published in that year, the first full translation of the work into English.

Lord Burlington became absorbed by the style, both as conveyed by Jones and in the original. In 1717 he built from his own first design, a garden building called a 'Bagnio' or 'Casina' at Chiswick, in the grounds of his Jacobean house. Two years later he asked Campbell to remodel his London town house in Piccadilly. In 1720/1 Burlington bought Inigo Jones's own classical designs, as well as the original drawings of Palladio, and subsequently made his own drawings for houses and features for his friends. From about 1720 Colen Campbell designed Mereworth Castle in Kent, the first and closest version of Palladio's domed Villa Capra or Rotunda at Vicenza. Around 1722 Lord Burlington built the Great Room for the Charlton Hunt which, despite its name, was on a small, experimental scale. Later, from about 1725, Burlington built Chiswick House, another memorable version of the Villa Capra. The Palladian style became increasingly popular. This was surprising considering that the buildings looked austere from the outside and with their shady classical porticoes, arched halls and marble floors were unsuitable for the English climate.

The 2nd Duke of Richmond must have been delighted by the existing family friendship with the great scholar-architect Lord Burlington, whose fourth foreign trip had been made in 1719, the same year as his own Grand Tour commenced. Moreover, through his marriage the Duke knew well one of the finest classical houses in northern Europe, the Mauritshuis at The Hague, which was the home of his parents-in-law. He began to fulfil his love of Italy in his patronage of Palladian architects, notably in a magnificent tomb monument to his mother for the nave of the fifteenth-century church at her family home, Deene Park, Northamptonshire, where she was buried in the family vault. The Duke may first have appealed to Lord Burlington for advice, as the design is based on the frontispiece, designed by Burlington's close colleague William Kent, of the *Fabbriche antiche disegnant da Andrea Palladio*. The designs inside were selected from Palladio's *Quattro Libri*, and were finally published by Burlington in 1730, about the date the monument was erected. The marble for the monument was carved by stonemason and woodcarver John Boson (c.1705–1743), while the bust of the Duchess was executed by Giovanni Battista Guelfi (fl.1714–34), a sculptor whom Lord Burlington had brought to England from Italy. The piece is signed by both Guelfi and Boson. This is a fascinating example of a collaboration by the Duke with the circle of Lord Burlington, following on from Burlington's building of the Hunt Club or Dome for the Charlton Hunt. It was also a prelude to works in London.

The Duke was eager to improve the old-fashioned house at Goodwood. Colen Campbell, architect to the Prince of Wales and known to the Duke through this circle, completed a survey of the old house and planned a new one for the 2nd Duke. It was to be in the type of Palladio's centrally planned villas, with two colonnades sweeping out to pavilions. Although drawings were made in 1724, of which four were published as three plates in volume III of his *Vitruvius Britannicus* of 1725, the building was not executed.[21] However, a new detached kitchen was built in the classical style. Monsieur de Carné told the Duke in August 1724 that he was waiting for Colen Campbell to come to Goodwood to check up on the building of the kitchen and to give him his orders.[22] In his next letter he commented sniffily that the building had been

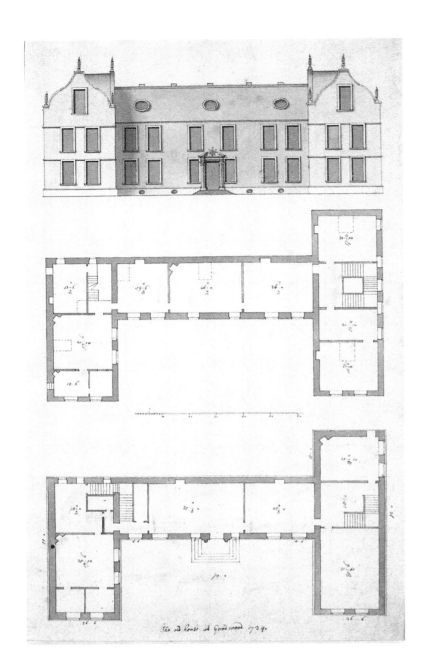

The old house at Goodwood. 1724.

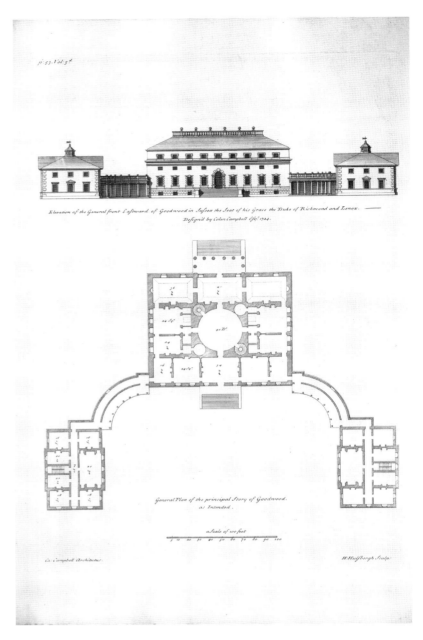

Elevation of the General front Eastward of Goodwood in Sussex the Seat of his Grace the Duke of Richmond and Lenox.
Design'd by Colin Campbell Esq.r 1724.

General Plan of the principal Story of Goodwood.
as Intended.

a Scale of 100 feet

Co: Campbell Architectus.

H. Hulsbergh Sculp.

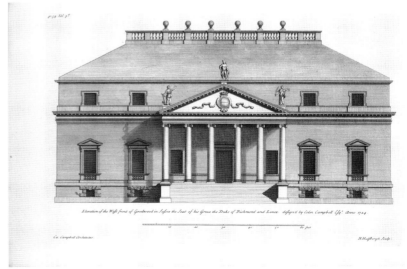

Elevation of the West front of Goodwood in Sussex the Seat of his Grace the Duke of Richmond and Lenox design'd by Colin Campbell Esq.r Anno 1724.

Co: Campbell Architectus.

H. Hulsbergh Sculp.

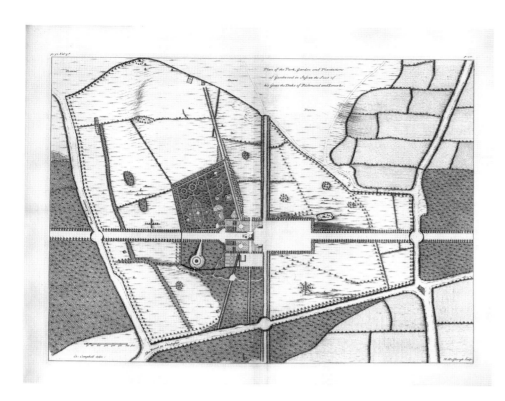

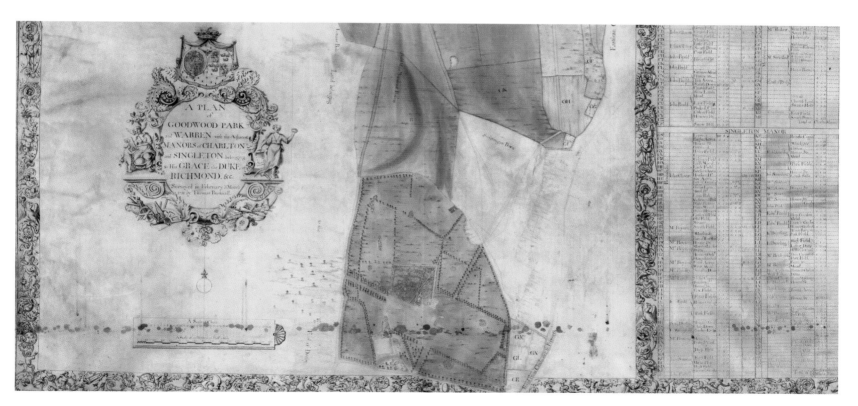

created more for looks than usefulness.[23] A drawing made soon afterwards shows a symmetrical two-storey building adjacent to the main house.

Even the kitchen for the proposed new house created a stir in the country, and in the autumn Lord Derby, who owned land adjacent to the estate, came to look over it.[24] In 1738 Daniel Defoe wrote that 'Godwood [*sic*] . . . is a very old ruinous Building, but his present Grace has built some new Offices lately, which are to correspond with a Mansion-House designed by Colin Campbell

and published by him in his *Vitruvious Britannicus* [*sic*].'[25] The antiquary Jeremiah Miller, who visited the house in 1743, also believed the kitchen to be part of Campbell's scheme: 'the Duke has had designs for some years to rebuild it according to a design of Colen Campbell in the *Vitruvius Britannicus*, and has already built up one of the offices, but I believe he will never do any more.'[26] Although, from the amateur drawing, the kitchen did not have at all the proportions of the pavilions of the proposed villa, it was clearly meant to relate to it. Perhaps the new Campbell

plans were unexecuted owing to high costs.[27] It certainly seems to have been intended as a fairly compact show building, like Campbell's Mereworth Castle or Burlington's Chiswick House.

Although he did not carry out Campbell's design, the 2nd Duke was already becoming known for his interest in classical architecture. James Brudenell asked him for a chimneypiece design for his own home at Luffenham in 1727, while in 1731 Sir Thomas Dereham requested his plan for a new church in Ireland: knowing the Duke's preoccupation with the Roman, he begged for 'no Porticoes'.[28] In a book in the library appears a sketch of what may be an idea either for Goodwood or for the proposed new Richmond House in London.[29] The Duke would find many ways of fulfilling his passion for architecture.

## THE DINING ROOM PAINTINGS

Through Owen McSwiny, the Irish promoter of musicians and painters whom he had met in Venice, the Duke began to receive a series of paintings that represented the allegorical tombs of illustrious Englishmen of recent history. The pictures were thus fanciful ideas, or *capricci,* representing tombs that did not exist, of famous statesmen and other figures who had contributed to the good of the nation at the time of the Glorious Revolution. They were principally an excuse for painting fine Italian architecture and sculpture: an urn representing the remains of the deceased would be surrounded by statues, figures and mythological beings alluding to his wisdom and stature. The notion was to make the imaginary Italianate scenes relevant to English viewers.

For the Duke, it meant that he would have a sophisticated room in the latest Italian taste. The paintings also had an important message. The images were not so much those of mourning, although they provided a Poussin-type nostalgia for the past, but were celebrations of the lives of the Whig faithful, who had so recently built the political structure on which the Hanoverian dynasty rested. The Duke was determined that there should be no

Cimaroli were the painters of the perspective and landscape on the images of the tombs of Archbishop Tillotson and Lord Somers.[31] McSwiny was far-sighted in the painters that he chose. This was one of the first appearances of work by the young Canaletto (1697–1768), and certainly his first commission from an Englishman. In the end only the Tillotson painting came to Goodwood.[32] McSwiny also commissioned Sebastiano and Marco Ricci, who had already worked in England, together with some well-chosen young painters. In 1723 he wrote to the new Duke about 'Twelve very Elegant pictures, painted or to be painted for his Grace of Richmond',[33] and in 1726 he told the Duke that he was 'overjoyed to find that ye pictures give you so much satisfaction.'[34]

The opportunistic McSwiny was always trying to sell the Duke as many paintings as possible, while excusing the constant delays. He suggested that the painting to go at the end was to be of King William, a constant reminder that the 2nd Duke was no Jacobite. In March 1727 the Duke paid McSwiny for eight pictures, all vertical, but, with the death of George I that year, he had to change his plans, to accommodate a large horizontal painting of the imagined tomb of the newly deceased king in the prime position at the end of the room. Exceptional care was taken over this image, which finally arrived in 1730. Realising that the Duke would not take any more paintings, McSwiny also sold some to Sir William Morice, a neighbour of the Duke in London. Subsequently McSwiny also tried to raise funds from an edition of prints of the series, published in 1741 as: *Tombeaux des Princes/Grands Capitaines/et/Autres Hommes Illustrées/Qui ont fleuri dans/Grande-bretagne vers la fin du XVII et le commencement du XVIII Siecle.*[35]

Instead of rebuilding, the Dule decided in the later 1720s to classicise his existing house by means of both art and architecture. The ten paintings were displayed in the Old Dining Room at Goodwood, where they were sketched and listed by the antiquary George Vertue (1683–1756) in 1747.[36] Over the doors were paintings of ruins by John Wootton. The room must have been a great source of pride to the Duke during the 1730s and 1740s. However, great baroque architectural scenes of heroic subjects were out of fashion by mid-century. The 3rd Duke kept them for a while, but removed them to the staircase. Nine of the paintings were sold by the 4th Duke in 1814.[37]

## Other Paintings and Improvements

Soon after inheriting, the young Duke augmented his art collection in other ways. A properly trained artist would consider it normal both to paint new pictures and to copy existing ones: nor did owners find it embarrassing to have a well-executed copy of a great master as part of their collection. Bills from the painter Enoch Seeman for 1724–6 shows two copies of paintings of dogs, together with a St Cecilia and 'a copy after Van Vitelli'.[38] New

doubt about his own allegiance to the King. The scheme was an extraordinary mixture of a Protestant message executed by Catholic artists from Italy.

McSwiny was already busy making Italian opera suitable for the English stage in London, and this was a similar means of importing Italian art and architecture. The idea was original and even eccentric. Whether it was in art or in music, McSwiny knew what he was about: one of the painters commented that he had 'as sound a knowledge of good pictures, books and antiquities as it is possible to have'.[30] He was an intriguing figure: roguish but scholarly, with brilliant artistic ideas and an intuitive sense of how to make high art appeal to the contemporary viewer.

Artists in Venice, Verona, Bologna and finally even Rome were engaged by McSwiny for his project, the plan being that three artists should collaborate on each work, painting the architecture, the landscape and the figures respectively. In 1722 McSwiny wrote to the Earl of March to say that 'A Canale' and

ABOVE *Sarah, Duchess of Richmond with Lady Caroline Lennox*, by Enoch Seeman, 1726, oil on canvas, 126 × 101 cm / 49½ × 39¾ in.

FACING PAGE, TOP 'The articles of cricket, drawn up for two matches between the 2nd Duke and Mr Brodrick', 1727. Mr Alan Brodrick, later Viscount Midleton, was the Duke's neighbour in London.

FACING PAGE, BOTTOM *Cricket and Cedars at Goodwood*, by Ann Witheridge, 2006, oil on canvas, 54 × 79 cm / 21 × 31 in.

portraits were also commissioned from Seeman: in 1726 the Duchess was painted with Lady Caroline, described as 'Mi Lady Duchess and a Child', for 14 guineas.[39] Sometimes a copy of a portrait was made for another member of the family: the Duke's portrait was painted by him for 10 guineas, together with 'a Copi of ye same', twice listed so presumably twice copied, for 6 guineas each.[40] He also had a copyist called Mr Graham who worked for him in the Duke of Parma's gallery in Bologna.[41]

A 'head after Vandick' appears on Enoch Seeman's bill in September 1724. A copy of Van Dyck's famous painting of the *Three Children of Charles I* may have been made at this time. It is one of many good copies of this image in the collections of old families, the paintings sometimes not being quite as early as the family would like to believe. Like his great-grandfather Charles I, who had used classical and religious images of majesty or heroism

to bolster the idea of divine right, the Duke was keen to emphasise his family's royal connections. There are two other medium-size royal paintings at Goodwood that are said to be by Van Dyck. *Charles II as a Young Man* may be another early-eighteenth-century copy, but *The Five Eldest Children of King Charles I* (see page 17) is of very high quality and probably from the original studio, perhaps one of a number of pictures given by the King to Louise de Keroualle. In 1726 the Duke's frame-maker, William Chisholm, regilded an old frame for 'ye Picture of the Royall famillie'.[42] A copy of 'Bacchanal by Rubens' also appears in Seeman's bills, as well as a Venus, presumably a copy of Titian's, no longer in the collection.[43]

Rooms were being improved and many of the decorations were being gilded. In 1726 a 'fine carved Chimney piece' was painted in a cinnamon colour, while its mouldings were picked out in gold leaf. Two years later, in 1728, a very large amount of gold leaf was used for the carvings in a newly painted room at Goodwood, probably the dining room where the paintings were being installed. Gilding and 'picking out of the ground' took two men ten weeks: they came specially from London, as did their foreman.[44] By 1732 'two New End pieces' had been provided and the frame of George II's picture (in another room) was repaired.[45] Over these years many picture frames were specially made for new portraits and pictures, and old ones were cut down or regilded. A number of frames for tables were painted and gilded, and chairs were made. A 'rich statuary Marble table stained with a landscape' was acquired, and paid for by another Goodwood agent, Richard Buckner, who was taken on at about this time and would stay for the rest of his working life.[46] Clocks were repaired.[47] Even the Duke's boat, which was kept at West Wittering, was painted vermilion.[48]

## CRICKET, GOLF AND RACING

Meanwhile a new team sport took place in the grounds. Goodwood is the first estate in England on which cricket was played with any regularity. As early as 1624 two young men were reprimanded for playing with a cricket ball in Boxgrove churchyard on a Sunday. In 1702 the 1st Duke of Richmond gave brandy for Arundel men following a cricket match, but the records do not say where the match was played. By the 1720s the Duke of Richmond's XI (or sometimes a different number) was playing all over Sussex, including a match against Sir William Gage's team at Firle Place near Lewes. In 1727 some laws or 'Articles' of cricket were drawn up for matches between the Duke of Richmond's XII (exceptionally) and Mr Brodrick's men, the first at Peper Harow, near Godalming, on 27 July 1727 and the second at Goodwood on 28 August. Despite the detail of the new rules, there was an easy let out for the two captains: 'These rules do not apply to the Duke of Richmond or Mr Brodrick.'[49]

From about 1730 the Duchess's housekeeping book shows payments 'To Lord Duke for his cricket match'.[50] In 1746 one

Articles of Agreement by & between His Grace the Duke of Richmond & Mr Brodrick (for two Cricket Matches) concluded the Eleventh of July 1727.

Imprimis,
'Tis by the aforesaid Parties agreed that the first Match shall be played some day of this Instant July in the County of Surry; the Place to be named by Mr Brodrick; the second Match to be played in August next in the County of Surrey; the Place to be named by the Duke of Richmond.

2d: That the Wickets shall be pitched in a fair & even Place, at twenty three yards distance from each other.

3d: A Ball caught, cloathed or not cloathed the Striker is out.

4th When a Ball is caught out, the Stroke counts nothing.

5th Catching out behind the Wicket allowed.

6th That 'tis lawfull for the Duke of Richmond to chose any Gamesters who have played in either of his two last Matches with Sr William Gage; & that 'tis lawfull for Mr Brodrick to chose any Gamesters within three miles of Pepperhara, provided they actually lived there last Lady Day.

7th: that twelve Gamesters shall play on each Side.

8th: that the Duke of Richmond & Mr Brodrick shall determine the Ball or Balls to be played with.

9th: if any of the Gamesters shall be taken lame or sick after the Match is begun; their Places may be supplied by any one chose conformably to the sixth Article, or in case that can not be done, the other side shall be obliged to leave out one of their Gamesters whomsoever They please.

10th: that each Match shall be for twelve Guineas of each Side, between the Duke & Mr Brodrick.

11th: that there shall be one Umpire of each Side; & that if any of the Gamesters shall speak or give their Opinion, on any Point of the Game, They are to be turned out & voided in the Match; this not to extend to the Duke of Richmond & Mr Brodrick.

12th If any Doubt or Dispute arises on any of the aforesaid Articles, or whatever else is not settled therein, it shall be determined by the Duke of Richmond & Mr Brodrick on their Honours; by whom the Umpires are likewise to be determined on any Difference between Them.

13th The Duke of Richmonds Umpire shall pitch the Wickets when they Play in Surrey; & Mr Brodricks when They play in Surry; & Each of Them shall be obliged to conform Himself strictly to the Agreements contained in the second Article.

14th The Batt Men for every One they count are to touch the Umpires Stick.

15th: that it shall not be lawfull to fling down the Wickets & that no Player shall be deemed out by any Wicket put down unless with the Ball in Hand.

16: that both the Matches shall be played upon, and determined by these Articles.

Richmond.
A: Brodrick.

---

J. Fuller was trying to arrange an annual match or 'Crickett Plate'. Each player would be paid one guinea, and the winners would have '11 black velvet caps'. Competition was to be fierce: 'a true cricket match should have as much solemnity as a battle.'[51] The game subsequently spread west from Sussex, via nearby Slindon, to Hambledon in Hampshire where it was famous from the 1750s. It also spread east to Knole in Kent, where it was played in the 1770s. It continued to be a favourite game of the 3rd Duke (who led an XI against Hambledon for £1,000 guineas in 1768) and of the 4th Duke.

Some twenty years after cricket was first regularly played at Goodwood, the Duke also seems to have taken up golf: in 1745 the Earl of Home sent him 'a Box with Gouf Clubs and Balls . . . You will find that the Clubs are of different sorts the meaning of which I shall explain.'[52] The Duke also enjoyed horse racing, following the tradition of his father and his grandfather. At the time 'match' races just between two or three horses often took place on private estates, in competition for a silver plate. His horses also ran at courses in Sussex, Surrey and Hampshire.

## Travel

While architecture and animals were his passions at Goodwood, and his life in London was becoming increasingly busy at court, in 1728 the Duke and Duchess went to the continent for an extended stay. It is remarkable how much those who could afford it travelled in the eighteenth century, bucketing from London to the country and from city to city across Europe. All this was achieved in very uncomfortable conditions: they were often 'overturned' in the carriage, causing consternation among relatives about their injuries.

*Lady Caroline Lennox with her pony and a groom*, by John Wootton, 1733, oil on canvas, 46.5 × 49 cm / 18¼ × 19¼ in. Wootton wrote to the Duke: 'I hope your Grace has received the little Picture of Lady Caroline safe and I wish it answers your Grace's expectation.'

Arriving together at Brussels, the Duchess, with the two little girls, took the waters at Aix-la-Chapelle before travelling on to her family at The Hague. The Duke had set off in a different direction. Accompanied by Thomas Hill and, while in France, by his secretary Labbé, as well as a couple of footmen and a valet, he seemed to be enjoying another, smaller, Grand Tour. They stayed first with his grandmother at Aubigny: 'I am here in the centre of France, with the Dutchess of Portsmouth, who is now completely fourscore years of age, and in humour, figure, spirits, memory and everything, has the appearance of a woman under fifty.'[53] After some partridge shooting there, the male entourage travelled on to Madrid, planning the journey via Orléans, Blois, Poitiers, Bordeaux and Bayonne. They arrived by early November, and then, enjoying the trip, extended the tour to Lisbon. There they were entertained by the cheerful ambassador, Lord Tyrawley, yet another Irishman who enjoyed convivial entertainment with the twenty-seven-year-old Duke, conversing with him in a casual mixture of English laced with French.

The plan, constantly delayed because the Duke was enjoying himself so much, was for him to meet up with the Duchess, then take the family back to Paris. When he eventually reached Brussels they were delayed there for three weeks, by now April 1729, owing to six-year-old Caroline having a cough and a fever. By the time they arrived in Paris in May, little Louisa Margaret had caught it. Sadly the little girl died, causing the Duchess the utmost distress.

The Duke wrote to Sir Hans Sloane saying that the Duchess had also miscarried, 'which proceeded meerly from the grief of that poor childs long illness and death.'[54]

The twenty-three-year-old Duchess had recovered enough to be presented at the French court in August: 'Her Grace is at present at Versailles, where she has received all the honours of the Court.'[55] She was given the great honour of the tabouret or stool: only a member of the royal family or a duchess could be seated in the presence of the King. Louise de Keroualle had been delighted to receive the honour herself two generations earlier. Both the Duke and Tom Hill were very concerned about the court fees. They stayed at Versailles and visited St Germain: a visit to the more private royal château of Marly was also projected. They stayed as guests of the Duc de Bourbon at Chantilly: 'Wee either stag hunt, boar hunt, wolf hunt or go a shooting every day . . .'[56] The Duke liked the shooting best, of both pheasants and partridges. They were also much diverted on rainy days by the French Duke's love of science, and of making mechanical inventions and experiments. In September they went on to Aubigny, possibly the first time that the Duchess of Portsmouth had met her grandson's bride. They finally returned to England in October, still 1729. By now Monsieur de Carné was one of the party, because of his old connection as retainer to Louise de Keroualle.

## HUNTING

While he was on his travels, the Duke was in constant correspondence about his horses. Hunting was his passion, just as it had been for his father. It meant long days in the open air, the challenge and courage of leaping fences at the gallop, and the conviviality of friends and farmers, grooms and huntsmen. For the Duke, it was, like cricket and racing, one of the ways in which he would get to know local people in a spirit of fun and mutual adventure. Before he left England in 1728 the Duke had begun to have a stable built for his horses in Charlton.[57] He continued with the building plans through his agent, Robert Sedgewick. Bills for the stable to the east of the present lodge continued through 1729.

While the Duke was abroad the Duke of Bolton resigned as Master of the Hunt at the entreaty of his new mistress, the actress Lavinia Fenton, bequeathing his hounds to his friend at Goodwood. Meanwhile, Charles Bennet, 2nd Earl of Tankerville, grandson of Lord Grey and the new heir to Uppark, was audaciously using his hounds to draw the coverts at Charlton. On the Duke's return to England that autumn, he agreed, after lengthy and difficult negotiations, to be joint proprietor with Tankerville. The following spring the Duke was buying a horse from the Duke of Bedford.[58] In March 1730, a grandly worded 'Treaty' creating the Duke and the Earl of Tankerville joint Masters of the Hunt was drawn up.[59] Tankerville (known in letters as Tanky) was only Master for a short time, after which the Duke was assisted by John

West, 16th Baron De La Warr (later 1st Earl): they corresponded regularly about the care, breeding and health of the hounds. It was in that year that the Duke finally took possession of estates at Singleton and Charlton, funded by his marriage settlement, and began to build his hunting lodge. He acquired additional stables and kennels at Findon on a lease in November 1731.[60]

The Duchess was also an accomplished horsewoman, and, as a young woman, even a wild one. Their neighbour at Petworth, the Duke of Somerset, described her as 'soe noble and soe Great a Huntress'.[61] The most famous day in the history of the Charlton Hunt took place on 26 January 1739, when, in 'The Greatest Chase that ever Was', hounds ran continuously from their first find at 8.15 a.m. until they killed at 5.50 p.m., a distance calculated at over fifty miles. The Duke, with only two other members of the field, was there until the end.[62] The Duke's hunting life is further remembered in a large memorial to his huntsman, Tom Johnson, in Singleton Church, who died in December 1744.

## The Heir?

In 1730 the twenty-nine-year-old Duke was settled with his little family, which still only consisted of the three of them, with one more on the way. Goodwood was already famous for its entertainment, not least the French cuisine and good wine. While the Duke was in Paris, the pleasure-loving Philip Stanhope, 4th Earl of Chesterfield (1694–1773), had written to him, appealing to his fine palate and requesting his help in finding a French chef.[63] Correspondents often sent good wishes to Jacquemar, the Duke's own chef. In the autumn William Pulteney, later created Earl of Bath (1684–1764), declined an invitation to Goodwood with these immortal words:

> Temperance and Regularity are still necessary for me to observe, and at Goodwood I believe no one ever heard of either of them, for my part I am determined not to come within a house that has a French Cooke in it for six months . . .[64]

At last, in October 1730, a son was born, to the great delight not only of his parents but also of his great-grandmother in France: 'I never recollect in my life having had so pleasant an awakening as when I learnt of the birth of your little son and the happy delivery of the charming Duchess.' She also thought of the little girl, now aged seven: 'Embrace my charming Caroline for me, tenderly, did she receive her brother graciously?'[65] Letters of congratulation poured in.[66] A 'Boys Coronet' (that of the Earl of March) was carved 'for the Great Parlour at Goodwood', and jubilantly gilded.[67] Life swung between highs and lows: events took another sad turn when the little boy tragically died. He was buried in the Church of St Martin-in-the-Fields, near their London home. This was the Duke and Duchess's fifth child, their fourth loss of a baby. They soldiered on.

# 3 IN THE SERVICE OF THE KING

LONDON LIFE AND RICHMOND HOUSE, 1727–1750

At court, honours abounded for the 2nd Duke of Richmond and Lennox. In 1725 George I revived the Order of the Bath, which had been dropped since the coronation of Charles II. The Duke was concerned that he might be awarded it in lieu of the Garter, which his father had held, but, through the Duke of Montagu, he was assured by the (de facto) prime minister, Sir Robert Walpole, that this was not the case. There was high excitement before the installation ceremony on 27 May, for which tickets were issued to friends and supporters. The Duke had an attack of smallpox and was unable to attend, but the illness was fortunately mild. The Duke was careful to record his elevation, acquiring twenty prints 'representing the Procession and Ceremonies observed at the Instalation [sic] of ye Knights Companions of the most Honourable Military Order of the Bath . . .'[1] He also had himself painted as a Knight of the Bath by both Joseph Highmore and Enoch Seeman.[2] The following year, on 16 June, the Duke was appointed to the Order of the Garter. The arrangement completed the ruse whereby Walpole, also a Knight of the Bath, could elevate himself too. Lord Cardigan was delighted at his nephew's elevation, but concerned about the expense, suggesting to him that he live at Goodwood until Christmas.

The Duke was interested in his family history and loved the trappings of Army and State.[3] He asked Robert Webber to make enquiries at the College of Arms into the history of the Stuart Dukes of Richmond, and had a copy made of a portrait of Charles Stuart, the last Duke of that line.[4] The Duke also had a family tree made of the succession of the Kings of Scotland.[5] The 'Embroyderer' not only made clothes such as smart waistcoats for him, but also items to do with ceremonial occasions.[6] Coats of

Books and oriental porcelain acquired by the 1st, 2nd and 3rd Dukes of Richmond, and their Duchesses.

arms were often being painted, engraved and applied to portraits for the Duke, who took his branding seriously. Possibly still slightly nervous about the stain of illegitimacy on his father, he was trying to aggrandise his family, giving them as many illustrious ancestors, portraits and honours as possible.

The Duke and Duchess were close both to George I and to the Prince and Princess of Wales. At the death of the King in 1727, they were ready and at hand. At the coronation of George II and Queen Caroline the Duke stood as Lord High Constable of England. Soon afterwards he was made a lord of the bedchamber, and the Duchess a lady: her salary was a useful £500 per annum.[7] As a lady of the bedchamber, the Duchess was normally on duty for about a week at a time, in constant attendance on the Queen. The duties were minimal but tiring: the ladies were not allowed to sit in the presence of royalty unless invited, or to leave the room unless dismissed. Perhaps it was to avoid the rigours of court life while the Duchess was having difficulties with childbirth that the couple went abroad for a long time in 1728–9. However, they were deeply loyal. The Duke commissioned Thomas Hudson to paint him a portrait of the new monarch, full length and seated on his throne, as well as an equestrian portrait from Highmore.[8] Court life was expensive: it could also be tedious. In 1733 the Duke commented that he was able to write letters while at Hampton Court, 'for I am here in waiting and have nothing else to do almost.'[9]

Although he was such a family man, the 2nd Duke of Richmond had grown up with a certain city sophistication. He does not seem to have been entirely faithful to his wife. In 1730, soon after his return from Paris, he received two notes from Paris from 'deux femmes qui vous aim [sic]'.[10] An intimate, witty, vulgar, and positively priapic letter, suggesting a world of misbehaviour and ready sex in Paris, was subsequently written to him by the celebrated French philosopher François-Marie Arouet, known as

ABOVE  *George II*, by Thomas Hudson, oil on canvas, 236 × 145 cm / 93 × 57 in, in one of the carved and gilded frames designed by or after William Kent for Richmond House.

FACING PAGE  *A Performance of The Indian Emperor or The Conquest of Mexico by the Spaniards*, by William Hogarth, oil on canvas (private collection). John Dryden's play is being performed by a group of children in the spring of 1732. The first performance, shown here, at the home of John Conduitt (Master of the Mint), was such a success that the children were asked to repeat it before the King and Queen at St James's Palace on 27 April 1732. The scene shows friends and family of the 2nd Duke. On the left the Earl of Pomfret, wearing the red sash of the Order of the Bath, leans past the Duke of Montagu to talk to a man traditionally identified as Thomas Hill, Secretary to the Board of Trade, possibly also the Duke of Richmond's friend and erstwhile tutor. The Duke of Richmond leans on the back of his wife's chair, while beneath the chimneypiece the royal children, William, Duke of Cumberland, and his sisters, look on. In the foreground their governess, Lady Deloraine, instructs one of her two daughters to pick up a fan lying on the floor. On the stage are, from left to right, Lady Sophia Fermor and her brother Lord Lempster (children of the Earl and Countess of Pomfret); nine-year-old Lady Caroline Lennox (speaking her lines) and Catherine Conduitt. The hosts, Mr and Mrs Conduitt, are shown only through their portraits. The Countess of Pomfret, who is not shown, was the great-niece of Louise de Keroualle, and therefore a second cousin of the Duke. The bust of the recently deceased Sir Isaac Newton dominates the wall, and the leading Freemason Dr Desaguliers is the prompter in the background.

Voltaire. The Frenchman had recently spent three years in London, between 1726 and 1729, and he would often have seen the Duke in the circle of Royal Society scientists. Writing in fluent English, Voltaire reported that news that the Duke had broken his leg (this was in 1732) had been heard in Paris, and that 'you are beloved my lord by the french no less than by the english, it seems every nation would claim you for its country man.'[11]

## FREEMASONRY

In the early days Freemasonry was often associated with Jacobitism; this was because through its system of lodges, Freemasonry enabled men from across the political spectrum to meet safely and in secret to discuss subjects of common interest.[12] However, largely owing to deliberate infiltration by royal agents, by the reign of George II Freemasonry had instead become associated with the Hanoverians. The role of the first two Dukes of Richmond in the origins of Freemasonry in England is only just coming to light. In Sussex it was believed locally that there had been Masonic meetings in a little building on the summit of St Roche's Hill, now known as The Trundle, from very early times. The 1st Duke is said to have led the last meeting of a very old order of Freemasons there in the 1690s and is known to have attended a private lodge in Chichester in 1696.[13] He is also believed to have given advice on the development of the early lodge at Chester. The first Grand Lodge in England was not created until 1717.

The 2nd Duke was especially involved. He knew the leading Freemason, Huguenot mathematician John Theophilus Desaguliers (1683–1744), who in 1723 helped publish a new set of *Constitutions* for Masons, shifting the old mysteries into a package of rational, moral values. The Duke was Grand Master in 1724–5 and became Provincial Grand Master of All England. In 1730, with his London neighbour, the Duke of Montagu, who had also been Grand Master, he once again held a lodge on St Roche's Hill, on the traditional date of the Tuesday in Easter week.[14] The Duke helped inaugurate the first lodge in France, in 1726, founded one at Aubigny in 1735 and held lodges at Goodwood in the 1740s. It was a condition that Masons had to believe in a 'Supreme Being', but not a specified deity, and they had to undertake charitable works, both of which were aspirations of early Enlightenment thinking. Freemasonry became fashionable among the aristocracy, and was regarded as a force for good. Of the subsequent Dukes of Richmond, the 4th, 5th and 7th were Freemasons. Through this as well as his links with Voltaire, the 2nd Duke was close to the thinking of the early French Enlightenment.

## OPERA AND THEATRE

One of the many attractions of London for the 2nd Duke was the opera. He already knew Owen McSwiny, who, only a year after the first Italian opera was performed in London in 1705, became associated with the theatre at Drury Lane. About one year later again McSwiny managed to gain the lease of the Queen's (later King's) Theatre in the Haymarket, thereafter using his own funds to import singers from Italy for the two theatres. One of his co-managers was the actor Colley Cibber (1671–1757), who became a friend of the 2nd Duke. McSwiny was also an early promoter in London of the work of George Frederick Handel.

After his first successes the unreliable McSwiny absconded from the Queen's Theatre in 1713 with the box-office takings. Owing to the ongoing row between George I and his son and the resulting uncertainty of court life, there was a lapse in operatic performances in London in the next few years. McSwiny reappeared in Venice, staying in 1720 with the English banker Joseph Smith. He now had the idea of acting as an agent to sell paintings by Italian artists to the English *milordi* on the Grand Tour. It was in Venice that he had met the young Earl of March.

Meanwhile in London the Royal Academy of Music (a performing company, not the present conservatoire) was founded in 1719 in order to establish regular seasons of Italian opera. Unlike other European countries, there was no court opera in London, so wealthy supporters were essential. Handel returned from abroad in time to be appointed master of the orchestra. Opera became extremely fashionable: Elizabeth Cadogan, Lord Cadogan's sister-in-law and daughter of Sir Hans Sloane, wrote to the Duke, 'I am just come from the opera, which had every Soul at it, that is in Town . . .'[15] By 1724 the persuasive McSwiny was again involved with the Italian opera in London, but from abroad and at arm's length.

This had considerable ramifications for the Duke. The Royal Academy of Music asked McSwiny to keep them informed about news of operatic productions in Italy and the feasibility of re-creating them in England, in return for which he would receive a reasonable salary. He also advised on the adaptation of libretti and hired singers for the Academy. The business was very competitive, with Italians in London trying to bring in their own friends. For reasons of his own, McSwiny declined to write directly to the Academy, addressing his information to the Duke. It seems to have been partly through McSwiny's influence that the Duke became so involved in the musical life of the capital, with the extraordinary situation of the Duke acting as a go-between for the roguish agent. The Duke's patronage was appreciated: in December 1726 he was elected Deputy Governor of the Royal Academy of Music, a position attained through a vote by the subscribers.

Arguments were rife in the musical world, especially over finance. After the end of the 1727–8 season, the Academy became bankrupt and had to close. McSwiny continued to write to the Duke, with news of Handel's search for a new company of singers. Although the Duke wanted to help, the next few years were very challenging in the operatic world, and he disengaged himself until 1733, when he joined the court of directors of the

Opera of the Nobility at Lincoln's Inn Fields. This was a breakaway, rival opera company, among the supporters of which were his Charlton Hunt allies, Lords Burlington and De La Warr; Thomas Coke, at the time titled as Lord Lovell; Lord Cadogan, and others. Nevertheless, the Duke's relationship with the persuasive but infuriating McSwiny continued through the 1730s.

The Richmond family also loved the theatre. Through the Charlton Hunt connection with the 3rd Duke of Bolton, the Richmonds must have been all too aware of the presence of Bolton's mistress, Lavinia Fenton, on the stage in John Gay's *Beggar's Opera*. Gay was part of the Duke's London cultural circle; Anne, Countess of Albemarle, reported to her brother Richmond in 1728 that Gay had written a second part to the play, which she believed to be very good, and that Colley Cibber also had a play that was in rehearsal.[16] In 1732 Cibber dropped a witty note to the Duke saying that he hoped the Duchess would be at his benefit play, and that she would have the first box on the stage.[17]

The children were also encouraged to perform plays. In 1731 John Dryden's *The Indian Emperor* or *The Conquest of Mexico by the Spaniards*, an heroic interpretation of the conquest of Mexico, was revived at Drury Lane. The next year a group of children, including Lady Caroline Lennox, were coached by the theatre's manager Theophilus Cibber (1703–1758), the son of the actor-manager, to perform the play privately at the home of John Conduitt, Master of the Mint, in Great George Street: the children were presumably friends of his daughter, Catherine. Conduitt was proud of his connections, commissioning Hogarth to paint the scene. The painting shows a delightfully intimate family scene, of parents admiring their offspring. The play was such a success that the children were asked to repeat it before the King and Queen at St James's Palace.[18]

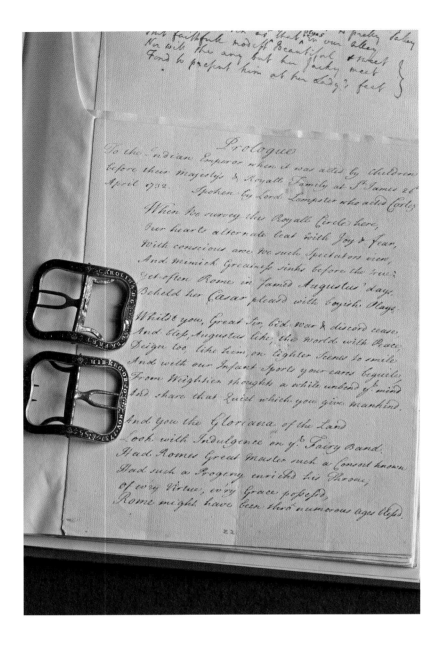

## FAMILY

On 6 October 1731 the birth of Lady Emelia was received with great joy.[19] The Duke and Duchess's only surviving child, Caroline, was now aged eight, and the arrival of Emily (as she was known) was much fêted. The King consented to be her godfather and gave a substantial gift: 'Two Hundred Ounces of gilt plate as a gift from his Majesty at the Christening of his Child to be made into such vessels and after such a fashion as his Grace shall direct.'[20] A circular Christening bowl and cover was made from this by Edward Feline of Covent Garden, in the baroque style with ornate cartouches, elaborate strapwork and wide handles with the lion and the unicorn as supporters. The whole was topped by the family crest, the Richmond lion on a ducal coronet. The child was named after the twenty-year-old Princess Amelia, the King's second daughter, who was also a godmother, as was the Countess of Tankerville from Uppark. After the baptism at St Margaret's, Westminster, a christening party was held, for which the steward made a payment of £10.0.0. for '8 cakes at ye Xning of Lady Amelia'.[21] These were expensive and elaborate offerings.

During their early married life the Duke and Duchess were often to be found at Greenwich, where they rented a house from Lady Vanbrugh, the widow of Sir John, the celebrated architect and dramatist. The purpose of this was mainly to keep the children out of central London, which the Duke believed was not good for their health, but it may also have been because they found the existing Richmond House unsatisfactory. In order to attend at court, the Duke and Duchess also had to keep an apartment at Hampton Court, taking their domestic staff with them.

## RICHMOND HOUSE

As befitted their close relationship to the monarch, the first three Lennox Dukes of Richmond lived for much of the year in central London, near to what had been the old Whitehall Palace. After most of the palace was destroyed by fire in 1698, royal relations and members of the aristocracy were granted ground leases to build and live in houses in the Privy Garden, the old garden area of the palace. Each monarch liked to retain control over the area, in which the royal Banqueting House by Inigo Jones was still the most prestigious building. Long-term leases were not granted: hence the history of dwellings in the area shows inhabitants applying and reapplying for the ground leases of houses built and funded by themselves.

Back in 1661 a small house had been built on the river bank, on one of Henry VIII's old bastions. By 1667 the enlarged house belonged to Charles Stuart, 3rd Duke of Richmond of the earlier creation. With his beautiful new bride, Frances Teresa Stuart, he lived at this, the first Richmond House, from August 1668, where they were visited by Samuel Pepys. In 1672 they were enlarging it again, but that December the Duke died, the last of the Stuart Dukes of Richmond. Frances Teresa continued to live there as a widow. Her neighbour at the time was Louise de Keroualle, who inhabited the nearest point of Whitehall Palace, separated from Frances Teresa's home only by the palace bowling green. Because she loved to entertain, kitchens were built for Louise immediately adjacent to Frances Teresa's house, across the green from her own forty-room apartments.

When Frances Teresa died in 1702, her house, still on royal land, was initially taken over for official purposes. In 1708 these riverside lodgings were being used by the two Comptrollers of the Accounts of the Army, Sir Philip Meadows and Mr Brodrick (later Lord Midleton). In 1710, Charles Lennox, 1st Duke of Richmond, applied to the Crown for the lease of 'old Buildings, Yards and Garden which he is now in possession of by her Ma(jesty's) favour . . .' A plan accompanying the lease shows a long strip, kinked in the middle, adjacent to the riverside house and ground. This was the site of his mother's kitchen and other offices. The property was therefore away from the river, parallel to it, but separated from it partly by the garden of the riverside house and partly by the house itself. The Duke's plot was sandwiched on the far (west) side by a third domain, 'the late Scotch Secretarys [*sic*] House'. This was the home of the Earls of both Loudoun and Mar, a handsome classical house with a pediment designed by Sir Christopher Wren in 1673, incomplete for many years, but by 1701 inhabited by both earls, who were joint Secretaries of State for Scotland. It was divided internally, the division running through the house to almost exactly the centre of the five-bay portico.[22]

The 1st Duke of Richmond built his house on the long thin site, but even in 1725 it was in a state of ill repair. The 2nd Duke decided to build a new mansion, the third with the name of Richmond House, on the site of his late father's property. Lord Hervey reported in October 1732 that the Duke was 'going to pull down and rebuild his house in town'.[23] Although the plot was long, about 200 feet, enabling a long courtyard at the north end, it was, at 70 feet wide, big enough for a substantial building, as his father's house had apparently been.

At the time of construction part of the immediate foreshore was clear, but did not belong to him. Slightly further south, away from the site of the old palace, some remains of Frances Teresa's house were annoyingly close on the river bank. This building was still subdivided between the two Comptrollers of the Accounts of the Army. The view to the river was clearly important, so the Duke applied in 1732 for a grant of the open ground. However, he only succeeded in gaining a strip 2 feet wide on which to build a wall. This meant that the new house had no option but to face north to Whitehall rather than east to the river.

Designs were made for Richmond House by Lord Burlington.[24] Documentation is scant, but the final version of the house probably had some amendments. The eleven-bay Wren house on the adjacent site clearly influenced the pediment-fronted design of the 2nd Duke's new seven-bay Richmond House by Lord Burlington. A staircase led to the first floor, with a grand colonnaded saloon proposed for the corner on to the Privy Garden. Three drawings for ceilings are in the Banqueting House tradition of broad bands, between which canvases could be placed.

In February 1733 the Duke and Duchess were trying to decide where to go while the house was rebuilt. The Earl of Pembroke found them a lease on Sir William Morice's house, near by, but in the event paintings, mirrors and other goods were removed early in May to a house on Pall Mall, while other possessions were taken to Greenwich.[25] The existing Richmond House was pulled down in May 1733.[26] In June, on exchange of contract, the bricklayers Churchill & Pratt were paid £400, while Mr Davis the carpenter received £350, and Mr Fellows the mason £200.[27] A supervisor was 'attending at ye new building Whitehall house' for the whole of July.[28] The money to pay for the works was a loan from Mr Anthony Isaacson, with whom the Duke had already dealt over the acquisition of land at Charlton, and from his relation Edmund Brudenell.

Facing north, the new Richmond House commanded the southern end of the relatively public area of the royal garden and

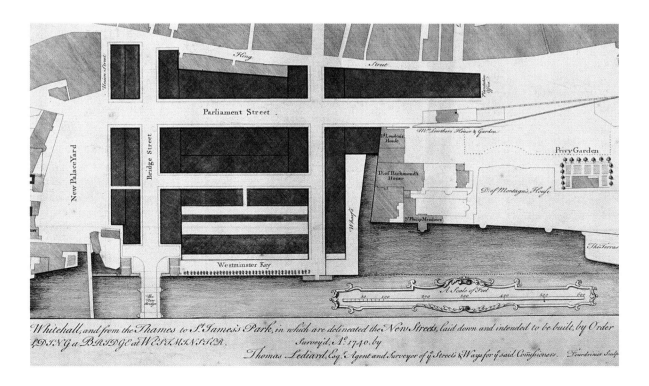

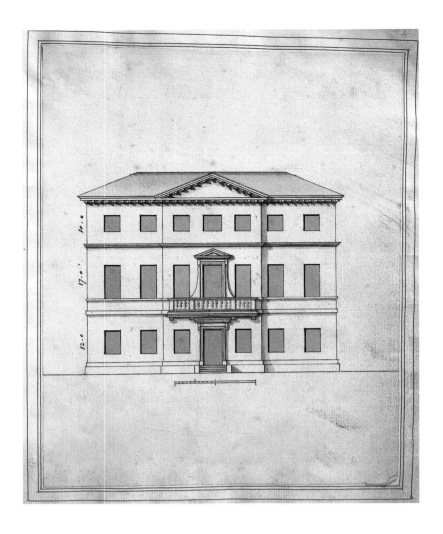

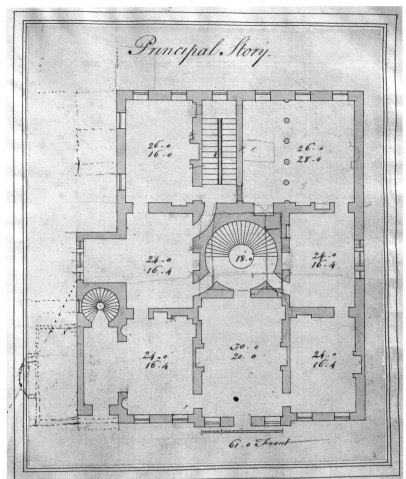

Principal Story.

26.0
16.0

26.0
28.0

24.0
16.4

18.0

24.0
16.4

24.0
16.4

30.0
20.0

24.0
16.4

61.0 Front

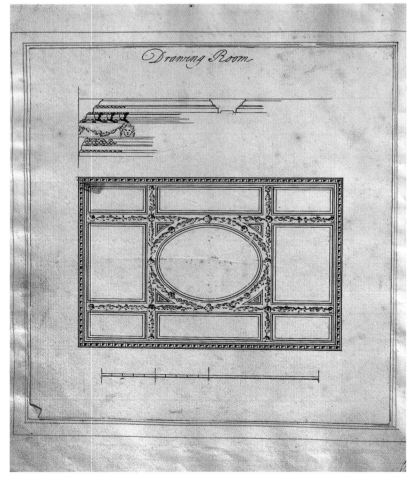

Drawing Room

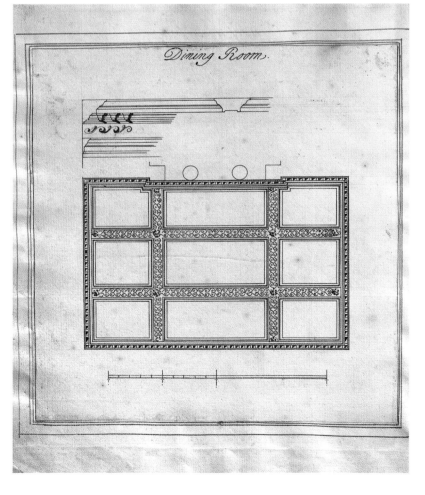

Dining Room.

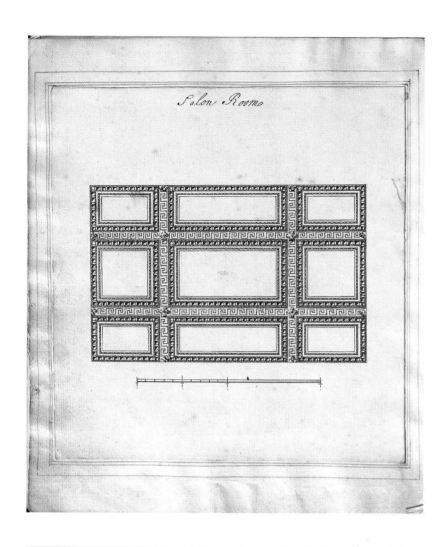

Salon Roome

FACING PAGE   Designs by Lord Burlington for Richmond House, pen and wash, drawn by another hand. The house as built may have had some amendments.
a) Elevation for the front, pen and wash, 220 × 180 mm / 8½ × 7 in.
b) Plan of the principal storey, pen and wash, 220 × 175 mm / 8½ × 6¾ in.
c) Design for the dining-room ceiling, pen and wash, 190 × 175 mm / 7½ × 6¾ in.
d) Design for the drawing-room ceiling, pen and wash, 190 × 175 mm / 7½ × 6¾ in.

LEFT   Design for the ceiling of the 'Salon', pen and wash, 200 × 180 mm / 8 × 7 in.

BELOW   *Whitehall View*, by Antonio Joli, *c.*1744–8, oil on canvas, 42 × 71 cm / 16½ × 28 in (private collection). The new seven-bay pedimented Richmond House, built 1733–6, is seen in the distant centre, just beyond the Banqueting House. Its style was clearly influenced by the earlier eleven-bay Wren house adjacent.

the Banqueting House, sharing this position with the Loudon & Mar house. The front of Richmond house projected into the Privy Garden beyond that of the two earls: this is best shown in a painting of *c.*1744–8, looking from beside the Banqueting House back to the two classical houses with their pedimented fronts.

Subsequently, in 1738, the 2nd Duke began a process to tidy up the foreshore beside Richmond House by obtaining the lease of the 'two old Houses' on the bastion, the earlier Richmond domain.[29] He was proud enough of the setting of his new house by 1744 to commission the Italian artist Antonio Joli to paint from it a 'View of St Pauls . . . a beautiful picture and veramente *di buon gusto*'.[30] It seems to have been the catalyst for other works by Joli of the Westminster bank, which yield much information about

the finishing off of Richmond House, in the area of the bastion. The Duke first demolished the part of the early house that was actually over the bastion. By 1745/6 he had built a new dining room, projecting out towards the river, abutting the remains of the old house belonging to Charles Stuart and Frances Teresa. A terrace was created on the waterfront, with the bastion levelled into it and arranged with garden seats, as shown in Canaletto's *The*

*Thames and the City of London from Richmond House*, painted from the window bay of the first floor dining room (see also page 45). Most of the old house was taken down in 1746 but a narrow line of buildings at the southern edge of the plot remained, appearing in John Rocque's map of 1746, adjacent to Todd's Wharf.[31] They may have been offices.

FACING PAGE, TOP    *The Thames*, by Antonio Joli, 1746, oil on canvas, 14.5 × 90 cm / 17¾ × 35¼ in (private collection), showing Richmond House, with its added dining room.

FACING PAGE, BOTTOM    Detail from *The Thames and the City of London from Richmond House*, by Canaletto (see page 45), showing figures on the terrace.

RIGHT, TOP    Chimneypiece and chairs by William Kent, from Richmond House, now in the Music Room. With a classical mask at the centre, deeply carved with bonny cherubs' heads in profile on acanthus-decorated brackets as caryatids, the classical detail on the chimneypiece is given an almost baroque setting amidst fruit and flowers. It is identical to those at each end of the Gallery at Chiswick House. The 3rd Duke did not keep his father's Italian-style armchairs by William Kent from Richmond House, giving them to the City of Chichester by 1785. They were bought back in 1996.

RIGHT, BOTTOM    Sketch of ground plan of Chiswick House, believed to be by the 2nd Duke.

## KENT AND BRETTINGHAM AT RICHMOND HOUSE

It is likely that much of the interior design for Richmond House was by William Kent. A ceiling painting of Neptune, Mercury, Zephyrus and Flora in a broken Venetian-style oval is believed to have been by him.[32] One chimneypiece now at Goodwood is certainly from Richmond House and its design is identical to the two by William Kent at each end of the Gallery at Chiswick House. They were made in 1727: the Duke ordered his version only a few years afterwards. Although the design was not published by Kent in his book of Inigo Jones's designs with some additions by himself, *Designs for Publick and Private Buildings* (1727), there is at Plate 65 in Volume 1 a similar chimneypiece design with the same theme of a central mask flanked by profile caryatids. It is marked *W. Kent inve*. The Duke was a subscriber to the publication: his copy is still in the Goodwood library. The quality of the carving on the Goodwood chimneypiece is superb, possibly even better than at Chiswick. Sketched on a later letter from Emily, there is a rough floor plan of Chiswick House, showing that the Duke was certainly interested in what had been carried out there.[33] Given that no documented payment to William Kent for architectural work on any of Lord Burlington's buildings exists, the chimneypiece is probably as close to being by William Kent as can ever be proved.[34]

Another Richmond House chimneypiece that is also now at Goodwood follows a design by Inigo Jones for the apartment of Queen Henrietta Maria at Somerset House. Dated 1636, it was not original to Jones, who admired the French use of Italian ideas and had copied it, with emendations, from a contemporary French design. The reuse of a design of French origin made for the 2nd Duke of Richmond's royal great-grandmother must have seemed especially suitable for Richmond House. Both drawings (now at the Royal Institute of British Architects) were in the Jones collection that had been bought by Lord Burlington, so they were available to his protégé William Kent. The design was subsequently published in John Vardy's *Some Designs of Mr Inigo Jones and Mr William Kent* (1744), Plate 10.[35]

Kent may have advised on the tomb monument at Deene Park. With Matthew Brettingham (1699–1769) he had recently been

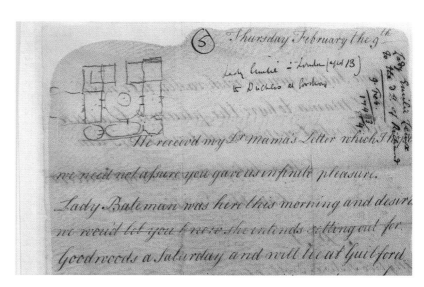

employed by Thomas Coke, later the Earl of Leicester (1697–1759), who, as a subscriber to the Great Room of the Charlton Hunt, had been a friend of the Duke from an early age, and had also supplied hounds to the Hunt. Coke, at the time Lord Lovell,

suggested that in order to gain experience Brettingham should survey Richmond House for the Duke when the builders had finished, a proposition on which he acted.[36] Although Kent may have been involved in the designs, Burlington's more hands-on protégé Daniel Garrett was clerk of the works for the building, having already worked with Roger Morris at White Lodge in Richmond Park and at Windsor.

After his original measuring, Matthew Brettingham did more work at Richmond House. According to an account, he made 'alterations and additions to the old and new part of the house, Garden and court walls': a subsequent insertion to the account adds: 'at Whitehall'.[37] It is therefore likely that the new dining room was built by him. A letter to him from the Duchess dated 1745 shows that there were still nine trades to be paid off at Richmond House. Soon after this, in 1748, Brettingham rebuilt Norfolk House in St James' Square for the Duke and Duchess of Norfolk. Mary Blount, Duchess of Norfolk, was a close friend of the Duchess of Richmond and the recommendation of this safe and solid classical architect may have passed between the ladies.

## FURNISHING OF RICHMOND HOUSE

In his usual peripatetic way, Kent seems to have left it to others to carry out the mundane work, dashing in with flashes of brilliance. Other items now at Goodwood that were originally at Richmond House were designed by him, in particular some very Italianate chairs with cherubs' heads. There may originally have been a whole set, possibly for a state room.[38] Four pedestals are also believed to be by Kent.[39] With the new rage for collecting 'marbles', these were ideal to support busts of famous people, of which the Duke certainly had a few. A pair of massive picture frames, surrounding the portraits of George II (by Thomas Hudson) and Queen Caroline (by John Vanderbank) may also have been designed by Kent.

Other furniture at Richmond House followed Kent's style of architectural furniture. A fine pair of mahogany commodes have cherubs' head terms at the sides in the same manner as the chimney-piece and the gilt armchairs. These are believed to be by William Hallett (1707–81/82), with the elaborate ormolu mounts possibly by John Boson. It is interesting to see just a hint of rococo creeping in to the Palladian designs, both in the long fronded scrolls on the sides of the pedestals and in these cartouche-type escutcheons.

There was also a set of the ever-popular Don Quixote tapestries at Richmond House (not the set now in the Tapestry Drawing Room at Goodwood, which were acquired later).[40] A sofa and eight armchairs were designed to match the five tapestries.[41] An inventory made in 1739 describes all the room contents at the time, while a later list shows the paintings to have been a classic mix of portraits, old masters, landscapes and topographical paintings.[42] More domestic furniture included various 'teaboards', or round tables with specially rounded compartments from which porcelain bowls and cups with saucers for tea could not slide. For use on them the Duchess had a number of sets of Chantilly porcelain.[43]

The new house was much needed. In 1735 the King appointed the Duke to the important role of Master of the Horse, the post which his father had held as a minor. The election was a great honour, one that the Duke undertook with much attention to detail, carrying a little vellum notebook which listed all the different horses in the Royal Mews. Eight royal coats of arms embroidered on red damask, which are still in the collection, may have been commissioned for ceremonial use at this time. He was also sworn in as a member of the Privy Council. To be politically detached was necessary in his new role, which involved attending the monarch on ceremonial occasions. However, the 2nd Duke of Richmond was clearly a Whig. He was a staunch supporter of Sir Robert Walpole, whose years as First Lord of the Treasury from 1721–42 ensured a long period of political stability. He was also close both politically and socially to Thomas Pelham-Holles, Duke of Newcastle (1693–1768), who from 1724 was Secretary of State for the southern department, exchanging it for the north in 1748 to achieve an unparalleled thirty years in that office. Newcastle's younger brother, Henry Pelham (1694–1754), MP for Sussex, was also a political ally, serving from 1730 to 1743 as Paymaster General and thereafter First Lord of the Treasury, succeeded after his death by Newcastle.

A 1736 map by John Rocque, commissioned by the Duke as part of his royal role, was dedicated in glowing terms 'To the Most Puissant Prince Charles Lenox Duke of Richmond Knight of the Most Noble Order of the Garter etc. etc.' The court was all-absorbing. A close colleague was Henry Herbert, the future 9th Earl of Pembroke (c.1689–1750), the great patron of architecture. Richmond and Pembroke were in a way related, Louise de Keroualle's younger sister having married Philip Herbert, the 7th Earl. They were certainly good friends, corresponding in a familiar manner: 'My best Respects Pray to the little Duchess who is I suppose as Mischievous and Fruitful as Ever', wrote Pembroke.[44] Mary Fitzwilliam, Countess of Pembroke (1709–1769), was also a lady of the bedchamber. Another colleague at court was the beautiful, blonde and discreet Henrietta Howard (née Hobart,

LEFT  Mahogany commode, one of a pair, believed to be from Richmond House, attributed to William Hallett, c.1735, the mounts possibly by John Boson, with Imari charger above, c.1700.

FACING PAGE, TOP  Chimneypiece from Richmond House, now in the Round Reception Room. From a design by Inigo Jones.

FACING PAGE, BOTTOM  Pedestal, by or after William Kent, veneered in mahogany with double shells and leaf pendants on the shafts; bearing Roman bust of boy, acquired in the eighteenth century with existing restoration; beyond, detail of giltwood mirror, George II c.1755.

*c*.1688–1767), Countess of Suffolk, mistress to the King both before and after his accession. At first a woman of the bedchamber, a role given to the untitled, she graduated on her husband's elevation as Earl of Suffolk to being Mistress of the Robes. In 1736, by now a widow, she became related to the Richmonds on her marriage to George Berkeley, younger brother of James, Admiral Lord Berkeley, the Duke's brother-in-law (who in that year died at the Duke's château at Aubigny). Sadly no correspondence survives to show the relationship between Henrietta and the Richmonds.

In 1737 there was a great upset at court when Frederick, Prince of Wales, infuriated by his unsympathetic and controlling parents, removed his wife from court when she was in labour with her first child. The King reprimanded his son, sending a message via the Duke of Richmond dismissing him from court. The sudden death of Queen Caroline in November that year further rocked the court, leaving the King isolated and despairing. For court mourning the Duke had gold shoe buckles, the gold lettering appearing through a black top coating. Four small skulls-and-crossbones on each one reminded the wearer of the ubiquity of death (see page 32). A small painting by an unknown artist shows the King standing in front of Queen Caroline's beloved library at St James's Palace.[45] The Duke had a similar portrait painted of himself.[46]

## FAMILY LIFE AT RICHMOND HOUSE

In 1735 the family entered a more secure and personally happy period with the birth of a son and heir. Charles Lennox, Earl of March, was born on 4 February. He was followed two years later by a brother, Lord George, who was to be his constant playmate, loyal supporter and firm friend. The Earl of March was born only months after the death the previous November in Paris of his grandmother, Louise de Keroualle, Duchess of Portsmouth and Aubigny, who had so longed for his arrival. Voltaire said of Louise: 'Never did woman preserve her charms so late in life. At the age of seventy she was still lovely, her figure stately, her face unfaded.' Louise died at the age of eighty-five, lonely and obscure, but drawing great strength from piety, and from the convent that she had founded at Aubigny. The Duke and Duchess went to

RIGHT, TOP    *Charles, 2nd Duke of Richmond, Lennox and Aubigny,* attributed to Charles Philips, oil on canvas, 74 × 61 cm / 29¼ × 24 in. The Duke is shown in his library at Richmond House. This small full-length portrait is by the same anonymous hand as one of George II at Marble Hill House, Twickenham.

RIGHT, BOTTOM    *Lady Caroline Fox, in Masquerade Costume,* by William Hoare of Bath, pastel, 59 × 44 cm / 23¼ × 17¼ in.

FACING PAGE    Eagle table, believed to be from Richmond House, with Imari bowls and covers, *c*.1700, acquired by the 1st Duke and Duchess. Above, portrait of Caroline, 5th Duchess of Richmond, by Sir Thomas Lawrence, 1829, oil on canvas, approx 254 × 160 cm / 100 × 63 in.

Aubigny in the summer of 1735, spending a few months there in order to sort out his inheritance. The Duke continued to go there each autumn, using La Verrerie as a hunting lodge. The Duchess would often travel with him to visit her family at The Hague on the same trip.

Inevitably the Duke's involvement in public duties brought further honours and appointments. He was a governor of Captain Coram's famous charity the Foundling Hospital, inaugurated in 1739. The painter William Hogarth was also a great supporter and, along with other artists, gave his work to the foundation, where in the large rooms it could be seen by aristocratic visitors who would give funds to the charity. Although the Duke was not a patron of Hogarth as a painter, he must have known the artist through this connection, and it was presumably he who

acquired the large collection of his first-edition prints now in the Goodwood library. In that year Richmond also became a governor of the Charterhouse, a charity endowed to care for impoverished gentlemen, soldiers, merchants or royal servants. Richmond was also President of the London Hospital in 1741, promoting its move to Whitechapel; Master of Trinity House 1741–5 and President of the Society of Antiquaries in 1750.

Sarah, Duchess of Richmond, was a perfect mistress of Richmond House. After the arrival of the two sons, a daughter, Margaret, was born in 1739, but died as an infant. Two further daughters followed in quick succession, Louisa in 1743 and Sarah in 1745. Frederick, Prince of Wales, consented to be Louisa's godfather. Despite his rift with his parents, the Duke and Duchess once again sought to be friendly with both generations, and indeed were sometimes able to calm the troubled waters between them. By now the two elder Lennox daughters were being brought into society. When the young Horace Walpole (1717–1797), youngest son of the Prime Minister, saw them all at a ball given by the Duke's friend 'long' Sir Thomas Robinson of Rokeby for Emily in the autumn of 1741, he reported: 'The beauties were the Duke of Richmond's two daughters & their mother, still handsomer than they; the Duke sat by his wife all night, kissing her hand.'[47]

BELOW    *Venice: the Rialto bridge seen from the north,* with the Palazzo dei Camerlenghi and the Naranzeria to the right, by Canaletto, oil on copper, 46 × 61 cm / 18 × 24 in. Commissioned by Owen McSwiny and sent to the Duke in 1727.

FACING PAGE    *Venice: a View of the Grand Canal to the north,* from near the Rialto bridge with the Fabbrichie Nuove di Rialto to the left on the far side of the canal, by Canaletto, oil on copper, 46 × 61 cm / 18 × 24 in. Commissioned by Owen McSwiny and sent to the Duke in 1727.

On 7 May 1744 Walpole reported: 'There is to be a great ball tomorrow at the Duchess of Richmond's for my lady Carteret: the [Prince of Wales] is to be there.'[48] This was not to be. The family was thrown into confusion by the elopement of their eldest daughter Caroline, hitherto so dutiful. Overwhelmed by love for Henry Fox (1705–1774), a much older, socially ambitious, womanising politician, to whom her father had already refused her hand, she had left Richmond House secretly, to marry him at the home of their friend Charles Hanbury Williams in Conduit Street. She then returned to Richmond House and did not tell her parents for another five days. When she did, a storm broke. The ball was cancelled. The Duke vowed that anyone who received the couple would be ostracised by them. As their other witness was the Duke of Marlborough, this meant that friends had to choose. Horace Walpole pontificated snobbishly: 'His grandfather was a footman: her great-grandfather was a King: *hinc illae lacrymae*. All the blood royal have been up in arms.'[49] The family rushed back to Goodwood to lick their wounds, which were very deep indeed. The Duke and Duchess declined society for a while, and especially refused to see anyone who entertained the Foxes. This state of affairs lasted for four years, by which time Henry Fox had become Secretary at War in Henry Pelham's administration and Caroline had borne her first son, Stephen.

## CANALETTO IN VENICE AND LONDON

In the hall at Richmond House the Duke had a total of three paintings by Antonio Joli, the Venetian topographical painter who worked in London between 1744 and 1748, primarily painting scenery at the King's Theatre, Haymarket. He had probably come to the Duke's attention through Owen McSwiny. As well as the view of St Paul's Cathedral, the Duke owned a vertical view by him of the church of S. Giorgio Maggiore in Venice, looking past the Customs House across the lagoon, and another horizontal view.[50]

The Duke also owned two smaller views of Venice, which hung in the library.[51] These were by the fashionable Venetian artist Giovanni Antonio Canale (1697–1768), known as Canaletto. McSwiny had already commissioned the artist to paint the architecture in two of the 'tomb' paintings proposed for the Dining Room at Goodwood (see page 23), and in 1727 he persuaded the Duke to buy these two small pictures on copper. As his first English agent, McSwiny had a considerable influence on the young artist, persuading him to paint small, sun-drenched pictures of piazzas and canal scenes that were attractive to the tourist, such as the two below, looking to and from the Rialto bridge. They replaced the larger, darker, slightly untidy close-up views with which Canaletto had commenced his career. McSwiny

wrote to the Duke in the winter of 1727: 'The two Copper plates done by *Canal* are very fine.'[52]

For delivery to Richmond House, the two views of Venice were sent by McSwiny to John Smith in London. He was the brother of McSwiny's friend Joseph Smith (*c.*1674–1770), an English banker and self-created art dealer. Joseph Smith had lived in Venice since about 1700, his palazzo on the Grand Canal becoming an essential visit for the British nobility passing through the city. The Duke and Thomas Hill had met him in Venice in 1721. By the mid 1720s Joseph Smith was showing great interest in Canaletto's work, commissioning him to paint larger views for himself, beautifully composed and coloured.[53] Soon most works by Canaletto were being commissioned through Smith, views and mementoes of their stay in the *Serenissima* for

the young English *milordi*. Whig patrons such as John Russell, 4th Duke of Bedford (1710–1771) and Henry Howard, 4th Earl of Carlisle (1694–1758), may have been attracted to the Venetian views because of an instinctive admiration for the political structure of the Venetian Republic.[54] Canaletto's popularity was such that prices began to go up. In 1727 the Duke declined the offer of two further landscapes.[55]

The 2nd Duke was instrumental in the appointment of Joseph Smith as Consul to Venice, in 1740 reminding his close friend and political ally Thomas Pelham-Holles, Duke of Newcastle, that he had promised two years ago 'for Mr Smith to succeed Consul Brown whenever he should dye or be removed', and chivvying him in three further letters to keep the promise.[56] Smith was appointed as Consul in 1744, with important ramifications. Because of the

War of the Austrian Succession (1740–48), the English could no longer travel on the continent, with a resulting fall-off in work for the painter. It was Smith who managed to keep Canaletto's career successfully on track for a few more years, in both Venice and Rome. Eventually Canaletto decided that he should go to England, where he believed there were patrons who would buy his work. He arrived in London by the end of May 1746, lodging at first near to the Duke's home in Whitehall. He brought with him a letter of introduction from Smith to McSwiny, of which the ultimate target was the Duke.

The Duke of Richmond was indeed pivotal in the artist's career in England.[57] His friend and former tutor, Tom Hill, learnt of Canaletto's aims at dinner in the house next door to Richmond House, the home of John, 2nd Duke of Montagu,

ABOVE   *The Thames and the City of London from Richmond House*, by Canaletto, oil on canvas, 101.5 × 117 cm / 41½ × 46 in. Next door, at the house of the Duke of Montagu, a lordly visitor knocks on the door. On the terrace beyond, a serving man sweeps. Near him can be seen a corner of the Chinese Pavilion, an exotic folly. Beyond lie the old buildings of the Savoy, stretching to Somerset House, whose trees run down to the Thames. Beyond, the Temple is seen in shadow. St Paul's Cathedral stands high above Wren's City churches, with the Monument round on the right. On the river itself can be seen barges of the City livery companies.

FACING PAGE   *Whitehall and the Privy Garden from Richmond House*, by Canaletto, oil on canvas, 101.5 × 117 cm / 41½ × 46 in. The view from an upstairs room shows the stable yard of Richmond House, the footman bowing to a visitor. On the far left runs Parliament Street, now incorporated into Whitehall, past the Holbein Gate on the left and the Banqueting House on the right, shown end on. Both were remnants of the old Whitehall Palace, which had been destroyed by fire in 1698. Immediately to the right of the Banqueting House are the spire of St Martin-in-the-Fields, and a dome of Northumberland House. The back of the Duke of Montagu's house is seen beyond the stable yard: it was here that Owen McSwiny and Thomas Hill first discussed the possibility of the commission.

where McSwiny was also a guest. The Irishman was somewhat drunk, according to Hill's subsequent report to the Duke; but Hill learnt from him of Canaletto's desire to work for the Duke. It was Hill's suggestion that Canaletto should paint a river scene from Richmond House. He wrote to the Duke:

> Canale, alias Canaletti, is come over with a letter of recommendation from our old acquaintance [Joseph Smith] the Consul of Venice to Mac [Swiny] in order to his introduction to your Grace, as a patron of the politer parts, or what the Italian understand by the name of *virtù*. I told him the best service I thought you could do him wd be to let him draw a view of the river from your dining room, which in my opinion would gain him as much reputation as any of his Venetian prospects.[58]

The Duke agreed to the request from his 'old acquaintance'.

In the event, Canaletto's earliest paintings in London were of Westminster Bridge, which was being constructed at the time. This was an important landmark, the only other existing bridge being Old London Bridge. One of the earliest versions of this was acquired by Ferdinand Philip, 6th Prince Lobkowicz. The Prince is believed to have met the Duke through another letter of introduction, sent by John Lindsay, 20th Earl of Crawford, from Brussels in January 1745.[59] By December that year the glamorous twenty-one-year-old Prince had become friendly with fourteen-year-old Lady Emily, and was due to arrive to stay at Goodwood. It is highly likely that it was the Duke who presented Canaletto to him.

The Duke of Richmond's London scenes are fabulous documents of contemporary life, as well as highly skilled works of art. The city and the gardens of the great London houses along the Strand and Whitehall looked on to the Thames, not away from it, and it was a popular waterway, buzzing with life. In his river scene, *The Thames and the City of London from Richmond House*, Canaletto shows the wide and brilliant river lapping its way towards

the City. As in Sir Hugh Smithson's version of the completed Westminster Bridge, he includes barges of the livery companies on the river. Out of another window Canaletto painted the Privy Garden, the old garden of Whitehall Palace that stretched away from both the Richmond and Loudon houses. Another, slightly later, painting by him shows it to be a muddy and disorganised area,[60] but in the painting for the Duke of Richmond it is tidily grassy, with figures both fashionable and humble.

When he first became popular, Canaletto was seen as a good topographical painter, working in an established tradition of producing good-quality views of whatever the patron wanted to see. He is little mentioned by other London artists at the time. His work has rightly come to be seen as so much more. One element that lifts Canaletto above other topographical painters is his use of light, combining a light blue sky with pale northern glimmer. Another is his clever juggling of perspective: he would often sketch from two viewpoints, combining them in the final version so that the viewer could see more than was possible from a single viewpoint. Thus the Thames is widened, to make it look perhaps more glorious and indeed somewhat Venetian, and to enable a dramatic balance of river and sky. Canaletto's little figures are also sensational. Perhaps surprisingly given the delicate rigidity of all the architecture, they are supremely if discreetly rococo. Against the carefully laid out topography of each scene are gathered small figures with tiny heads and huge swirling skirts or frock coats.

The two paintings of London scenes were probably always intended for the Duke's revamped main hall at Goodwood. They are, unusually, square: most of Canaletto's paintings of London scenes were rectangular, but in this shape these pictures would fit well above the Duke's classical chimneypieces by Roger Morris. One of two preliminary sketches for the landscapes is a panorama, from which Canaletto modified the central section to fit the canvas; another is also a horizontal view, showing the river, for which he also condensed the composition for the square format.[61] The present frames are rococo, a style that was very much in the latest fashion in 1747, but the paintings may originally have been let into the panelling.[62] In London the Duke had the real views from the windows. At Goodwood he could be reminded of this good fortune.

## Firework Finale

One of the best surviving views of Richmond House is provided in a 1749 engraving, *Fireworks and Illuminations on the Thames*. In April, to celebrate the peace Treaty of Aix-la-Chapelle, which ended the War of the Austrian Succession, the King commissioned a magnificent firework display to accompany Handel's first performance of *Music for the Royal Fireworks*. A special viewing pavilion was constructed for the royal family. The English weather was disobliging, providing a continuous downpour. The fireworks were drenched and did not explode. The Duke of Richmond bought the whole supply, dried them out, and six weeks later used them for his own party on the riverside. The fireworks were assembled on barges on the river, from which they were discharged, allowing a safe stretch of water between them and the house, with a handsome viewing pavilion constructed on the shore.

For fourteen years between 1736 and 1750 Richmond House was the glittering London home of the 2nd Duke and Duchess of Richmond. The Duke was one of the great men of the day, serving on four occasions as one the Lord Justices of England during the King's absence on the continent. He was a staunch supporter of the Hanoverian succession and of the Whig politicians who ensured its security. The Duke and Duchess were also still regularly at Goodwood, where the Charlton Hunt was at the height of fashion. In Sussex he acted on behalf of the Duke of Newcastle, trying to control West Sussex, through political appointments, in which he was more successful at Chichester than at Arundel and Shoreham. Although they were in the first rank of society, they enjoyed the company of family and senior members of their household as much as that of the smart and fashionable. In London they dined more with close members of the family than with other dukes or earls. In 1743 Henry Fielding addressed his poem 'Of Good-Nature' to the Duke.[63] 'Excellence of heart', a quality ascribed to the Duke, became the central theme of his celebrated novel *Tom Jones*, published in 1750. The Duke's friend Martin Folkes described the Duke as 'the most humane & best man living'.[64]

ABOVE   *A View of the Fireworks and Illuminations at his Grace the Duke of Richmond's at Whitehall and on the River Thames, on Monday 15 May 1749* (Victoria and Albert Museum: Theatre Collection). Richmond House appears to the left, with its pedimented front facing into the Privy Garden and its new Palladian three-light dining-room window looking to the river. An elaborate viewing stand is seen on the river bank. The engraving is by George Vertue, who had already made an engraving of Chichester Market Cross for the Duke in 1747.

FACING PAGE   Sketch for the stable yard, believed to be by the Duke, from his copy of Lord Burlington's *Designs for Richmond House*.

# 4 FABRICATING FOLLIES

## ROGER MORRIS IN SUSSEX, 1729–1743

The 'Great Room' created by Richard Boyle, 3rd Earl of Burlington in about 1722 for the hunt in the neighbouring village of Charlton (see page 12) was well known to the 2nd Duke. It was an emotive spot to those who loved hunting, with a proud flagstaff bearing a gilded weather vane of a fox planted in front of it, to show the direction of the wind and help consideration of the scenting conditions. This had been given by Henrietta, Duchess of Bolton, who, as the natural daughter of the Duke of Monmouth, was also, like the Duke of Richmond, a grandchild of Charles II. Two other grandsons of the Merry Monarch also hunted at Charlton: Charles Fitzroy, 2nd Duke of Grafton (1683–1757), and Charles Beauclerk, 2nd Duke of St Albans (1696–1751). The 2nd Duke of Richmond loved the hunting and the company; and he even loved the architecture of the existing hunt building, because he requested Lord Burlington to design him three separate buildings in the new Palladian style.

## GOODWOOD HOUSE

However, it was Burlington's pupil, Roger Morris (1695–1749), who made the first alterations inside Goodwood House. Probably via Colen Campbell, architect to the Prince of Wales, Morris had already gained the patronage of Lord Herbert, later 9th Earl of Pembroke, with whom he had collaborated to build the ravishingly elegant villa at Twickenham, Marble Hill, from 1724.[1] Like Burlington, Pembroke was absorbed by architecture and was an important influence in court circles. The Thames-side villa was for Pembroke's colleague in the royal service, Henrietta Howard, at the time the mistress of the Prince of Wales, and it was discreetly paid for by the Prince. Morris also collaborated with Pembroke on the royal White Lodge at Richmond (1727–8), as well as on other buildings and follies in the new Palladian style.

Morris worked closely with Campbell throughout the 1720s, and may even have been the draughtsman of his plans for a new Goodwood (see page 20), the design of which was not dissimilar from that for Henrietta's beautiful new house at Marble Hill.[2]

On their accession as king and queen in 1727, George II and Queen Caroline continued to patronise Palladian architects. Houses tended to be simple and stern on the exterior, with a riot of sophisticated carving and gilding within. The Duke of Richmond was at the forefront of this fashion, taking every opportunity he could find (and afford) to build in the Palladian style.

By 1729 Campbell and Morris were working together in Sussex, at Compton Place, near Eastbourne.[3] After Campbell's death in September 1729, Morris took over much of his work. Having already transformed the dining room at Goodwood by the introduction of the tomb paintings, the Duke had returned from his travels in October 1729 to focus his attention on the main hall and the adjacent parlour. The dividing wall, and possibly a screens passage, were removed in favour of one large, long room, symmetrical around the front door: this is now known as the Long Hall. Jacobean carved chimneypieces in each room were also taken away. An account for plastering work, including 301 feet of cornice, was dated March 1730 and signed by Roger Morris as the surveyor.[4] The work in the house started soon after the Duke's return, perhaps at the New Year. The 301 feet could well be for the three rooms above the Long Hall, which have fine Palladian cornices: the measurements roughly correspond. A corner cut in a cornice further suggests there was a chimneypiece in one of the rooms, possibly inserted by Morris for whom this was a favourite idiom.[5] The actual chimneypiece may now be the one in the Duke's room on the south front, the guilloche banding on it being very similar to that in other designs by Morris. In the hall a pair of new classical

scrolled chimneypieces in carved stone replaced the old ones: these would also appear to be by Morris. Thus, although he did not have his desired new house in the centrally planned manner, the Duke had a handsome new Palladian interior in his older house.

When the house was insured by Sun Insurance in 1732, with a tiny insignia positioned on the façade above the Garter Star, it was referred to as the Duke's 'new house'.[6] This was possibly a reference to the relative newness of the flinted exterior and of the classicised interior.

## THE HUNTING LODGE AT CHARLTON

One of the main purposes of living at Goodwood was still fox-hunting. At this date hunts started very early in the morning. Now that he was a Master of Foxhounds, the Duke needed to start each hunting day in Charlton. This gave him a practical excuse for an architectural *capriccio*: a hunting lodge. The finances to buy further estates had been provided in his marriage settlement of 1719, under which his father-in-law, Earl Cadogan, had agreed to buy him land to the value of £60,000.[7] This payment was now

called in: indeed, following the Earl's death in 1726 some of his chattels had had to be sold to pay for the settlement. On 2 September 1730 the manors of Singleton and Charlton, including a farm in each village as well as the forests, were purchased from the Earl of Scarbrough, whose seat was some five miles to the west at Stansted Park.

As part of these acquisitions, the Duke had gained the forests to the south of Charlton, and the rolling fields on the edge of which sat the Great Room. In order to pursue his passion for architecture, the Duke had his new lodge built adjacent to Lord Burlington's hunt club. This lodge is believed to have been a single-storey building with a dome and possibly a three-light Palladian window (see page 12).[8] It was known as Fox Hall. The Duke expected to be there daily when he was hunting, for he kept there his own personal silver cutlery for dining, namely a knife, a fork, a spoon and a tumbler.[9] This first building was very important in its own time, both because of its novel design and because of the rich and powerful men who subscribed to it.

For his hunting lodge and stables (which are nowadays known as Fox Hall), the Duke chose a site across the lane marginally to the

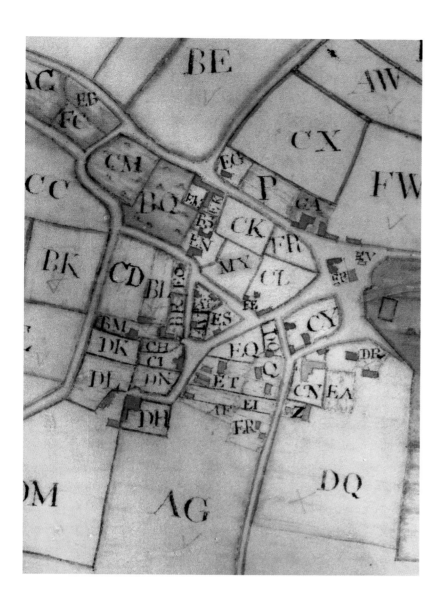

south-east, making sure that the two buildings together created an elegant ensemble. The architect for the Duke's lodge is believed to have been Roger Morris. A design by him made at about this time shows a domestic dwelling with features and proportions very similar to the lodge, and the internal decorations are commensurate with his style.[10]

The Duke's work in Charlton had commenced with the building of the stables in 1729. Throughout 1730 and 1731 the bricklayer sent in bills for work on the house.[11] Labbé, the Duke's steward, was organising the funding, for which in August 1730 the Duke sent in £150, his considerable winnings from horse racing at Tunbridge Wells. This was to pay for the 'Bricks, and timber I have taken upp, for my building at Charleton', which he felt had not been expensive.[12] Decorative items were being prepared in the autumn of 1731, notably 'Gilding the three frames at Charlton'.[13] A contemporary document summarised: 'The house at Charlton, walls finished and covered in at Michaelmas 1730; the inside of it was finished by Michaelmas 1731 and it was furnished and the Duke and Duchess of Richmond lay in it November 22nd 1732.'[14] A payment of 2 guineas made to Morris

ABOVE, LEFT The 2nd Duke's hunting lodge at Charlton – the second Fox Hall – from the south-east, with the *serliana* (window) on its south side.

ABOVE, RIGHT Fox Hall, the north and west fronts, from the lane. The 'Dome' or Great Room for the Charlton Hunt, designed by Lord Burlington, was probably located just to the right of the lane at this point.

FACING PAGE Fox Hall, interior, with original bed recess.

in August 1732 'to distribute amongst ye workmen that reard ye Building' has usually been assumed to be for the Chichester Council House, but from the dates it is just as likely to have been for Fox Hall, with a payment of 5 guineas to Morris himself in October.[15]

The hunting lodge is shown as the Duke's House on the 1732 map, proudly inscribed *A Plan of Goodwood Park and Warren with the Adjacent Manors of Charlton and Singleton belonging to His Grace the Duke of Richmond &c . . . Surveyed in February and March 1731 by Thomas Bucknall*.[16] The anonymous poet who subsequently presented his doggerel to the Duke in 1738 stated that the Duke had the finest house:

A warm but small Apartment, each one has,

the Duke's alone appears magnificent,
conspicuous, it stands, above the rest
And uniform, & nearest to the Dome.[17]

The lodge was certainly conspicuous, rising high above a thatched farmhouse near by. With its severe lines, superb brick-work and creamy quoins, it was quite different from anything else in the locality, except for Lord Burlington's Great Room.

The Duke's hunting lodge comprised one main first-floor room with a high ceiling, with chimneypiece and overmantel and a fine recess for the bed, and offices downstairs. Here his servant could sleep and prepare his breakfast: in the lodge his silver comprised a coffee pot, a pair of candlesticks, six teaspoons, a strainer, a pair of tea tongs and a cream pail.[18] It was normal in Georgian houses for rooms not to be overlit, so the main room on the first floor had one sash window to the west and one to the south, with the other two lights of a Palladian window or *serliana* on the south side blocked in on the exterior, giving the lodge the pattern of this stylish window but not the function. On the north façade there are also a number of what appear to be blocked-in windows: these would never have been open and were a way of articulating the otherwise blank areas adjacent to the main chimney stack.

In 1735 a neighbouring cottage was given up so that the Duke could 'make a beautiful Green before his hunting seat at Charlton'.[19] A map of *c.*1767 shows that a handsome avenue indeed ran away from the lodge to the west, directly across the lane: it would give a view from the main chamber to the setting sun.[20] It is likely that when arriving from Goodwood, the Duke used this as an avenue, riding straight up to the proud main façade with its heavily articulated ground-floor window. The Dome and the nearby lodges were remarked on in 1751 when Dr Richard Pococke passed through Charlton and noted 'several lodges of a Society of Hunters with a large room in which they dine'.[21]

## OTHER PATRONS OF ARCHITECTURE IN CHARLTON

The importance of the little architectural ensemble in Charlton should not be underestimated; nor should the forum of the Charlton Hunt for discussions on architecture. Smaller buildings could often be used to try out ideas for greater schemes. Original subscribers to the Great Room *c.*1722 had included men who either were or went on to be celebrated architectural patrons in their own right. The Earl of Carlisle had already commissioned Vanbrugh to build Castle Howard, while through

other subscribers there were many contacts with the Marlborough family. Even Sir Robert Walpole had a house in Charlton.[22] Thomas Coke, subsequently Lord Lovell and Earl of Leicester, was a subscriber: with the help of Burlington and William Kent he created one of the great icons of English Palladianism at Holkham Hall, on the neighbouring estate to Walpole's Houghton Hall in Norfolk.

A more local subscriber was Sir William Gage, 7th Baronet. Installed on the same day as the Duke as a Knight of the Garter, he was soon encasing Firle Place, Sussex in a neat classical design. The Duke's friend and political ally Thomas Pelham-Holles, Duke of Newcastle, and his brother the Hon. Henry Pelham were also subscribers. Their homes were nearer to London but, closer to Firle, their cousin Sir Henry Pelham used Palladian architect Nicholas Dubois to build him a fine house at Stanmer. In the 1740s Sir William Gage did more work at Firle, creating two stunning Palladian interiors.

By 1738 the Charlton Hunt had become so fashionable that it was necessary to create a proper club, not least in order to exclude some people who would have liked to join. It is possible that the enthusiasm for the hunt was partly fuelled by the attractive little pair of perfect buildings. New members were elected by ballot, and the vote tended to go to the rich and fashionable.

ABOVE Carné's Seat, the 2nd Duke's Banqueting House and 'one of the finest Rooms in England' (George Vertue, 1747).

FACING PAGE View from Carné's Seat, with sphinx.

Charles Spencer, 5th Earl of Sunderland and subsequently 3rd Duke of Marlborough, added to the roll-call of dukes, while Francis Seymour Conway, later created Earl of Hertford, was also elected. Through its heyday in the years 1730–50, the Charlton Hunt was perfectly housed, not just with the buildings by Burlington and Morris, but also with other lodges that sprang up through the village.

## THE CHICHESTER COUNCIL HOUSE

In 1730 the Duke asked Lord Burlington to draw him plans for a Council House in Chichester, reminding him in June, 'I am very sensible how troublesome I must be to your Lordship about these plans, and am really quite asham'd of it but I must once more beg of you to send the plan for the Town house as soon as possible for

the Subscription is full and . . . I dare not go [to Chichester] without a plan.'[23] Burlington did produce a design for the façade of the Council House, but otherwise it seems to have followed the designs of Roger Morris.[24] George Vertue, visiting Chichester in 1747, commented on 'the new great Room for a hall of business or meeting erected by benefactions. – the Duke of Richmond the greatest promoter & Mr Roger Morriss designed [He was] the architect.'[25]

The Duke's friend Martin Folkes met Roger Morris at this time, probably soon after Morris's return from Italy and before Folkes himself headed off to Venice: he later recorded a discussion they had about Italian architecture.[26] Folkes, a wealthy squire and patron of science, enjoyed his tour of Germany and Italy but found that the conversation was better at Goodwood and that English houses were better maintained: 'I think I shall if possible come home with a far greater notion of my own nation . . . Architecture and painting the Nations far exceed us in, but that is all, and even if I may say it the finest palaces I have yet seen want something of a neatness that we have in very indifferent dwellings in England.'[27]

## CARNÉ'S SEAT

About two years later the Duke was begging the elusive Lord Burlington for a design for a banqueting house, writing *c.*1734 'Don't forget my Casino and pray remember to keep the opening to the buffet in the dining room as wide as possible. The dining room Kitchen and Cellar being the apartments I have always most at heart.'[28] There was some delay before this was built: in the 1730s, the Duke was concentrating his building activities in London where he had to spend so much time at court. The banqueting house was eventually built by Morris in 1743, a two-storey classical pavilion, comprising one single cube room with a coved ceiling and a loggia above service rooms. It is high on the hill behind Goodwood House, commanding a sensational view across the park to Chichester, the sea beyond and the Isle of Wight.

The building was called Carné's Seat, because it replaced or was near to a cottage that had been lived in by Louise de Keroualle's old retainer, Monsieur de Carné. It is inscribed on a lintel in the ground-floor loggia: *Carnès* [*sic*] *Seat/Ligneam invenit, lapideam fecit/Carolus Richmondiae Leviniae et Albiniaci Dux/ MDCCXLIII* (Carné's Seat/he found it wood, he left it stone/

Charles, Duke of Richmond, Lennox and Aubigny/1743). The attribution to Morris is based on a drawing, believed to be in his hand, of the floor.[29] It is reinforced by a note in the letter book of the mason Andrew Relfe, which shows that Morris was dispatching stone to Goodwood in 1742.[30] The newly demolished church tower at Hove provided much of the material for the building. On 5 December that year the Duke declared that 'A great deal of stone is cutt for my building.'[31] However, nothing much more could happen until March.

A fine pair of stone sphinxes on the parapet at Carné's Seat are very similar to those designed by William Kent for Chiswick House. These were later removed to Devonshire House on Piccadilly (see page 78), on the destruction of which they were moved with the gate to the Green Park side, where proudly they remain.[32] The source for all the Chiswick sphinxes, of which there are known to have been five, is believed to have been one of the Arundel marbles, which had been restored by G.B. Guelfi at Easton Neston, Northamptonshire: Guelfi was also the sculptor used by the Duke for his mother's tomb monument at Deene Park.[33] The Duke may have known all of these versions, especially as the Countess of Pomfret, whose home was Easton Neston, was Henrietta Louisa Jefferies, Louise de Keroualle's great-niece and his own second cousin. The choice of the sphinxes was completely in line with the current classical thinking and also tied in with his new interest in Egyptian antiquities.

In 1747 Vertue both sketched and described the Duke's new banqueting house: 'His Grace the Duke of Richmond since, has there erected a beautifull building of stone, fronted with an Archade rooms & other agreeable conveniencys, for to entertain company. & over it a most beautifull room for a dineing room – finely adorned with stucco's carvings marbles &c. in the finest and most elegant taste'.[34] It was once described as the 'Venetian Room', and there was gilding; to what extent it was painted or frescoed is not known, but there was clearly a flat, bordered area in the ceiling to take a canvas.[35] The 'buffet' requested from Lord Burlington was presumably the window area. The window pattern of small elongated octagons was newly fashionable at this time, and the making of the frames in bronze was a device to help them withstand the elements. The Duke thought of having a carpet made, noting in his little booklet that it should be 12 feet 6 inches by 7 feet 3 inches.[36] This size would cover the area beneath a long dining table for ten or twelve people.

The Duke and Duchess were always concerned for their children, and they incorporated their affection for them into the banqueting house. In the rooms on the ground floor, mainly intended to be for service, a pretty single room runs along the front. Low in height, it has an oval band of decoration in the ceiling and a small but smart fireplace. The floor is in marble, a small version of what would be in a grand ballroom. This could also have been used as a buffet, but could double as a miniature saloon for the children, where the eight-year-old Lord March and his brother Lord George could play, with their two little sisters, at being dukes and duchesses.

Over the main entrance doorway was another conceit. In a little domed ceiling to the portico a painting was made of the planets as they had been aligned on the Duke's day of birth. This was something that he may have seen in the Old Sacristy of the church of S. Lorenzo in Florence: the device was subsequently used in the late 1750s at the Casino at Marino, Dublin, for the architect William Chambers, who derived the idea either from Goodwood or directly from Florence. A written description was made of it, dated 28 August 1747: *A Description of the Coelestial Hemi-Sphere delineated in the Ceiling of the Portico at Carnè's [sic] Seat in Goodwood Park*.[37]

## EMILY

The pavilion had a romantic association for the family. In 1746 an episode occurred between Emily and James Fitzgerald, 20th Earl of Kildare, who had just succeeded in gaining agreement for her hand in marriage. Emily referred to it in a letter to her husband

written some sixteen years later: 'If you are at Goodwood, and the sun shines as bright as it does here, I hope you will take a walk up to Carné Seat, sit down in the little room and think of that you took with Lady Emily Lennox, just returned from Bognor Church, sixteen years ago, and I believe that I love you sixteen times better now than I did then.'[38]

Her parents were initially less than enthusiastic about the match. Although Kildare was a peer and very wealthy, they felt that he held a lower rank than his English equivalent and was not good enough for their daughter. However, love prevailed. The Duke and Duchess grew to recognise the affection between the couple. They may also have come to realise that as their daughter would have a smallish dowry of £10,000 payable only on their deaths, her prospects were not so exceptional. Emily married her earl on 7 February 1747, in a magnificent ceremony at Richmond House. She was fifteen years and four months old.

To celebrate, the King created Kildare Viscount Leinster of Taplow, an English title to give him a seat in the House of Lords. The couple were still in England in May, staying at Goodwood, where Emily said that she was very happily married, with 'the best and kindest of husbands.'[39] Their marriage was passionate and fruitful: Emily bore him nineteen children (though the youngest, George, was probably by William Ogilvie, the children's tutor). In 1766 Kildare, by now a Marquis, was made Duke of Leinster, becoming the senior peer in Ireland. He was also a leading Freemason.

## THE GROTTO OR SHELL HOUSE

In the area close to the new pavilion one of Goodwood's hidden jewels was nearing completion. Sir Thomas Robinson, a family friend and Governor of Barbados, had heard about it: 'I am now making a collection for the Dutchess of Richmond of Shells – as we hear her Grace is fitting up a Grotto under one of the finest Rooms in Britain built lately in Goodwood Park by Your Grace.'[40] The 'finest Room' was Carné's Seat and the Grotto was what is now called the Shell House, erected soon after Emily's marriage and departure to Ireland. Robinson wrongly assumed it to be underneath the pavilion, but it was a separate little building, constructed near by. Emily referred to it in August 1748, a year after she had left for Ireland: 'I fancy you don't chuse to tell me what improvements there is at Goodwood since last year but I am sure the Grotto is not the only one . . .'[41]

The Shell House is rectangular, 15 feet 6 inches by 10 feet 6 inches, with a barrel vault, culminating in an apse containing three niches. The impeccable Palladian architectural arrangement, both sterner in its lines and far superior in quality to that in most shell houses, suggests that it was probably also designed by Roger Morris. Its walls were encrusted with shells brought back from voyages of discovery by sea captains, one of whom would have shipped the Barbados shells on behalf of Sir Thomas. A huge number was needed and usually the Duke simply paid for

RIGHT *Sultan, a Chestnut Hunter, the Property of the 2nd Duke of Richmond, Carné's Seat beyond,* by John Wootton, 1743, oil on canvas, 100 × 125 cm / 39½ × 49 in. One of the six paintings of hunters commissioned for the main hall of the house.

BELOW *Lady Emily Lennox, in masquerade costume,* by William Hoare of Bath, pastel, 60 × 44 cm/ 23½ × 17¼ in. Emily wrote from Ireland to her father in 1748, 'Goodwood I shall always be happy to go to, for there are few places I love so well.'

them, as he did for his stuffed birds. 'I have a small ship load of shells for the Dukes of Bedford and Richmond,' the captain of HMS *Diamond* had written in 1739.[42] The project took many years. In September 1748 the boys' tutor, Mr Gibberd, was still trying to buy shells in London:

> I have been trying to get some Shells of the same sort with that my Lady Duchess gave me, at every place I knew or could hear of, both at this end of the Towne and in the City, but without success. There are indeed about fourscore at the shop in Marylebone Street, but many of them are larger and of a much redder colour than I have; and they are besides so very dear (some of them being six pence and others a shilling apiece), that I don't think it would be right to send them without further orders from her Grace.[43]

By the time that the work was put up, the Duchess had so many shells that she did not know what to do with them.[44]

The shellwork is exquisite, the design including superbly simple areas formed to look like basketwork, perfectly rounded vases on plinths, a cornucopia over the arch, with coral pink and cream coffering in the ocular window surrounds. While molluscs provide black and silvery colours, and borders of tiny black mussels range with rows of pale, almost white, cockles, many of the shells add tones of pink, cream, straw and sienna. Although the grotto was always said to be by her, it is likely that the Duchess called in professional help to create such a perfect shell interior. In the same way that paid embroiderers existed, there were craftsmen who did specialist shellwork. Some sections of wall are so

ABOVE The Shell House, interior. Shells were being collected from 1739; the panels were finally put up in 1748. The floor was made of horses' teeth.

LEFT The Shell House, detail. Lady Diana Cooper described a picnic there in 1928: 'We would often move our Sundays to the Shell House at Goodwood, a temple-folly guarded by two stone sphinxes. We would take our lobsters and meats, fruit and wine, roses and candles, to this delightful pavilion, and there by sun or moonshine revel and sing.'

FACING PAGE, LEFT The Shell House, detail of initials CF for Caroline Fox, who married in 1744. (Opposite, a similar EK for Emily Kildare reveals that she must also have completed her panels after her marriage in February 1747.)

FACING PAGE, RIGHT *The Temple of Neptune and Minerva*, by Lady Louisa Tighe, 1850, watercolour, 7 × 24.5 cm /6¾ × 9½ in. 'Ye Duke has fixed up the Roman Inscription wch was found at Chichester . . . On each side of it he has placed the statues of Neptune, & Minerva, and over it the busto of King Cogidubnus mentioned in the inscription . . .'(Jeremiah Miller, 1743). The temple was to the north of the house, presumably visible from the old Jacobean cross wing.

uniformly and evenly encrusted that they could not have been executed by an amateur. The Duchess and her daughters certainly did some of the panels, probably working on them in the main

house before the building was put up. It is possible to identify which these are. At the sides of the arch the initials CR and SR appear on the paired pilasters, denoting Charles Richmond and Sarah Richmond, with CF and EK on the sides of the columns. This was Caroline, who became Caroline Fox on her marriage in 1744, and Emily Kildare, who gained her new surname in 1747. Below the carefree Emily's initials is an especially rough piece of shellwork, while beneath those of the more perfectionist Caroline a more accomplished but still slightly wobbly area can be seen.

Emily recognised that the shellwork she had done before leaving for Ireland was not good, writing to her doting father, 'I am glad the work looks so well now it is put up I doubt nothing but your partiality makes you think the middle Nitche tolerable but I don't despair of altering it sometime as I think it quite a disgrace to the rest of the work.'[45] There was certainly some problem with the outer niches, which the Duke planned to have redone, but he declared that he was charmed by Emily's niche.[46] The work in these two niches is now restored, but the centre one is indeed rather amateur. The Duke's notebook reveals a sketch of a simple rectangle for 'over the door of the grotto at Carnès [sic]'.[47] This was presumably for the exterior, which was later covered up by a crude restoration. By the 1760s shell houses or grottoes were all the rage, especially as they were a good outlet for the fashionable rococo style. As with the buildings in Charlton and his home in London, the 2nd Duke of Richmond was in the vanguard of fashion; but it was still a few years before he could make much impact at the old-fashioned Goodwood House.

## OTHER FOLLIES

In the mid-1740s the Duke had a small classical temple constructed to the east of the house. It was built in order to house a tablet of Roman origin, that was inscribed with the words *Neptuno et Minervae Templum* . . . (The Temple of Neptune and Minerva erected for the health of the Imperial Family by the authority of King Cogidubnus, the lieutenant of Tiberius Claudius Augustus in Britain.) This had been found in Chichester, in 1723.[48] For a time it was fixed in the wall of the house in which it was found, but the site was cleared when the Council House was built, and the marble slab was given to the Duke. The Duke decided to build his own little Temple of Neptune and Minerva. He had two statues carved, of Neptune and Minerva.[49]

Peppering the grounds with follies that reminded the viewer of ancient Rome, the Duke also had an ice-house dug out, topped by a classical arch. He had as well a 'thatched hut' in High Wood, 'where ye Duke dines sometimes in summer'.[50] However, these little buildings mostly did not have the enduring quality of those designed for the Duke by Roger Morris.

## MORRIS'S ACHIEVEMENT IN SUSSEX

It is still extraordinary to think that Burlington and Morris, designers respectively of houses as important as Chiswick and Marble Hill near to London, were so well represented on a smaller scale in rural Sussex. Given Burlington's subsequent lack of interest in Sussex, Campbell's death, and the considerable extent of the Duke's architectural projects, it seems likely that it was Roger Morris who carried out most of the building work for the Duke outside London. As a result there are three extraordinarily sophisticated follies surviving in a remote corner of West Sussex, one at Charlton and two at Goodwood (if the Shell House is included), and an impressive Council House in North Street, Chichester. All are surprises and delights of English Palladianism.

# 5 NURTURING NATURE

ANIMALS, BIRDS, TREES AND PLANTS, 1725–1750

*All my plantations in general flourish prodigiously . . . our verdure here is beyond what I ever saw anywhere & Carne's Seat as well as the whole park & gardens are in the highest beauty.*[1]

At Goodwood works were also being carried out in the grounds. Campbell's plan for the new house (see page 21) included a semi-formal landscape garden running away up the hill to the north. This comprises about 35 acres and is known as High Wood. A map drawn by Thomas Bucknall in 1732 shows the garden, with a pale ground plan representing the house that Campbell (now recently deceased) had designed (see also page 21).[2] Perhaps the Duke had not yet entirely decided to reject the scheme. Over the whole area lines and avenues of trees, criss-crossed with straight paths, are shown skirting an eight-sided star-shaped area. The star was surrounded by a looser area of planting between the avenues comprising both straight and serpentine paths, in the manner of the fashionable new 'natural' garden. An inspiration to the Duke could have been the Spring Garden at Hackwood Park in Hampshire, created in the late 1720s, which similarly had straight alleys with the serpentine paths in between. Its owner was the Duke's friend and previous Master of the Charlton Hunt, Charles Powlett, 3rd Duke of Bolton.

However, judging by the plan of avenues shown on maps from the 1780s by Yeakell and Gardner, this scheme was not carried out.[3] Instead the Duke installed a roughly triangular scheme, tipped to the right, of three straight avenues, with three extra parallel paths crossing over at the southern end. The plan roughly survives, with modifications. The principle was similar to that at Hackwood. High Wood is a natural garden, with free planting around the three main avenues.

## THE ROYAL SOCIETY

*His doors were always open to men of learning, science, and ingenuity.*[4]

It is hard to resist the notion that the Duke was interested in everything. Not only was he absorbed by art and architecture on the one hand, but an interest in the science of the natural world was also developing rapidly. During his childhood leading men of science were pushing back the frontiers of all forms of knowledge, sharing their discoveries at the Royal Society in London. This had been founded in 1661, under the patronage of the Duke's grandfather, Charles II. It had become especially respected under its president Sir Isaac Newton (1643–1727). Under his leadership the Society led the intellectual quest for the gaining of knowledge through observation, experiment and verification.

Thus for a wealthy young man who was interested in natural history, the opportunity and encouragement to develop this passion were provided through the world of the Royal Society. A huge demand was developing for rare natural specimens, which sea captains were bringing in through the Port of London and selling as 'curiosities' to wealthy collectors. The timing and opportunity were fortuitous. The Age of Enlightenment, of man learning to understand his natural environment through reason, is usually seen as having started at about the time of the death of Louis XIV in 1715. The young Duke's interests were to run exactly in line with its prevailing philosophies.

## SIR HANS SLOANE

The Duke's love of science was stimulated by the remarkable physician, naturalist and collector Sir Hans Sloane (1660–1753). As a physician, Sloane had attended Queen Anne: as a naturalist, he had published a treatise on the plants of Jamaica. He married an heiress and in 1712 made the shrewd move of purchasing the manor of Chelsea. In 1721 he founded the Botanic Garden in London. While also making a great fortune, he never turned away a patient who could not pay. Sir Hans was secretary to the Royal Society from 1693 to 1712, and was thus at the forefront of the new emphasis on observation and factual recording. He was president of the Royal College of Physicians (1719–35) and first physician to George II. On the death of Newton in 1727, Sloane became president of the Royal Society.

In 1717, two years before the Earl of March married Lady Sarah Cadogan, Lord Cadogan's brother Charles, younger than him by thirteen years, married Sir Hans Sloane's daughter. This meant that Elizabeth Sloane became Lady Sarah Cadogan's aunt, although the two were not far apart in age. Sloane was Lord Cadogan's physician, treating him in 1724 for a 'violent Feaverish Fit'.[5] Already in his sixties, Sir Hans became not only the Duke's physician but also his veterinary surgeon, treating both his family and the wild animals in his menagerie. Despite his undoubted genius, many of Sir Hans' prescriptions and concoctions were typical of the day: when Lady Caroline was ill in 1728 he recommended bleeding, with doses of oil of sweet almonds and syrup of maidenhair.[6] Charles and Elizabeth Cadogan continued to be very much part of the Duke's circle.

The Duke was elected as a Fellow of the Royal Society on 6 February 1724. His early election was probably due to Sir Hans Sloane, though the introduction was made by the leading Freemason, John Theophilus Desaguliers. The new Fellow was only twenty-two years old: he must have been elected for his interests and potential, not to mention the influence that accrued from his titles. In 1728, when attending George II on a visit to Cambridge, he was made a Doctor of Law. Then, in the same year, in a move that would seem even more extraordinary to us today, given his apparent lack of appropriate qualifications, Sir Hans also put the Duke up to be a Fellow of the Royal College of Physicians, to which he was elected on 25 June. In September he was invited to attend a meeting of the Académie Royale des Sciences in Paris. He thus joined in the active exploration of trees and plants, animals and birds, anatomy and medicine.[7] It was animals that were to excite his curiosity first.

## Wild Animals

Now about [this time] was brought to Goodwood the Great Novelty of many wild Beast, Birds, and other Animals, and there kept in Dens, with iron grates made for them to be seen through, which draw'd a gret number of People Thither to see them, a Lion, Tiger, man Tiger, Bears, Egles, Ostrich etc. etc.[8]

The late-eighteenth-century reminiscences of James Spershott (b.1712), a joiner from Chichester, include this all-too-

brief description of the 2nd Duke's menagerie. Menageries had traditionally belonged to royalty, the first recorded in England being established by Henry I in Woodstock Park, Oxfordshire. Since the sixteenth century wild animals had been kept at the Tower of London, with just a few rarities in some royal gardens in the late seventeenth and early eighteenth centuries.[9] Exotic beasts had more recently been fashionable at the court of Louis XIV at Versailles, where the royal children each had their own small zoo, but the 2nd Duke of Richmond was one of the first private owners to have one in England. The wild animals kept at Goodwood from the late 1720s became famous. The Duke's menagerie was in the true scientific spirit of the eighteenth century, when biologists and botanists were beginning to classify the various species, hitherto largely unknown outside their own country of origin.

In his menagerie at Goodwood the Duke housed at various times a lioness, wolves, racoons, Indian pigs, a wild boar, an armadillo, a baboon, an African squirrel, a civet cat, a jackal, husky dogs, ostriches and monkeys. The earliest surviving reference to the animals among the Duke's accounts is to a monkey in March 1726.[10] When Sir Hans Sloane tried to send him a sloth, he was rather disappointed to find that it was just a 'common young black bear', of which he already had five: he also had them in brown and white. He did not want any more 'Bears, Eagles, Leopards or Tygers' because he was already overstocked with them.[11] He was an avid collector, keeping lists of his species, and was always eager to obtain a rare type, entering into lengthy correspondence with his friends to ask them to find him particular varieties on their travels abroad. He was especially keen to obtain an elephant: one intended for him died in a fire at sea in 1730. The variety of species was impressive, and with animals not bred for captivity, accidents were not infrequent. The lioness died a few months after her arrival in 1729. She was buried in a magnificent tomb in High Wood, and commemorated by a stone statue above. The tomb is at the apex of the two main avenues, in the woodland garden scheme.

The animals were mostly housed in metal cages above ground, as was usual in eighteenth-century menageries. In 1726 a cage was built for the tiger, at the huge cost of £93. It was to be 15 feet square, with a covering on the top. The tiger also wore a chain, as did the eagles and the monkeys. Separate cages or houses for the eagles, ostriches and monkeys were also constructed. Feeding was a formidable task: the carnivorous animals in one of his lists ate 36 pounds of beef a day and 39 pounds of horse flesh. In 1729–30 the Duke was paying for between 140 and 156 loaves of bread a week for the bread-eating animals. A huge variety of food was offered to the animals, including barley and oatmeal for the fowl; greens, apples, carrots for the monkeys; offal for the eagles; and hay, oats and turnips for the sheep. However, the care of them does not seem to have been very good. In 1730 there were so many animals that Henry Foster, who was in charge of them, was concerned both about space and about feeding them. He also complained about lack of funds. It is clear from correspondence with

The Lioness. 'One of his Lyoness's he has buried in his garden at ye end of one of ye walks, & has erected a monument of Portland stone over her' (Jeremiah Miller, 1743).

Sir Thomas Robinson, who was sending him animals from Barbados, that the Duke was still receiving them in the 1740s. Robinson acquired 'the oddest Creature I ever beheld he sleeps hanging by his tail . . . he had fine long hair when he was brought to me . . . and is called Ginn.'[12]

Travel arrangements for the animals were complicated and expensive. They mostly arrived in London, from where in 1729 the lion was transported at least part of the way from Bishopsgate Street in a cart. This must have been hugely exciting for onlookers. A baboon was sent by boat from Deptford and a tiger from Tower Hill, presumably after residing in the menagerie there, while, the following year, a fox, a mountain cat and a bear were all collected by boat from Southwark. The animals attracted great interest. Local visitors came to see them, but unfortunately could be rough and unruly: Foster reported that 'we are very much troubled with very rude company to see ye animals. Sunday last week we had about 4 or 5 hundred good and bad . . .'[13] Family and friends were also intrigued to know how individual animals fared, constantly asking about them in letters.[14]

The Duke also loved small natural 'curiosities'. He acquired goldfish from China, having a special earthenware vessel made in which to transport them. Beautiful Kanxi bowls were acquired for their display. Even an interest in insects must have been stimulated by Sir Hans Sloane, a first edition of whose *History of Jamaica* is in the Goodwood library. A three-day sale of possessions after the Duke's death shows that, in his 'museum' at Richmond House, he also had vast numbers of curiosities such as dried scorpions, centipedes, and a salamander from Surinam; a 'monstrous large Tarantula' and another 'long legged Spider', together with other scorpions from Bengal.[15] It is not surprising that his widow wanted to be rid of them as rapidly as possible.

The Duke was especially keen on collecting birds, both live and dead. Birds of prey in his collection included vultures, eagles,

a kite and owls. He spent many years trying to obtain a macaw; Lord Tyrawley promised to send him two from Portugal. The Duchess and Emily were especially fond of the tamer birds. Writing from London before her marriage, Emily told her father, 'Mama begs you would send her an account of her Pea Chicks and Canary Birds.'[16] There was in High Wood (though it could have been built later) 'an elegant little Building called the Parrot House, once the receptacle of a choice collection of those beautiful though noisy birds.'[17] The Duke also had a large collection of stuffed birds, brought back by traders from the little Dutch colony of Surinam in Central America. Sir Hans Sloane had many of these birds, and watercolours of others. The Duke may have developed this collecting link through the Cadogans' Dutch interests, as most items from Surinam came back with the Dutch, rather than the English, East India Company.

## THE ROCK DELL

Another novelty in the grounds behind the house at Goodwood was the Rock Dell. At the lower right, or south-east section, of Bucknall's 1732 map is marked an oblong, a formal shape with concentric lines, looking like an amphitheatre. This was presumably, like the villa and the star-shaped garden shown on the map, a proposal. In the event, near this location, on the eastern edge of the main triangle of formal avenues, the Duke created a mysterious scooped-out hollow of shell buildings and follies, linked by tumbling steps and brick paths. The shellwork was being inserted as late as 1747/8: writing from Carton, Emily complained 'I am grown by the accounts I hear of it [the shellwork] so jealous of that in the rock dell . . .'[18]

A little shell house at the head of the Rock Dell, facing south to the rear of Goodwood House, is classical in design, with a broken

Ionic column found near by. From its back wall water trickled down from a fountain into a brick-lined rectangular pool, making it a kind of antique shower house. To the right, or clockwise, is a small, rustic, two-cell building in flint. A third edifice, clockwise again from the first two, was known as the Ruined Abbey, owing to the details of Gothic tracery, of which a fraction survives. Completing the circuit was another tiny shell edifice, not of standing height, and a ground-level structure made around a terracotta urn, of a type used for olive oil, tipped towards the onlooker. These are adjacent to what may have been a cascade. Finally, completing the circuit is a second, larger, two-cell flint structure, which could be entered from each side.

The buildings in the Rock Dell were for animals. The little classical shell house has the remains of iron bars stuck into its exterior in many places, suggesting that there was a cage in the front of it, perhaps for a semi-aquatic creature. There are several openings in the top, safely covered with grilles. The two rustic buildings may be the 'dens' mentioned by Spershott, and therefore constructed earlier. They must have had tall iron entrance grilles, of which the suggestion of a couple of bolt-holes remain. Their very curvy lines, with no right angles, were suitable for animals that were prone to curling up or skulking. Early engravings of animals such as beavers in other locations certainly suggest that they were kept in rustic dens of this type. Little niches were incorporated high up in the dens for candles or lamps when needed. Oculi in the roofs assisted ventilation. Possibly they also had cages extending outside. In the double-cell structures, there are hooks in the ceiling of the left cell, perhaps for a hay net. Even the half-size shell structure may have had a cage in front, making it suitable for the display of a small jackal, or perhaps the agouti or civet cat.

## THE CATACOMBS

An underground tunnel, lined in brick, runs into the Rock Dell, opening into the Ruined Abbey. In 1747 the antiquarian George Vertue described 'other Ruins erected (lately) artfully with stone cells under ground and dark recesses – or passages – subturane. which are as wel contrived as curious, vast stone porpheryes sea pebbles &c. varyously disposed.'[19] At its other end the tunnel emerges into a large underground brick-lined cell, fronted by fine iron-grille doors, which opens on to a wide ditch running about 50 yards to the north, traditionally known as the lion run. In the brick vault there is a small oculus as an air vent, filled with a grille. Two further tunnels run northwards from this area, both bricked in. Southwards from the brick cell another tunnel leads down towards the back of the main house, about 50 yards from where, its lining changing from brick into flint, it opens out into a short ditch.

The question of how these tunnels were used in relation to the Dell has excited much curiosity. Living animals certainly ran in them, running through the narrow tunnel up to the grille at the back of the Ruined Abbey, where they were viewed in the

manner suggested by Spershott. This arrangement may have been designed in imitation of the way that wild beasts had been kept below the Colosseum in ancient Rome, a fact that the Duke would have known from his Grand Tour. The wider tunnel running southwards to the house must also once have terminated in bars. Running freely in the long tunnels in High Wood and out into the special run would certainly have given any animal some good exercise.

In 1743 Jeremiah Miller, another visiting antiquary, wrote that 'The Duke had formerly a good menagerie at Goodwood but within these few years he has disposed of allmost all his beasts.'[20] This may explain why Emily wrote from Ireland in 1748 that 'I have often thought that since these Catacombs have been in fashion at Goodwood my poor birds have decreased daily and that I had even some suspicion of there not having had fair play for their lives.'[21] Emily's implication was that the tunnels were used for dead animals in the manner of the catacombs in ancient Rome, where bodies were stored. It would seem that she was referring to the gradual closure of the menagerie, with the storage of skeletons in the tunnels, which were then filled in. Seven weeks later she returned to her theme: 'I find the fate of all the unlucky animals that come to Goodwood is to be burying them in the Catacombs and an epitaph by Sam Chandler . . .'[22] Chandler also wrote the epitaphs for the burial of children's pets in the Rock Dell, perhaps similarly towards the end of its time as an arena for the display of animals. A 1741 tablet for a spaniel called Miss, belonging to 'Aunt Anne' Keppel, Countess of Albemarle, was in a delightfully mock-heroic vein: 'I once was Miss, the mildest, best of Misses,/Nursed and brought up by Keppel's care and kisses,/But now no more than Argus, or Ulysses.'[23]

The 'natural' garden, with the Rock Dell in its midst, thus for a time provided a setting for the special display of animals kept in the menagerie, before becoming their burial place. The combination of wild animals and classical follies seems extraordinary, but is typical of an eighteenth-century 'enlightened' mind seeking to

The Menagerie, later the Pheasantry, signed *S H Grimm fecit 1782* (British Library). The old chalk pit was made into a menagerie, probably for wild animals, by the 2nd Duke. It was modified by the 3rd Duke in the 1760s to rear pheasants and to house rare birds. He also added the obelisk at the top of the quarry, to act as a chimney for the little house below, and the little Gothic summerhouse to the top at the right.

acquire all possible knowledge, and to display the findings in a setting redolent of the past. At Wentworth Castle, Yorkshire, in the late 1720s, Thomas Wentworth, Earl of Strafford (1672–1739), also constructed his menagerie garden in a sunken quarry, with a classically inspired banqueting house overlooking it, in which he could entertain his guests. The Duke used the Rock Dell for the viewing of animals in a similar way, but not necessarily for the permanent keeping of them.

## THE LOCATION OF THE MENAGERIE

*Pray order all the Bears and Tygers to be Muzl'd* [24]

It is unlikely that the family would keep dangerous wild animals, so risky to their young children, so near to the house all the time.

The effect of tigers growling behind bars within sight of the house would have been terrifying, and the strange noises by day and night needed to be kept out of earshot. The smell would have been unbearable. The permanent menagerie, with all its necessary paraphernalia of cages, hutches, sheds and feeding troughs, was probably sited further away up the hill, to the north of the house. The animals were said to be kept 'in ye grove',[25] which could also describe the small area of tightly planted trees inside an old quarry, used from the 1760s as a pheasantry, and still known by this name today.[26] In December 1733 a bill of work for a carpenter includes work 'up at ye live creatures in ye Grove', a day each for two men on a bear house and several more for housing leopards and wolves. The whole area is surrounded by a high flint wall, as was normal for eighteenth-century menageries. That the Duke kept only rather tamer animals in the park close to the house is suggested in a letter he wrote to Sir Hans Sloane in 1739: 'I am most extreamly obliged to you for the two most curious creatures you have sent me: which are by farr the oddest of the kind I ever saw. They are arrived in good health & are in a piece of ground of almost an acre. Butt if I find they are not at all mischeivous [*sic*] I will let them run in my parke.'[27]

The location of the main zoo up the hill is suggested by the reports of three late-eighteenth-century visitors, and by a drawing from a separate source. In 1787 John Marsh, the gentleman composer from Chichester, commented that the area that was now 'the Pheasantry, a beautiful little romantic spot' had been made by 'ye former Duke out of an old chalk pit', though he does not mention its earliest use.[28] In 1788 Viscount Palmerston named the same spot as the old menagerie:

> at some distance from ye house, which stands low, is a menagerie now going to decay, but originally very pretty, and a little further up is a building called Carney's Seat, from which there is a very fine view of Chichester and al ye adjacent country with the sea, Spithead and the Isle of Wight.[29]

Later, in 1795, a young lady traveller called Anne Rushout, the daughter of John Rushout, 1st Baron Northwick of Northwick Park, Worcestershire, similarly named it as the menagerie, though she clearly knew that by then it was used for birds. She wrote:

> We drove by the house & ascended a steep hill to get to a building which is very highly situated & which commands a fine view of Portsmouth, Isle of Wight, Spithead &c. [Carné's Seat; she then describes the Shell House].We next went a little way further to the Menagerie which is in the most sheltered situation. I fancy it must formerly have been a stone quarry for it consists of a pretty lawn, surrounded on three sides by steep banks. There is an narrow path which brought us down to the bottom. There were a great many Pens going to ruin but very few Birds. At one end of the lawn there is a very pretty painted Room which has a charming view through the only opening there is.[30]

A sketch dating 1782 by S. H. Grimm shows the little classical folly containing the painted room at the top, and the surrounding fir trees. As the sketch shows, a grille was put along the top of the stone-capped flint wall, making it clear that the area had to be entirely enclosed.

Other elements of the menagerie still survive today, including the lawn.[31] Delightfully, a door described by Anne Rushout at the top of the quarry also survives to this day, a perfect 'Secret Garden' entrance covered with lichen and ivy. Through it she walked down the steep path, straight into the painted room.

## The Complete Pleasure Grounds

As with the Rock Dell, the menagerie is another example of an owner combining architecture and exotica, with a glamorous and safe little room from which the wilder elements of what was probably a zoo could safely be surveyed. There was moreover a steep-sided pit beyond the menagerie, known as the Stone Dell: buildings in its base could be used to house dangerous animals. The dens and tunnels in the enclosed High Wood therefore seem

to have been for the viewing of wild animals on special occasions and public days. A few animals would be transported down from the menagerie or Stone Dell in cages on carts. The carriage would leave the menagerie through the brick arched doorway, trundling through the field across to High Wood, at the top of which a special tunnel entrance for the animals has now been discovered. This is set low in the flint wall, and arched with brick. It must have run directly into the large brick chamber some 50 yards away. Leopards or tigers could thus be released from outside the wall into the tunnels. They could either run down to be contained in the brick chamber, for which the great iron grille provided a viewing point, or could be released from it into the open air in the lion run.

The Duke's reference to wild animals being allowed to 'run in my parke' introduces another aspect of eighteenth-century animal keeping, namely that many owners had a rather idyllic view of how wild animals could be allowed to roam free. This resulted in many animal deaths and disasters. The Duke seems to have been cautious. As well as using the tunnels and brick chamber, animals were contained in their dens in the pit of the Dell. There was also another pit near by, which survives as a recess but without trace of dens or follies. The Duke knew that different species of animals had to be kept apart, with dangerous ones far removed from the main house.

The flint wall surrounding High Wood on three sides could therefore have been as much for keeping dangerous wild animals out as for keeping other ones in. This is confirmed by the fact that the wall is set low on the northern wood side, like a ha-ha, down which an animal could easily jump out, near to the entrance tunnel, but it could not jump in. Each animal would thus have had several layers of security to keep it away from the family and the house; the pen in the menagerie, and/or the collar and chain; the wall around the menagerie itself; and the wall around High Wood.

Despite the practical problems of animal husbandry, the actual display of wild animals at Goodwood was thus a very organised affair. The display was much enhanced by the building of follies and tunnels. Visitors could watch the animals in the Rock Dell, peering at the dark little cells and the Ruined Abbey. They could also walk round to see them from the other viewpoints. They could then promenade out through the tall decorative iron gates at the north-east corner of High Wood and across to the menagerie itself. Alternatively they could walk straight up to Carné's Seat, where a woman was installed to pour tea, admire the Shell House, and then pass down through the 'secret' hilltop door into the Menagerie, staying in the Painted Room if the ladies were nervous.[32] It would be an extensive and exciting walk, leading from one point to another, giving a much larger dimension to the Duke of Richmond's remarkable pleasure grounds.

Soon after constructing some of the new arrangements, the Duke began to lose interest in keeping wild animals. The grounds would be used in a different way by the 3rd Duke. From the late

ABOVE AND RIGHT  Cork oak tree, introduced to Goodwood by the 2nd Duke. After the Duke's death Dr Richard Pococke described '30 different kinds of oak and four hundred different American trees and shrubs' in the park at Goodwood.

eighteenth century the area was marked on maps as 'The Hermitage'; in 1838 someone even wrote to the Duke to ask if he could be the hermit.[33] The 3rd Duke probably simply did not know what to do with the exotic zoo that he had inherited from his father.

## TREES AND PLANTS

The 2nd Duke was very interested in trees, planting up not only High Wood but also other areas around the house. Many of his earliest trees were provided by the remarkable horticulturist and writer Philip Miller (1691–1771), who from 1722 ran the Physic Garden at Chelsea for the Society of Apothecaries, initially under the benefaction of Sir Hans Sloane. Although he considered him a 'puppy & coxcomb', the Duke gave Miller £20 per annum to provide seeds and plants 'of his own raising' and to go down four or five times a year to Goodwood to inspect the results.[34] The third edition (1737) of Miller's *Gardener's Dictionary*, first produced in 1732, is still in the Goodwood library, the first volume dedicated to Sir Hans Sloane and the Royal Society: the second volume, dated 1740, is dedicated to Lord Burlington, showing the closeness of that fashionable, aristocratic, intellectual circle. Later manuscript notes by the 3rd Duke on the title page of Volume I record 'On the Bowling Green was planted The Collection of Evergreens in the year 1734–1737-: 1738' and 'Tulip Trees and Virginia Oakes on the Arbor Vitae Grove planted 1739'. This grove was to the south-west of the house.[35] Miller also reported in his

*Dictionary* experiments proposed by himself for serpentine walls at Goodwood, constructed to protect delicate fruit trees and to aid the production of fruit. They were not a success, and the trees were replaced with vines and figs, also difficult to grow.

The Duke acquired many of his trees through Peter Collinson (1694–1768), a wealthy Quaker cloth merchant, who was also a colleague of Sir Hans Sloane. Collinson collected rare trees and shrubs for his own garden, first at Peckham and then at Mill Hill. He discovered an especially useful American contact in the botanist John Bartram (1699–1777), a Quaker farmer in Philadelphia. Through Bartram, Collinson initiated a regular import of American plants quite new to Britain. Like the Duke, Miller subscribed annually to receive plants and support Bartram's travels: the Duke paid Bartram 5 guineas per annum, in return for which he received 'a great deal of good seed'.[36] The Duke wanted a myrtle hedge, so in February 1743 he ordered forty or fifty 'broad leaved Myrtles' from Collinson, requesting them to be small in order to keep the cost down.[37] The Duke also planted cork oaks: ten survive on the estate, with a group of good specimens near the house. From his oak trees at Aubigny he brought back acorns to sow at Goodwood.[38]

Collinson also collaborated on the import of plants with the 8th Baron Petre (1713–1742), a young Catholic peer who created a plantation of about forty thousand trees and built hothouses for plants at Thorndon Park in Essex. Many of the trees were catalogued by Miller in 1736. As two of the principal arboriculturists in the country, it is not surprising that the Duke and Lord Petre were in correspondence. Petre had already completed the design of a garden at Worksop Manor in Nottinghamshire for Edward Howard, 9th Duke of Norfolk, and his wife Mary, the Duchess of Richmond's friend. When the Duke acquired 'the True Cerrus Oake from Nottingham' (a Turkey oak), it probably came from Worksop: from it he planted sixteen acorns.[39] In a letter to the Duke dated March 1740, Petre said that he was sending him two small magnolias: these were still very rare, and he only had a few of them.[40] A *Magnolia grandiflora* at Goodwood had already died in the hard frost of 1740, reported on by Miller. Petre told the Duke to ask for anything he wanted.[41] Sadly, Lord Petre died in 1742 at the age of only twenty-nine. His collection was broken up, and his sorrowing widow offered 'turkey-buzzards' from the aviary and plants and trees to the Duke: 'her Ladyship is so good as to say that I may have some of the curious plants from Thorndon.'[42] Collinson became the intermediary for the arrangements. First the Duke wanted Chinese thujas, swamp pines and 'some more of that small firr with leaves like the common Yew'. He knew all about the best time to dig them up, insisting they were not moved until the end of March (1743). Quickly realising that there was an opportunity to acquire large numbers, he offered to pay in order to acquire sixty to eighty tulip trees.[43]

Just after Christmas in 1742 the Duke wrote to ask for some cedars: 'I don't so much as mention the numbers of cedars of

Lebanon, because the more I could have the better, for I propose making a Mount Lebanon upon a very high hill . . .'[44] Collinson confirmed that 'his Grace intended clothing all the bare hills above the house with trees.'[45] This means that he at least commenced the planting of the huge plantation behind Carné's Seat, later replanted with beech and now known as Birdless Grove, not inhabited by birds because the trees grew so close together. He also wanted a hundred thujas. He became impatient for the tulip trees, writing in January, 'now you know is the best time for the Tulip trees.'[46] Two weeks later, by mid-February, they were planted:[47] by 1746, one was already 33 feet 6 inches high. Collinson visited Goodwood from time to time, and in 1745 the Duke asked him to come down for four or five days in late March. In 1748 the Duke was again desperate for some trees to arrive from Thorndon for planting in March.[48] At the same time the next year, the Earl of Hopetoun sent him fourteen baskets of Scots pines.[49] The Earl praised his new plantations: 'How well soever your Grace may think you praise the Plantations of Goodwood, forgive me to say you fall much short of what I have heard from others of them.'[50]

## BOOKS ON NATURAL HISTORY

The Duke was acting as a patron of natural science by helping ground-breaking authors to publish their books. In the library he had a copy of the first French edition of Mark Catesby's *A History of Carolina*, published in 1741, to which he was a subscriber. Catesby had spent some years in America (1710–19 and 1722–6), travelling far afield to find specimens in their natural habitat. Both Sir Hans Sloane and Peter Collinson had helped finance his travels. He returned to live in Hoxton, London, where he published his work in sections from 1731 to 1743, etching all the drawings himself. In an appendix dated 1747 he included an agouti or Java hare, a South American rodent that belonged to the Duke, who was pleased by its inclusion. Catesby was especially interested in birds. Some rare unbound original plates by him that are still in the library were given to the Duke by Emily in 1749, she having acquired them in Dublin.[51]

Names were given to many of the species that appeared in Catesby's volumes by the Swedish natural historian Carl Linnaeus

(1707–1778), who came to England in 1736 to visit Sir Hans Sloane. He was the founder of the modern binomial system of the classification of plants and animals, the first part of his *Systema Naturae* having appeared the previous year. It is possible that Voltaire may have introduced Linnaeus's work to the Duke. In an undated letter probably from the 1730s, he mentioned 'a Swedish history which I took the liberty to send lately to yr grace . . .'[52] During his stay in England between 1726 and 1729 Voltaire had been especially interested in the work of Sir Isaac Newton, in the Royal Society and in natural science. The animals newly classified by Linnaeus included the Duke's agouti, but he derived this from Catesby. There is no record of Linnaeus and the Duke having met.

## BIRDS, BOOKS AND RARITIES

As well as pursuing his interests at Goodwood in horses and dogs, exotic animals and birds, and gardens and trees, at Richmond House the Duke had an aviary, as did Lord Burlington at Chiswick and the Duke of Montagu at Blackheath. The Duke of Richmond went even further: he was also the patron of more books on exotic birds. Through the good offices of Sir Hans Sloane he became a supporter of George Edwards, whose work *A Natural History of Birds* became very famous. Edwards had an astonishing talent. He came from a middle-class London family, and spent his early twenties travelling in Europe, often rather aimlessly. He began to sketch flora and fauna, developing an extraordinary facility. After his return he became a tutor in drawing, living with his parents at West Ham where he was near enough to the Port of London to be able to view the many rare specimens that were being imported by sea captains from voyages of discovery to the Caribbean, Central America and the East Indies. Exotic birds and animals were news. Edwards's drawings began to be in demand among rich collectors of natural specimens and came to the attention of Sir Hans Sloane, for whom he did many drawings, of items belonging both to the physician and to his friends.[53]

As President of the Royal College of Physicians, in 1733 Sloane managed to have Edwards appointed as bedell (or Beadle), in charge of the College's fine building in Warwick Lane, near St Paul's Cathedral, and its possessions. This gave Edwards, a corpulent, sociable figure, an income of £12 a year and an elegant, free town house. He not only ran the College, but with the support of Sloane and the Physicians, was free to pursue his drawing.

Edwards increasingly worked on illustrating exotic birds that had not previously been recorded or described, drawing them from the stuffed specimens that were being imported. He also began to acquire his own birds through the Bartram family in Philadelphia, as well as others from contacts in Gibraltar and Lisbon. Aware that a stuffed specimen would appear to have no life, Edwards did sketches of each bird from three or four different angles, combining them into one final, painstaking drawing.

Each specimen was shown with a little of the local greenery or topography behind it, his favourite support being a lichen-covered bough. He drew both live and stuffed birds belonging to the Duke, who wrote to him, 'I shall send you up in a day or two a small bird . . . which I desire you would draw and then prepare him with feathers so that I may put him in my collection.'[54] He also drew a butcher bird for the Duke's aunt Lady Albemarle, who had bought a cage full of them back from Copenhagen.[55]

The Physicians encouraged Edwards to publish his drawings, probably by promising to subscribe individually to the book, as was normal for the publication of any book at the time. Rather than give his drawings to a commercial engraver, which he felt would be expensive and would never capture the spirit of the original, George Edwards was taught by Mark Catesby how to etch, becoming a pioneer in his use of etching at a time when engraving was more prevalent. Eventually he became so skilled that he often drew directly from nature on to the waxed copper plate, printing all his work himself. He turned his home at the College into a studio, producing all his work from there. Edwards hand-coloured his own work, producing at least twelve personally coloured versions of each print, including one master version to be kept at the College, available for future copyists. Edwards wrote all the text, prefaces and notes about the birds himself. From someone who appeared to have started adult life in rather a relaxed way, Edwards had developed into a driven perfectionist.

The first volume, published at the College in 1743, was entitled *A Natural History of Birds, most of which have not been Figured or Described*. The work was dedicated to the President and Fellows of the College. Edwards also wrote the text, describing each bird very carefully. Sometimes he added a more imaginative or exotic setting, such as Stonehenge in Plate 74 (Volume II) as a background to the hen bustard. At the end of each entry he always gave the provenance. Some of the Duke's birds and animals were included. At Plate 5 is a Black Parrot from Madagascar which Sir Charles Wager had presented to the Duke: Edwards described it as 'a very gentle bird, always choosing to be on the Hand . . .' At Plate 10 A Swallow-Tail'd Kingfisher 'inclosed and pasted up in a Glass' had come from Surinam via Holland, as had the Blue Creeper and the Golden-Headed Black Titmouse in Plate 21.

Volume I further includes, at the back at Plate 51, after all the birds, a Greenland deer that the Duke had in his menagerie at Goodwood. The second volume, published in 1747, was dedicated to Sloane, who had by then retired to live at his manor of Chelsea, where Edwards visited him daily to update him with news. At the same time, Edwards decided to publish a French edition of the two volumes: French was at the time a more international language than English and scientific literature was very popular in France. His work was translated and published as *Histoire Naturelle de Divers Oiseaux*. The same birds are shown, in the same order, but each is in reverse to that in the original volume.[56] The first French volume, published in 1745, which was Edwards's second actual

book, was dedicated to the 2nd Duke of Richmond, and the second volume, in 1748, to the Duchess, showing that, through the descent from Louise de Keroualle, they were still very much thought of as leading Francophiles. Both dedication copies are in the Goodwood library, with eulogies to their dedicatees: in the foreword the Duke was described as 'true Maecenas' (from the Roman patron of the arts). Edwards especially noted the Duke's knowledge of French and of natural history, and complimented him on his menagerie.

ABOVE  *The Natural History of Birds* illustrated and written by George Edwards, London 1743–51, showing (clockwise) an illustration of an artist sketching (a classical personification of Edwards himself), painted by Bartholomew Dandridge, facing the title page to Volume II; a bird belonging to the Duke, above an insect; the dedication of the French translation, *Histoire Naturelle de Divers Oiseaux*, to the Duchess; the toucan (which appears on the slop basin in the Sèvres tea service of 1765). The books are surrounded by blue and green plates from the Sèvres service, 1765–6, on which the birds were copied. Of the twenty- two green plates at Goodwood, eleven are signed by the painter Chappuis.

RIGHT  The Greenland Deer, from George Edwards, *A Natural History of Birds*, Volume I, London 1743, Plate 51. At the end, after all the birds, is shown this animal that the Duke had in his menagerie, having received it from Sir Hans Sloane, who in turn had acquired it from a sea captain. The 3rd Duke also became interested in rare types of deer, acquiring over the years at least five different moose, a caribou and a Himalayan deer.

In 1744, the year after the publication of his first volume, Edwards was put up for fellowship of the Royal Society. His supporters including Martin Folkes who in 1741 had succeeded Sir Hans Sloane as president of the Society, Mark Catesby and Peter Collinson. That all were friends of the Duke of Richmond shows what an intertwined group they were, each one bent on scientific discovery and colleagues rather than rivals. Most were polymaths, extremely interested in more than one subject, or in Folkes' case, interested in encouraging others through generous patronage. Surprisingly, Edwards declined the honour, but he continued to be widely admired by his peers. After the publication of his second English volume of *Birds*, Collinson wrote about it to his friend Carl Linnaeus in Sweden. Edwards and Linnaeus also became close colleagues, Linnaeus using his descriptions of birds as being the best. Faced with what they saw as the challenge of categorising every known species, between all these naturalists there was an extraordinary spirit of co-operation.

After the success of his first two volumes on birds, George Edwards decided to continue. The third and fourth volumes appeared in 1750 and 1751 respectively, the third again dedicated to the President and Fellows of the Royal Society, and the fourth rather charmingly to God. The third is in the Goodwood library, but not the fourth, having appeared after the death of the 2nd Duke. Edwards was exhausted by his work after the production of a total of four English and two French volumes. However, he later started again, producing *Gleanings of Natural History*, with volumes in 1758, 1760 and 1764 (to which the 3rd Duke was a subscriber). This time the French translation was set parallel to the English on the page. In the 1758 volume Edwards noted four patrons 'who were perhaps the greatest promoters of learning, science and arts of any in the present age'. The first of these was 'the late Most Noble Duke of Richmond, noble in his lineage and descent from the Royal house of these kingdoms, but still more noble and great from the innate magnificence, generosity, and goodness of his soul. Though, by his high offices, his time was taken up by the important affairs of the public, yet his doors were always open to men of learning, science, and ingenuity.' The other patrons were Sir Hans Sloane, Martin Folkes and Dr Richard Mead, Fellow of the Royal College of Physicians. These volumes were acquired for the Goodwood library by the 3rd Duke, who was to take the work of George Edwards yet one step further by having his exotic birds painted on to china.

As well as rare animals, the Duke became interested in rare humans. He owned a painting by Joseph Highmore of an Irish dwarf named Owen Farrell, who with a height of 3 feet 9 inches was celebrated for his deformities. Also known as Leather-coat Jack, Farrell was the porter at the notorious brothel in Drury Lane, the Rose Tavern, immortalised by William Hogarth in his series *The Rake's Progress*. He had extraordinary strength and became one of London's best-known characters of the 1740s. The Duke presumably commissioned the painting as Highmore

worked for him on several occasions, but Leather-coat Jack was famous enough to be painted by three other artists.[57] After the dwarf's death in 1749, the Duke acquired his skeleton.[58] He also had a wax model of a hermaphrodite and a 'skeleton, with the muscles raised, of a Robber, found in a chimney at Paddington'.[59] Richmond also supported the work of early inoculators against smallpox in Sussex, a hazardous process as it involved catching a mild form of the disease; he collected information on the Chichester smallpox epidemic in 1739 for the Royal Society, for which he also wrote descriptions of a local earthquake in 1734. The Duke was one of the founder members of the short-lived Egyptian Society (1741–3). In 1742 the Society invited scholars to Richmond House to watch the unwrapping of an Egyptian mummy that the Duke had acquired through Dr Richard Pococke (1704–1765): Edwards was commissioned to draw one of these.[60] The Duke also acquired ancient Egyptian pots, one containing an embalmed ibis.

## THE BENTINCKS

Another main influence on the Duke's interest in the natural world came from Holland, via his brother-in-law Count Bentinck. The Hon. William Bentinck, known in Holland as the Count de Rhoom, or as Count Bentinck, was the second son of the 1st Earl of Portland, the Dutchman who had advised William of Orange. Bentinck lived just outside The Hague with his younger brother Charles, on a wonderful country estate called Sorgvliet. The mansion was surrounded by vast formal gardens, massive greenhouses arranged in a semi-circle, and extensive topiary. The Count married the Duchess's sister Margaret, or 'Titie', and had two sons. As a consequence of his interest in science, Count Bentinck had become a curator in the University of Leiden. With considerable forethought, in 1736 he took into his magnificent home a young scientist called Abraham Trembley, with the idea of his being the future tutor to his children.

Adrian Trembley (1710–1784) was to become one of the leading educators of the age. Born in Geneva, in the 1730s he worked as a tutor to a noble family at Leiden. While waiting for Count Bentinck's boys to be old enough for lessons, Trembley worked in two other grand households, and also spent his time on biological research. He returned to Sorgvliet in 1739, and the next year, through the empirical methods of observation and experiment, which were used at the university, made the discovery that a freshwater 'polyp', or what we would now call a hydra, was an animal rather than a plant. In 1742 his findings were published in the preface to the sixth volume of the French naturalist Réamur's *Mémoires pour servir à l'histoire des insectes*. The Royal Society in London became interested. The president, the Duke's friend Martin Folkes, wrote to Bentinck, and in January 1743 two sessions were devoted to the findings of the *Chlorohydra viridissima* or green hydra. The Duke had seen his work at Sorgvliet, and reported on him to the Society: 'I need not, I believe, tell you with what Satisfaction I passed my time, and that Mr Trembley is one of the most agreeable Men I have known. He is particularly handy and dextrous in his operations, and explains himself about them with great Exactness and Perspicuity.'[61]

Trembley's discovery had made him famous, and in May that year he was made a Fellow of the Royal Society.

Trembley was modest about his achievements and spent much time fulfilling a familial role in the Bentinck household. In the summer of 1745 he brought his two charges, Antoine and Jean, to London to stay with their grandmother, the Countess of Portland, with whom he was in regular correspondence. He then installed the boys back at the University of Leiden, returning to England in 1747. Here Trembley met the 2nd Duke again, who found him a role as an envoy to the Treaty of Aix-la-Chapelle. After the successful signing of the Peace, Trembley was given a pension of £300 a year by the King for life. The Duke also planned to take him on his proposed embassy to Paris.

In the autumn of 1748 Trembley was at Goodwood, making experiments. He found another specimen that was believed to be a plant and proved that it was animal, writing to Bentinck: 'At Goodwood I have shown two good botanists a kind of marine plant belonging to the corallines . . . Both of them acknowledged that it was not a plant . . . I should have the wherewithal to amuse myself for a long time with these animals, if I lived beside the sea.'[62] This specimen is now called the *Sertularia polyzonias*. At this stage Trembley's future was slightly uncertain. He went back to The Hague in 1749, before travelling to Geneva to see his family. He met the Duke in Paris and travelled with him via Brussels to London. Early in 1750 the Duke decided that he should become tutor to his son. The influence of Abraham Trembley was to have a radical effect.

# 6  ENTERTAINMENT AND EXPANSION

THE SOUTH WING, 1735–1750

*Good God! How I will rejoice with you! For who can want spirits at Goodwood? Such a Place, and such company!*

*Why should not wee with convivial familiarity concellebrate the Rights of Jovial Festivity?*[1]

In 1736 John Collis, Mayor of Hastings, described a magnificent dinner at Goodwood. This took place during the Duke's term as Mayor of Chichester, serving for one year from September 1735.[2] The dinner started at the usual time of 4.30 p.m., continuing to the considerably extended hour of midnight. The guests comprised '27 Sussex Gents', including the Duke of Newcastle, the Earl of Wilmington, Lord Abergavenny and Lord Ossulston, son of the Earl of Tankerville from Uppark. Food was served on silver dishes by twenty-four footmen, eight wearing the Duke's own livery and sixteen the royal livery, to which his position as Master of the Horse entitled him. There was a 'fine desert', laid out for all to admire. The Mayor was very impressed by the display: 'In short, the Dinner Sideboard, Desert, and grandeur surpassed everything I saw.'[3] The house was 'vastly fresh finished': this was the dining room with its proud paintings celebrating English heroes and the newly classicised hall, as well as the flinted exterior.

In September that year the Duke also entertained the Moroccan Ambassador and his suite. Colonel Pelham, the MP for Hastings, was invited to meet them; he jovially told the Duke to muzzle all the bears and tigers in his menagerie for the occasion.[4] Some ten years earlier another Moroccan ambassador had been a friend of the Duke: they had exchanged letters, the ambassador writing in Arabic with an accompanying translation.[5] Both friendships reveal the Duke's hospitable nature and his desire to show English life to exotic foreigners.

In 1738 the Duke and Duchess gave a ball at Goodwood. Aged fifteen, Caroline was allowed to attend, though her partners may have been rather older. The guest of honour was Monsieur de Cambis, the French Ambassador to the Court of St James, with his wife. They had already visited Goodwood and were ecstatic: '*nous vous accompagnerons au bout du monde*.'[6] Lady Tankerville, from Uppark, was there, as was Lady Hervey, the beautiful Molly Lepel: she was the wife of the foppish bisexual courtier Lord Hervey, who was at the time pursuing an affair with Caroline's future brother-in-law, Stephen Fox. Lady Hervey was a regular visitor to Goodwood, while the Duke saw much of her husband at court. Hervey teased the Duke about his animals, comparing them, and their couplings, with those of courtiers.

On 26 September 1740 the play *Les Dehors Trompeurs, où l'homme du Jour* by de Boissy was presented at Goodwood, before a small but noble audience, presumably in the Long Hall. Caroline (aged seventeen), Emily (nine) and Charles March (five), all took part.[7] It may have been for this or a similar occasion that the actor/manager Colley Cibber came to stay, writing to the Duke, 'Good God! How I will rejoice with you! For who can want spirits at Goodwood? Such a Place, and such company!'[8]

By this date the Duke had acquired a large amount of silver.[9] In the nursery each child had its own personal silver knife, fork and spoon. The Duchess's dressing-table set comprised six round and two square boxes, a pin box, four brushes, two basins, two cups, a looking glass and a basin and ewer. From Louise de Keroualle the family had inherited a generous set of four dozen octagonal plates, with over thirty spoons and forks, as well as salvers, salt cellars, sauceboats and sugar casters. The Duke was also collecting items of sculpture, loosely known as 'marbles'. At the sale of Edward Harley, 2nd Earl of Oxford (1689–1741), between 8 and 13 March 1741 he bought a large number of items, including various figures of Jupiter, one of which was a *Leda and the Swan* in marble, a very pretty small relief.[10] He bought figures of Saturn, Apollo and Mercury, busts of Sappho and Flora, Roman marble urns, dishes and inscriptions. He also acquired some Egyptian items, including a laris (or household god) and figures of Isis and Osiris in touchstone, mounted on bronze.[11]

Behind the scenes the Duchess paid close attention to the children's clothes and medical needs. For the latter, Sir Hans Sloane was still the chief adviser; also treating the animals in the menagerie. A bathing house was built, suggesting that the family was in the forefront of the new fashion for fresh air and swimming in the sea. The couple still had the same French chef, Jacquemar, as well as a clerk of the kitchen, Mirande: special chefs for dessert and confectionery were also French, and there was a pastrycook. Other French servants included a female housekeeper called Dubois at Hampton Court. François Liegois was the Duke's valet, while his wife Elizabeth was a housekeeper, who worked both at Hampton Court and Goodwood, often making arrangements for provisions. Payments were made to the poulterer at Hampton Court, the gardener, the butcher, the man who lit the lamps. Mrs Bryon was paid for teaching Lady Emily to make artificial flowers. Cockades were purchased for 'my Lord Duke's horse'.[12]

## The Wider Horizon

In 1739 war broke out, first against Spain, and later against France, with Prussia joining in. England and Austria were alone against a group of both major and minor powers. As Master of the Horse, the Duke accompanied the King to the Battle of Dettingen on 15 June 1743, organising the huge transport train required by the monarch. This was the last time that a British monarch would personally lead his army into battle. Fighting the French must have posed a clash of sympathies for the Duke, given his own French ancestry and his estates at Aubigny. The King's second son, William, Duke of Cumberland, also fought at this battle: he was thus a military colleague of the Duke, and would become a political ally of the 3rd Duke. His portrait hangs at Goodwood.[13]

At the time of the Jacobite rebellion in the summer of 1745 Richmond was already an enthusiastic loyalist. Quite unexpectedly Prince Charles Edward Stuart arrived off the west coast of Scotland in July, raising his flag in August. The Duke was made a full general with responsibility for the defence of London. He served with the Duke of Cumberland in the first stages of the campaign, travelling north with the intention of stopping the progress of the rebels southwards. Edinburgh fell to the Jacobites, and, in December, Derby. The rebels were turned back at Derby but when the Duke arrived there he marched on, seeing action in the recovery of Carlisle and ensuring their retreat. He did not follow the Jacobites into Scotland and thus was not involved in the butchery at Culloden in 1746.[14]

The Duke was always careful to show his loyalty to the Crown. When he went north to fight, the Duchess thought she might go to stay with her friend, Mary, Duchess of Norfolk; but the Duke, being sensitive to the fact that the Duke of Norfolk, England's premier duke, was also the leading Roman Catholic, persuaded her not to go.[15] The Duke clearly felt that no risks could be taken. Once Bonnie Prince Charlie's rebellion had been halted, he could worry less on this account. Even the acquisition of a trio of marine pictures was a message championing the house of Hanover.[16] Painted in 1737/8 by Thomas Allin, two of them show the ship that had brought William III to England fifty years earlier, and continued to be used by George II, and one the *Royal Caroline*, another of the King's yachts.

## John Wootton: *'where ye Wines in ye Witts out'*

Meanwhile, from *c.*1743–6, the Duke was having his horses painted. John Wootton (*c.*1682–1764) was selected for the commission. As a friend of William Kent and a protégé of Sir Robert Walpole, Wootton was a natural choice for Richmond. He had already contributed two overdoor paintings of ruins to the Old Dining Room, and had painted a small picture of Lady Caroline with her pony. The Duke had also asked the artist to paint one of his favourite hounds, Tapster, with all his pedigree. Wootton wrote to his patron in a humorous, respectful but teasing mode that was typical of many of the Duke's correspondents, and says as much about the Duke as about the writer:

> I hope your Grace has recd the little Picture of Lady Caroline safe and I wish it answers your Grace's expectation . . . and now my Lord give me leave to return your Grace my moste hearty thanks for the noble present of Venison you pleas'd to send me, it came safe and sweet and proved a delightfull repast, I invit'd some friends to partake of your Grace's bounty and wee did eat and drink your Grace's good health and each man look'd like a new-varnish'd portrate, I had some artists with me but they were observ'd to draw nothing but Corks, thus my Lord your Grace sees where ye Wines in ye Witts out . . . but I know your Grace is so good as not to expose the nakedness of your Grace's most oblig'd humble Servt.
> to comand
> J. Wootton[17]

Wootton had become very popular among the aristocracy. He had painted a large hunting portrait for Sir Philip Meadows, the Comptroller of the Army, who lived in the house adjacent to Richmond House and hunted with the Charlton.[18] In 1733 he had painted great hunting scenes for the hall at Althorp, inherited that year by Charles Spencer, hitherto 5th Earl of Sunderland and now also 3rd Duke of Marlborough. The great hall at Longleat in Wiltshire was similarly embellished, as was that at Badminton in Gloucestershire. At about the time that he started to paint again

*Sheldon, A Chestnut Hunter, the Property of the 2nd Duke of Richmond, Goodwood House beyond*, by John Wootton, 1746, oil on canvas, 102 × 125 cm / 40 × 49¼ in. To the left of the house can be seen as a blank block the building works that were being carried out in 1746, taking shape as the south wing. The Temple of Neptune and Minerva is to the right of the house.

for the Duke of Richmond, he also painted another hunting scene, set in a fabulous fictitious classical landscape, for the Duke of Marlborough, who was a member of the Charlton Hunt.[19]

The six scenes painted for the Duke of Richmond show his favourite hunters. Wootton had been to Rome and was much influenced by Claude Lorrain; often in this series a local beauty spot, such as Carné's Seat, Halnaker Hill or Petworth House, is shown in the background, providing the resonance of a classical scene. As in the other, grander, houses, the paintings were probably designed to hang in the main hall (now the Long Hall), where their frames exactly fitted the four panels adjacent to the chimneypieces, with two wider panels opposite. Wootton also painted a hunting scene that showed the Duke himself: possibly this work and *Tapster* were meant for the overmantels until they were displaced in 1747 by the two Canalettos.[20] In 1822 the six Woottons and two Canalettos were all hanging together in the room.

## THE SOUTH WING

In the background of Wootton's painting of *Sheldon* is Goodwood House, still with its two old-fashioned Jacobean gable ends. The following year, at the Duke's invitation, the antiquary George Vertue visited Goodwood. His sketch of the house shows

ABOVE Devonshire House, Piccadilly, designed by William Kent and built c.1744. The south front at Goodwood seems to have been modelled on this very plain classical façade. The sphinxes on its gateway, taken there from Chiswick House, were also copied by the 2nd Duke of Richmond to flank Carné's Seat.

FACING PAGE Goodwood, the south front, built by Matthew Brettingham from c.1745. The round towers were added by James Wyatt in 1799.

that the original east-facing façade was still the principal front. However, he does not show the house exactly as it was; there is, surprisingly, a central pediment, an extra embellishment over the front door and completely uniform windows. The drawing may have been an invention, a proposal, or, more probably, an inaccurate sketch from memory. The projecting wings are still shown, although the Dutch gables are not sketched on. However, both Wootton's and Vertue's images show the beginning of another wing to the left, indicated as a blank end wall in Wootton's painting and in just a few lines in Vertue's sketch. This was the dramatic new south wing.

The pair of stone sphinxes at Carné's Seat, in place by 1747, reflected the couple's admiration for William Kent, imitating a pair by him at Chiswick, later moved to the Devonshire House gate on Piccadilly (see page 55). Between 1746 and 1750 the Duke and Duchess further showed their enthusiasm for Kent by building an impressive new extension to Goodwood House, of which the very plain façade copied Kent's Devonshire House, built as recently as 1744.[21] The architect is believed to have been Matthew Brettingham, whom Thomas Coke, Lord Leicester, had recommended for work at Richmond House.[22] Brettingham was paying off the London bills for the Duchess as late as 1745.[23] In turn the Duchess may have suggested Brettingham to her friend the Duchess of Norfolk for her new town house in St James's Square, constructed from 1748. Another Charlton Hunt member, Charles Fitzroy, 2nd Duke of Grafton, soon afterwards also employed Brettingham, at Euston Hall, Norfolk (where the 1st Duke of Richmond had reputedly been conceived in 1671).

This was the 2nd Duke's second major stage of classicising Goodwood House. Wootton's 1746 painting shows a square grey area to the left of the Jacobean house. Close viewing suggests that it is a simple indication of what would at the time have been building works. The wing is in Portland stone, its plain façade with unadorned windows topped by a pediment, in the style of extreme severity so promoted by Palladian architects.[24] In 1748 Emily was enquiring anxiously from Ireland how the building works were going: 'I hear there are great improvements in the House . . .'[25] Only three days later she chided her mother: 'I fancy you don't chuse to tell me what improvements there is at Goodwood since last year . . . for I think we never left it for any considerable time that there was not something pretty and new at our return.'[26] She had clearly been told that something massive was being built: 'I must confess I have a great curiosity to know what building you are about at Goodwood in the style of Westminster Hall, I am told there are vast improvements there since I saw it . . .'[27]

The evidence for Brettingham's hand at Goodwood is revealed in just a few letters. In February 1750 he wrote to the Duchess, 'Agreeable to your Grace's commands, I have look'd out and bought the several Apartments of stuff, proper for finishing the new building at Goodwood.' He pointed out that owing to 5 per cent river tax, the prices of the items had gone up: they could be bought more cheaply but he suggested that less expensive ones 'are not proper for Your Grace's business'.[28] He also mentioned a deadline: 'the sooner they are sent to Goodwood, the better with the materials befor use this summer'. He had also now investigated how to make the brass window sashes; these must have been for the more exposed windows at Carné's Seat, to resist the weather up at the top of the hill. He had found a less expensive supplier for them. Her response, written on 18 February from London, was sent to him at Sheffield Park in Sussex, the home of their hunting friend Lord De La Warr, and shows her practical involvement: 'as to the sashes I have wrote into the country for the exact dementions, & when I have them will be glad to speak to you about them.'[29]

The new extension comprised a 'Great Room', a designation that was fashionable at the time: this later became the Large Library. A ribbed ceiling was applied in true Palladian manner, following in fact a design by Serlio, another sixteenth-century Italian architect. Adjacent, an anteroom gave on to the room through paired doors. Above, a fine suite of bedchambers have classical detailing. Domestic offices were built beneath the new extension, with a handsome pillared Servants' Hall, the columns for which have always been said to have come from HMS *Centurion,* the warship in which Commodore (later Admiral Lord) Anson made his famous circumnavigation of 1740–44, accompanied by the Duke's nephew the Hon. Augustus (later Viscount) Keppel (1725–1786).[30] The separate kitchen was still in use, and indeed this arrangement, with the other domestic offices in the basement, continued into the early nineteenth century.[31]

## GRANDCHILDREN

When Emily had married in February 1747, she immediately took her husband to visit her sister Caroline, whom she had not been allowed to see for three years. The next year a reconciliation was effected with the Duke and Duchess. This was not, according to the Duke, who was a great stickler for filial obedience, as a result of any intervention by Emily but because of what he described as their own 'tenderness', together with the encouragement of her grandmother, Lady Cadogan.[32] The Duke and Duchess were longing to see Caroline's son, Stephen. To celebrate, Henry Fox gave the Duchess a Meissen snuff box with a portrait of Caroline on the lid. George Vertue told how many of the family were at home in that year, after Emily had left for Ireland: the two boys, aged twelve and eight, and the two 'young Ladyes his daughters Louisa & Sarah both fine young children.'[33] They were four and two. In May 1748 Walpole reported that 'the Duchess of Richmond . . . does not go out with her twenty fifth pregnancy.'[34]

Gold-mounted snuff box, Meissen, 1748, 3.4 × 6.8 × 5.2 cm / 1⅜ × 2¾ × 2⅛ in. In 1748 Henry Fox commissioned his friend Charles Hanbury Williams, Ambassador to the Court of Saxony at Dresden, to oversee the making of three porcelain boxes at the Meissen factory, of which this one, for the Duchess, was a reconciliation gift four years after his elopement with Caroline. The miniature of Caroline was painted by Gervase Spencer (*fl.*1740–63) and was delivered to the factory on 5 May 1748, its glass broken in transit. The lid had to be fired seven times before Hanbury Williams was satisfied. In her will, the Duchess bequeathed the snuff box as a precious object to her sister Lady Margaret Bentinck, but it remained with the family.

## The Paris Project

Despite all the building activity, in 1748 the Duke was very occupied with preparations to become British ambassador to Paris. This was an appointment to support the renewed relationship with France following the peace treaty of Aix-la-Chapelle to end the War of the Austrian Succession. The preparations are especially interesting for what they reveal about the Duke's household. He made lists of the staff he would need, including six 'gentlemen', not least his old tutor and friend Tom Hill, M. Trembley (who was to become his son's Grand Tour tutor), his chaplain, the Revd Robert Webber, Robert Sedgewick, the steward and a gentleman of the horse. The gentlemen would be accompanied by four pages, while the Duke would have four footmen, one of them French, and the Duchess also three or four, of whom most would be French. François Liegois was by now *maître d'hôtel*. The family would also take a butler, an under butler and four valets de chambre; a coachman, helper and postillion, and a French groom.

In Paris, under his head chef Jacquemar (who earned more than double the salary of Liegois), they planned to recruit specialist kitchen staff; a *rotisseur*, a *patissier*, a *marmitor*, a confectioner, and an under confectioner. The confectioner had to be able to make 'chocollate [*sic*], sweetmeats, liqueurs, and all sorts of ice'. The Duke was now so famous for his table that friends would often compliment him on the fare; among them Martin Folkes was an especial *bon viveur*.

The staff were loyal and long-serving. Elizabeth Liegois was still 'woman to Lady Duchess'. Louisette the chambermaid was also to go to Paris, as well as a governess and a maid for the children. The boys were to stay in London for their education, joined by a Keppel cousin. The final list of servants numbered sixty-nine. On the road the Duke was to travel in a party of eighteen, with twenty horses.[35] However, in January 1749 the Duke was still in England.[36] In the event, although he went first to Holland and then to Aubigny, where he had arrived by August, he never became ambassador to Paris. This seems to have been because it was anticipated that an ambassador of equally high rank would be sent to London; but in the event only a marquis was dispatched. The Duke was also said to be concerned about the expense. The position was given instead to his brother-in-law, William, 2nd Earl of Albemarle.[37] Walpole commented: 'I was surprised to see that the Duke of Richmond would not go as ambassador to France, thinking he would like it of all things.'[38]

At home the Duke was always very committed to the city of Chichester, where he controlled one of the two parliamentary seats and exercised great influence over the city council. In 1746 he paid for the complete restoration of the old Chichester Cross, at the centre of the city: it was engraved by Vertue the following year. In particular he had the clock moved, to make each face look down one of the four streets to north, south, east and west. His grandfather, Charles II, had previously repaired it in 1674, placing a bust of his own father, Charles I, in a niche facing east.[39] Thus the Duke was very much acting in the spirit of his royal forebear, and was proud if the locals made the connection. In 1749 he succeeded the Duke of Somerset as High Steward for the city.

## Thirty Years of Marriage

Despite discreet infidelities, the Duke's passion for his wife was unremitting. Horace Walpole reported in 1743/4:

I drove to the other end of town, where I heard lived a constant couple – I found a man and a woman, Duke and Duchess of Richmond, both handsome enough to have been tempted to every inconstancy, but too handsome to have ever found what they would have lost by the exchange. I begged this happy charming woman to tell me by what art she had for twenty years together made herself beloved . . . She coloured with a sort of mild indignation that made her ten times more beautiful, and replied, she knew not what I meant by art – that she had always obeyed, been virtuous, and loved her husband; and was it strange he should return it . . .[40]

Although she was now over forty and had borne eleven babies, with six children living, the Duchess would bear one more child. Walpole wrote in February 1750: 'The Duchess of Richmond . . . again lies in, after having been with child seven-and-twenty times: but even this is not so extra ordinary as the Duke's fondness for her, or as the vigour of her beauty: her complexion is as fair and blooming as when she was a bride.'[41] The baby, Lady Cecilia, was her seventh child to survive infancy. Emily dutifully wrote individually to each parent to congratulate them.[42]

Sadly, the little girl was hardly to know her father (nor, for long, her mother); nor was the Duke to see his 'Great Room' completely fitted out. In the autumn of 1749 Emily was worried about his 'growing so thin and that disorder continuing so long.'[43] For five months in 1750 he suffered from cancer of the bladder, bravely enduring operations by his surgeon, Francis Tomkins, and unable to join the Foxes to stay with Emily at Carton.[44] He died in August 1750, followed just one year later by his Duchess. His deathbed was at his halfway home between London and Goodwood, at Godalming. Abraham Trembley, who witnessed the couple's distress, described him as 'an amiable, virtuous affable man, endowed with that urbanity and frankness that give lustre even to virtue, and whose kindness I had often experienced . . .'[45] The Duke asked for his funeral to be carried out 'with as little expense & show as possible in his vault just made at Chichester.'[46] The body of his father was moved at his request to the vault, as were those of his five deceased children.

# 7 MAN OF SCIENCE

## CHARLES, 3RD DUKE OF RICHMOND, 1735–1806

When his father died in 1750, the new Duke was only fifteen. From his deathbed, the 2nd Duke asked Abraham Trembley to be the tutor to his two sons. He had been impressed by Trembley's scientific discoveries, his modest nature and good character, and by his care and education of Count Bentinck's sons. The young 3rd Duke's five guardians during his minority included his uncle, William, 2nd Earl of Albemarle, who was in Paris, and his older brother-in-law, Henry Fox, who, despite being very busy in London, was very diligent, writing him many letters. Left with a grieving mother, surrounded by younger sisters and with just his brother Lord George for everyday family support, the young Duke found himself in the care of an extremely capable tutor, who was also at the forefront of new ideas on education.

### Teenage Years

The Duke was very close to George, with whom he attended school at Westminster, very near to their home at Richmond House. The boys had been boarders, writing letters home, or apologising for not writing them, and leaving Goodwood for school after Christmas when everyone else stayed in the country. The young Earl of March's letters to his parents reveal devotion, duty, obedience and affection, qualities which were expected of him. While the rest of the family was abroad in 1749, the boys lodged at Wandsworth, from where a tutor from Westminster, Mr Gibberd, took them on an educational tour. This included the Cadogans' estate at Caversham, near Reading; Oxford; Rousham in Oxfordshire; and Lord Cobham's Hagley Hall. The trip was clearly designed to teach them about great houses and English history.

*Charles, 3rd Duke of Richmond, Lennox and Aubigny,* by Pompeio Batoni, Rome, 1755, oil on canvas, 135 × 98 cm / 53¼ × 38½ in.

However, the boys' preferred occupation was larking around with horses and dogs. Lord George had a 'pretty little monkey' and kept a pet fox in town, causing their neighbour, the Duke of Montagu, to complain about the smell.[1] The fifteen-year-old March was more interested in girls, proudly relating his amorous exploits in the Vauxhall and Ranelagh gardens to Fox.[2] They were naturally high-spirited; as related by the poet William Cowper, March set fire to the greasy locks of a Latin master at Westminster, and then boxed his ears in order to extinguish the flames. Although his parents would have liked him to stay at school for one more year, March enlisted the aid of Henry Fox to persuade them to let him leave before reaching the sixth form. However, it was decided that serious study was needed. Following his father's death, in the autumn of 1750 the Duke set off with his tutor for Trembley's home town of Geneva. The widowed Duchess believed that it would be good for him to stay there for two years, but was greatly distressed by his departure.

Not only was Trembley an accomplished scientist, but he could also teach most other subjects. Above all he was kind, sympathetic and family-minded. Some of his views accorded with those of Jean-Jacques Rousseau, such as that children's mental capacities must not be overtaxed, and that a child's individual interest must be developed. Unlike Rousseau he believed in discipline and that moral principles should be instilled rather than learnt by self-discovery. Rousseau published his ideas in *Emile* in 1762; later Trembley spoke out against his views on morality, saying that they were very damaging. The tutor's training was to have a powerful influence over the Duke's entire life, developing him as a scientist and a radical. However, although he was an intelligent young man, the method of education may have led him to develop as something of a dogmatist and not necessarily as a great intellectual. He was trained more

ABOVE  *Lord George Lennox*, by Pompeio Batoni, Rome, 1755, oil on canvas, 96.5 × 71 cm/38 × 28 in. Lord George had a distinguished military career. He was MP for Chichester 1761–7 and for Sussex 1767–90.

FACING PAGE  *Charles, 3rd Duke of Richmond, Lennox and Aubigny*, by Antonio Mengs, Rome, 1755, oil on canvas, 127 × 94 cm/50 × 37 in.

to follow his own convictions than to look at the other side of an argument.

The Duchess was never to see her son again: in the summer of 1751 she died at the age of forty-five. The family crisis deepened. The Duke's eldest sister, Caroline, was offended to find that the guardianship of the younger sisters, Louisa, Sarah and Cecilia, was left to her next sister, Emily, Countess of Kildare, until they were fifteen. This meant that the younger girls moved to Ireland, and for a time the whole family was together very little. Lord George left in September 1751 to join his brother in Geneva. There Trembley commented that the Duke 'loves dogs prodigiously . . .

and also the human race and the feminine race.'[3] They were still there in September 1752, when the Duke wrote to Albemarle, begging to be allowed to return. They were bored: the Calvinist city state was dull, parties were few and public diversions banned. The Duke was nearly eighteen: he wanted to see other countries, but first he wanted to return to England to see the family, not least Emily whom he had not seen for four years.

## GRAND TOUR

However, on 16 September 1752 Trembley set off again with both boys for a tour of France. Trembley's fame as a scientist and the Duke's rank meant that they were well received everywhere. They travelled first via Lyons to the south of France, reaching Marseilles and then going west via Montpellier to Bordeaux, to make contact with the English wine merchants and try the famous claret. Here they stayed with the French philosopher Baron de Montesquieu, who had known the 2nd Duke.

By Christmas they were in Paris, staying for three months in the rue de Condé. Trembley enjoyed this less, but he introduced the Duke to leading intellectuals, including the famous elderly scientist and naturalist René-Antoine Ferchault de Réamur (1683–1757), whose method of temperature measurement was in widespread use. They also met the mathematician Charles Etienne Camus (1699–1768), who was especially interested in cartography and the measurement of the earth; Charles-Marie la Condamine (1701–1774), explorer of the Amazon; and the young liberal aristocrat Baron Malesherbes (1721–1794).

By the end of February 1753 they were back in London, and in the spring went down to Goodwood. Then they returned to the continent, travelling via Tournai, Brussels and Strasbourg. At Sarre they found troops on manoeuvre: here the Duke was able to pitch his tent and join in, an early taste of army training. That autumn they went to Leiden, where Trembley had studied twenty years earlier. The Duke entered the university, where he carried out scientific studies under the overall direction of the Swiss

botanist Professor Frédéric-Louis Allamand (1736–after 1803), who like other naturalists was trying to define the various species. These studies, especially in anatomy, were to be a very formative influence on the Duke, his interest in equine anatomy being the reason he later chose to commission the unknown painter George Stubbs. In the New Year Lord George joined the studies. That spring they were off again, being presented to Frederick the Great in Berlin en route for Bohemia and Moravia. In the autumn of 1754 they were in Vienna, where Trembley spent much time in the museums, working on natural history.

Finally, Italy beckoned. The travellers went to Venice, and in February and March 1755 were in Rome studying 'Antiquités and virtû'.[4] Here they were both painted by Pompeio Batoni, predictably shown not with their books and urns, but with their beloved dogs.[5] The Duke was also depicted by Antonio Mengs, again in a three-quarter-length portrait, this time a handsome swagger pose. At Naples they studied the ancient city of Herculaneum, the excavation of which had started some twenty years earlier, and were lucky enough to see Vesuvius in eruption. They went north to Florence in May, where the British representative Sir Horace Mann was very helpful, 'the best kind of man in the world'; thence to Pisa; and then in the summer to Milan, which the Duke enjoyed the most because of the great hospitality received in country houses.[6] Thence they went to Turin, where Trembley spent much time in discussion about natural science, and on to Berne where they met Albert Haller (1708–1777), the famous anatomist who was the first scientist to make animal physiology an important subject in its own right. He had a great influence on the Duke. From there they travelled through the old duchy of Nassau and along the Rhine. Study was now at an end: after a visit to Holland to see their widowed aunt, Lady Margaret Bentinck, the young men reached London in January 1756.

The Duke seemed to enjoy it all more than Lord George and was in no hurry to return. The eventual impact on him was certainly an abiding interest in science, and in how things worked. Ultimately his whole approach to life was more that of a scientist than of an artist. Another major insight was that military preparations were being made for war in Europe, about which he showed considerable curiosity, requesting pamphlets and maps. Trembley was generously rewarded for his considerable pains and never had to work again.

## Majority and Marriage

The Duke turned twenty-one in February 1756, at which stage Trembley gave up his duty of care. Lady Diana Spencer, the eldest daughter of Charles Spencer, 3rd Duke of Marlborough, was seen as a possible bride for the young Duke. An album of classical drawings by her, still in the collection, may have been given to him at this time. They were perhaps an indication of his taste for classical drawings as expressed in his subsequent sculpture gallery. Instead, on 1 April 1757 he married Lady Mary Bruce (1740–1796), third and youngest daughter of Charles Bruce, 4th Earl of Elgin and 3rd and last Earl of Ailesbury (1682–1747).

The Duke selected his bride for himself, finding that tongues were wagging before he really even knew the girl: 'I was told t'other day that I had proposed myself *en mariage* to Lady Mary Bruce and that on my account she had refused Lord Bruce [a cousin]. . .'[7] In fact, he had danced with her at Norfolk House, presumably in the famous house-warming party of 1756, and had admired her at the opera. He decided to press on: 'I will try to get acquainted with her and see how it is . . .' Showing much embarrassment, he applied to her stepfather, Major-General the Hon. Henry Seymour Conway, assuring him that 'Every time I see her I like her better and find in her everything I could wish.'[8] Conway replied that he had spoken to Lady Ailesbury, and she to Lady Mary, and that 'as Your Grace seems interested to know her answer I have great pleasure in telling you it was such as I believe you wou'd most approve . . .'[9]

Caroline was surprised at his choice, finding her an odd character. Lady Mary was not well educated or cultured. She was very natural and lacking in etiquette. There was already an existing contact between the couple's families, which may have made the Duke feel safe, in that Mary's aunt, Lady Elizabeth Bruce (1689–1745), had married George, 3rd Earl of Cardigan, the Duke's great-uncle.[10] He was, moreover, very taken with his bride, giving two balls to celebrate the engagement. The wedding, by special licence, took place at Conway's London house in Warwick Street. The groom was twenty-two and the bride seventeen. As the nephew of Sir Robert Walpole, Conway was the first cousin of the acerbic wit and connoisseur Horace Walpole. In his correspondence Walpole had made many comments about the 2nd Duke and Duchess and their children, and would now become even closer to the family. Not unnaturally, he was beside himself with joy at the match, pronouncing it 'The perfectest match in the world; youth, beauty, riches, alliances, and all the blood of all the kings from Robert Bruce to Charles II. They are the prettiest couple in England . . .' He qualified the last comment: 'except the father-in-law and mother.'[11]

The Duchess was certainly devoted to the Duke: in 1758 she travelled a hundred miles to Weymouth just to greet his arrival with the fleet, only to find that he had already sailed again. She would travel 'day and night to be with him an hour sooner', and at one stage camped in a tent in Surrey to be near him on army manoeuvres.[12] In 1759 she travelled with him to Holland as he set off for war in Germany.

## The Conways

Mary's mother was the lively socialite Caroline, Countess of Ailesbury (1721–1803). The daughter of John Campbell, 4th Duke of Argyll (c.1693–1770), Lady Caroline Campbell had been married at the age of eighteen, unwillingly, to the sixty-year-old twice-widowed Charles, 3rd Earl of Ailesbury, later 4th Earl of Elgin, who was furious when he discovered that she had no fortune. In her early years Mary lived at his fine new Palladian mansion, Tottenham Park, in the Savernake Forest. Only a few months after his death in 1747, when Mary was only seven, Caroline married Henry Seymour Conway (1721–1795), whose elder brother Francis, at the time Lord Conway of Ragley, was created Earl of Hertford in 1750. As was normal for a noblewoman, Caroline continued to style herself as Lady Ailesbury after her remarriage. Henry and Caroline acquired Park Place, Henley, where they made many improvements to the house. Their decorations were in the forefront of fashion. Mary was therefore brought up in cultured circles, centred on London society, so it was extraordinary that she should be so little interested in the arts, especially as she often went to stay with her family at Henley.

The Conways had a younger daughter. Anne Seymour Conway (1748–1828) later became famous as the sculptress Anne

ABOVE, LEFT  *Charles, 3rd Duke of Richmond, Lennox and Aubigny*, by Joshua Reynolds, 1758, oil on canvas, 126 × 97 cm / 49½ × 38¾ in. The portrait shows the Duke in the military uniform of which he was so proud, and in a pose typical of the painter's work at this time, imitating the ancient statue of the Apollo Belvedere.

ABOVE, RIGHT  *Mary, Duchess of Richmond*, by Joshua Reynolds, mid-1760s, oil on canvas, 75 × 62 cm / 29½ × 24½ in. The Duchess is depicted wearing a brown riding habit and doing her embroidery. There was a particular tendency in the mid-1760s for ladies in the country to wear their habits all day rather than changing their clothes both before and after riding, and one to which the Duchess and her sister-in-law Lady George were especially inclined. The custom was frowned upon by more fastidious friends.

Seymour Damer. In the early 1750s she used to stay with her relative Horace Walpole at his new home at Strawberry Hill, his Gothick mansion on the Thames at Twickenham. She would pretend with amusement that she was his wife, a situation that was clearly unlikely. Anne would later make an unfortunate marriage to the Hon. John Damer, who shot himself in 1776 at the age of thirty-two.[13] However, she developed her talents as a sculptress, creating figures of Isis and Osiris on the bridge at Henley, which had been built at her father's expense, and to which they would drive down the hill from Park Place. Anne was an important part of the extended Goodwood family. She sculpted

Walpole's *Two Sleeping Dogs* in terracotta with such success that they were repeated for the Duke; they were also admired by James Wyatt. Walpole commented that 'She has a singular talent for catching the characters of animals . . .'[14] He was so delighted with his that he said he would never part with the original. When Walpole died in 1797, by which time he had succeeded his nephew as 4th Earl of Orford, he bequeathed Strawberry Hill to Anne.

## PORTRAITS

In another three-quarter-length portrait, after his return to England, the Duke was painted in 1758 by Joshua Reynolds. Reynolds already had a close link to the family: having been brought up in south Devon, where he trained under Thomas Hudson, he had the good fortune to sail from Plymouth to the Mediterranean in 1749 with Captain the Hon. Augustus Keppel, the Duke's first cousin. Through this link Reynolds not only managed to see Rome, but also gained for himself an indulgent patron in the form of Keppel, whom he would paint seven times, as well as the patronage of the Duke.

The Duchess was also painted by Reynolds in this year, in profile, and again in 1759/60, in a three-quarter-length seated portrait.[15] The latter painting was given to Lord Holland in 1768, for the picture gallery. The Duchess was painted by him a third time, in a modest half-length seated pose, *c.*1764–7, looking rather workaday in a brown riding habit and doing her embroidery very demurely. In their usual family manner of making the same choices, Lord George was also painted by Reynolds in 1760.[16]

The Duke's aristocratic good looks were commented on by Walpole, always one to mind about appearance, at the time of the Reynolds portrait: 'his figure was noble and his countenance singularly handsome.' At the coronation, he found that 'it required all the beauty of the Dukes of Richmond and Marlborough to make them [the other peers] noticed.'[17] Similarly Sir Nathaniel Wraxall, not always a generous commentator, said that 'His person, manneres and address were all full of dignity, and that personal beauty which distinguished Mademoiselle de la Querouaille was not become extinct in him.'[18]

## Lady Mary Bruce, Duchess of Richmond (1740–1796)

With the Duke married, Goodwood once again became a lively family home. In late May 1757 Conway was staying there, together with Fox's elder brother the Earl of Ilchester, and their sister, Henrietta. Expected soon were Lady Kildare (Emily) and the rest of the Fox family, together with their hostess, the Duchess, who had apparently not yet arrived. 'Never was such a collection of roots and branches,' Conway remarked cheerfully.[19] By June the Foxes had changed their mind, but Louisa (now aged fourteen) and Sarah (twelve) were there, with Emily who was their guardian.

Although they mostly wintered at Goodwood in the early years of their marriage, for the Duke's shooting and hunting seasons, the couple spent much time in London, which Mary clearly preferred, and especially in early summer, when the social season really got going. There they attended masquerades and balls, plays and concerts. Caroline groused that they partied too much, returning home late in hackney (i.e. hired) carriages, and that in the Duke's absence abroad Mary imprudently stayed in a box at the opera with men only, and was generally 'racketing about . . . always five or six men about her.'[20] At first Caroline did not really like Mary: she found her irritating, though good-humoured and easy to live with. After a ball at the Conollys' (their sister Louisa's town house), Walpole reported that he was 'fetched back to sup with Prince Edward and the Duchess of Richmond, who is his present passion'.[21] This is simply a description of a flirtation, to which the Prince was inclined and at which the Duchess was adept. Walpole further commented: 'he pursues [her] with great earnestness, but meets with so little encouragement from Her Grace that I fancy he will soon grow weary.'[22] It was all quite harmless. Caroline found that 'She is so simple! It provokes one, but at the same time so excessively good-humoured, one is angry at feeling provoked with her.'[23] She had to admit that 'The Duchess seems to pass thro' life more happily than most people, very good health, great good humour, and very little sensibility.'[24]

Being so close to the Conways, Horace Walpole often spent time with mother and daughter, as when they visited him at Strawberry Hill in 1759, together with the beautiful, widowed Elizabeth Gunning, Duchess of Hamilton, who in that year married Lady Ailesbury's brother, John, 5th Duke of Argyll. Walpole declared: 'Strawberry Hill is grown a perfect Paphos; it is the land of beauties.'[25] However, reading between the lines, Walpole's admiration of Mary was not as long-lasting as that for her late mother-in-law, Duchess Sarah; nor indeed as genuine as that for Caroline Ailesbury herself, nor as profound as that for the beauty of Emily. He wrote semi-critically to Henry Seymour Conway after the royal marriage in 1761, 'Your daughter was much better dressed than ever I saw her', making a similar comment about her lack of effort with clothes, shoes and hair after seeing her at the coronation.[26] This is confirmed by Caroline's comment that 'There is a roughness in her that is not pleasing at all.'[27] Caroline concluded that one could not form a settled opinion of her sister-in-law.

Finally, the unkindest cut of all. Walpole said of reports of her appearance in Paris in 1763 that 'The last (Lady Ailesbury's daughter) is in all the bloom of youth and beauty, but awkward and unfashioned.'[28] Mary had an extraordinary confidence and a natural prettiness: she did not seem to care what people thought. Indeed, Caroline described her as travelling there in a grubby old dress, looking like a housemaid. No children had arrived, but she was as cheerful and good-natured as ever. Mary would simply deflect adverse comment with the remark that people should always do things their own way.

Meanwhile, on Christmas Day 1759 Lord George married Lady Louisa Kerr (d.1830), daughter of the Earl of Ancram, later Marquis of Lothian. As her father did not approve, they had to elope from her Scottish home. At first the two wives did not get on very well, but relations settled down and they all became very close. Although she was rather masculine, Lady Louisa was extremely amusing, and always made the family laugh. At first the Lennoxes lived with the Duke and Duchess both at Richmond House and at Goodwood, but in 1764 the Duke bought for them the manor of Stoke, which they made their family home.

## Military and Political Career

Commissioned as an ensign in the 2nd Foot Guards in 1751, the 3rd Duke was made a captain in the 20th Foot two years later. His enthusiasm for military matters was especially stimulated by having met Colonel (later General) James Wolfe in Paris in 1752, and on his return from the Grand Tour the two corresponded. In 1756 war broke out again when the balance of power in Europe was once more disrupted. The Empress Maria Theresa, dissatisfied with the Treaty of Aix-la-Chapelle that had made her give up Silesia to Prussia, broke away from her traditional alliance with England to side with France. They were joined by Russia and

Saxony and some smaller states, with the result that England, eager still to protect Hanover, joined forces with the militaristic Prussia. The Duke was made lieutenant-colonel commanding the 33rd Foot, with which he served in the Netherlands and Germany in the spring and summer. In 1758 he was made colonel of the 72nd Foot, in which role in August he took part in the raid on Cherbourg, one of several coastal raids designed to keep some of the French forces away from Hanover. The following year, when there were great British victories by sea and land, he served as ADC to Prince Frederick of Brunswick in his great triumph for the English in repulsing the French at Minden on 1 August. Hanover was secure, and England no longer feared invasion by the French. The Duke was praised by the Prince in his despatch. Although he left active service as early as 1760, he emerged from the war with the rank of major-general.

As a young man, the Duke believed that his career would be in politics. However, from the accession of the young George III in 1760 he would find himself in a very different situation from that of his father. The Whigs had been instrumental in bringing the Hanoverians to England in 1714 and had governed the country largely through a network of great Whig houses throughout the reigns of the first two Georges, keeping royal power in check as they felt was properly in line with the Glorious Revolution of 1688. However, George III felt that he was more truly British: he wanted to be more authoritarian and to create a party of his own, not to be held in·check by the Whigs, whom he in turn felt were usurping royal authority. The Tories had for some years been unpopular because they were identified with the deposed Stuarts and the rebellion in 1745; but under the new king a succession of Tory prime ministers of a new type would break Whig power. The party to which the 3rd Duke adhered was therefore usually in opposition. It also had the normal Whig tendency to break into factions.

At first the King was prepared to look kindly on the Duke, not least because he was very fond of Lady Sarah Lennox, who had arrived from Ireland in November 1759 to be in Caroline's care. She was presented at court and the King, as Prince of Wales, had fallen deeply in love with her.[29] This relationship was not allowed to flourish, resisted by the King's mother in collaboration with his former tutor, the Earl of Bute. In November 1760 the Duke was appointed as a lord of the bedchamber to the new monarch. However, his impetuous and demanding nature quickly proved his downfall at court. The following month his brother Lord George was not given an army promotion that both his wife and his brother thought should be his. The Duke dashed up from Goodwood to be granted a twenty-minute audience by the King, who summarily refused his request. Feeling that his situation was now untenable, the Duke resigned his court position, declaring to his uncle that 'there are some things I think I have a right to'.[30] He later appeared annoyed with himself, but he would never fully regain royal favour.

Nevertheless, at the coronation in September 1761, the Duke held the Sceptre with the Dove ready for the King; this was the traditional role of the Dukes of Richmond. When the war ended in 1763, he became Lord Lieutenant of Sussex, a post which he held for life. This gave him a welcome new position in which he was able to assume leadership of the Sussex militia. He was often away from Goodwood to attend their camps or training. He spent two years hoping for political office, but, according to a later report, offended the King again.[31] The control of ministers still rested with the King, but an appointment was anyway unlikely while the Tory Marquis of Bute or George Grenville was first minister. However, when the Marquis of Rockingham was appointed to the prime position in July 1765, the Duke was finally offered a post, that of ambassador to Paris. The King was reluctant when, after the Duke's return the following year, the Marquis of Rockingham gave him the very senior position of secretary of state for the south, while Conway, whose military career had ended two years earlier, was given the same position for the north. However, the administration lasted a short time, so the Duke only held this appointment for a year. He was not reappointed in the next government.

## Fashionable London Life

After his return from overseas service the Duke seemed especially happy with his wife. Mary was completely focused on her husband. Caroline was much relieved: 'She has the most perfect confidence in him, tells him everything in the world, the least trifling event, loves him as well as she can love anything, and grows more formed a good deal. He loves her ten times better than ever he did. It's a vast pleasure to me to think that will be a happy marriage'.[32] The Duke himself often referred to Mary in his letters to Henry Fox as 'the lovely'.[33]

Parties to celebrate family occasions continued to take place at Richmond House. Early in 1760 a ball was given for the just-married Lady Louisa Conolly, with her husband, Tom Conolly of Castletown, the wealthiest man in Ireland. Louisa was fifteen. In 1762 the Duke and Duchess much enjoyed a visit to Ireland, where they visited the family homes of the Duke's sisters as well as other great houses. In 1763 Walpole described a ball that took place at Richmond House, which he attended dressed in a 'sober purple domino'.[34] The ball went on until 6 a.m.

> Last night we had a magnificent entertainment at Richmond House, a masquerade and fireworks. . . . A masquerade was a new sight to the young people, who had dressed themselves charmingly . . . The Duchesses of Richmond and Grafton, the first as a Persian sultana, the latter as Cleopatra, and such a Cleopatra! were glorious figures, in very different styles. Mrs Fitzroy in a Turkish dress, Lady George Lenox and Lady Bolinbroke [sic] in a Grecian girl's, Lady Mary Coke as Imoinda and Lady Pembroke as a pilgrim, were the principal beauties of the night . . . The whole garden was illuminated and

the apartments. An encampment of barges decked with streamers in the middle of the Thames, kept the people from danger and formed a stage for the fireworks, which were placed too along the rails of the garden. The ground rooms lighted, with suppers spread, the houses covered and filled with people, the bridge, the garden full of masks, Whitehall crowded with spectators to see the dresses pass, and the multitude of heads on the river, who came to light by the splendour of the fire-wheels, composed the gayest and richest scene imaginable; not to mention the diamonds and sumptuousness of habits. The Dukes of York and Cumberland, and the Margrave of Anspach, were there, and about six hundred masks.[35]

Among the guests who were picked out for mention Lady Bolingbroke was the Duke's old flame, formerly Lady Diana Spencer; in 1768 she would scandalously divorce her husband to marry Topham Beauclerk. Lady Pembroke was her sister, wife of the 10th Earl, formerly Lady Elizabeth Spencer. The Duchess of Grafton was Anne Liddell, married to Augustus, 3rd Duke of Grafton, who was, like Richmond, a great-grandson of Charles II. Anne would eventually leave her unfaithful husband, taking up with the Earl of Upper Ossory, also a friend of the Richmonds, whom she in turn married after her divorce. Lady Mary Coke was the fourth daughter of John, 2nd Duke of Argyll. As the second cousin of Lady Ailesbury, and a single woman (separated from Viscount Coke and then widowed), she would see a good deal of the Richmonds in London.[36] Mary, Duchess of Richmond, was always regarded as having a rather risqué set of friends. Another regular guest at Richmond House was the witty George Selwyn (1719–1771), a close friend of both the Fox family and Horace Walpole.

The area close to the old Whitehall Palace was still the smart place to live. Next door to Richmond House lived the new Duke of Montagu. Like his predecessor, he was close to the Duke of Richmond, but they were also blood relations. The Duke of Montagu of the new creation was George Brudenell, 4th Earl of Cardigan (1712–1790): his father, George, 3rd Earl of Cardigan, had been the brother of Richmond's grandmother Anne Brudenell.[37] The 10th Earl of Pembroke lived slightly further down the Thames, replacing the house that his father the Architect Earl had built with a new one by Sir William Chambers.

Richmond House was always available for the Duke's nephews and nieces. In September 1765, having left Eton, Emily's eldest son, George, Lord Ophaly, was staying. He had just been commissioned into a cavalry regiment. Suddenly he was struck by a fever. The Duke obtained the best medical attention for him, but tragically the young man died. The Duke had to inform the boy's father and arrange the burial at the nearby church of St Martin-in-the-Fields. Everyone was deeply distressed by the death of Emily's favourite child. Thereafter she brought her children back from England to Ireland for their education. It was organised at her large seaside home in Dublin Bay, named by her Frescati, at Blackrock, under the auspices of the Scottish tutor William Ogilvie, who was well versed in the latest theories of the Enlightenment. Rousseauistic ideals were applied in combination with kind but firm Scottish discipline.[38]

The Duchess of Richmond was constantly sociable and by 1760 was also receiving large houseparties at Goodwood.[39] It was hardly surprising if, in the absence of the longed-for children, she and her husband enjoyed the company of others in order to divert themselves. The Duchess herself seems to have been quite unaffected by her surroundings. Surprisingly, Lady Sarah later described Richmond House as being cold, damp and uncomfortable. Despite the hospitality and generosity that were traditional for guests at both homes, at Goodwood Friday was at least sometimes a *jour maigre* or a day of fasting, a leftover from the old idea of eating only fish on that day of the week. The Duke was also attacked for 'domestic parsimony', his kitchen being said to be 'the coolest apartment in his house, both at Goodwood and in Privy Garden'.[40] Hospitality on high days and holidays may have been modified by a modicum of abstention in between.[41]

## EXTENDING THE ESTATE

The Duke had inherited just 1,100 acres of land, including a park around the house of 200 acres. When he was not away from home for military or political reasons, he was very busy on the estate. After his return from the Grand Tour he took his country responsibilities seriously, immediately writing to his father's friend Peter Collinson in the spring of 1756 about trees. In 1759 Collinson returned to Goodwood after a gap of nine years. He was 'agreeably surprised with the wonderful progress and growth of so many exotic trees that I remember in their infant state', and commented that they now needed skilful pruning.[42] He had seen the nurseries at Charlton (the plantations of young trees next to the hunting lodge) and was busy 'forming great designs for future planting'. Collinson was delighted that the young Duke planned to carry on where his father had left off, seeing it as 'noble work worthy of the noble Lord and will be what a glorious scene to see these barren mountains shaded with verdant woods.'

'The true Richmond spirit' did indeed, as Collinson presaged, carry on. The Duke carried out a huge planting programme, adding to the plantations behind the house. Like his father he used exotica such as tulip trees and magnolias, and he added more cork oaks. From 1761 he planted a thousand cedars of Lebanon. Two years later, in one plantation he was sad to see that 'there are not five of the five hundred left with one leaf on.' He immediately ordered another hundred. Some of the evergreen plantations over to the right of the road up to the racecourse had grown well up by the 1830s,[43] but the area at the top of the hill was later replanted with beech, becoming known as Birdless Grove.

An early cedar tree at Goodwood. The first cedars at Goodwood were planted for the 2nd Duke in the 1740s. The culmination was a planting of a thousand in 1761 for the 3rd Duke.

In the 1760s the Duke had a tennis court built at Goodwood, about a quarter of a mile to the south of the house. A walled garden was established around it. In London the Duke played tennis almost daily, usually early in the morning; he probably did the same in the country.

In 1765 the Duke paid £48,000 for Halnaker House and its park, to the south of Goodwood. The main Chichester–Petworth road ran uncomfortably in front of Goodwood House, past Molecomb and Pilley Green to East Dean, so he diverted it to run further east, through Halnaker and its park to the south-east of Goodwood, to join the old road at Upwaltham. The acquisition extended his holdings into many parishes or manors, including Boxgrove, Walburton, Barnham and East Lavant. By that year he had also acquired land at Westhampnett, West Lavant, Tangmere, Singleton and East Dean.[44] Thanks to the careful stewardship of his funds by his guardians while he was young, he would eventually manage to extend the estate to 17,000 acres in total.

# 8    ART AND ANATOMY

1755–1775

Freshly returned from his Grand Tour, the twenty-year-old Duke threw himself into new projects. He had a magnificent London house, and a well-placed country seat: the question was how he would best use and enhance these to express his own priorities. As his father's son his sympathies were naturally with the Whig aristocracy. Its members especially espoused a love of the Antique in art, both because of their intensely classical education and because they believed in the high moral and civic virtues of Republican Rome, where government lay in the hands of the Senate. The better Roman emperors could be seen as prototypes for good kings of England, where the ideal of a monarch who was subject to parliamentary controls had been established at the Glorious Revolution. Instinctively, the young Duke decided to embark on two ventures that combined practical needs with the noble qualities of the Antique. Taking place roughly contemporaneously, one was in sculpture and was public-spirited, and the other in architecture for private but status-enhancing usage.

## The 3rd Duke's Sculpture Gallery

As a child the Duke would have known about the sculpture collection at Wilton House near Salisbury of his father's close friend the Earl of Pembroke, and of that at Holkham Hall in Norfolk of the Earl of Leicester. Although Holkham was far away, there were strong links both through the Earl, a long-established member of the Charlton Hunt, and through Matthew Brettingham, who with his son had acquired much of the Holkham sculpture. The Duke would also have heard about Sir Robert Walpole's collection at the neighbouring Houghton Hall in Norfolk. All these great patrons of arts were Whigs.

Most of this generation had now passed on. The Duke may have been aware that in the mid-1750s his future political ally, the young Marquis of Rockingham, had been collecting sculpture for his home at Wentworth Woodhouse in Yorkshire. The new Duke of Richmond approached the collecting of sculpture in a different way again. His aims were in the spirit of science, experiment and improvement, of wanting artists to make better depictions of the human form and of enabling this to occur in London. In 1758 the *Daily Advertiser* announced:

> We hear that His Grace the Duke of Richmond has ordered a room to be opened (for the use of those who study painting, sculpture, and engraving) in which is contained a large collection of original plaster casts from the best antique statues and busts now at Rome and Florence; where any painter, sculptor, carver, or other artist, . . . will have liberty to draw or model at any time . . . On Saturday Messrs Wilton and Cipriani are to attend to see what progress each has made, to correct their drawings and models . . . At Christmas and Midsummer annually . . . a large silver medal will be given for the best design . . . and another for the best model in basso relievo. A small silver medal for the second best design . . . and one for the second best basso relievo.[1]

The Duke of Richmond's new sculpture gallery at Richmond House was widely reported, because it filled an important need. Since the Renaissance it had been felt in Europe that an artist could only gain merit by being able to draw the human form. This was usually attained by learning to draw from antique statues, in which human physiognomy and anatomy had been idealised to show perfect and elegant proportions. From this students could proceed to drawing from live models. There were academies in Rome, Florence and Paris, but in England there were very few establishments where training was possible. In the early eighteenth century Sir Godfrey Kneller had inadequate casts

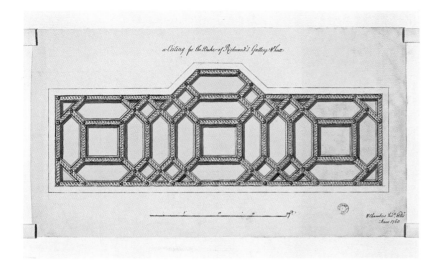

Drawing by William Chambers for the ceiling of the sculpture gallery at Richmond House, 1760 (Sir John Soane Museum). The drawing gives an idea of the proportions of the gallery, with a wide niche on one side, looking out over the river, which was usable for special displays. It is not known if the design was carried out.

in his private academy and, at the St Martin's Lane Academy, popular from the 1730s, students could only work from live models. The sculpture galleries and collections owned by the nobility and by connoisseurs were not open to the public.

The 3rd Duke's gallery was designed mainly to be a training space, in which he also recognised the values of viewing, in that competition and prizes would stimulate young artists. The initiative was much admired. It was the 'first school opened in this country, where the beauties of the antique could be studied', enthused the painter Edward Edwards (1738–1806), who had been a student there. He described how 'It consisted of a gallery or great room, fitted up with every conveniency requisite for the accommodation of students, and furnished with a number of gesses, or casts in plaster of Paris, moulded from the most select antique and modern figures at that time at Rome and Florence'.[2] To have a rich and eminent duke as patron would surely determine the success of the new academy. The students were 'permitted to draw there for several years'.[3]

The gallery was run by the sculptor Joseph Wilton (1722–1803), who selected the casts, and the painter Giovanni Battista Cipriani (1727–1785). The Duke must have met both artists when he was in Italy on his Grand Tour. Wilton, the son of a successful ornamental plasterer in London, was the first English sculptor to receive an academic education on the continent. In Rome he established a lucrative trade in making and procuring copies and casts of antique sculpture for English noblemen. In 1751 he moved to Florence, being paid to show private collections to English *milordi* and helping with acquisitions for their collections. He met Horace Mann, Horace Walpole's relation and reg-

ular correspondent and, through this ever-obliging contact, may well have been the guide to Florence for the Duke and his brother when they arrived in May 1755. The idea for the gallery could have been suggested to the Duke at this time.[4] Wilton knew Matthew Brettingham the younger (1725–1803), who had returned to England the previous year, and whose father had worked both at Richmond House and at Goodwood. Brettingham was himself hoping to find subscribers for a gallery, for which he could acquire good moulds for casting the statues in plaster. Wilton would use him as a major source.

Certainly Wilton was best placed of anyone to select the statuary. Cipriani was a member of the Florentine Academy of Drawing, a perfect qualification to be a drawing master in London. He also had many patrons among English tourists. William Chambers, who befriended both Wilton and Cipriani in Italy, was the third in the important trio of influential classicists to assist the Duke in the foundation of his academy. Chambers had previously met in Rome a young Irish peer, James Caulfeild, 1st Earl of Charlemont, whose home in Dublin was near Emily's, and who was already voicing ideas about creating an academy of art. That Wilton, Cipriani and Chambers travelled to London together in the early summer of 1755 is an indication of a new momentum. These three professionals were at the forefront of classical design, which could now draw on a wider repertoire than that used by early-eighteenth-century architects.

Chambers helped create the gallery building at Richmond House, a long room running down to the river, parallel to the new dining room extension. The gallery was formed out of some of the offices of the old Richmond House. Chambers made an impressive geometric design for the ceiling. This related well to the Jonesian-style compartmented ceilings of the drawing room and salon, but was based on more fanciful octagon shapes. Dated 1760, the drawing gives an idea of the proportions of the gallery. Chambers also designed therms, or pedestals, for Richmond House, and a gateway into the Privy Garden.[5] It is not known how many of these designs were executed.

On his return to England early in 1756, the Duke's initiative may also have been stimulated by a new society, founded in 1754 by noblemen and gentlemen, which had begun to give drawing classes. This was also based on the Whig ideals of mercantilism and patriotic self-improvement. It eventually became the Royal Society of Arts, with premises off the Strand.[6] Walpole wrote to Horace Mann in February 1758, enthusing both about the Society and about the Duke's project for an academy:

There is now established a Society for the Encouragement of Arts, Sciences and Commerce, that are likely to be very serviceable; and I was pleased yesterday with a very grand seigneurial design of the Duke of Richmond, who has collected a great many fine casts of the best antique statues, has placed them in a large room in his garden, & designs to throw it open to encourage drawing.[7]

The Society obtained permission from the Duke to use his gallery for their own students. The gallery opened on 6 March 1758. As well as in the notice in the *Daily Advertiser* on 28 February, entry was advertised in the *London Chronicle* on 25 February and in the *Gentleman's Magazine* on 1 March. The gallery would be open every day, from 9 to 11 a.m., and from 2 to 4 p.m. During this year the Duke sat for his portrait to Joshua Reynolds, who would become a key figure in the ultimate realisation of a gallery that was also an academy.

Every contemporary commentator noted the casts in the Duke of Richmond's gallery as being of the highest quality. Contemporary lists suggest that there were twenty-four casts of free-standing statues round the room.[8] A dozen busts sat on brackets on the walls, with a few smaller busts and bas-reliefs on the chimneypiece, and casts of hands and feet on tables. Numerous casts of Trajan's column were fixed to the wall behind the entrance. Most were after Greek or Hellenistic originals or after Roman works which had copied the Greek, often the only way by which non-surviving Greek sculpture was known. These were sculptures which had been famous for many centuries, and each was a particularly revered example of its type.

The works included statues showing perfect female form, such as *Cupid and Psyche*, *Venus Washing her Feet*, and the *Venus de Medici*, the original marble of which in Florence the Duke had particularly liked, declaring, 'I am in love with the Venus and take great pleasure to stroke her bum and thighs.'[9] Venus's companion, the *Dancing Faun*, was a marble copy by Wilton himself, as was one of the two *Apollo Belvederes*.[10] The Duke also had the masculine statues of great warrior athletes, the *Dying Gladiator* (recumbent), the *Borghese Gladiator* (upright), the *Wrestlers* and *Discobolus*, all seen as depicting the perfect male form. To this end he also had *Meleager*, *Antinous* and *Mercury*. A painter who needed to depict a draped figure should, it was believed, understand the anatomy underneath, and this was how to learn about perfect bodies. Three of the statues were copies after figures that were already in English collections.[11]

The Duke also had copies of 'modern', Renaissance sculpture, namely Michelangelo's *Bacchus*, Sansovino's *Bacchus* and his *Ganymede*, and *Santa Susannah* by Duquesnoy, which was from a church in Rome. Emotive Counter-Reformation baroque sculpture was not included; in line with the prevailing taste, and not least with that of Chambers, the gallery aimed at a return to the idealised austerity of the Antique. Edwards stated that the aim should be for young men to acquire a 'purer taste in the knowledge of the human form, than had before been cultivated by the artists in England.'[12] As well as emphasising beauty and proportion, the inclusion of many heads suggest that Wilton, the first English sculptor to execute classically inspired portrait busts, was promoting the ideal of character and expression. These were skills that would be needed by both history and portrait painters.

Unfortunately the enterprise foundered, mainly owing to the prizes not being awarded as planned. Having been called away to serve in the army in 1759, the Duke returned to find a sarcastic note about the lack of prizes pinned to the gallery door. Furious, he closed the gallery. Many students had anyway become disaffected and had deserted their splendid studio. Wilton and Cipriani resigned as directors, probably because they were unable to countenance some of the more liberal views of the Society of Arts. Chambers also ceased to work for the Duke at Goodwood at about this time. The landscape painter Thomas Jones (1742–1803) described how he went to the Gallery in 1761–2:

> being thought sufficiently qualified, I was introduced by Mr Shipley [a drawing master in the Strand] to the Duke of Richmond's Gallery in Privy Gardens, to draw after those fine Copies of the most celebrated Antique Statues which were collected by His Grace and deposited in a handsome Appartment erected for the purpose, & dedicated to the use of Students in the Art of Design – But this noble Institution was now on the Decline . . . However the Gallery was still open to all young Artists upon proper Application.[13]

The gallery did re-open, for the classes of the Society of Arts, of which the Duke became vice-president in 1761. The gallery was used by the Society until about 1767. The Duke's gallery thus lost its independence but was a crucial part of the campaign for artists to be able to learn to draw from the Antique, to compete and to exhibit. In 1765 the Duke was further elected as a member of the Dilettanti Society, which encouraged the study of classical antiquity. The movement to help artists was gaining momentum. Exhibition space was another issue. Following the decline of the use of the Foundling Hospital to display paintings, the first regular art exhibition was opened by the Society of Arts in 1761, in their own premises off the Strand. Although provision of exhibition space in London is not mentioned in documents as a principal aim of the Duke, his father's involvement with the Foundling Hospital meant that he would also be very aware of the need for artists to be able to exhibit their work. It is not surprising that this first occurred in the Great Room of the Society of Arts under his vice-presidency.

As well as a few continuing students, not least George Romney, the gallery also had other uses. In 1761 Joseph Wilton made a life-size marble copy there of Michelangelo's *Bacchus*, from a version owned by the Duke, on behalf of another great patron of the arts, Hugh Smithson, Earl (later Duke) of Northumberland.[14] The whole teaching situation was finally remedied when the Royal Academy was opened in 1768, under the patronage of George III, with Joshua Reynolds as the first president. Thus what the Duke of Richmond had begun to do was more fully realised. The initiative was enthusiastically supported by Chambers and Wilton, who had by now been appointed respectively as Clerk of the King's Works and Sculptor in

Ordinary to the King. In 1782 a portrait of Chambers, Reynolds and Wilton all together was painted by J.F. Rigaud.[15] That all three artists had been working for the Duke fifteen years earlier shows how important were the initiatives that he had taken then.

The Duke allowed his collection of casts to be used in the 1770s by another breakaway group, the (Incorporated) Society of Artists, but gradually the group became isolated and the gallery was again closed when students mutilated some of the casts. It had been pulled down by 1782. The casts survived intact until the fire at Richmond House in 1791. They were then dispersed, with a few marble items ending up at Goodwood. Many were sold by the 5th Duke at Christie's in 1820. However, a number may well have ended up in the Antique Room at the Royal Academy's premises, newly built by Chambers, at New Somerset House in the Strand.[16]

The Duke had shown himself to be deeply interested in both art and science, seeing the two combined in the art of depicting human anatomy. His motives in creating and supporting the gallery were both aesthetic and philanthropic. He was recognised for this by being included in James Barry's mural of 1780 for the Great Room at the Society of Arts' new specially built premises by Robert Adam, part of the Adelphi complex, near to the Strand. The mural shows some of the great patrons of the arts of the period. At his school successful painters such as George Romney, John Mortimer, William Hodges and Tilly Kettle had studied at various times, along with miniaturists Richard

Cosway and Ozias Humphry, and, in the first year of its opening, the sculptor Joseph Nollekens.

However, for the moment the Duke was preoccupied at Goodwood with an architectural project that was more for his own personal use. This was the construction of a new stable block, to house his hunters.

## THE CHARLTON HUNT IN THE 1750S

After the shock of the 2nd Duke's death at the age of forty-nine, the Charlton Hunt went into a decline. The Hunt Club had been his creation, and all the members his friends. Hounds were dispersed to other packs. Hunting ceased at Charlton altogether, with the lodges deserted. The Great Room fell into disrepair, and was eventually demolished by the 3rd Duke, by about 1785.[17] He may never have occupied his father's hunting lodge.

However, in 1757 the 3rd Duke decided to revive the hunt. He was helped by Sir John Miller, a Chichester luminary and Charlton Hunt supporter, whose daughter later married the Duke's cousin, George, 3rd Earl of Albemarle (1724–1772). Sir John began to acquire hounds from other packs. Some came from far afield, while others were from nearer to home, including some from a cousin of the Duke of Bolton in Hampshire, and a few from 'Mr Gibbon', the father of the historian Edward Gibbon, who lived near by at Buriton, also in Hampshire. (Gibbon himself stated that he did not hunt or shoot, preferring when at Buriton the pleasures of the kitchen garden and the wooden bench.) As many new hounds as possible were descended from the old Charlton bloodlines. The Duke was very interested in quality and pedigree, and became deeply involved in breeding them for the future. However, the crowds of grand and aristocratic hunting men never came again to Charlton. Other packs such as the Beaufort and the Quorn were now changing from hunting deer to foxes, and consequently were becoming fashionable. The Duke decided to move the base of the hunt from Charlton to Goodwood, where it became known as the Duke of Richmond's Hounds.

## THE NEW STABLES

The Duke began in 1757 to build a magnificent new stable block adjacent to the eight-year-old pedimented Portland stone south front of Goodwood House. His father had also considered building new stables, for which a plan had been drawn up by Colen Campbell for a U-shaped quadrangle, roughly on the present site, but this was never carried out. In 1757 William Chambers drew 'two large figured Plans and Eight different Elevations with Various Alterations'.[18] He visited Goodwood again in February 1758, subsequently completing a 'large finished drawing of the South front', with a separate design for the triumphal arch and alterations to the design for the east front. Chambers also charged 5 guineas for teaching the Duke about architecture.

The grand new block in dark knapped flint with contrasting creamy stone dressings looked even more glamorous and sophisticated than the façade it was meant to support. It is a virtuoso performance, showing off his understanding of Roman architecture, and his pleasure in large-scale, high-quality, intellectual adornment. On the garden side to the house the stables could be entered through a pedimented arch adorned by elaborate rustication (not dissimilar from Campbell's original design), while the

main entrance into the stables from the south was a grandiose tri-umphal arch in Tuscan Doric. The visitor walked beneath a long barrel arch into a vast brick courtyard which housed fifty-four hors-es. The north wing, not so easily visible from the front, was also fin-ished in brick on the exterior, while the west wing had a looser flint, both as economies rather than the more expensively worked flint. By 1799 horses were still so important to the Duke that there were twenty-nine staff in the stables alone, including eleven grooms.[19]

Chambers also billed the Duke for 'Various designs for fin-ishing the large Room at Goodwood'; this was the 2nd Duke's Great Room, which had sat incomplete after his death.[20] Chambers' work involved bookcases decorated with a small run-ning flower-studded guilloche, with similar but grander frames for the handsome pier glasses. This was all the work that he did inside the house. Chambers also made a design for the Duke in 1760 for the principal entrance to Goodwood Park.[21]

GEORGE STUBBS AT GOODWOOD

A third artistic venture by the young Duke again showed his orig-inality. In 1759 a little-known painter called George Stubbs (1724–1806) came to Goodwood. Stubbs was the son of a currier (a leather dresser) in Liverpool. Showing early talent, he had managed to get himself apprenticed for a while to copy paintings at Knowsley Hall, the home of Edward, 11th Earl of Derby (1689–1776), near to his own home at Liverpool. He subsequently worked for a while in the family's leather business while teaching himself to paint. He managed to obtain commissions for portraits locally before moving to York, where he studied and taught anatomy, eventually publishing some etchings. In 1752 he had moved to Hull, where he had painted more portraits. To date his career had been diligent but unexceptional.

That Stubbs stayed at Goodwood for some time is known only from the memoir of Ozias Humphry, an artist and miniature painter who was already a friend:

> The first commission of importance Stubbs received came from the Duke of Richmond, and it obliged him to take up residence at Goodwood, where he worked hard at his plates. In nine months there were several pictures painted, among them a hunting piece, 9 feet by 6 feet, with many portraits. Of these was one of the Earl of Albermarle [sic], painted whilst he sat at breakfast, the day before embarking on the ever-memorable and successful expedition to the Havannah, when it was taken.[22]

The 'plates' on which Stubbs was working are extremely interest-ing in themselves. They were engravings from drawings of horses he had made over a period of eighteen months between 1756 and 1758 while living outside Hull at Horkstow. Lodging in an isolated farmhouse, he had dissected dead horses in a barn, stripping off the skin and hanging the corpse from hooks in a

beam, so that he could minutely observe the muscles and bones. His aim was to provide a completely scientific anatomical description. Humphry claims that when in Rome for a two-month trip in 1754, Stubbs had insisted that 'nature' was more important than art. He must have learnt in Rome that it was by dissecting and observing human corpses that the great Renaissance artists Leonardo da Vinci and Michelangelo had made such advances in the study of human anatomy. Stubbs tried to get some of his drawings engraved in London in 1759 but the engravers had not been interested in reproducing images of dead horses. Instead, having learnt the rudiments of engraving while at York, Stubbs began to engrave them himself, a long process involving incising the lines of the image on to a copper plate.

Some of the plates that were finally published as *The Anatomy of the Horse* in 1766 were executed at Goodwood. It is possible that Stubbs would have resided in the newly built stables while he was at Goodwood, where ample lodging space was pro-vided above the loose boxes. Alternatively, if no section of them was complete, he could have been in one of the single row of old cottages near by, in what is now known as Laundry Green. His studio would probably have been in the same area. According to Humphry, he worked so hard in the years up to the publication of the plates that he would be painting all day and working on the plates 'early in the Morning, & in the Evening and sometimes very late at Night.'[23] He only completed three plates a year, so while he was at Goodwood he may only have worked on two or three.

Although it is remarkable that the twenty-four-year-old Duke could be so far-sighted as to commission such an unknown painter, there are various avenues through which he could have heard of Stubbs, or indeed Stubbs of him. A very probable point of contact was Joshua Reynolds, who in 1758 asked Stubbs to pro-vide him with an image of a war horse for a portrait. The Duke sat to the portrait painter in that very year (see page 89). Although Stubbs actively disliked being considered merely as a 'horse painter', that was exactly what the Duke wanted.[24] Sir William Chambers could have been a point of contact, having met Stubbs in Rome, where the young artist may also have heard Matthew Brettingham the younger talk about his father's recent work at Goodwood.

There are other possibilities. It is very likely that both the Duke and Reynolds actually met George Stubbs at the 10th Earl of Pembroke's riding school, which was run by an Italian called Domenico Angelo.[25] This was located near to Pembroke's home in Whitehall, and therefore very close to Richmond House. It was frequented by Stubbs soon after his arrival in London: indeed, the war horse requested by Reynolds was defined as a 'Portrait of a Manèged Horse' and Domenico's son Henry claimed that it was through his father's influence that Stubbs got most of his early commissions.[26] The Duke may, but less probably, have been told about Stubbs in London by Lord Derby, who until 1752 was the owner, through his wife, of the Halnaker estate adjacent to

*The 3rd Duke of Richmond with the Charlton Hunt*, by George Stubbs, 1759–60, oil on canvas, 140 × 246 cm / 55 × 97 in. The Duke, the tall figure on the horse at the centre, is turning towards his brother, Lord George Lennox, whose back is slightly towards the viewer. On the left is General (or Captain?) Jones, his horse leaping over a gate. The gentleman at the gallop beyond may be Sir John Miller. Every hound is a portrait. The hunt is seen beyond, in full cry.

Goodwood. Finally, the painter had already been hawking the drawings round London to find engravers: the attention of the Duke may have been drawn to them at this time in a coffee house.

## STUBBS'S CELEBRATION OF THE CHARLTON HUNT

The principal purpose of Stubbs's visit to Goodwood must have been to paint the Duke's 'hunting piece', to celebrate the newly revived hunt. Science and observation continued to be paramount to the Duke, and with his new pack of well-bred hounds he would have sought the best painter of horses and dogs that he could find, a man who could understand and reveal the finer points of pedigree. He already owned the series of paintings of hunters by John Wootton, and would want an artist who was at least as skilled. Of the three sporting scenes in the Goodwood collection, *The 3rd Duke of Richmond with the Charlton Hunt* is also believed, on stylistic grounds, to be the first executed on the estate.

*The 3rd Duke of Richmond with the Charlton Hunt* shows the Duke on his black hunter, accompanied by his dog and gesticulating to his brother, Lord George Lennox, who sits his horse with especial ease. The figure on the left was said to be General Jones, possibly a misnomer for Captain Jones, the gentleman Groom of the Bedchamber to the 3rd Duke.[27] Another figure gallops beyond, his horse with the legs at full stretch in the way that artists painted them prior to photography.[28] It is now believed that Stubbs was embarrassed by this arrangement, as he did not use it very often. The rider is probably Sir John Miller, 4th Baronet (1712–1772), an old family friend and hunt member, who had helped the Duke restart the pack. All four horsemen are in Charlton livery, but only three (the Duke, Lord George and Sir John, but not Mr Jones) have the gilt hunt buttons showing that they were full members. The Duke as Master is accompanied by a huntsman, who wears the red and yellow equestrian livery of the Duke of Richmond.

All the figures are portraits: the huntsman may well be one of the Budd family, who lived next to the hunt building at Charlton and had already been hunt servants for many years.[29] They are surrounded by ten couple of hounds, each one an individual portrait. As many as fifty-seven couple had been amassed for the 1757 season,[30] so these were presumably selected as being the best hounds. Beyond, the hunt is in full cry, with the Master and hunt staff leading the field. That the hunt appears

ABOVE *Racehorses Exercising at Goodwood*, by George Stubbs, 1759–60, oil on canvas, 127.5 × 204 cm / 50¼ × 80¼ in. Mary, Duchess of Richmond, is at the centre, mounted side-saddle, with her sister-in-law Lady George Lennox near by, in a similar location to that of Lord George in the hunting picture. The estate steward, probably Richard Buckner (d.1776/7), dressed in green livery with gold frogging, is pointing out the three horses hooded and blanketed for exercising. The jockeys wear frock coats, their yellow and scarlet ducal livery matching the horses' colours. To the right a horse is being rubbed down with straw, surrounded by grooms who may include members of the Budd family from Charlton. The spire of Chichester Cathedral is in the background, with the Isle of Wight beyond.

FACING PAGE *Shooting at Goodwood*, by George Stubbs, 1759, oil on canvas, 140 × 203 cm / 55 × 80½ in. The 3rd Duke loved shooting from an early age. Two of his favourite relatives are shown; he described his brother-in-law Henry Fox, the portly man at the centre, as 'my second father' and 'my best friend'. George, 3rd Earl of Albemarle, shown with his back to the viewer, was his first cousin (and the oldest of his cousins). The black servant wearing the yellow and scarlet livery, holding the Arab horse, may either be Thomas Robinson, who came to Goodwood in the 1740s and was named after the Governor of Barbados, or a footman named Jean Baptiste, who came from one of the French colonies. The gamekeepers wear the green estate livery.

twice in the scene is an example of the kind of continuous narration that Stubbs would have observed in Renaissance art when he was in Rome.[31] A small oil sketch for the hunting picture shows Lord George only, but with a different hound, perhaps a favourite.[32]

## RACING AT GOODWOOD

With the desired picture complete, it is likely that the next commission was for another equestrian sport, and one in which the Duchess could be included. Racing was already a sport popular with the Dukes of Richmond by the 1750s, following the tradition of their royal ancestor, Charles II. Early races, starting from Newmarket in the late seventeenth century, had usually been 'match races', literally a match between two horses. The racehorses were often quite small, measuring from 15 hands high downwards. Racing became central to country life in the early decades of the eighteenth century, and little racecourses sprang up near many small towns. The 2nd Duke often had runners in local races in the 1730s, notably at Steyning and Lewes in Sussex, and at Stockbridge in Hampshire. At first the speed was usually a canter, with an acceleration over the last half mile, but from about 1760 the distances became shorter, the horses younger and the speed greater. Breeding of thoroughbred racehorses became a great skill, owing to the import of Arab stock, and the test of that breeding was racing.

Race management skills increased under the patronage of the Jockey Club, founded in 1750 in London and soon afterwards relocated to Newmarket. The Duke was an early member, along with eight other dukes. Race meetings, lasting between two and

four days, became very sociable events, at which mounted spectators would gallop along beside the race. There are relatively few entries in the *Racing Calendar* for horses in public race meetings owned by the 3rd Duke. It is therefore likely that his horses may have been used more for the private match races, held on country estates.

The racing painting would not quite be a pair with the hunting one, as this canvas is less wide, but they were the same height and would relate to each other. *Racehorses Exercising at Goodwood* shows the Duchess of Richmond at the centre, with her new sister-in-law Lady George Lennox beside her, both wearing the dark blue livery of the Charlton Hunt. While Stubbs was working at Goodwood, Lord and Lady George eloped, marrying in Scotland on Christmas Day 1759. Lady George (who, as the daughter of the Marquis of Lothian, could use her own title and was often known as Lady Louisa) loved horses and dogs and after a cautious start would become firm friends with the Duchess.[33] The estate steward points out the three horses being put through their paces, each one hooded and blanketed up, to make them sweat. The jockeys do not wear silks, which were already the norm for races, but frock coats for exercising. To the right a horse being rubbed down with straw throws up its head and kicks out in annoyance. The main groom in attendance may be William Budd, who had accompanied the Duke on his Grand Tour, with Christopher

Budd junior as the stable lad, together with other servants portrayed from life.[34] This little cameo shows Stubbs excelling himself in painting a horse scientifically, whereas on the left his three horses again reveal the contemporary lack of knowledge of how to paint horses' legs at speed. Always scientific, Stubbs has tried to express the speed by showing a little dog bounding along with them, and yapping.

The racing scene has a more specific location than the other two scenes, looking to Chichester, with its cathedral spire, and across the Solent to the Isle of Wight. There are *capriccio* elements too, with some loose water shown in the foreground before Chichester, and a romantic old seaside fort or mill. To the right a large light-coloured house looks nothing like Goodwood at the time, which was still an erratic rectangular shape. The Duke would soon embark on plans to enlarge it, and it is possible that he told Stubbs to make it look grander. The beautifully painted trees and the rough foliage and fallen branch in the foreground show Stubbs at the beginning of his career as a landscape painter, creating an idyllic, lyrical scene, underpinned by careful composition.

## Stubbs and the Shoot

*Shooting at Goodwood* was probably the third scene to be painted, the main equestrian subjects having now been documented. The

Duke was already a keen shot, having developed an enthusiasm for it while staying with his uncle Count Bentinck near The Hague. His diary a couple of years later shows him shooting at Raby Castle, County Durham, and he had by now converted his father's menagerie up the hill into a pheasantry, where Elizabeth Stout was paid £5 8s a month for many years, well into the 1780s, to rear and care for the young birds. Every year about 500–800 partridge eggs were bought.[35]

The main figure at the centre of the scene is Henry Fox, the husband of the Duke's eldest sister Lady Caroline, to whom the Duke was devoted. Fox was doing well as a politician, his marriage was happy and he was part of the family. He was also passionate about shooting.[36] The other figure, with his back to the viewer, is the Earl of Albemarle.[37] Behind Fox stands the loader, with the keeper mounted: this may be Henry Budd.[38] The more senior grooms, holding the two horses for the guns, are again in the yellow and scarlet livery. The horses would be needed between the drives.

On the left the black servant has been given a magnificent Arab horse to hold. He may be Thomas Robinson, who was at Goodwood in the 1740s, where he was referred to by the actress Peg Woffington as 'my little Orinooko', suggesting that he was still a lad.[39] He had presumably been sent by Sir Thomas Robinson of Rokeby, the family friend who was at the time Governor of Barbados: it was normal to name orphans after their saviours. Thomas is probably the same servant to whom the 2nd Duke gave a full classical education. Louise de Keroualle had been shown with black servants in two portraits and the family tradition continued. They were regarded as rather exotic and special, and were often given fine clothes or liveries to draw attention to them, as shown in all these portraits.

A portrait never in the Goodwood collection was also painted by Stubbs at Goodwood. This is *The Countess of Coningsby Wearing the Livery of the Charlton Hunt*; in the background is the 2nd Duke's banqueting house at Carné's Seat.[40] It is possible that two 'portraits' that were dispersed at the 4th Duke's sale in 1814 were by Stubbs; one was of 'a Pug Dog in a landscape' and the other 'of a White Hare'.[41]

## 'THE ROCKINGHAMS'

From Goodwood Stubbs went on to paint for other Whig grandees, notably Charles Watson-Wentworth, 2nd Marquis of Rockingham (1730–1782). It has usually been assumed that Stubbs made these contacts while in London before coming to Goodwood: there is no evidence of a contact with Rockingham during the earlier years in Yorkshire. However, given the Duke's close friendship with Rockingham, it is equally possible that there was a word-of-mouth recommendation from him.

Indeed, in 1761 the Duke visited Rockingham's home at Wentworth Woodhouse in Yorkshire. The Duke's diary for that year shows that in July he went on a visit to the north of England.[42] On the way up, on 3 July, he stayed at the home of another Whig grandee, John, 4th Duke of Bedford (1710–1771), at Woburn Abbey. The next week he 'call'd to see the Duke of Portland's House at Welbeck'. On the 7th and 8th he stayed at the home of Edward Howard, 9th Duke of Norfolk (1685–1777), at Worksop. Then, on the 9th he arrived to stay at Wentworth Castle, where the next day he went round the park, gardens and plantations. On 11 July he visited Rockingham's 'House Park and Gardens' before arriving the next day at Richmond, where he still owned the Castle. On the way south he spent some time at Chatsworth, before returning by way of Woburn to London. It is unfortunate that this is the only year for which the Duke's diary survives. It reveals a fascinating country house tour, a huge opportunity for gaining ideas for his own homes and estates.

Like the 3rd Duke of Richmond, the young Marquis of Rockingham inherited his title in 1750. He was only twenty. His father had been a friend of the 2nd Duke's ally, the Duke of Newcastle. Both young men had been educated at Westminster, Rockingham as the older of the two entering eight years earlier. Like the Duke he was very interested in science, in his case especially in agricultural developments on his vast estates in Yorkshire. Both men were elected to be Fellows of the Royal Society, Rockingham in 1751 and Richmond in 1756. His political supporters, called 'the Rockinghams', tended to be young, rich and landowning, and to be progressive. They were snobbish about the relatively new Hanoverian dynasty, whom they saw as conditional monarchs, believing they could stay in place for only as long as they agreed with traditional English values of freedom and toleration.

Stubbs would prove to be the ideal painter for the wonderful horses and vast acres of this very powerful man. The Duke also treasured his friendship, which continued for many years.[43] After Rockingham's death in 1782 the Duke commissioned a bust of him, executed from a death mask.[44] He also owned a miniature of the Marquis.

## ART AND ANIMALS: GEORGE STUBBS AND DR WILLIAM HUNTER

Although he did not ever become as obsessed with collecting exotic animals as his father, the Duke was interested in rare species. It may have been partly due to the influence of the Swiss scientist, Albert Haller, that he was so determined that animal physiology should be correctly understood and represented. It was an interest that he shared with Dr William Hunter (1718–1783), a Scotsman who first came to London in 1741, leaving to study anatomy in Paris and Leiden, after which he worked hard to extend the teaching of both human and animal anatomy in London. Hunter became a fashionable obstetrician, attending Queen Charlotte at the births of her children. He also attended the Duke's sister Sarah when she gave birth in 1768, and Caroline,

*The Duke of Richmond's Moose* by George Stubbs, 1770, oil on canvas, 62 × 73 cm / 24½ × 28¾ in (Hunterian Art Gallery, Glasgow). Commissioned by Dr William Hunter as part of a scientific study, the painting shows the young animal, the first male moose to enter England, together with an inset image of the antlers of a fully grown moose.

on her deathbed, in 1774. In 1767 he was made a Fellow of the Royal Society and in 1769 he became first Professor of Anatomy at the newly established Royal Academy.

From the late 1760s the Duke acquired four different moose from North America. This was an animal of great interest to the King, who enjoyed investigating the acclimatisation and inter-breeding of rare species, and to various members of the aristocracy and intelligentsia. In 1766 a young female was sent to the Duke from Quebec by General Carleton, Governor-General of Canada, later Lord Dorchester. The next year the General followed up with a caribou. The Duke was very pleased with them: 'this frosty weather agrees with both the creatures orignal [orignals, another kind of deer] and carabou exceedingly: they are now got into exceedingly fine order, their coats very fine and thick and they grow apace.'[45] After living at Goodwood for about ten months, the moose died, in 1767. The Duke then acquired another female, which also died, the following year. The Revd Gilbert White (1720–1793), the naturalist, visited from nearby Selborne in

Hampshire and saw its corpse hanging in a sling for inspection, as if it were still standing.[46]

Unperturbed, the Duke acquired a male moose from the General in 1770, the first to enter England. The Duke acquired a rare female deer in 1771, and a second male moose in 1773, by which time Rockingham also owned a male, and Lady North, the wife of the Prime Minister, a female. A female moose acquired by the King had also been given away to Horace Walpole, and now belonged to the Countess of Upper Ossory at Ampthill Park in Bedfordshire.

In 1770, the year of its arrival, the first male moose was painted by George Stubbs. The picture was commissioned by Dr William Hunter, who wanted a first-hand visual description, in order to establish its precise species. The painting also shows a separate pair of antlers, copied from a pair provided by General Carleton, to indicate what the moose's antlers would be like when the year-old animal was fully grown. It was Hunter's mission to prove that the great French natural historian Buffon was wrong, as were earlier historians, in believing that the North American moose was descended from the ancient Irish elk. Hunter correctly believed that the giant Irish deer was extinct. He thought that this could best be shown by comparing the antlers, as large horns from the ancient Irish type had often been excavated. From Stubbs's painting, probably intended for use as an illustration for a presentation to the Royal Society, Hunter hoped to show how different the antlers of the moose really were.[47]

Presumably it was the Duke who originally suggested Stubbs to Hunter for this task of recording rare animals. Stubbs had already painted a *nilghau* or antelope for Hunter in 1769, and sketched a blackbuck in oil for him. He also drew the Duke's second male moose in 1773, the third one to enter the country.[48] When Dr Hunter went to view this second animal, he even took the painting by Stubbs of the first moose with him. In fact Hunter was such a perfectionist that he never completed his intended paper on the moose for the Royal Society.[49] In another negotiation with the Duke, Hunter acquired for his collection of medical curiosities both the unusual skeleton of Owen Farrell and the painting of this famous dwarf. Both had belonged to the 2nd Duke but were unsold at his sale of 1751. They may have been gifts from the 3rd Duke.[50] The Duke certainly gave Hunter great encouragement. Hunter even founded a School of Anatomy in Great Windmill Street, London, where he lectured until his death in 1783. A pair each of antlers of the Irish elk and the moose were in the Goodwood Collection in the early nineteenth century.[51]

The Duke continued to be interested in natural history. In the mid-1770s Charles Reuben Riley did a number of sketches of wild animals on the backs of envelopes of which some bear the Goodwood address. Although these are mostly copies from Bernard Picart's *Recueil des Lions*, prints after Rembrandt, possibly borrowed from the Goodwood library, a few are of live domestic animals.[52] That an artist working at Goodwood should be sketching rare breeds is in itself intriguing. That the Duke continued to keep at least some rare species is proved by the fact that a wolf 'from his menagerie' attacked him on one occasion, forcing him to let rip the skirt of his coat to get away.[53] In 1790 there was another accident, this time involving Emily's husband:

> Poor Mr Ogilvie has been very near killed at Goodwood by an astonishing indiscretion of his own. He went, yes, and with one of his daughters, and without even a stick, into an enclosure where the Duke keeps an elk. The animal attacked him, threw him down, gored him, bruised him – in short he is not yet out of danger.[54]

The so-called elk was presumably really another moose. Dr William Hunter's younger brother, the surgeon Dr John Hunter (1728–1793), was called down from London to attend him. On another occasion the Duke sent John Hunter a *moschus*, a musk deer from the Himalayas or Siberia, to dissect. In the posthumous sale of paintings by Stubbs there was also one of a tiger that had formerly been 'in the possession of the Duke of Richmond'. This may also have been for the purpose of examination, as in the 1790s Stubbs worked on a project to compare human skeletons with those of animals, not least tigers.[55]

Just as the 2nd Duke of Richmond had given Canaletto a springboard from which to launch his career, the 3rd Duke did the same for George Stubbs. However, it is important to remember that this type of painting was not held in very high regard at the time, and that the Duke and his friends simply regarded Stubbs as a brilliant technician, who could give them images of the things they loved best. The commissioning of Stubbs to make what was really a scientific image of a rare animal confirms this view, especially with the added close-up image of the antlers, denying the picture any chance of being considered as a work of art. The Duke's own paintings by Stubbs did not hang in a smart drawing room at Goodwood, but were first recorded in 1822 as being on the first floor, at the north end of the Long Hall, in the Old Billiard Room, where they had probably been installed when this wing was built in the 1770s.[56] However, the Duke admired Stubbs enough to buy a painting later in his career, for Richmond House, of *Lions and a Lioness*.[57] The painter was successful in his own lifetime but his reputation would fade after his death in 1806, only being slightly revived in the late nineteenth century and, more effectively, in the 1950s, since when he has become one of England's best-loved painters.

## ART AND LANDSCAPE: FROM CLASSICAL TO SUBLIME

In the early 1760s the Duke acquired landscape paintings by local artists John and George Smith of Chichester. Their elder brother William was a portrait painter, for whose training the 2nd Duke had paid. In 1760 John Smith won a prize for his landscape at the Society of Arts (see opposite). The two canvases by him and three by George Smith still in the collection are accomplished classical scenes, *capriccio* views, usually looking beyond a pastoral idyll to a city. With the way the composition is created, looking across a streak of sea to an island, these views are always said to look like the view to Chichester from Goodwood, though the imaginary city's architecture is in fact different. Indeed, one early commentator said that the view down to Chichester looked like a Claudean landscape.[58]

Two close-up rustic views by George Smith represent a new strand in the Duke's interests. Another aspect of the Swiss anatomist Albert Haller's influence may have emerged in how the Duke used the Rock Dell at this time. Haller also wrote poetry and was one of the first people to see the beauty of wild, untamed Alpine scenery – at the time not at all fashionable in England. In the 1760s the Duke had a pair of paintings done of his father's Rock Dell by George Smith of Chichester, showing respectively the little shell bathing house and the ruined abbey. Instead of appearing as the polite, amusing and interesting architectural animal dens for which they had originally been intended, the abbey was now shown as a wild, even more ruined location, with ghostly hooded monks seated on the steps surrounded by boulders in a consciously fantastic, primitive, medieval setting. The romantic and dramatic allure suggested that not just antiquity but also mystery, wildness and even superstition were the characterisations that were now meant to be associated with the Rock Dell. Edmund Burke's essay *Philosophical Enquiry into the Origin of our Ideas on the Sublime and Beautiful* had been published in 1757 and was already enlarging the repertoire of what was considered beautiful. It would seem that the 3rd Duke was abreast with the latest thinking, picking up on his father's love of old buildings to suggest that something religious, ancient and slightly sinister could be as appealing for its romantic associations as a building that was elegant and classical.

In this way landowning, country sports, love of the Antique, interest in science and Whig political allegiance were all expressed in the art collecting and other activities of the 3rd Duke of Richmond. Like his peers, he was proud of being wealthy and influential, wishing his house at Goodwood to be enlarged not just in order to accommodate more guests and to entertain more grandly, but also in order to have a country residence that reflected his high status. Even when he used his seat in the House of Lords, he found himself in political opposition to the government. This gave him more time to spend in the country. With his restless nature, he enjoyed developing his estate. He had not yet made up his mind on improvements to the house.

*Romantic Landscape with Trees around a Lake,* by John Smith of Chichester, oil on canvas, 100 × 126 cm / 39½ × 49½ in.

Le ROI des

CET Oifeau eft à peu près de la groff
que nos Vautours de la plus grande e
tion. Le Bec eft raifonnablement fo
croc & furpaffant la mandibule inférieure,
au deffus & au deffous des Manibules eft
s'élevant de chaque côté jufqu'au haut de la
Narines de figure oblongue. Entre les N

Edwards delin.

# 9 FRENCH CONNECTION

## PARIS AND AUBIGNY, 1765–1780

The Richmonds' ties with France were constantly interrupted during the eighteenth century by war. After Louis XIV's War of the Spanish Succession (1702–14), there was a brief period of alliance from 1716–31. However, the struggle for power in Europe still needed to be resolved, and triggered further conflict in the War of the Austrian Succession (1740–48) and the Seven Years War (1756–63). Next, the American War of Independence (1775–83) involved France from 1778. The long contest of arms was completed by the French Revolutionary Wars (1792–1802) and the Napoleonic Wars (1802–1814, and 1815).

### Ambassador to the Court of Louis XV

The Duke and Duchess were first able to travel to Paris together in 1763. John Russell, 4th Duke of Bedford (1710–1771), had been instrumental in negotiating the Treaty of Paris which ended the Seven Years War and was the first ambassador to Paris after the peace. He was followed in 1763 by the Duchess of Richmond's step-uncle, Francis Seymour Conway, 1st Earl of Hertford (1718–1794), whose appointment naturally gave the Duke and Duchess the best of contacts.

In September 1765 the Duke and Duchess were again at Aubigny, making an inventory and sending back paintings and furniture to England. They arrived in Paris in November for the Duke to take up his appointment as ambassador. Although the Duke had

Sèvres wine coaster, *seau à bouteille*, 1766, and hand-coloured engraving of 'The King of the Vultures', by George Edwards, from his *Histoire Naturelle de Divers Oiseaux*, Vol. I, Plate 11, 1745, dedicated to the 2nd Duke, from which the image on the coaster was copied. Sèvres painters used images of real, rather than imaginary, birds for the first time on this service. The view of Stonehenge is copied from Vol. II, Plate 74.

been hankering for a post in government, a foreign appointment was not what he wanted, and at first he declined. He also insisted from the outset that he would return home in January.[1] The Richmonds were preceded in their travels by Horace Walpole, who arrived in September, seizing the opportunity to be there with them. He was planning to use their residence, vacated that month by Lord Hertford, while he found himself accommodation, envisaging that their house would be his second home.[2] Before the Duke and Duchess arrived, Walpole had already struck up a large acquaintance, which included the French philosophers Baron d'Holbach (1723–1789) and Denis Diderot (1713–1784), as well as the Scottish philosopher David Hume (1711–1776), secretary to Lord Hertford. The Richmonds would not be nearly so sociable.

The Richmonds' home was the Hôtel de Brancas, a great mansion constructed between 1722 and 1726 for the Marquis de Lassay, standing at the west end of rue de l'Université, which runs parallel to the river, on the left bank, just south of the long arm of the Louvre. This area was both central and fashionable, the many new town houses having fine rococo interiors. It had been taken over by the aristocracy after the end of Louis XIV's long reign from Versailles. For the Richmonds it also had some personal history. Louise de Keroualle had lived towards the end of her life round the corner from the far end of the street, in rue de Verneuil. Louise's sister, Henriette de Keroualle, in her second marriage to the Marquis de Thois, had lived until her death in 1728 not far away at 56 rue de Varenne, a house newly built for them.

Walpole's letters suggest that they did not mix well with the French in Paris, preferring at first to remain *à quatre* with the Duke's brother, Lord George, and his wife. The diplomatic world in Paris was anyway subdued owing to the illness of the Dauphin, the heir to Louis XV, who died on 20 December at Fontainebleau.

Walpole visited the Duke and Duchess daily, often taking the Duchess shopping, especially to buy china, or escorting her out in the evening to theatre and opera. He enjoyed the whole family group, continuing himself to meet all the fashionable French, such as the Prince de Conti and Madame de Luxembourg, and attending their cultivated, amusing and salaciously witty *salon* evenings.

Of particular interest to the Richmonds was the family of Fitzjames. They were descended from James II and his mistress Arabella Churchill, whose elder illegitimate son James had been created Duke of Berwick (1670–1734), a title that was subsequently attainted in England. He had continued to be known as 'Berwick' in France. In 1707 he was created Duke of Liria y Xerica in Spain, titles which were inherited by his elder son, James, and in 1710 was created Duc de Fitzjames in France, which title was inherited in turn by two younger sons. The Duchesse de Fitzjames, wife of the youngest son, Charles, 3rd Duc de Fitzjames (1712–1783), politely called on the Richmonds on 10 November, very soon after their arrival. Her son, the twenty-two-year-old Marquis de Fitzjames (1743–1805) (the Duke's third cousin), dined with them on 21 November. After Christmas the Richmonds moved more into their stride. On 2 January they gave a dinner for the whole Fitzjames family, the 3rd Duke of Berwick (1718–1785) and his Duchess now joining his uncle and aunt, the Duc and Duchesse de Fitzjames and their two sons.[3]

The Duke, ever restless, was certainly impatient with mere social life. His sisters were subsequently damning about their time in Paris. Caroline, never the greatest supporter of the Duchess, wrote, 'contempt of their own set of people is their fault in this country as well as France. They have no desire to please, and of consequence do not.'[4] Similarly Edward Gibbon complained, 'Instead of keeping anything of a public table, he hardly asks anybody; while the Spaniard gives balls every week, the magnificence of which is only exceeded by their politeness and elegance.'[5]

The Duke and Duchess were indeed in Paris for only a very short time. Their conduct was more a result of their general disinclination to meet new people than from anti-French sentiment. Lord and Lady George particularly did not treat the French with sympathy and courtesy, even though as a young man Lord George had loved France, yearning to go there from Italy. Sarah reported that 'My two brothers and their wives are arrived in town from Paris, where I hear they behaved very ill, especially the Lennoxes, who shut themselves up, saw no French, kept late hours, and laugh'd at everybody.' The Duke and Duchess preferred dining with extended family and close friends, or families who were of particular interest to them, and that way of life continued in Paris. The Duke was always following political events in England, with the result that his ambassadorship never really acquired momentum.

## THE GOODWOOD SÈVRES PORCELAIN

Within a week of their arrival in Paris the couple purposefully visited the new porcelain factory at Sèvres, with Horace Walpole in tow. There they bought three vases and ordered a magnificent dinner service. It was reported by the Revd William Cole, a travelling English cleric: 'The Duke and Duchess of Richmond, who were attended one morning, while I was at Paris, by Mr Walpole, bespoke a service of this manufacture for their table which was to cost 500 pounds. I mean Mr Walpole went with their Graces to Sèvres.'[6] The factory had been owned since 1759 by Louis XV, who, with his mistress Madame de Pompadour, was keen to promote its wares. Every New Year at Versailles there would be an exhibition of the new porcelain, the idea being that the royal factory was promoted in court and diplomatic circles. The price paid by the Duke was enormous.

There are two probable English influences at work in the Duke of Richmond's acquisition of such an expensive set of Sèvres china. One was the service given in gratitude by Louis XV for her husband's ambassadorship to France to Gertrude, Duchess of Bedford. It is likely that the Duke of Richmond saw the service where it was first used, at their London home at Bedford House after their return in 1764. In that year the Richmonds and Bedfords became quite closely related, when Francis, Marquis of Tavistock, heir to the Duke of Bedford, married the Duke's first cousin Lady Elizabeth Keppel, one of the fifteen children of 'Aunt Anne' Albemarle. She was the sister of George, Earl of Albemarle, and of Augustus Keppel, the cousins to whom the Duke was so close.

An even more direct influence was a Meissen dinner service of birds and animals ordered by Charles Hanbury Williams, the close friend of Henry and Caroline Fox, who in 1763 and 1762 respectively (i.e. Caroline first), became Baron and Baroness Holland.[7] In Hanbury Williams' absence abroad on diplomatic duties, the service was delivered piece by piece into Caroline's care at their home at Holland House, where Hanbury Williams had an apartment. The soup plates were all painted with birds, taken from an English book, *A Natural History of Birds* by Eleazar Albin, which was obtained by Meissen in 1745. Caroline would certainly have known it and may even have seen it unpacked, as the exciting unwrapping of new china was invariably done with people watching. It is likely that she suggested to her brother that he have a similar service made at Sèvres, from their own George Edwards bird books, to which the 2nd Duke had been a subscriber.

The Duke may have gone to France already equipped with the bird books from his own library, for in January 1766, the painters François-Joseph Aloncle (1734–1781) and Antoine-Joseph Chappuis *jeune* (1743–1787) from the Sèvres factory arrived at his residence to copy the birds on to china.[8] It is likely that preparatory enquiries had been made, and some items may have been ready for decorating; the two painters copied 100 birds, for which they were paid a *livre* for each one. The large blue and green

Garniture of three vases, 1765, Sèvres, soft-paste, comprising a *vase à couronne* (35.5 cm / 13 in high); and a pair of vases *Danemark à gauderon* (21.7 cm / 8½ in high), the latter bearing factory marks of interlaced Ls, one with date letter for 1765 and the other for 1766. Painter's mark for Jean-Louis Morin, *fl.*1754–87. Believed to be those purchased by the Duke and Duchess of Richmond on their first visit to the factory on 12 November 1765.

dessert service is decorated with birds and flowers, of which the green is marked M for 1765 and the blue N for 1766. The service was original at the time of its creation and remains extremely rare. To have real, tropical birds painted on to china was a break with the past at the Sèvres factory. Prior to these services, any birds painted on Sèvres china had been imaginary and fantastical. George Edwards' exotic birds, with their bold colours and extravagant shapes, gave the service a new style and daring, as well as being of great ornithological interest, because few people had ever seen such rare birds. The French edition of his volumes was used, dating from 1745 and 1748 (see page 70), and dedicated to the 2nd Duke and Duchess of Richmond.

The linking of the two colours was also unusual. The magnificent underglaze blue or *bleu lapis* may simply have taken longer in preparation than the green (*vert*), giving it the later date letter. Clients would normally order one colour only, but four little sweetmeat baskets in blue and green bear witness to the combination of the two colours, and to the 3rd Duke's taste and originality. The service would have been seen on white damask tablecloths, which would show up the colours and decoration. It

is probable that they used silver plates or other porcelain for the first two courses, and that the Sèvres service was just used for the elaborate desserts that were so fashionable. Sixteen compotiers were supplied, shaped as shells, rounds, ovals and squares: there are four in each shape for soft-textured delights such as compotes and jellies. Round stands, which have small feet, would be piled high with fruits, one type in each dish, studded with delicious little nuts, dates or marzipan. The blue ice-cream cups, set on a tazza, would contain the half-melted, sorbet-type ice-cream that was so popular at the French court. Four elongated bowls with covers, set on trays, were supplied in blue for sugar, some of the fruit being quite sour. Four wine coolers were supplied in green.

The services are believed to have been supplied through Jean-Jacques Bachelier (1724–1806), the factory's artistic director and an occasional *marchand* or dealer.[9] Some of the blue pieces have the marks of the flower painters Guillaume Noël (1734/5–1804) and Charles-Louis Méreaud *jeune* (*c.*1735–1780). The Duke also ordered a rare matching green tea and coffee service with an unusually large teapot that he must have commissioned specially. It is painted on one side with a magnificent owl and a parrot, and

ABOVE Sèvres service, laid out for tea, comprising (clockwise from right) a teapot or *théière Calabre* of extra-large size; double-ogee cup or *gobelet Hébert*, with matching five-lobed saucer; a sugar basin or *sucrier Bouret*; and a slop basin, variously 1765–66. Of the eighteen teacups at Goodwood, fifteen were painted by Chappuis. This service is entirely green but the service used at the dinner table for the dessert course is both blue and green.

FACING PAGE Sèvres vase, presumably the vase 'Bachelier à serpents, first recorded in 1766 and designed by Jean-Jacques Bachelier, Artistic Director at Sèvres'. The mazarin-blue beaker is Chelsea.

on the other with two more colourful birds. Elegant jugs were designed as *cafetières*. The double-ogee teacups in this service were mostly painted by A.-J. Chappuis. Like the Bedford service, the Richmond one has a large quantity of plates, in both blue and green. Where the Bedford service has 'biscuit' or white figures for the centre of the table, as was normal in France, the Richmonds may have used some of their coloured vases for the centre of the table, sixteen '*pièces d'ornament*' being part of the order.[10]

The 3rd Duke of Richmond was England's greatest patron of Sèvres porcelain. Apart from the Duchess of Bedford's service (now at Woburn Abbey) and Lord Melbourne's (now at Firle Place, Sussex), the other main English collectors of Sèvres, namely the Hertford descendants and the Rothschilds, acquired their porcelain some years after it had been made, at the time of the Revolution or in the nineteenth century. The Richmond service is unique in England because it was actually commissioned at the factory in 1765 and because the Duke played a decisive role in the choice of decoration. Whereas most eighteenth-century porcelain was intended for a town house in London, the Duke's Sèvres service was intended for Goodwood, whither, in 1768, the master potter Josiah Wedgwood (1730–1795) sent his artist to draw vases.

In mid-February the Duke and Duchess came home from Paris, supposedly on leave but in fact for good. The Duke was in such a hurry to return, in order to help the new Whig government in Parliament over the American issue of the repeal of the Stamp Act, that he crossed the Channel in a fishing boat, leaving the Duchess to find a calmer crossing. He left Lord George to hold the fort in Paris, and did not return, staying at Goodwood that spring in the hopes of getting a government post. In London afterwards, their guests at Richmond House often revealed their French connections: in 1767 at a 'very fine dinner', all but two guests were French.[11] Despite the brevity of their time in Paris, France was important to the Duke.

The Aubigny dukedom, encompassing the *seigneurie*, had been created for Louise de Keroualle, and was inherited on her death by her grandson, the 2nd Duke. The question of its legitimacy for a non-national was always a slight problem. In 1749, as ambassador to Paris, William, 2nd Earl of Albemarle, had managed to get the 2nd Duke's right to the title agreed. From as early as 1752 the 3rd Duke was considering paying the necessary homage to the French king.[12] The issue became delayed over the question of whether or not homage was acceptable from a non-Catholic. After much effort, he finally managed to render his French peerage 'more complete and unquestionable' by paying the necessary homage to Louis XV in the summer of 1777 and having it registered by the Parlement de Paris.[13]

## SARAH IN PARIS

For the winter after the Duke's embassy, that of 1766–7, the Hollands were accompanied in their visit to France by Sarah, the Duke's youngest sister. She was married to Sir Charles Bunbury, 6th Baronet (1740–1821), but the marriage was cold and she found life in Suffolk dull. To Caroline's distress, during that winter Sarah

acquired a considerable reputation for flirting. She was pursued, not only by the cultured Frederick Howard, 5th Earl of Carlisle (1748–1825), but also by the notorious rake Armand de Gontaut, Duc de Lauzun (1747–1793), who, despite his own arranged marriage the previous year, continued to be an active seducer of women. He was a popular and amusing member of Parisian society.

The Duc de Lauzun claimed in his *Memoirs* first to have had an affair with Madame de Cambis, who would later become the Duke of Richmond's mistress. He reported having sat between her and the newly arrived Sarah at supper with the Prince de Conti.[14] He then suggested that Madame de Cambis had been furious as he abandoned her for Sarah. Lauzun's *Memoirs* were written to impress other ladies and were prone to vast exaggeration, but there was certainly a close relationship with Sarah. On the Bunburys' return to England in February 1767, Lauzun accompanied them north. Subsequently he followed them to England, to stay at their country home at Barton in Suffolk. Wisely or unwisely, Sir Charles then went away for three weeks, leaving the ground clear for Sarah and her French duke.

Lauzun reported these to have been the happiest days of his whole life. He bragged that Sarah wished him to run away with her, a proposed course of action in which he claimed to have counselled caution. However Sarah's cousin, Susan O'Brien, and her own sister Caroline both believed the relationship to be an innocent one. Whatever the nature of the affair, it ended when the trio went to London, Lauzun departing to Bath for a few days with Sir Charles and returning to find that Sarah had set off for Goodwood with the Duke and Lord Carlisle. The Duke had no doubt got wind of the problem, and was protecting his sister, letting her be accompanied by a more appropriate male friend.

However, the following winter, while Caroline and Henry were again in Paris, Sarah embarked on a love affair that was to be her ruin. Lonely and unhappy in Suffolk, she took up with the red-headed Lord William Gordon, whom she had met the previous autumn. The younger brother of Alexander, 4th Duke of Gordon, he had come to stay with the couple at Barton because of his poor health. A child was born in December 1768, whom Sir Charles accepted as his own, though after his eight childless years with his wife, little Louisa was clearly the daughter of Lord William. Casting all cares to the world, early in 1769 Sarah openly ran away with Lord William. This was the ultimate *faux pas* for a young woman in her position. Initially they rushed to Knole in Kent, the great rambling mansion of the Duke of Dorset. The family was aghast. The story was all over town, with the 'distracted' Duke of Richmond due back immediately. Worse, in an astonishingly modern-sounding and unconcerned statement, Sarah declared that she was not planning to marry Lord William because he had a bad temper, but that she intended to proceed with the relationship for the moment.[15] The couple went to live together near Southampton.

The Duke of Dorset had himself aroused comment by staying at Richmond House as a guest of the Duchess while the Duke was away. For this reason the Duchess of Richmond was felt by the Duke's sisters to be complicit in Sarah's affair, and great distress was caused to all. It was even reported that the Duke and Duchess were 'not well together'.[16] Indeed, the Duke was often moody and even depressed over the next few years, his sisters often referring to his 'illness', which may have been the beginning of a liver complaint.

## 'All of his French ladies'

The Duke and Duchess had no children: that the Duchess was 'irregular' was mentioned in letters.[17] There is no evidence of any infidelity during the 1760s, and it may be that the couple continued to be very wrapped up in each other for the time, but in the 1770s the Duke had more than one mistress.

At some stage between about 1770 and 1774 the Duke had an affair with a young girl locally. His sister Sarah wrote, 'I did not at all approve of his flirtation here with a little dab of a miss 20 years younger than himself, & he allows it was very ridiculous.'[18] The girl seems to have embarrassed him, insisting against his wishes

on going to a ball, presumably at the Assembly Rooms in Chichester, when she was 'not well', just so that she could show off in front of the officers of the militia. Sarah may have been hinting that she was in the early stages of pregnancy. A child was born at about that time, as Louisa reported in the summer of 1776 'the death of a poor little girl that he and the Duchess had taken into the house, whom perhaps he may have told you of. There was a mystery about where she came from, but my brother and the Duchess were kind to her.'[19]

A baby girl born on 28 October 1773 has always been identified as the Duke's natural daughter. She was to become an integral part of the Goodwood family. Little Henriette Le Clerc was certainly French, but the identity of her mother remains uncertain. Her descendants have always believed Henriette's mother to have been the sister of Victor Emmanuel le Clerc, who was subsequently one of Napoleon's generals and who, by marrying Pauline Borghese, became Napoleon's brother-in-law.[20] In fact the whole Napoleonic connection was probably wishful thinking. The name Le Clerc was probably grasped at random, as an average French name, before it was made famous by the connection with Napoleon. It is much more likely that Henriette was the daughter of another French lady.

## Madame la Vicomtesse de Cambis, Princesse de Chimay

In the summer of 1776 the forty-one-year-old Duke was enjoying a passionate love affair in Paris. The object of his affections was the attractive and amusing Louise Françoise Gabrielle d'Alsace-Hénin-Liétard, Princesse de Chimay (1739–1809).[21] She was the daughter of Alexandre, 12th Prince de Chimay, whose family lived at the Château de Chimay, in the Ardennes, on the borders of north-eastern France and what would later become Belgium. She had married in 1755 Jacques François, Vicomte de Cambis. This was certainly a grand liaison and no doubt an arranged one, made when she was only sixteen.

The Duke could have met Madame de Cambis, as she was always known, through any number of contacts, including an old family connection. His father, the 2nd Duke, had known the Vicomte's father, Monsieur de Cambis, when he was French Ambassador to the Court of St James between 1738 and 1740 and had offered him and his wife various marks of hospitality.[22] In 1739 the senior Monsieur and Madame de Cambis attended a ball at Goodwood. In the next generation Thomas, 13th Prince of Chimay, was killed at the Battle of Minden in 1759, where, as Colonel of the French Grenadiers, he may well have met the Duke.[23] As the elder brother of Madame, this could subsequently prove quite an emotional link.

Madame de Cambis was an integral member of the sociable Parisian smart set. As early as 1763 the Duke's sister Caroline Holland met Madame de Cambis' sister-in-law in Paris: 'There is a daughter of the Duchess Fitzjames, a little Princess Chimez, about eighteen, so pretty.' This was Laure de Fitzjames, who was married to the next brother, Philippe, now 14th Prince de Chimay (1736–1804). The Prince dined with the Duke soon after his arrival in Paris in 1765. Madame's uncle, her mother's younger brother, the Prince de Beauvau (1720–1792), was taken by Walpole to the Fitzjames' dinner that January and in April her sister, the Comtesse de Caraman, was praising 'cette divinité' from the Hôtel de Brancas.[24]

At the time of the Duke's embassy to Paris, Horace Walpole met the famous salonnière, Madame du Deffand, who some ten years later was to report closely to him on the love affair between the Duke and the Vicomtesse. In 1765 Madame du Deffand was sixty-eight and blind, but full of spirit, entertaining fashionable friends at her home on the left bank to supper at least twice a week. She and Walpole became such close friends that thereafter he used to go over to Paris every two years to visit her.

The Parisian circle was more sophisticated and more dissolute than the Richmonds' usual London circles. Women such as Madame du Deffand had a history of innumerable lovers. She managed to survive socially because she was witty and smart, rich and well connected. Madame de Cambis' aunt and frequent companion, the beautiful Marquise de Boufflers, also had a long history. Marie Françoise de Beauvau-Craon (1711–1787) had been widowed at the age of forty-one, thereafter taking many lovers, including King Stanislas, the ruler of Lorraine. Love affairs between married people were conducted quite openly in Paris, without the discretion more usually shown in England, as the French were even more obsessed than the English about not marrying below one's rank. It was thus quite rare for an aristocratic couple to be happily married in France, whereas in England families tried to ensure at least a degree of affection between couples.

From the autumn of 1769 Madame du Deffand often mentioned Madame de Cambis. Walpole was in Paris again that autumn; the Duke and Duchess of Richmond were also visiting and must by now have met the Vicomtesse during their stay. On 9 October Madame du Deffand went to the theatre with the Richmonds, describing the Duke as 'le meilleur homme du monde' and the Duchesse as 'la plus naturelle, la plus gaie, la plus facile'.[25] Afterwards she entertained them to a supper for ten. Together with her aunt and her cousin, Madame is described as a 'bird of passage', flitting in and out of Paris: Madame du Deffand felt that the aunt especially was dangerously addicted to gambling.[26]

Over the next few years Madame du Deffand made various references to Madame de Cambis, who lived near to her. By 1773 she was 'ma meilleure amie' (my best friend).[27] The younger Madame's connections were impeccable. As daughters of the Prince de Beauvau, her aunts had married according to their station. The eldest was the Marquise de St Martin; another was the Duchesse de Mirepoix; another was a senior nun, the Abbesse

de St Antoine; and the Marquise de Boufflers led her into that enormous clan, which included the mistress of the Prince de Conti and the wife of the Duc de Lauzun. Madame's own elder sister Marie Anne Gabrielle married the Comte de Caraman, whose son would in the end become the next Chimay heir: the surviving family is now Chimay-Caraman. The Comte de Caraman had a country home near to Paris at Roissy, where the Vicomtesse would often stay for weeks at a time.

In 1774 Walpole asked the Duke's mother-in-law Lady Ailesbury, who was visiting Paris, if she had heard the Vicomtesse sing a certain French song. Lady Ailesbury replied in her praise: 'Madame de Cambis is our intimate acquaintance, and we seldom pass a day without seeing her. She is uncommonly sensible and lively, and sings "Sans dépit et sans légèreté" charmingly.'[28] In that year Madame de Cambis also became friendly with Lady Mary Coke: the two loved to make jokes together. Lady Harriet Stanhope became another friend, as did Lady Ailesbury's younger daughter, Anne Seymour Damer. Madame du Deffand commented on how much she was cultivating her English ladyfriends, rather than her French ones. Her husband the Vicomte de Cambis is only ever mentioned once, when, in May 1776, he was with his wife at an ambassadorial supper party in Paris.

In April 1776 the Duke prepared to travel to France, both to pay homage to the new king and to make his château at Aubigny available to his sister, Emily. The widowed Duchess of Leinster had married her children's tutor, William Ogilvie, at Toulouse in October 1774. With the scandal of duchess and tutor being too hot for polite Dublin society, the Duke offered them his French château so that they could live a secluded family life. He met them there early in May: this was the first time that he had met his sister's new husband. When Emily finally dared to move in Paris society that July, Madame du Deffand was extremely scathing, saying that one did not marry such men and that the Duchess of Leinster should have simply kept Ogilvie as her lover.[29]

The day before the Duke's departure for France, his youngest sister Sarah, now living at Goodwood, wrote to Emily about his forthcoming visit, telling her that their brother was not in good health. She asked her to beg 'all of his French ladies' to send him home early to bed: 'For though we spare him very willingly to them (vu que they have taste enough to like him) for a little while, we expect he should be nursed up and sent home at least as well as he goes.'[30] This could corroborate the evidence that he had more than one affair in Paris, but it may also cover flirtations and friendships. Sarah then mentioned 'his friend Madame de Cambise', saying that she 'is sick, so I hope she will have proper attention to his health.' This probably was a genuine illness, not a pregnancy, as the Vicomtesse might otherwise have fled to the country. Madame du Deffand would first report on the progress of the affair throughout that summer of 1776.

Initially the Duchess was intending to travel with the Duke to Paris: the couple were to go over with her half-sister, Anne Seymour Damer. In fact the Duchess returned from Goodwood to London when the Duke left for France in late April. However, the Duchess must have found out about the affair before long. Louisa reported on her sister-in-law's philosophical approach to her husband's love affairs: 'As to my brother's flirting, she don't mind it one bit.'[31] After nineteen years of marriage, the Duchess had obviously recognised that she would not bear children. A rather insensitive woman, thick-skinned and good-natured, she also seems to have been confident of the Duke's respect for her, and of taking first place: 'she is very sure of being that with him', commented Louisa. While tolerating infidelity to some extent, women had their own individual rules for the extra-marital behaviour of their husbands and brothers. The Duchess could accept her husband's affairs providing they were only 'creditable and genteel'. Louisa was amused by her approach: 'She is vastly comical upon that subject, for jealousy is not in question, but her pride is and she is discomposed if she thinks he likes anything frippery and vulgar.'[32] The Duke had not always been so scrupulous.

The Duke enjoyed his summer in Paris so much that Madame du Deffand thought he would delay his departure. He was finding Madame de Cambis '*fort a son gré*' (much to his taste).[33] The Vicomtesse responded with enthusiasm, maximizing her French charms for his benefit: '*Celle qui chante si bien . . . elle a joint à ses grâces naturelles toute la coquetterie possible, et il m'a paru que c'était avec beaucoup de succès.*' (She who sings so beautifully . . . has added to her natural graces all the flirtatiousness possible, and it seems to me with much success.)[34] Not having seen him for seven years until this summer season, Madame du Deffand declared that the Duke had an excellent heart and that everyone found him more '*aimable*' on this trip than on his previous ones. During that summer Madame had watched a passion develop between the Duke and the Vicomtesse.

In the autumn the Duke remained in France, travelling in mid-September to Aubigny. By now a heaviness hung over him: '*On n'a jamais vu personne aussi profondément triste.*' ('I have never seen anyone so sad.')[35] Claiming that he was not well (which Madame du Deffand deemed to be lovesickness), he returned to England via Paris. After his arrival in England, the Vicomtesse was anxious for news, begging Madame du Deffand to ask Walpole for reports. That month she began to learn English. Progress was excellent, driven, according to Madame du Deffand, by love.[36] Similarly that winter the usually tetchy, impatient and hot-tempered Duke was more relaxed. Sarah told Emily that 'Love, you know, is like the chameleon and takes its colour from the object. Of course, while he is in love with Madame Cambise he is "*aimable*".'[37] Two people had used the same word to describe the Duke: softened by love, he had himself become lovable.

## 'Poor Mary is entirely forgot'.

Although Madame de Cambis was accepted by the sisters from at least as early as 1776, they may not have anticipated that the relationship would become such a serious passion. The Duke left England for Paris again late in the following April, 1777, accompanied by his nephew Charles Lennox and the boy's tutor. That May the lovers often dined with Madame du Deffand, who was delighted by their company. Madame de Cambis had already learnt enough English to be able to translate Lord Chesterfield's *Portraits* into French. She was naturally 'dry and silent, totally concentrated on one single object'[38] while the Duke had a sadness about him.[39] He did, however, enter into Parisian life, visiting Sèvres on a commission for Walpole and dining with Baron Necker; but Madame du Deffand found him very preoccupied.[40]

The historian Edward Gibbon was in Paris that summer. Walpole introduced him to Madame du Deffand, of whose generous hospitality he wrote to a friend, 'When you see the Duke of Richmond . . . he will give you an account of that house where I meet him almost every evening. Ask him about Madame de Cambis. I am afraid poor Mary [the Duchess] is entirely forgot.'[41] Gibbon reported how very happy and alive the Duke seemed to be: 'Your favourite, the Duke of Richmond, has fallen in my way infinitely more than he ever did in England and I do assure you that the air of Paris agrees perfectly well with him. He is easy, attentive and cheerful, pays court to young and to old women, and is extremely popular and even fashionable in the Society of Paris.'[42] However, Horace Walpole was shocked by the affair, not believing that such a scrupulous and virtuous man would fall prey to such a passion. Madame du Deffand, writing regularly to him on Sundays, insisted against his denial that the Duke was '*fort épris . . . et de la plus profonde tristesse*' (completely smitten . . . and in the greatest sadness).[43]

In the autumn Sarah reported that he planned to see Madame de Cambis yet again the following spring: 'There is a fine lady there too, whom I hear the French say "*qu'il aime avec passion*", & he don't deny it, but tells us all he must go & see her again; I knew her & think her very pleasing, & quite a proper age for him.'[44] That winter Madame du Deffand expressed warm affection for the lady: '*Celle ici qu'il aime le plus, est celle aussi que j'aime le mieux.*' (She whom he loves the most is also the one whom I love the best.)[45] The only person who did not take to Madame de Cambis was the sarcastic and clever educationalist Madame de Genlis (1746–1830), who found her haughty and snobbish but could not deny that she was known for her gaiety and wit.[46]

In late 1777, the situation was complicated by political events when France supported the American colonies in their battle for independence from Britain. In January 1778 Emily arrived in Paris from Aubigny. She sent notes to Madame du Deffand and

Madame de Cambis, who rushed to see her within an hour of receiving them. 'I cou'd not help comparing their easy, polite, pleasant, chatty manner with the stiffness and conceit of our English ones,' Emily told Sarah.[47] The Duke was expected in Paris in May, taking a house in the rue de Grenelle, but the ladies were nervous about the approach of war.

## The Mystery Mother

The Duke's third and younger sister, Lady Louisa Conolly, surmounted travel difficulties to go to Paris in March 1778 for three weeks, to see her belovèd sister Emily and to meet Madame de Cambis. Being childless herself, unselfish and 'an angel', she was the one who was always given the family's emotional chores. Intriguingly, she and Emily, who was awaiting the arrival of her twenty-second child, went to stay at the country residence at Roissy of the Comtesse de Caraman, the sister of Madame de Cambis. When she was about to return from Dieppe on 6 April, Louisa described bringing a child from Paris to the coast. She was going to bring her on to England, heading for Lord George's home at Stoke. The child was Henriette Le Clerc:

> We have had most heavenly weather and our journey went off vastly well, *all to the* poor little French girl, who 'spued' all the way; but it is so miserable at having left its friends, as is quite terrible; it said so many moving things and looked so meek, that it set us all a-crying; but we have bought it playthings, and it is growing more used to us.[48]

From Stoke she reported that she was expecting the Duke and Duchess to settle at Goodwood for the summer, 'which I don't wonder at' (presumably both because of the war and of the child), but a week later she was beginning to think that the Duke might be about to go off to Paris after all.[49] She told Emily that 'Madame Cambis I really feel an affection for.'[50] The Duke was sending the lady some books via his nephew's tutor. On 21 April she made a telling comment to Emily, who was still in Paris: 'Pray thank Mme de Cambis for her kindness in telling me what I ought to do . . .'[51] Louisa clearly wanted to be friends with Madame: she had also left some poems in Paris for Emily to give her.[52]

A month later Louisa reported further to Emily:

> Perhaps I never told you of the good luck of that poor little French child, which is, that instead of its going to a boarding school in Chichester, my brother and the Duchess let it stay at Goodwood. Mr Jones has got a maid for it, and they have undertaken the care of it, 'til its father comes to England. I say 'they', because it is impossible for a child or animal to live in the house with my brother without his 'tutoring' it or 'teaching' it, which Lady Louisa [Lord George's wife] prophesied would be the case, the minute she heard of my bringing over the little creature.[53]

The Duke travelled down to Goodwood on 16 April because the Duchess was ill: the little French girl was also very unwell at about this time. The Duke was torn in different directions. Madame du Deffand archly told Walpole that she had 'a friend' who was longing to see the Duke.[54] He seems to have gone over in late April.[55] His absence abroad was hinted at in Louisa's report.

Was Madame de Cambis the mother of Henriette Le Clerc? It would certainly seem so. In December 1773 Madame du Deffand had reported her as being '*dans un état effroyable*' ('in a terrible state'), during eleven days of illness: that this was only weeks after the birth of Henriette may have been no coincidence.[56] That Madame de Cambis was well established in the sisters' correspondence by 1776 may well indicate that she was indeed the secret mother. An unsubstantiated editorial note in the *Memoirs* of the Duc de Lauzun states that she was in love with the Duke of Richmond by 1774.

There also seems to have been a deliberate cover-up. Sarah insisted on referring regularly to Henriette as 'the little protégée of Mr Jones', the Groom of the Bedchamber, who was supposedly entrusted to care for her education, as if her sister Emily had never heard of the child.[57] Louisa similarly called her 'Mr Jones little girl'.[58] Captain Jones, who had been with the Duke in the army, was in Paris in 1777 looking after Charles Lennox and was often detailed off with complicated family tasks. Madame de Cambis and Henriette are never ever connected in family letters: this could have been in order to ensure secrecy. Letters were often read aloud, and the sisters might have been preserving the appearance of discretion, perhaps even laying a false trail. There is no discussion between them of Henriette's parentage: they seem to have known the facts and deliberately suppressed them. The 'friends' that the little girl missed were probably her mother and her nurse. The sisters were writing in a loose code.

## 'Sa coquetterie est sèche, froide et picquante . . .'

After the outbreak of war, Louisa was pleased to report in August 1778 that Madame de Cambis was well settled in Paris.[59] Although interrupted by the American War, the affair somehow continued, by means of a long and intimate correspondence.[60] In March 1779 Madame du Deffand was longing for peace, so that the Duke could return to Paris.[61] That summer the Duke was receiving reports, clearly from Madame de Cambis, about the activities of her brother, the Prince de Beauvau, who was leading an expedition that, to the Duke's concern, anticipated a Franco-Spanish alliance.[62] The next year Madame du Deffand commented on how attractive, striking and witty the Vicomtesse was, saying that she made more conquests now than when she was young: '*sa coquetterie est sèche, froide et picquante*' (her flirting is dry, cold and piquant).[63] Even Gibbon had been rather smitten by her. Madame du Deffand admitted that she herself liked the Vicomtesse for her spirit, her 'truth' (which presumably

means that she was not affected) and for other excellent qualities. Madame de Cambis was certainly educated, sophisticated and interesting, commanding both affection and respect.

The affair continued for many years. In July 1783 Madame de Cambis was again in England, sailing over in the Duke's yacht and dining with Walpole at Strawberry Hill. In 1786 she was at Goodwood, where she met Emily's son, Lord Edward Fitzgerald, who commented: 'I like her very much what I saw of her the few days she was at Goodwood.'[64] There is no mention of her meeting the young Henriette. Madame then went away, but returned to Goodwood a few weeks later with the Duke. While the Duke was going off on a tour of Portsmouth and Plymouth for about ten days, she was going to stay at Stoke, the residence of Lord and Lady George, whom she may also originally have met when they were part of the Paris Embassy. The Duke and the Vicomtesse were apparently being treated as a couple. In 1789 Madame de Cambis moved to England permanently.

A miniature in the collection that probably dates from the 1780s is likely to be of Madame de Cambis. It is inscribed with a

dramatic and mysterious verse, that may describe one of their frequent partings: 'Though parted now/Perchance for life/In viewing this/Behold thy wife.'

## Henriette Le Clerc

The little girl was a great success at Goodwood. Sarah's daughter, Louisa Bunbury, wrote a polite thank you letter in French to her Aunt Emily, saying: '*Mon oncle et ma tante Richmond se sont chargés du soin de l'éducation de Mademoiselle Le Claire qui est une charmante enfant.*' (My uncle and aunt have taken on the education of Mademoiselle Le Claire who is a charming child.)[65] Sarah was delighted to have Henriette as a companion for Louisa, who was then aged about ten and was also an aristocratic love child. Sarah told Emily in July 1778 that Henriette was:

> by far one of the most enchanting little creatures I ever saw. She is lively and passionate, yet orderly and submissive . . . beautiful and agreeable . . . and not the least obstinate . . . Every mortal attaches themselves to her – servants, strangers and all.[66]

Henriette could teach young Louisa not only French , but also 'submission and humility'. Sarah looked after Henriette a great deal, taking care not to spoil her and overseeing both her health and her education: 'my pretty little Henriette is my child now while she is in my care.'[67] She took her bathing at Itchenor, and in 1780 the child was reading Molière with enthusiasm. The Duke adored her, letting her sit with him in his study at Goodwood while he worked:

> Although he does not spoil her I confess (for he makes her obey instantly) yet she gets so about him that, do you know, she has liberty of staying in his room while he is busy, she always will sit next him, be helped by him and in short, she makes a complete nurse of him.[68]

It is an intimate image: the Duke in his devotion is compared to a child's nanny.

The Duchess was 'as fond of her as he is'. Indeed, Sarah reported more than once that 'every mortal takes to her.'[69] She was very generous in her treatment of Henriette, whom she adopted as her own. Although described as 'The Poor Orphan' Henriette was treated as a little celebrity. Her august pedigree on both sides may have helped.

## French Furniture

While he was in Paris, both in 1765 and in the mid-1770s, the Duke bought many items of furniture made by the latest and most fashionable cabinet-makers. Unfortunately, receipts do not survive for the Duke's magnificent French furniture. It is also

LEFT  *Bonheur-du-jour*, stamped Feuerstein JME, *c.*1785. Joseph Feuerstein (1733–1809) was received Master in 1767. The 'Sèvres' plaque seems to have been inset in the nineteenth century.

ABOVE  Detail of *bonheur-du-jour* by Feuerstein.

FACING PAGE, TOP  *Coiffeuse*, stamped RVLC JME, *c.*1770. Roger Vandercruse (d. 1799), called Lacroix, was received Master in 1755. The right-hand middle drawer inscribed in black ink '3 pièces Argentées, Poirier', showing that three silver boxes were to be made as inserts, and that the item went through the hands of the famous *marchand mercier* Simon-Philippe Poirier.

FACING PAGE, BOTTOM  A giltwood *fauteuil* by L. Delanois.

impossible to know how much perished in the Richmond House fire of 1791. However, it would appear that he bought some items in the rococo style while he was ambassador.

The rococo was a style that was to be found inside classical houses, such as the Hôtel Biron at the end of rue de Varenne near St Germain-des-Près, or the remodelled Hôtel de Soubise in the once-again-fashionable Marais. It took the form of carved panelling (known as *boiseries*) but mostly did not actually use the classical language itself. Starting from the 1720s, the rococo repertoire derived from *rocaille*, or shell-like decoration, and many of its motifs were abstract, but were drawn from nature and not from classical art. One of the earliest examples of *rocaille* in Paris was the huge carved stone overdoor of 1723 at the home in rue de Varenne of the Marquis de Thois, the husband of Louise de Keroualle's sister, Henriette. Staying in this *quartier* of Paris as ambassador in 1765–6, the Duke simply could not have missed the many new interiors in the rococo style. The small drawing rooms of the *salonnières* were often modelled in this way.

The Duke's Sèvres porcelain of 1765 and 1766 was still very much rococo in feel. The style was also often expressed in mirrors, commodes and chairs. The Duke certainly acquired serpentine-fronted commodes by Latz and Dubois in Paris[70] (see page 181), as well as a stunning japanned cabinet by Bernard van Riesenburg.[71] His suite of furniture by Delanois was also made just at the end of the period when the rococo was most fashionable, as were some elegant armchairs. He also acquired a more transitional commode, just moving towards the straighter leg design, stamped by Couturier and Moreau, as well as two transitional *coiffeuses*. It is noticeable that there are no pairs of commodes. This may be because some were lost in the Richmond House fire or because the Duke enjoyed spreading his spending across a variety of objects. About half the surviving collection, including some elegant neoclassical pieces, was acquired after his ambassadorship, in the 1770s. Thus it seems that it is the Duke's relationship with the irresistible Madame de Cambis that accounts for much of the French furniture at Goodwood.

# 10 NEOCLASSICAL NOVELTY

1770–1790

The Duke had already increased his estate and planted many trees, but the most impressive building on the estate was the stables, supporting the taller and sleeker south wing in Portland stone, to which it was adjacent. However, from the main entrance on the eastern side, with its Garter Star over the front door, the house looked lop-sided, with the new wing to the left contrasting with older Jacobean gables. From time to time visitors to Goodwood made rude remarks about it not being fit for a duke.

The Duke decided to rectify this. In the early 1770s the rising architect James Wyatt began to work for him. Wyatt had just attracted attention in London with his design for the Pantheon, and was in danger of being enticed abroad. Instead, a group of English noblemen clubbed together to pay him to stay, making designs for them. A drawing by him exhibited at the Royal Academy in 1771 of an 'elevation of a house intended for a nobleman in Sussex', is believed to be the one now in the RIBA collection, and to have been for Goodwood.[1] The elevation shows a rotunda with free-standing columns imposed on a long low classical façade: this could have been a grand proposal for fronting the old Jacobean house, using it as the centre of an H-shaped plan, with the principal façade still facing east.

The façade design was not carried out, but a new north wing, designed by Wyatt to balance the 2nd Duke's south wing, was built. In a handsome but rather pedestrian classical manner, not unlike the second-generation Palladian houses of the 1760s, its pedimented façade looked north to High Wood. The extension, in red brick, provided a drawing room to the west of the Long Hall, built partially over the footprint of the Jacobean extension. Beside it, a short passage from the end of the hall gave access to a state bedchamber looking westwards, with an accompanying dressing room overlooking High Wood. These rooms

ABOVE *Goodwood House*, by Samuel H. Grimm, 1782, watercolour (British Library), showing the entrance front of the original Jacobean house, with the new north wing, its pediment peeping out from behind a modified right-hand gable. The original Dutch gable remains on the left. On the extreme left can be seen the end of Brettingham's 1740s south wing. Further left remains the 1720s kitchen, entirely separate and connected to the house by a tunnel.

FACING PAGE The Kennels, for the Duke of Richmond's hounds, by James Wyatt, 1787.

were on the ground floor, in the sequential apartment mode that had become fashionable in France. Upstairs further rooms included a billiard room.[2] The famous firm of Bromwich & Co. provided wallpaper for the new apartments.

A watercolour by Grimm shows the extension from its side, on the east front. For the outside, in 1775 orange trees and tubs were being bought.[3] These were presumably to be housed in the Duke's

The Orangery, designed by James Wyatt.

new Orangery, also by James Wyatt. From this attractive building, Wyatt would develop a particular style that he would use across the whole estate.

## THE LARGE LIBRARY AND SIR WILLIAM HAMILTON'S FIRST VASE COLLECTION

The first interior to be completed in this phase of building was that of the existing Large Library (see page 81). At the death of the 2nd Duke, the 'Great Room' in his new wing had only completed up to dado level. In 1757 William Chambers provided pier glasses to go over matching tables. Bookcases were added, their tiny running flower-studded guilloche decoration echoing that of the more formal banded oval rosettes adorning his looking glasses, and converting the room into a handsome library. Swags were then

added, presumably by Wyatt, above the earlier entablature. Between about 1772 and 1775 antique figures were painted on the dado cupboards. These were copied from prints of the sides of vases belonging to Sir William Hamilton, who since his appointment in 1764 as British consul at Naples had made a vast collection of ancient Greek vases. There had been a Greek colony at Naples well before the Romans conquered the area and, with recent excavations on a variety of local sites, it was possible to acquire such ancient artefacts.

Hamilton was keen to teach artists about the classical world and he wanted his pots to be made known to a wider audience through prints. The collection of more than two hundred ancient vases was painted two-dimensionally on canvases and first published over a ten-year period as 456 engravings in a luxury folio by Baron d'Hancarville, *Collection of Etruscan, Greek and Roman Antiquities* (Naples, 1766–76). If broken or fragmentary, the pots were shown as reconstructed, and the designs were sometimes made slightly more elegant or sinuous, believed to be an improvement on the original. The engravings were intended to be models for artists, to enable them to make images of the Antique. It was all seen by the benevolent Hamilton as a great educational project. The publication of his vases was a revelatory addition to what was known about the art of the ancient world.[4]

There was a personal link in the use of the vase designs at Goodwood. In December 1765 Hamilton had written to the Duke from Naples to congratulate him on his appointment as ambassador to Paris. As he signed off, Hamilton commented 'Do not forget that we have both great reason to be ever the humble servants of the Goodwood family . . .'[5] The relationship may have been formed when Hamilton was MP for Midhurst in 1761, or it may have been due to the fact that the Conways had acquired the home in which he was born, Park Place, Henley. The following winter the Duke's two nephews, Charles James Fox and 'Fitzy', William, Marquis of Kildare, were extensively entertained by the Hamiltons in Naples, together with the Hollands. The boys remained abroad and in 1767 Fitzy wrote to his mother to praise the publication of the vase designs, of which he bought several copies, saying it was 'a very good ornament to the library and a pleasant book to dip in to, as there is very pretty figures, and vases to draw from. It'll also oblige Mr Hamilton, who has been very civil to me.'[6] He recommended it to his aunt Lady Louisa Conolly, to whom one copy went at Castletown. The publication was certainly of interest to the whole family and in 1773 Lady Louisa described the Goodwood library as 'one of the prettiest rooms I ever saw', saying that she hoped to finish their gallery at Castletown in Ireland in the same manner.[7]

Hamilton was also highly interested in the excavations of the Roman cities of Herculaneum and Pompeii, the latter begun only since 1760. Both had been left frozen in time by the lethal eruption of Mount Vesuvius, which was also a source of much fascination to him, producing a constant stream of lava at the time. Drawings by Hamilton of Vesuvius and Etna subsequently found their way to Goodwood.[8] All information pertaining to the volcanoes would have been of great interest to the Duke, with his penchant for science.

James Wyatt himself first used the Hamilton vase designs for a whole decorative scheme in England as early as 1771, to decorate a temple on an island in the Thames at Fawley Court, Henley.[9] The Duke and Duchess would have known the house and the temple, as they were near her parents' home at Park Place, just south of the Henley bridge. It may have been because he knew this scheme that the Duke decided to use James Wyatt as his architect, rather than the better known Robert Adam. The Duke's library therefore suddenly took a radical turn to the newly fashionable style known variously (and inaccurately) as 'Etruscan' or 'Pompeian'.

The painter of the decorations on the Large Library cupboards was Charles Reuben Riley (1752–1798), who also provided numerous classical figures painted on canvas for insertion into the Serlian-

Figures copied from illustrations of vases belonging to Sir William Hamilton, by Charles Reuben Riley, on dado cupboards in the Large Library.

style banded ceiling. These were copied from engravings of Herculaneum published in the *Antichità di Ercolan esposte*. For the overdoors Riley copied paintings of Bacchus and Ariadne by Giles Hussey from the Duke of Northumberland's newly remodelled house at Syon Park, Middlesex, reportedly using the Duchess's own features in the depiction of Ariadne. The effect of the decoration of the library was, as in so many other schemes of this date, that images that were in fact ancient appeared startlingly new. Riley also did other drawings while at Goodwood.[10] By June 1775 he had left Goodwood to paint the Castletown decorations.

## THE ENGLISH NEOCLASSICAL STYLE AND THE FRENCH INFLUENCE

In the winter of 1776 the Duke appeared to be especially cheerful, spending only ten days in London and almost giving up politics. It must have been his love affair with Madame de Cambis that was making him 'better altogether this year than ever I saw him', as his sister Sarah reported.[11] That winter he was having his elegant new drawing room fitted out.

Despite its plain exterior, the interiors of the Duke's new wing were also in the latest style, subsequently known as neoclassical, which involved elaborate plaster ceilings and painted decorations. English neoclassical architects went back past the sixteenth-century buildings of Palladio that had been the source for early-eighteenth-century architects, in order to draw on genuinely ancient designs. As revealed in the library, they could make

use of the wider repertoire enabled by more recent excavations in Italy at Herculaneum and Pompeii. The first and most famous exponents of this style were William Chambers, who had already worked for the Duke, and Robert Adam, who, from about 1760 to 1780, was the most fashionable architect in Britain.

Although the Duke did not use either of these architects for his drawing room, French influence prevailed. Adam's interpretation of the Antique was much admired in Paris, where French designers were already developing their own version of neoclassicism. Just as the English aristocracy had been very influenced by the French since 1763, in the 1770s English styles were all the rage in Paris.[12] As Horace Walpole commented, 'Our passion for everything French is nothing to theirs for everything English. The two nations are crossing over and figuring in.'[13] It is likely that the ideas for the new drawing room were influenced to some degree by Madame de Cambis. The Duke had waited more than ten years to hang some new tapestries.

## The New State Apartment

The Duke had first bought a set of four tapestries from the Gobelins factory, on the edge of Paris, in 1763. These were from a series of eight called *Les Portières des Dieux*, illustrating the elements and the seasons. They were now hung in the newly added Tapestry Bedroom in the north wing (see page 128).[14] In 1776 a damask curtain was bought for its 'Canopy Bed', over which the Duke's ambassadorial canopy of state from his Paris days was re-erected, complete with the emblems of George III. Steps were covered in crimson velvet to lead up to the bed.[15] In 1763 he had also acquired one tapestry that showed an episode in the ever-popular story of Don Quixote, the deluded Spanish knight of Cervantes' novel.[16] The latter was for Richmond House, where his father's set of five Don Quixote panels was already hanging.

ABOVE, LEFT   An aerial view showing the north wing by James Wyatt, by 1776. Unusually, windows were not inserted on the right-hand side to complete the set of seven needed for an otherwise symmetrical façade. This was because the room was the Tapestry Bedroom, designed to take four Gobelins tapestries (additional to those in the adjacent Tapestry Drawing Room), for which wall space was needed, as well as a setting with not too much light.

ABOVE, RIGHT   Wyatt's north wing. Dry rot meant this had to be removed in 1968–70, along with a few rooms on the west of the house.

FACING PAGE   The Tapestry Drawing Room. The ceiling, by James Wyatt, is similar to designs executed at the time by the Adam brothers, but Wyatt uses a slightly more masculine interpretation of the Antique. The suite of furniture is by L. Delanois.

In 1766 the Duke was given by Louis XV a set of four new tapestries, again illustrating the story of Don Quixote, together with a matching floral piece to go over a door and a Savonnerie rug. These were paid for by the French King.[17] The Duke's tapestries came from the fifth out of nine different series of the tapestries. Between 1717 and 1794 a remarkable 174 tapestries of these subjects were woven, each taking two years. Designed as central pictures shown against a background within a wider border, the narratives were copied from a series of twenty-eight paintings by Charles Coypel, most of which were published as engravings between 1723 and 1734. The fifth series comprised thirty different scenes woven in the workshops of Michel Audran and Pierre-Francois Cozette between 1752 and 1764, of which the first six were completed quickly in tandem for Louis XV's château at Marly. Only a further twelve went to Marly, leaving the King enough to make a gift to the Duke of four. His other known gifts were from the later, eighth series, which, like the seventh, has a *damois cramoisi* or pink background, whereas the backgrounds of the Goodwood tapestries are a pale golden yellow.[18] The outer border was modified for each different series, depending on the client.

The Tapestry Drawing Room at Goodwood is a classic example of a new type of drawing room introduced by the architect Robert Adam, in which neoclassical ornament combined with the more rococo French style of the Gobelins tapestries. A hybrid French–English decorative scheme was first seen at Croome Court in Worcestershire, also a second-generation Palladian house. The room there was put together by Robert Adam for George, 6th Earl of Coventry, who had commissioned a set of tapestries from the Gobelins factory as soon as the war was over in 1763. These were hung in 1771, set off by light and elegant seat furniture, of the fashionable French type. The Duke may have known of it, as Lord Coventry was one of his political allies at the time.

Another scheme possibly known by the Duke was Osterley Park to the west of London, where the banker Robert Child was having his Gobelins tapestries hung in the room prepared for him by Adam in that summer of 1776. Adam designed tapestry rooms for five of his clients, the new elegance enabled by the

ABOVE   Gobelins tapestry, c.1763, with scene from Don Quixote, copied from Charles Coypel, this one *The Enchanted Head*, 372 × 434 cm / 12 × 14 ft. Events in the life of Don Quixote are depicted as in framed paintings, surmounted by a peacock and supported by a cartouche of a warrior. These are set against a yellow mosaic ground with floral trophies, surrounded by a further picture-frame border.

FACING PAGE, LEFT   Doorcase, the Tapestry Drawing Room, by James Wyatt.

FACING PAGE, RIGHT   Chimneypiece by John Bacon RA, in the Tapestry Drawing Room, 1776. It is said to depict male and female beauty. The female figure demurely requires a cushion beneath her feet in order to stand at the same height as the male. Originally a separate painting or mirror in a gilt frame probably hung above. The marble *Sleeping Dogs* by Anne Seymour Damer sits below.

introduction of these light and prettily coloured tapestries, with literary or mythological subject matter set in central cartouches to give the effect of a painting.[19] They could be made to line medium-sized or smaller rooms, the idea of the smaller *salon* emanating from the eighteenth-century French town house. The tapestries had illusionistic gilded borders which gave them a neat edge, fitting in well with the straighter neoclassical lines of the rooms. They were then usually hung under a frame in the French manner, like a painting, so that the overall effect was of a painting within a painting. The Duke's drawing room was designed to take all four tapestries, the usual number in a set, with the little overdoor panel for good effect. They were hung in the autumn of 1777.[20]

It seems extraordinary that Wyatt should create a drawing room that was so like those by Adam, and it is likely that he was deliberately trying to compete. Wyatt's ceiling is a perfect example of the scholarly use of the classical language, including tripods, urns and antique figures. With its decorative circles surrounded by an oval, light bands of running decoration and a range of bluey-green and pink colouring, the ceiling looks very like the work of Adam at the same date. However, Wyatt's is in some ways more masculine. The plasterwork was done in the summer of 1775 by the leading plasterer Joseph Rose, who also worked for Adam.[21] Like his rival, Wyatt took his design to the doorcases, window surrounds and shutters, which are beautifully

and intricately carved, removing the need for curtains and pelmets. He also provided a set of very sophisticated girandoles, or wall lights. The room was furnished with the Savonnerie carpet, part of the original gift.[22]

The chimneypiece, commissioned in 1775, departs from the Adam style of the room, and was included at the wish of the Duke, whose interest in sculpture was already established. It is by the sculptor John Bacon (1740–1799) who may have come to the Duke's attention through the Society of Arts. Bacon was also a modeller for Mrs Coade's manufactory of artificial stone at Lambeth, in which role he may have seen, or even have worked, on a Coade stone for the Duke from as early as 1771. His fame was assured by a bust that he made of George III for Christ Church, Oxford, in 1770. The marble chimneypiece at Goodwood depicts 'male and female Beauty standing in the attitude of drawing aside a drapery which unveils the fire-place . . .'[23]

The Tapestry Drawing Room was formally arranged in the French manner, with chairs around the walls and very little in the centre of a room. The chairs were carved and gilt, covered with white satin 'richly embossed in various colours'.[24] This shows that the room always had a number of patterns in play and the chairs referred to may be the suite by Delanois of eight *fauteuils*, two *bergères* and a *canapé* that is in the room today, with multi-coloured upholstery, in a Lyons cut velvet, on a white satin back. The Duke continued to like the classic French open-sided armchair or *fauteuil à la reine* with a curving back and slightly cabriole legs, of which he had a large number, not replacing them with anything more strictly straight-sided and neoclassical. Indeed, as the Duke completed his new wing, war with France was imminent, and only a few of his purchases, such as a little *bonheur-du-jour* by Feuerstein (see page 119), were completely neoclassical.

The only surviving drawing by Wyatt that was definitely for Goodwood was for a bedroom ceiling, presumably in the new wing. It was also suitably antique, and very light and graceful. However, Wyatt was accomplished enough not to imitate Adam too directly. Wyatt admired only Chambers, who, he felt, was

LEFT   Design by James Wyatt for a bedchamber at Goodwood (Metropolitan Museum of Art, New York). There is no record of this having been carried out, but it again shows Wyatt working for the Duke in a style similar to that of Robert Adam.

BELOW   The Tapestry Bedroom, with tapestries from *Les Portières des Dieux* series, illustrating the elements and the seasons, photographed in 1932. The bedhangings with their royal monograms were made out of the 3rd Duke's ambassadorial canopy. The bedcover was made later by 'Aunt Lina'.

FACING PAGE   *Charles Lennox*, the nephew and heir of the 3rd Duke of Richmond, as a youth (he later became the 4th Duke), by John Downman, watercolour, oval, 20.5 × 17 cm / 8 × 6¾ in.

more accurate. For a long time he would not admit any Adam influence, complaining furiously in 1794 that the brothers had accused him of plagiarism.[25] Years later he finally conceded their influence on his work, telling the King that 'when He came from Italy He found the public taste corrupted by the Adams & He was obliged to comply with it.'[26]

Next to the Tapestry Bedroom, in the central section of the new wing, a dressing room was fashionably painted on the ceiling with 'subjects from the Antique'.[27] Of this, a small oval painting of classical figures by Cipriani may be a survivor. There was also probably a closet, with the dressing room doubling as a second

bedchamber. For his labours, Wyatt was paid the large amount of £125 in April 1777; he had probably also received earlier payments.[28] Thereafter he was salaried, receiving £50 a year, or £12 10s from the Duke every quarter for the next twenty years. By 1778 the Tapestry Drawing Room was ready to take over as the main drawing room of the newly extended house.

## THE FAMILY

Given her lack of style, it is unlikely that the Duchess was involved in the extensions made to Goodwood House in the 1770s, or in the refurnishing with French furniture of Richmond House. The Duke seems to have carried out all the building and collecting himself. However, the Duchess spent more time than before at Goodwood, largely on her own.[29] Her friend Lady Melbourne would come to stay every year.[30] At least Mary began to show an interest in gardening. In 1776 Sarah reported that: 'The Duchess has taken more to planting and Goodwood than ever I saw her do.' Although she had begun to show interest in the improvements to the house, it was not a passion, and certainly 'not in the Lennox way yet'.[31]

It was tacitly recognised from the 1770s that Charles Lennox, the son of Lord and Lady George, was to be the Duke's heir. Louisa and Sarah wrote of him affectionately in their letters to Emily, commenting on his progress and his manners. From the autumn of 1777 regular disbursements were made to him by the Duke, mostly for clothes from his tailor, shoes and books.[32] In the summer of 1777 Emily's husband, William Ogilvie, came to Goodwood. This was the first time that the rest of the family had met him: they were enchanted.[33] From 1778 the Duchess was much cheered by the presence of little Henriette Le Clerc. She also worked tirelessly in London to look after Emily's son, Lord Henry Fitzgerald, when he was very ill.

A 'public day', when anyone could visit (but only the genteel were expected), is first recorded at Goodwood in 1779, in order to show off the Duke's smart new decorations. Nevertheless, in about 1781 one Silas Neville still reported that the house was 'the meanest I ever saw', though he admired Carné's Seat, a 'tea-drinking place built on an eminence by the late Duke'.[34] John Marsh, the gentleman composer from Chichester, also took tea at Carné's Seat in July 1787, where a woman 'residing there' provided 'cream, bread and butter and boiled the water'.[35] Public days in the house were on Mondays while the Duke was at Goodwood, and in March 1789 Marsh attended one: 'Mrs M and I dined for the first time at Goodwood, it being one of the Duke's public days . . .'[36]

After tea (drunk straight after the mid-afternoon dinner), Henrietta Le Clerc (aged fifteen at the time; the anglicised form of her Christian name was now usually adopted) and others went to the Music Room and performed two of Marsh's symphonies. Subsequently Marsh would often visit Goodwood, both to dine on public days and to play music with the band of the Sussex militia,

who, when not on active service, were kept there by the Duke, their colonel, at his own expense. Some of them worked as grooms in the stables. The Duke paid for good music teachers of both string and wind instruments. The band rehearsed each day between 11 a.m. and 1 p.m., and were accomplished enough to be taken to London to play at the Duke's theatre at Richmond House.[37]

Meanwhile Lord George's family at Stoke were very self-contained, enjoying simple country life. Their social life revolved around the regiment, which was based at Winchester, and they made little other effort to be fashionable. Lord George would ride every day into Chichester. They were often away: whenever Lord George went off to fight, Lady Louisa would follow.[38] Similarly, with the threat of French invasion especially looming in 1779, the Duke was often away from Goodwood, organising the militia. The Duchess followed his regiment to Exeter in order to be with him at such a dangerous time.

## THE SERVANTS

While running two large houses, the Duke and Duchess managed in the 1770s with a permanent staff of about thirty to thirty-five, some of whom moved from one house to the other. They each had two footmen, who would attend them everywhere, standing behind their chairs at meals and accompanying them on journeys. This was quite modest given that the Duchess of Northumberland had eight, exceeding the Queen's seven.

The senior female staff were the two housekeepers, one in each house, supported by one permanent housemaid in London and three at Goodwood. There was a laundry maid for each house, plus one each of pantry, kitchen and dairy maid, the latter presumably being only for the country. Probably temporary kitchen maids were brought in for London. On the male staff Richard Buckner was still the most senior, as the Land Steward, but he died in the winter of 1776–7.[39] His son the Revd John Buckner became Bishop of Chichester, while Captain Buckner, presumably another son, received a good salary of £25 a year, as the forester. Often three generations would work for the family: even 'C. Buckner', possibly a child, was paid for posting letters.

## SARAH AND MOLECOMB

The year 1770 began gloomily at Goodwood with the family grieving for the death of the youngest Lennox sister, Cecilia. Brought up in Ireland by Emily, she was sent to London both in order to be with Caroline and to seek the best medical help for her failing health. It became clear that she had consumption, so Caroline took her to France hoping that the milder climate of the south would help her; but Cecilia died in Paris in November 1769.

A picture of Goodwood throughout the 1770s emerges from the many letters of Sarah, who had more time than anyone to put pen to paper. After her passionate love affair with Lord William Gordon, there was no possibility of a reconciliation with Sir Charles Bunbury. Sarah was forced to retire from society. Uncontrollable passion was seen as uncouth and ill-bred, and an open flouting of the conventions was ruinous to the reputation of a young woman. Her husband who, she admitted, had never wronged her, was eventually granted a divorce by an Act of Parliament, the only way that a marriage could be terminated.

The Duke took Sarah under his wing, letting her stay at Goodwood. However, when there were guests or a 'public day' at the house, she had to move away, sometimes to Lord George's home at Stoke, where her strait-laced brother was not very helpful. Indeed, the Duke's own attitude seems to have caused Sarah a good deal of hurt. She might also go down to his newly acquired estate at Halnaker, which may been where her old flame the Duc de Lauzun visited her, declaring that 'dressed in a plain blue gown, her hair cut quite short and unpowdered [she] was more beautiful, more seductive than she ever had been.'[40] If she were allowed to go to London, she would be parked out of the way at the top of Richmond House. More happily, she often used the old seaside house which the Duke had acquired at Itchenor (now Jetty House) to bathe in the sea. Sea-bathing was very fashionable among the aristocracy at this date, and was believed to be good for the health. Little Louisa braved it even in December. Sarah spent eleven years at Goodwood, bringing up her daughter, writing letters, going for walks, building her house; and trying not to be a nuisance to anyone.

Early in 1777 Sarah was told by her brother to choose a location for her house. Sarah, who was easily demoralised, was indecisive about where she wanted it to be. She wanted her own private patch, not too close to the main house, and was largely relieved when it was decided for her: 'He [the Duke] has at last fixed upon my house being at Molecomb, where it will be beautiful and in some respects convenient.'[41] As James Wyatt had now been working at Goodwood for some years, it was natural that he would make the design. Once building started in the summer of 1777, Sarah became more enthusiastic. With the roof partly on, she declared that 'You never saw anything so pretty as Molecomb is, the house & one wing all done & covered in, the colonade [*sic*] is going to be done . . . It is the most Chearful warm good airy house that can be, in short it is *just* what I like . . .'[42] The only problem was that the Duke would not let her have the cupboards she wanted. In general she was very grateful to him: 'next summer 12 months I hope to inhabbit it, & enjoy the comforts of a *home*, a *pretty* home, & one given to me by the best of brothers . . .'[43] She spent the winter of 1779–80 in the seaside house at Itchenor, waiting to move in and busying herself with the furnishings.[44] In the meantime she spent much time looking after 'my pretty little Henriette', whom she loved like her own child.

Sarah's tenancy of Molecomb was short. In August 1781, aged thirty-six, she had the good fortune to marry the Hon. George Napier, who was twenty-nine. He had admired her at a distance some time earlier, when he was still married: the subsequent death of his wife and of two of his three children from yellow fever in New York placed him in a new situation. With a daughter named Louisa apiece, they were married at Boxgrove, moving to live at Celbridge in Ireland, near to Louisa and Emily. Sarah bore Napier five sons, of whom three became generals, one a captain in the Royal Navy, and one a fellow of All Souls, Oxford. There were also three daughters: Emily was adopted by her aunt Louisa Conolly, but the other two Napier girls died.

## ITCHENOR PARK: THE YACHTING VILLA

In 1773 Louisa reported that the Duke had 'taken to the sea and sailing', an interest which would develop over the next ten years.[45] In the summer of 1776, he acquired a farm by the sea at Itchenor, comprising over two hundred acres, together with some farm buildings.[46] Late that year the Duke began building works on this small new estate, which from then on featured in his accounts for every quarter. The farm was developed on the flat peninsula, and was probably also used as a base from where his racehorses could be exercised in the sea. As well as his yacht *The Falcon*, he had a cargo sloop called *The Goodwood*. He also had a barge built at Itchenor, presumably intended for the Thames.[47] To have his yacht made ready for him, the Duke's man would go up to Carné's Seat, from where he could signal down to Itchenor. In 1777 his yacht was in a match race from Brighton via Worthing to Beachy Head

Molecomb, designed by James Wyatt, built by the 3rd Duke for his sister Lady Sarah Lennox, 1777–80.

for 1,000 guineas. He built a row of cottages on the main street at Itchenor, and magnificent new stables and an indoor riding school on the farm, crowned with the Richmond arms on a Coade stone dated 1783.

A new house was completed on the farm, known as Itchenor Park, for which the Coade stone gives the date of 1784. This was his yachting villa, but it may also have been intended for Madame de Cambis. Local tradition has always suggested that it was for the Duke's mistress, but that she never came to live there. Madame did indeed visit England in 1783. It is not impossible that she came to Itchenor to see Henrietta. The bathing house was accessible from the park through a field, and it was both a private place to stay, eleven miles from Goodwood, and a perfect holiday location. With its immaculate four-square geometry, the house is believed to have been designed by James Wyatt. In 1786 the Duke paid for expensive 'white bricks', presumably belated payment for the pale yellow ones that were used for this handsome but modest country villa.[48]

## GEORGE ROMNEY

In the 1770s the Duke commissioned a number of portraits from George Romney, a Cumbrian artist who was just becoming known in London. Romney had sketched in the Duke's sculpture gallery from 1762, and a painting by him of *The Death of General Wolfe* may have been executed with the specific aim of getting the Duke's attention, the Duke having already bought a small full-length portrait of the military hero and commissioned a statue. Romney's advertising efforts bore fruit. In 1776–7 the Duke had his own portrait painted by the artist. This is not the glamorous image of the younger years, but an informal view of a middle-aged, balding man reading a book. This suggests that the artist may already have known the Duke, having the confidence to paint him as he was.[49] He also commissioned Romney to paint his brother, Lord George.[50] The Duke moreover acquired portraits of his cousin the naval hero, the Hon. Augustus Keppel, now an admiral, and of his sister, the matronly and sensible-looking Lady Louisa Conolly, both painted in 1776.[51] These may have been gifts from the sitters to the Duke: commission details do not survive. All these portraits were executed just around the time when

ABOVE, LEFT *Lady George Lennox (Louisa)*, by George Romney, 1777, oil on canvas, 96.5 × 71 cm / 38 × 28 in.

ABOVE, RIGHT *Charles, 3rd Duke of Richmond, Lennox and Aubigny, reading*, by George Romney, 1776–7, oil on canvas, 75 × 61 cm / 29½ × 24 in.

FACING PAGE, TOP The Kennels, the side facing away from the house.

FACING PAGE, BOTTOM *The Kennels as seen from the House*, engraving published in 1793. The chimneys appear to be over the cross wings, serving both the feeding stoves and the fires for the heating system.

Romney's talents were being generally recognised in London, partly engendered by a move to a better studio in Cavendish Square in November 1775 and perhaps partially a result of the ducal patronage.

Starting in January 1777, in the week in which the Duke was still having sittings, the artist also painted the Duchess. She sat to him no less than eight times that year, with a further seven sittings ending as late as 1789. It is not known what became of this portrait, which perhaps had its problems, nor of that of the Duchess's dog, painted as a finale, the artist sending it to her as a gift.[52] Romney liked to have many sittings, completing only when the work was fully paid for, and with the sitter before him in a final creative rush. Two further paintings from that year were more successful. Lady George Lennox also first sat to him in

January, a classic, perfectly composed painting, showing the feeling for grace and elegance in a sensitive, romantic way that could sometimes elude the artist's more literal rival, Sir Joshua Reynolds.[53] An even larger canvas than those of the pair for his parents was selected for the young Charles Lennox, the heir to the titles and estate, who followed the family tradition of having his spaniel at his side.[54] These three portraits were presumably commissioned by the Duke as a family group.

Romney's work was admired by the Duke over a long period, perhaps suiting his instinct for quality and classic elements in art, while also displaying a slightly free and different spirit. In 1795 the Duke was again painted by Romney, at his own request, though the idea may have originated from William Ogilvie, this time in a three-quarter-length military portrait in the uniform of a lieutenant general. For this he had an astonishing eleven sittings. Four copies were also made in his studio.[55]

However, the artist was increasingly nervous and fragile, often unable to complete his work. When the Duke asked him in 1796 to paint Henrietta Le Clerc, he was initially reluctant. Eventually he agreed to do so, undertaking the commission near to Goodwood at Eartham, where he often came to stay with his friend the poet and biographer William Hayley (1745–1820), who had generously provided him with a painting room. His romantic portrait of Henrietta shows the liquid use of paint that he had begun to exploit

in the late 1770s after his return from Italy, seen in the white strokes of her dress and bonnet (see page 143). The sitter was now twenty-three and perhaps not quite the little shepherdess portrayed. The background of the portrait (and maybe more) was completed by Martin Archer Shee in 1801; that of the military portrait of the Duke is also believed to have been painted by him.

The Duke continued to be a useful patron to other artists, lending classical items to the clever entrepreneur and manufacturer Matthew Boulton (1728–1809) to inspire his designs. The Duke also introduced him to Horace Walpole, enabling Boulton to visit Strawberry Hill.

## The Kennels

Having done so much work on the main house, and having designed the Orangery, Itchenor Park and Molecomb, James Wyatt was found a new commission by the Duke between 1781 and 1783 in return for his regular salary. This was to add a New Assembly Room to the Council House in Chichester. Richmond then sprang yet another ambitious new project on the architect.

What had once been the famous Charlton Hunt was now known as the Duke of Richmond's Hounds. The Duke was still enthusiastic about hunting: in the 1770s John Downman executed for him a set of pastel portraits of members of the hunt.[56] Thirty

years after reviving the hunt, the 3rd Duke asked James Wyatt to build kennels for the hounds. Wyatt created a superbly handsome building in pale straw-coloured brick with facings in knapped flint. Corresponding to the classical ideals, with function and form blending into one perfectly thought-out shape, it was a substantial eye-catcher from the grand new state rooms of the house. The cost was £6,000.

The building comprised a central, four-square cube-shaped house for the huntsman. Just inside the front door a flight of stairs

ABOVE    The Kennels, seen through the bastion-like wall, also by James Wyatt.

FACING PAGE, TOP    A Coade stone from one of the Pilley Green lodges. James Wyatt particularly liked to use Coade stones, made by Mrs Eleanor Coade's factory at Lambeth. The Richmond arms at this date were the royal arms of England with a wide border, denoting that the 1st Duke had been a natural son of Charles II. A shield applied at the centre bears the arms of the Duchess (Mary), daughter of the Earl of Ailesbury.

FACING PAGE, BOTTOM    The Pilley Green lodges, with the unusual knapped flint quoins on the corners that are particular to Goodwood. The door surrounds are faced in the same pale yellow brick that is used at the Kennels. The lodges abut what had once been the main road from Chichester to Petworth, until the 3rd Duke had it moved further east.  They are dated 1794 on their Coade stones. Each has a charming little carriage house adjacent.

led straight up ahead, dividing halfway up into two in order to access four 'sleeping Rooms' from two separate landings. Tom Grant (1754–1839), huntsman both to the 3rd and the (absent) 4th Duke, lived there for many years. In 1799 there were just three hunt servants, himself and two whippers-in, and, as an important member of staff, he may have had the house to himself and his family.

To each side of the house were long low wings, not directly accessible from the house. These were subdivided into two hound 'lodges' each side, running away from the central house and entered from the far end. The inner section of each lodge had a timber floor, over which there was a slightly raised wooden 'bench', a wide platform on which the hounds slept on straw bedding. The other half of the lodge had a stone floor for the hounds to run around. A passage running at the end of each pair of lodges enabled hounds to be let out through arched flint porches into one of two open-air yards in the forecourt on the west side, from which the most appropriate hounds could also be selected for each day's hunting. Two small projecting wings provided breeding rooms and a boiler room, at the north end, and a two-stalled stable at the south. Natural freshwater tanks below the building contained '7000 hogsheads' of water, providing the deep tanks in the airing yards and possibly the main house.[57] The water level would have risen in line with the River Lavant.

The Kennels were especially remarkable for their heating: 'The dogs were quartered in large rooms, one side of which was lined with iron plates heated from behind by huge fires in the coldest weather.'[58] The plates would have been on the inner sides. Judging by the location of the chimneys at the time, the heat probably came through pipes from the furnaces in the feeding rooms at the end.[59] Each feeding room had a stove, used mainly to heat the very smelly offal cooked for the hounds.

Owing to Wyatt's very careful and yet simple plan, all the main areas needed on a daily basis were thus contained in one long, elegant, rectangular building. Some way beyond, Wyatt designed a handsome pair of houses for the whippers-in. These are still known as 1 & 2 Kennel Lodge. On the side of the Kennels facing the main house, the Duke built a flint wall, set in a ditch. This was created to look rather like a bastion, running into a point, with impressive arched entrances at each side, reflecting his interest in military architecture.

The Kennels are adorned by a Coade stone with the Richmond arms, dated 1787. The two Kennel lodges (not to be confused with hound lodges) have a facing pair of Coade stones dated 1789. There is also one on a row of cottages in East Dean (1786) and one on a little flint house beyond Stoke (1791), as well as a facing pair on the two Pilley Green lodges, also by Wyatt (1794). These ornamental plaques had been made for some years by Mrs Eleanor Coade's workshop at Lambeth in London. They are fabricated stone, a clever invention created by her and widely used for capitals, coats of arms and other decorative motifs. All the buildings with Coade stones were built at the instruction of the 3rd Duke.[60]

The Kennels were much admired. Viscount Palmerston said that the main house was just 'an irregular old house of the Duke of Richmond with some comfortable rooms, but little worthy of

particular notice . . .' but he was very enthusiastic about the Kennels: 'ye Duke is making a dog kennel which is an object from ye house and which both within and without is in a style of elegance unknown hitherto to that species of building.'[61] The first exact and detailed description of the Kennels was published thirty-five years after they were built, by Dennett Jacques, the Goodwood librarian, in 1822.[62] The Duke of Richmond's Hounds, as they were now known, returned to Goodwood in 1790 to be the best quartered in the country. The western avenue from the house to the Kennels was terminated at the ha-ha by an obelisk, with a sphinx on top.

## THE ESTATE

Although the menagerie had become a pheasantry, the Duke still took the trouble to make amendments to the little viewing house there. It had been very smoky because the chimney came right up against the side of the old quarry. The Duke seized the opportunity to build an obelisk at the top of the hill, re-routing the chimney flue through it: 'his grace, consistently with his system on blending the *utile* with the *dulce*, took the opportunity of erecting an ornamental object.'[63]

The Duke also owned the public house at Waterbeach, where he had a tennis court. He was also still extending the wider estate, in 1785 buying land at Strettington (£120), Lavant (£269) and Westerton (£100). In 1787 he acquired more land in East Lavant.[64] When he could not acquire a freehold, he often took a lease or a copyhold, obviously hoping to make his acquisition good at a later date. By about 1790 he also had land at Barnham, Birdham and Wittering. He ran the estate very efficiently, checking that work was under way very early in the morning. There was a standing notice at Chichester that all tradesmen had to send in accounts for settlement without delay.[65]

## THE RICHMOND HOUSE THEATRE

Meanwhile the Duke also made considerable changes to Richmond House, to which in 1782 James Wyatt added a staircase and two rooms. These may have been the first stage in arrangements made to accommodate theatricals. In 1765 the Duke had financed the building of a little theatre in South Street, Chichester; this had to be rebuilt in 1791, a modest but attractive brick building with a pediment.[66] The city theatre was for visiting professionals, but the family were well used to putting on their own theatricals at home. Amateur theatrical performances by aristocratic families often took place in country houses, a left-over from the days of the travelling royal court.

It was probably in order to entertain Henrietta that theatricals were inaugurated at Richmond House. They were carried out to a very high standard. For the first season James Wyatt converted two rooms of the south side of the house on the first floor into a 'Play-house' with a large saloon as an ante-chamber. Double doors were thrown open in the ante-chamber when the play was about to start, so that visitors mounted temporary steps into the back of the auditorium, going through a grand doorway and down rows of graduated seats to get near to the stage.[67] The royal box was in a recess on one side, with a gallery in the bow window opposite holding about fourteen people. The decoration was designed by the Duchess's artistic half-sister, Anne Seymour Damer. Columns were gilded for the royal box, while canvas for scenery, printing, lamps, upholstery and iron columns were all bought in.[68] The scenery was painted by Thomas Greenwood of Drury Lane, with portrait figures by John Downman.

Performances took place in the spring of both 1787 and 1788. Music was provided by the wind ensemble of the Sussex militia. The actors were fashionable amateurs and *dilettanti*, relations and friends, including Anne Seymour Damer and the Earl of Derby. In 1788 the celebrated actress Mrs Siddons gave advice to the ladies on their costumes, which were always superb. Owing to the unexpected success of the venture, there were seven performances in the first season. Special friends were allowed to attend an open rehearsal. Tickets, which were of a different colour for each night, were distributed in small batches, which were given to actors or to friends. The recipients had to write the name of their guest on each ticket, seal it with their arms and send in the names of their guests the day before. Each performance would start at 8 p.m. The theatricals became so popular that an important motion in the House of Commons was postponed for the opening night on 19 April. The Prince of Wales was the guest of honour, seated between the Duchesses of Richmond and Devonshire. Mrs Fitzherbert also attended, as well as the Duke and Duchess of Cumberland, the Sheridans, Mrs Garrick, and political foes William Pitt and Charles James Fox. On the last night, on 17 May, the King and Queen attended, with four of their daughters.

Rehearsals for the next season began just before Christmas, with Emily's son Lord Henry Fitzgerald as one of the principal actors, and his brother Lord Edward and stepfather William Ogilvie also playing parts. This year the theatre was in a new location. The Duke had bought the adjoining house on the west side (formerly the home of the Earls of Loudoun and Mar) for Lord George and his son Charles Lennox. In this house Wyatt designed a new theatre, again on the first floor, but carving up the levels to use the floor as the stage with the orchestra and pit sunk below. There was a large central box high up opposite for the Duke and Duchess and their guests, with a canopy for the King in the centre. There were also side boxes. The seats all had backs, displacing the usual benches, and were lined in pea green. The capacity was 100. The Prince of Wales attended the first night on 7 February, together with the Dukes of York, Gloucester and Devonshire. The ladies were invariably covered in jewels, but, as the previous year, high headdresses were banned. Four different plays were performed that year, largely because of the great success and good looks of the dashing Lord Henry. The King and Queen attended three of the four, sweeping in through Lord George's own residence, specially decorated.

The family attended in their large numbers, including Fitzgeralds, Ogilvies and Keppels. Horace Walpole was a regular attendee, writing reports back to his friend the Countess of Upper Ossory, who had also started giving theatricals at her own home at Ampthill Park in Bedfordshire. The actor John Philip Kemble and the intellectual 'Blue-Stockings' Hester Piozzi and Hannah More also attended. One performance was interrupted by the late arrival of Charles James Fox, Lord North and General Burgoyne, who, with General Conway, had supported the venture from the start.

After June 1788 there were no more performances at Richmond House. The King's mental breakdown that November cast a great gloom over the court. It was decided to dismantle the theatre, which was subsequently converted into 'a dwelling house for Colonel Lennox and Lady Charlotte'.[69] In a similar way to that in which the neighbouring house had been earlier divided for the Earls of Loudoun and Mar, it was now divided between Lord George and his son, with Charles Lennox and his bride, Lady Charlotte Gordon, living on the side immediately next to his uncle. The scenery was given to the little theatre in Chichester.

The beautifully arranged dramatic performances at Richmond House owed their success entirely to the Duke. Cast lists for each production were announced in *The Times*, with a review usually appearing a few days after the opening night. Each performance had a very personal air, with special prologues and epilogues for royal visitors in the first season. Ices and other refreshments were presented at suitable intervals. Supper was served for selected guests afterwards and, accompanied by songs and toasts, could last until 4 a.m. The Duke was always trying to improve the detail, managing to create a glittering, fantasy world for his guests, where family and fashionable could mingle at ease. These were not just social events but were also a forum for intel-

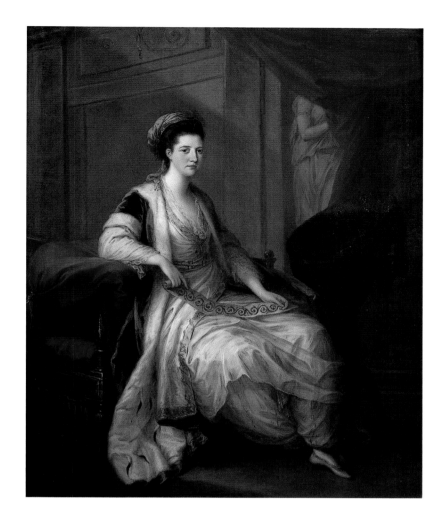

*Mary, Duchess of Richmond, in masquerade costume*, by Angelica Kauffman, 1775, oil on canvas, 75 × 62 cm / 29½ × 24½ in. In the first years of their marriage, the Duke used to refer to his Duchess in his personal letters as 'the lovely'.

ligent discussion about the plays and the individual performances. The Richmond House Theatre showed the 3rd Duke of Richmond at his best; working on a project, organising, directing, and achieving perfect results.

# 11 WEAPONS, WAR AND WOMEN

1790–1800

In politics the Duke always thought for himself. This was to some extent true of all Whig politicians, but he went his own way more than most. While many people overcame their initial doubts about the young George III, the Duke of Richmond continued to regard him as a threat to British constitutional monarchy. After he ceased to be a secretary of state in 1766, he was the main Opposition speaker in the House of Lords, so vociferous that the Duchess complained that he returned home hoarse. In turn the Duke was rebuffed by the King. As a local grandee the Duke was obliged to attend a royal visit to Portsmouth in 1772, but 'he was not invited to dine with the King as you may imagine,' reported Lady Mary Coke. She continued sniffily, 'I hope he [the Duke] will on every occasion receive marks of his displeasure which he well deserves.'[1]

## 'THE RADICAL DUKE'

The Duke was always a promoter of liberty, consistently defending what he saw as natural rights against challenges, whether it was for Americans, Irish, Catholics or voters. Although he was in favour of the American colonies keeping some kind of a link with the British Crown, once he saw the situation escalating into war he supported their independence, in opposition to the King. In the mid-1770s he 'sailed in a yacht through the fleet when the King was there, with American colours at his mast-head.'[2] The British fleet was anchored off Portsmouth to give a show of strength: the Duke was defiant indeed. An image of this is shown

in a contemporary painting of the royal visit.[3] Not only did the Duke feel that the Americans had a national character of their own, but also he especially disliked the violence that was being inflicted overseas, and he dreaded the entry of the French into the war.

An unfortunate incident in the House of Lords in 1778 added to the view of the Duke of Richmond as a dissident. The contretemps occurred when the elderly William Pitt, Earl of Chatham, had spoken for the Crown: 'Lord Chatham came down to the House today . . . a feeble, shocking sight, a wreck . . . yet he made a spirited short speech . . . A few minutes after he sat down, & whilst the D. of Richmond was speaking, he . . . fainted, fell back, & was carried out.'[4] Chatham later died. The Duke, who had been proposing the removal of British troops from America, was partly blamed. The scene was painted by J.S. Copley, with the Duke brandishing a document showing earlier, pro-American comments made by Chatham.[5] Although the old man had really been too frail to attend the House anyway, the Duke was subsequently even more notorious for his contrary opinions.

The Duke was a man of great moral principle, with a zeal for hard work, who longed to act on behalf of his country. In 1780 he tried to introduce his *Declaration of the Rights of Englishmen*, a great bill to reform Parliament, giving universal manhood suffrage to those over twenty-one. This did not receive very much attention. His next cause was Ireland, where, like his late brother-in-law the Duke of Leinster, he felt the English Protestant ascendancy in Dublin was too strong. His views were often ahead of his time, but he also wanted to preserve the subtleties of traditional links and connections, where they were valuable. His sister Sarah commented astutely that she could not understand his politics, and that 'he will try to be so very right that he will be very wrong.'[6]

Flint wall to the Hat Hill estate (now the home of the Cass Sculpture Foundation). Tradition says that these walls were built by French prisoners of war in the 1790s.

## MASTER OF THE ORDNANCE

When his great political ally the Marquis of Rockingham came to power for the second time in 1782, the Duke was appointed Master General of the Board of Ordnance. The post gave him responsibility for fortifications, military defence and small arms and munitions. It was the Duke's misfortune that four months later Rockingham died, leaving the Whig party in a state of internal discord. Initially the Duke continued in post under the Earl of Shelburne. However, when the ministry collapsed in favour of a coalition between the Tory Lord North, whom he despised, and his own nephew Charles James Fox, he resigned. In turn this uneasy coalition crumbled, with the Duke turning to support the Crown. He was then reappointed to the post of Master of the Ordnance in the ministry of the twenty-three-year-old William Pitt, feeling able to turn to the Tories because of Pitt's interest in parliamentary reform. The Duke accepted the new challenge as chief military adviser to the cabinet with enthusiasm. For once he had pleased the King, who was reported to have said that 'There was no man by whom he has been so much offended, and no-one to whom he was so much indebted, as the Duke of Richmond.'[7]

The Duke made many innovations as Master of the Ordnance, especially in the modernisation of small arms. In 1782 he began an investigation of the defences of Portsmouth and Plymouth. The project was enormously expensive, and the overall scheme was defeated in the House of Commons by one vote. However, the Duke made some improvements at both ports, including an innovative and beautifully designed star-shaped Fort Monckton at Gosport, which was also practical.[8] In 1785 he advised the Admiralty that a set of land signals should be established on projecting headlands to convey information about the approach of an enemy. Hitherto invasion warnings had simply been made by means of beacons. This far-sighted recommendation was slowly accepted, so that by 1795 most signalling stations between Kent and Portsmouth had been completed, with a new system of squares on boards. As Master of the Ordnance the Duke was briefly in correspondence with a young naval captain, Horatio Nelson.[9]

## THE ORDNANCE SURVEY

Always a scientist at heart, the Duke especially loved topography. He commissioned a map of Richmond in Yorkshire as early as 1755.[10] From 1758 the Duke was employing his own surveyor on the Goodwood estate, the Dutch engraver Thomas Yeakell, who had served under him in the army. He was later joined by the surveyor William Gardner, a Sussex man. These men were to become the first great British mapmakers. Before this, most local maps were extremely inaccurate, viewing an area very much from the focal point of the person who commissioned the map. Their 6-inch maps, embracing 72 square miles of the Goodwood estate, mostly dating from post 1765, are very beautiful and precious documents. For all the Whig magnates science was as much an aesthetic as art. In 1770 Yeakell and Gardner set out as part of their private work to survey the whole of Sussex at a scale of 2 inches to 1 mile, of which they initially completed only the southern part, four out of eight sheets.

The Duke was very interested in the work of General William Roy (1726–1790), who had been commissioned by George II to make a military map of the Highlands after the 1745 rebellion.[11] Roy based his maps on an accurate system of triangulation (by measuring one

side of a triangle and then finding the internal angle at all three points the length of the other two sides could be calculated), using high ground to gain lines of sight to the country around them. This method eventually led to the construction of the trig pillars which still exist on many hills and mountains today. Roy believed that the whole country should be mapped, presenting a paper on the subject to the Royal Society. In the event the Duke took charge of the project. Taking Yeakell and Gardner with him to the Ordnance, which was housed in the Tower of London, in 1785 he commissioned the first proper survey of Britain under the direction of William Roy. After Yeakell's death in 1787, Gardner became chief draftsman to the Ordnance. In 1787 the 'Duke of Richmond's Survey' was carried out by him in Guernsey, with that for Jersey published by various mapmakers in 1795, the islands being especially vulnerable to any threat from France. Gardner was joined at the Ordnance by another Sussex mapmaker, Thomas Gream, who assisted him in completing the map of Sussex. In 1795 it was published as a 1-inch map under the patronage of the Duke of Richmond, making Sussex the first county to be properly mapped.

The prime aim of the map-making was military defence. Work on other counties became increasingly urgent following the Revolution in France in 1789 and the subsequent very real fear of invasion. In July 1791 two officers were designated to take charge of the practical work of the trigonometrical survey of the whole country. The Duke authorised the purchase of a huge theodolite, 3 feet in diameter, which was purpose-built by Jesse Ramsden, to record the angular differences with a new and remarkable accuracy. From this time onwards the Duke named the map-making department the Ordnance Survey. The first Ordnance Survey 1-inch map, of Kent, was published in 1801. Mapping of England and Wales at the 1-inch scale took until 1870 to complete.

## Watershed: 1789

The rest of the Duke's time in government was not easy. At the time of the King's madness in 1788 he refused to support the Prince of Wales and the Duke of York over the Regency Bill. As a result, in May 1789 his nephew Charles Lennox was rashly involved in a duel with the Duke of York. The link with William Pitt should have been strengthened further in September that year when Charles Lennox married Lady Charlotte Gordon, whose mother, Jane, Duchess of Gordon, was the leading Tory hostess in London. Pitt's importance to the family was marked by the acquisition of his portrait, copied from Gainsborough's prime version by his nephew Gainsborough Dupont in 1790, for which the Duke paid one guinea.[12] A studio bust of Pitt by Nollekens dated 1808 was later acquired by the 4th Duke. However, when a new government leader was appointed in the Lords in 1790, the Duke felt displaced. He began to attend cabinet less and less.

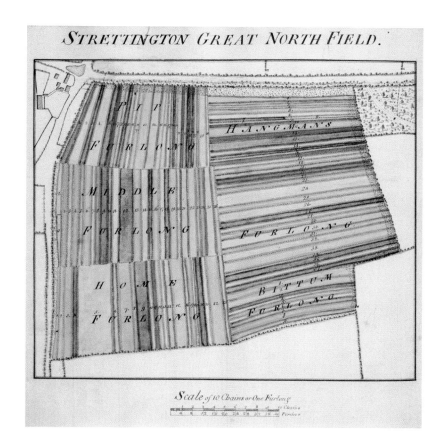

STRETTINGTON GREAT NORTH FIELD.

Scale of 10 Chains or One Furlong

The Revolution in France in 1789 was greeted with mixed opinions by the English aristocracy. The Whigs had not been supporters of the authoritarian Bourbon kings, and now rejoiced in a new era, which they saw as the political culmination of the French Enlightenment. They hoped that the same arrangement that the English had made in 1688 would follow, that of a monarch bound to his people by mutual contract. However, the Duke, now a Tory, was sceptical. In October that year Madame de Cambis left Paris for England, accompanying the Duchesse de Biron. This was Amélie de Boufflers, whose husband, the roguish Duc de Lauzun, had become the Duc de Biron. A relation reported on their escape: 'I ascribe it entirely to Mme de Cambis, who, no doubt, turned her head by frightening her, and was probably delighted to take advantage of the opportunity for going to see the Duke of Richmond on cheap terms.'[13] The Duchesse subsequently made several visits to England, showing that travel continued to be possible. However, Madame de Cambis settled on Richmond Green, where a large community of emigrés developed around her and her aunt, the Marquise de Boufflers. From 1793, presumably when her own finances dried up, the Duke paid her something over £200 per annum, amounts which she returned to him between 1802 and 1805 when his finances were dire. However, he was sufficiently good-natured toward her to note that if he should die before the debt was paid off, it should be cancelled.[14]

The Duke's nephew Lord Robert Fitzgerald held a post at the British Embassy in Paris in 1791, writing home to his uncle with a fascinating account of the position of the French royal family.[15] In late 1792 events in France took a more serious turn. The Duke took steps to have Lord Robert moved to Switzerland. The Duchesse de Biron fled Paris for the last time, without any attendants. She persuaded a seaman to let her go on his boat to Portsmouth, where she was found wandering confused on the beach. A message was sent up to the Duke, who took her in to Goodwood, summoning Madame de Cambis to take care of her 'cousin'. The following year the Duc de Biron was guillotined. When the French royal family tried to escape from Paris late in 1792, they may have been heading for the Château de Chimay, the family home of the Duke's mistress.

In January 1793 Louis XVI was executed. Revolutionary France declared war on Britain and Holland. Oral tradition says that during the long conflict with France, French prisoners of war worked at Goodwood, building huge flint walls on the estate. Surrounding an area known as Hat Hill, these walls are several miles in length. The prisoners are variously said to have come from Lewes gaol or from prison ships in Portsmouth harbour. Tradition also says that they were well housed in the stables, and far better fed than they would otherwise have been. No documents have yet been produced to substantiate these claims.

## THE RICHMOND HOUSE FIRE

Events at home continued to go badly. Between 8 and 9 a.m. on the morning of 21 December 1791 fire broke out at Richmond House. The disaster was reported by the *Public Advertiser*, *The Times*, *The Annual Register* and the *Gentleman's Magazine*, as well as in the diary of John Marsh, who must have read about it in the newspapers.[16] The Duke was taking breakfast in the library and writing a letter. A spark burst out from the fire in Miss Le Clerc's room on the second floor, igniting the bed hangings. The fire took hold quickly, engulfing the top of the house. The Duke, the Duchess and Henrietta left within minutes. The ladies took refuge in the house next door which, since the death the previous year of George, Duke of Montagu, had become the home of his son-in-law and daughter, the 3rd Duke and Duchess of Buccleuch. The Duke of Richmond returned to the blaze. The servants were too stunned to know what to do but, led by an unknown gentleman, some helpers ran up the great staircase. They rescued three huge looking-glasses out of four, while other furniture was lowered over the rails of the balcony. Although much was lost, all the furniture from the first floor was saved, as were books from the library, which, at the direction of the stranger, were thrown down on to mattresses. Two large cabinets containing the Duke's private papers were lowered down and rescued, as was the 'model of the new house intended to be built at Goodwood'. His 'valuable museum' was also saved, as were 'the valuable paintings' and the busts from the library.[17] All the papers were also retrieved from his ground-floor Ordnance office.

At one o'clock the whole roof of the house fell in. Floating fire engines on the river tried to drench the flames. The Duke of York brought along his own military river fire engine and about three hundred Coldstream Guardsmen. The Duke of Clarence (later William IV) arrived early and stayed all day, sometimes up to his knees in water to assist the fire engines. Colonel Lennox was there to watch his inheritance go up in flames, with his home next door partly on fire as well. Meanwhile, seeing his own favourite spaniel yapping at an upstairs window, the Duke offered a reward to anyone who could get him down. One of the watermen fastened two ladders together, climbed up, threw up the sash, and brought the dog down. The Duke paid him ten or eleven guineas (the reports differ), more than a year's salary, with two guineas for the man holding the ladder.

Richmond House was not insured against fire. Work to clear the ruins began on 2 January 1792. The Duke took up residence in Lord George's home next door, the far side of Charles Lennox's house. It took a few years for him to decide what to do. Already worried by debt, he did not have enough cash to commence an extension to Goodwood immediately. In the summer of 1792 there was a further setback for him when he was attacked in the House of Lords by Lord Lauderdale: a duel was just averted.[18] Luckily in that year the Duke was given the highest army rank of field marshal, and soon afterwards he embarked on a different distraction.

## THE ROYAL HORSE ARTILLERY

Given that the abiding interests of the Duke were now defence and horses, science and engineering, it was appropriate that he should lead the development of the first substantial horse-drawn gun in England. Until the introduction of mounted horses to transport guns, which was already established in Europe, the movement of guns had been very slow, with the gunners trudging along beside them. As Master General of the Ordnance, the Duke automatically had overall responsibility for artillery, and, war with France being imminent, he was enthusiastic about the proposals for the new guns. Two troops of horse artillery were created by royal warrant early in 1793. The Duke decided to take a personal interest, summoning the 'A' troop to Goodwood so that he could train it himself. The horses, traditionally chestnuts, were housed alongside his hunters in the magnificent stables, with the guns parked in front of the house.[19] From 1795 to 1806 he had another military interest as colonel of the Royal Horse Guards.

## THE END OF POLITICS

In January 1795 the Duke was removed from his position as Master General of the Ordnance by Pitt's reorganisation of the government. The process was excruciatingly slow and painful. Having heard that his non-attendance at cabinet had been criticised, he wrote first to Pitt in December 1794. Pitt responded with a very cool holding letter. The Duke sent a second letter, this time of acknowledgement, and then, ever impatient, a third begging for a reply, followed by a fourth in desperation. He was not used to being kept waiting. Finally Pitt announced very sharply in late January that the Duke could not continue in post as the other members of the cabinet would no longer work with him: 'From the sentiments of some of those Persons . . . I see that your resuming a seat in the Cabinet must prove equally unpleasant and embarrassing to Public Business.'[20] He gave no clear reason for the dismissal, but criticised the Duke for failing to maintain communications with him.

The Duke was greatly offended, returning to the subject years later to discuss how badly he had been treated. He was received graciously by the King and was allowed to remain active as a general, commanding the southern district. In 1796 he busied himself with preparations for a 'Grand Review' of the troops at Brighton, in the presence of the Prince of Wales, who gave a dinner at the Royal Pavilion afterwards.[21] Despite declaring in 1797 that 'when a man has passed his 60th year it is time for him to retire and live in the country as a private gentleman . . .',[22] the Duke was desperate to be of use in such difficult times. He remained deeply hurt by his premature retirement from government at the age of sixty, and in 1799 wrote a pamphlet on national defence.

## Henrietta Le Clerc

The Duke's 'adopted' daughter was taken into society by the Duke and Duchess in London, where at Richmond House in 1783 a trio of lively girls were 'all playing upon the pianoforte, singing and dancing, and making such a noise'.[23] By 1787 more and more bills were being paid for Henrietta, for lessons in singing, dancing and Italian, gloves, shoes and hats, and a piano.[24] This was at the time when the Richmond House Theatre was in full swing.

At the time of the fire at Richmond House, Henrietta was described first as a 'companion to Her Grace', but this was upgraded quite definitively the next day to 'a lady of fashion and received in the first circles'.[25] When the Duke was dismissed from the cabinet in 1795, he asked the Duchess to tell Henriette, as he himself always called her, what had happened. The next day he wrote again from Goodwood to say that 'I should like to have Henriette here for this week . . . for I confess I do want some of my females just now . . .'[26] At about the time that she was painted by Romney, a bust of Henrietta was sculpted by Nollekens. Early in 1796 the diarist Joseph Farington reported: 'Nollekens also shewed me his Bust of Miss Le Clerc, natural daugr. of the Duke of Richmond. She is abt. 20 years old, is tall & handsome. She lives at the Dukes, & the Duchess is very fond of her. She has been introduced at Court. The Duke comes with her sometimes to Nollekens & seems very fond of her.'[27] Sadly, according to Farington (who also openly referred to her as the

*Henriette Le Clerc*, by George Romney, 1796 (the background completed in 1801 by Sir Martin Archer Shee), oil on canvas, 125 × 100 cm / 49¼ × 39¼ in.

Duke's natural daughter on another occasion), she started to go slightly deaf at the age of only twenty-three.[28]

Henrietta's beautiful and romantic portrait by Romney hung on the main staircase at Goodwood.[29] Colonel Lennox's fourth son, William Pitt Lennox, remembered her as a constant visitor at his parents' home at Stoke. It is not inconceivable that she used to go there in secrecy to meet her mother. She grew into a great hunting lady, of whom the children were in awe: 'Tall, thin, muscular, and endowed with a masculine mind, this lady never allowed cold or wet to interfere with her favourite pursuit . . .'[30] Unfortunately, her haughty demeanour and hot temper made her unpopular locally. In 1800 a property was bought in her name at West Wittering.

## Death of the Duchess

Henrietta was also often at Goodwood with the ailing Duchess, playing music after supper and behaving as a dutiful step-daughter, although she was not ever openly admitted by the family as being a blood relation. The Duchess's health was declining from about 1793. Apart from the military activity, Goodwood in these years seems to have been quiet. At some stage the Duke had his father's paintings of *The Tombs of the British Worthies* removed from the old dining room to the main staircase.[31] Outside, the estate buildings were not always in perfect order. Visiting in 1795, Anne Rushout described how the pens in the pheasantry had gone to ruin. Up the hill, Carné's Seat was deteriorating and, by 1802, Marsh saw it as 'a small parlour, with a saloon over it', as if the downstairs room were now the one to be visited.[32] By 1822 the upper saloon was in disrepair.

After his dismissal from the Ordnance, the Duke stayed at Goodwood all the time in order to be near to his wife, devoting himself totally to her until her death on 7 November 1796. Walpole was greatly saddened: 'I had loved [her] most affectionately from the first moment I knew her, when she was but five years old; her sweet temper and unalterable good nature had made her retain a friendship for and confidence in me that was more steady than I ever found in any other person to whom I have been the most attracted. It is a heavy blow.'[33] The *Gentleman's Magazine* for 1796 paid a public tribute: 'a woman whom neither titles could dazzle nor pains depress; who bore her honours so modestly upon her, that, while her dignity enforced respect, her gentleness inspired love.'[34]

## The Gothick Dairy

During the later decades of the eighteenth century, or the first few years of the nineteenth, a romantic dairy in the picturesque style of the Gothic revival was built at Goodwood, facing the main axis from the house to the Kennels. Given the close family relationship with Horace Walpole (who died in 1797), it is likely that this was built under the influence of his enthusiasm for the Gothic. Originally it had stained glass and coats of arms of the main ancestral families. An L-shaped range of service buildings adjacent was also given a romantic battlemented flint façade, facing away from the private gardens. A charming little square Gothick cottage, known as Huntsman's Cottage, was added to the scheme. These 'two sides of a square' appear on maps from *c*.1780 and were seen by John Marsh in 1802, when he described them as being 'workshops for all sorts of artificers, the duke having all his repairs and alterations made under his own eye'.[35] However, he did not mention the Gothick element, leaving it unclear whether or not this had already been applied. The laundry was also in this area.

## Lady Elizabeth Foster

Soon after the death of the Duchess, the Duke began an affair with Lady Elizabeth Foster. She was notorious for her long relationship with the Duke of Devonshire, by whom she had borne three children, while also being the intimate friend of his duchess, Georgiana. Bess, as she was always called, had visited Goodwood while Mary, Duchess of Richmond, was still alive, no doubt a sympathetic friend but also possibly a predator on the soon-to-be bereaved Duke. Her father, the fanatical builder-collector the Earl Bishop of Bristol, wrote to his daughter twice from Naples early in 1796 begging her to send him a plan of the proposed new building works at Goodwood, 'of that model of a house you admired so much and prefer to mine'.[36]

Lady Elizabeth decided that she would like to marry the Duke of Richmond. This caused consternation even in her own group. Georgiana's sister Harriet, Lady Bessborough, wrote of her 'great anxiety concerning Bess if she marries the D. of Richmond', though she was relieved that 'Nothing is settled.' She continued: 'It seems quite a separation from us all, and changing the habits of fifteen years' standing is always a serious thing, especially at our age . . .'[37] The 'habits' were presumably the affair with Devonshire. However, Bess was prevented from any marriage by two forceful ladies. Lady Charlotte, the wife of the Duke's heir Colonel Charles Lennox, wanted to make sure that no sudden late heir would prevent her husband becoming a duke, and Henrietta Le Clerc did not want to be displaced in her father's affections. In 1798 Louisa Conolly saw Bess at Goodwood, but the affair ended early that year. Elizabeth returned to her former lover, eventually becoming his second duchess. She was commemorated at Goodwood by Anne Seymour Damer's bust of her, a copy of that by Joseph Nollekens.[38]

## Lord Edward Fitzgerald

In 1798 the entire Lennox family was devastated by the death of Emily's son, Lord Edward Fitzgerald. He had been a particularly favourite nephew, who in 1786 had spent some months at Goodwood and for whom the Duke had tried hard to find a good position. Lord Edward was a 'patriot' who believed in a separate, united Ireland and was engaged in planning an armed uprising. He was arrested on 19 May in Dublin on a charge of high treason. In the ensuing scuffle he was wounded by a bullet. He was first carried to Dublin Castle but the Lord Lieutenant had to yield to pressure for him to be removed to Newgate Gaol in Green Street, Dublin, where he died on 4 June. The rising took place as planned on 23 May, but without its leader had no hope of success. Murder and arson were inflicted by both sides.

The tragedy was heightened when Lord Edward was subsequently attainted for his part in the rebellion: this meant that his widow and daughters were prevented from inheriting his estates. They would thereby be cast into poverty. Although the Duke did not condone Lord Edward's treason, letters flew among the relatives to try to find the best way to prevent the attainder. In a devastating response to the Duke's considerable efforts, Lord Cornwallis wrote back to him describing Lord Edward as 'the

The Gothick Dairy. This may have been built in the 1790s, as a private part of the service courtyard, perhaps for the Duchess (Mary) during her long illness. It is also possible that it was slightly later, to the design of John Nash, who in 1807–8 worked on the Market House in Chichester, having already carried out unspecified work at Goodwood.

great author and contriver of all the Mischief and Treason which has already cost so many Lives, and which had nearly reduced to Ruin and Beggary the Wives and Families of every Man of Property, and deluged the whole Island with Blood . . .'[39]

That summer the grieving Emily and Ogilvie stayed first at Goodwood and then at Itchenor Park, where the Duke had created for them a tent room in the latest fashion. They distracted themselves by driving out in the cabriole, while the children spent their time riding, boating and racing. Before his capture, Lord Edward's wife Pamela had escaped from Ireland and came to live

at Goodwood. As the illegitimate daughter of Philippe Egalité, Duc d'Orléans, and probably of Madame de Genlis, she was an intelligent if unusual character. By now the Duke had earned an heroic reputation among his sisters for looking after whichever member of his family might be in distress.

The 1790s, although mostly spent at Goodwood, were not good years for the Duke, haunted as he was by war and debt, disaffected from the government and suffering from gout. He had been at his happiest when running substantial practical projects. Those opportunities had now gone. He liked power and aimed to do good on a wider stage, but now acted mostly for his many nephews and nieces. As the diarist Joseph Farington summarised 'He has been very kind to his relations, and retains his servants long, – is of an irritable temper but good natured at bottom.'[40] However, the low spirits of these years were lifted when he began a huge new building venture and even embarked on a new relationship.

# 12  PICTURESQUE VISION

## THE REGENCY HOUSE, 1800–1806

From the ashes of the Richmond House fire the new Goodwood House arose like a phoenix. In order to rehouse his art collection, most of which had been saved from the fire, the Duke began by 1800 to build a vast extension. Although nothing was pulled down, Goodwood effectively became a new house. In June 1799 John Marsh, the gentleman composer from Chichester, took a ride to Goodwood and 'look'd at 2 round towers the Duke was then building at the SW and SE corners of his house, one of which was to be an observatory.'[1] These flanked the existing south wing. Soon afterwards, work began on two new wings beyond. The use of flint provided work for poor itinerant labourers, who would collect and cut the stones for the builders.[2]

### THE OCTAGON QUESTION

It used to be believed that the 3rd Duke of Richmond had been intending to build a fully octagonal house. However, there is no contemporary evidence for this. When John Marsh visited again in September 1802, he found the house 'in an unfinished state, forming three sides of an octagonal figure, of which the middle one seemed to be the principal front . . . having a portico with a double tier of columns erected in the middle of it.' Although he found the circular towers 'singular', and concluded that the building was of 'so noble an appearance', Marsh could learn nothing of the intention: 'Of what figure the house is to be, whether the octagon is to be complete (which will, however, make an immense building) or whether no more is to appear from the park than what is now visible, we could not learn . . .'[3]

FACING PAGE   Goodwood House, by the Earl of March

RIGHT   Round tower at Goodwood, by the Earl of March

It is probable that the Duke did not know himself. James Wyatt, his architect, was experimenting with asymmetrical ground plans in other locations at the time. Views were very much part of the new notions of the picturesque, and those from the house to Boxgrove Priory and the Solent were particularly attractive. If he had meant to build more, he would have had time to start on another wing before his death four years later.

Although it was agreed that the house was incomplete, the first house librarian, Dennett Jacques, did not comment on any octagon in the first guidebook, even when he described 'a large Model in Wood for Goodwood House'.[4] When J.P. Neale published Country Seats in 1829, including an engraving of the newly enlarged house, he made no mention of any intention for an octagon to be built. In 1839 W.H. Mason, revising Jacques' guidebook, ignored any idea of an intended octagon. The first person to suggest that the house had been meant to be an octagon was John Kent, the racehorse trainer, in his Memoirs, published much later, in 1896. Kent was guessing. In fact, the only full octagonal structure ever created by the Duke was a barn, near to the pheasantry.[5]

It is more likely that the Duke was aiming to build a house that looked like an octagon from the front without going to all the expense. He was certainly worried about funds. Before he started to build in 1799, the Duke had debts of £90,000.[6] In that year he sold his coal tax dues back to the government for the enormous sum of £728,333, which was achieved by Act of Parliament. This gave him an annual income of £19,000 and enabled him to enlarge the house. However, he also had further debts and his outgoings were considerable. Knowing his financial position to be stretched, he wrote to his nephew and heir in the spring of 1806 begging him to be economical. When the Duke died later that year, he was in debt to the tune of £180,000. Completing even four or five sides of an octagon would have been a vast extravagance. In the eighteenth century, architects did not build the back of something if it was not necessary. The Duke had already practised this kind of economical architecture when he had just two façades of the stables built in the best knapped flint, with the third in looser flint and the fourth in brick. The new house was designed to be first seen from exactly the same angle as the stables. An element of artistic deception was normal. The items from Richmond House would fill the two new wings exactly. Had the Duke gone any further, he would have had vast empty wings and even larger debts.

Only one major room in the new extension had been completed when the Duke died. The front hall had been fitted with columns of Guernsey granite and was in an acceptable state. The first room to be completed internally was something completely novel.

## THE EGYPTIAN DINING ROOM

The Duke had inherited an interest in ancient Egypt from his father. From the sale of the goods of Edward Harley, Earl of Oxford, in 1740 the 2nd Duke had acquired various statuettes, including those of Isis and Osiris. He had also commissioned two magnificent sphinxes to flank Carné's Seat (see page 55).

In the first part of the first wing to be added, the Duke created his Egyptian Dining Room. Egypt was an exciting new source of decoration following Napoleon's recent campaign on the Nile. The French fleet had been spectacularly defeated by the English at the Battle of Aboukir Bay in 1798, but Napoleon hung on by land. By the time he left Egypt his scholars had made drawings of Egyptian temples and decorations. These were published in two huge volumes by the French artist and archaeologist Vivant Denon (1747–1825) as Planches du Voyage dans la Basse at la Haute Egypte pendant les Campagnes de Bonaparte, first printed in French in 1802. The room was started soon afterwards. The sum of £300 was paid at midsummer 1804 for the vast expanse of sienna scagliola created by Joseph Allcott.

In looking to Egypt the Duke was probably simply looking for a new form of classical decoration. Details of the room are known only from Dennett Jacques' guidebook of 1822, written less than twenty years after it was created.[7] Jacques suggested that the scheme had particularly used the temple discovered by Denon at 'Tintyra' or Dendyra, but this in fact was a generic name that tended to be given from afar to most of the new temples.

Jacques described how 'The walls are of scagliola, resembling a rich polished sienna marble, with a cornice and skirting of grey and white marble, adorned with classical ornaments in bronze;…' These 'ornaments' were perhaps four vast gilt bronze trophies of Egyptian objects which, from the dark shadows on the scagliola, seem to have been on the walls. To allow for the possibility that there were other bronze ornaments, and for the sake of added strength, a new cornice was created in the recent restoration, based on a design newly selected from Denon's work. It was bronzed and gilded. The lower band, the 'grey and white' frieze, was re-created according to surviving pieces, and was left plain.

Jacques went on to describe the far end of the room: 'at the upper end is a large looking-glass, nine feet by five, inserted in a fascia of grey marble, before which, on a pedestal, stands a vase of Egyptian porphyr; and on each side are small tables of choice granite.' The tables may be a pair of granite ones supplied earlier, by John Devall in 1781, which never seemed to be part of the more Napoleonic style of the room.[8] Jacques further described 'girandole figures of Isis and Osiris in bronze and gold' (these were probably made up from the existing statuettes). The original floor had oak marquetry, which he described as being, with the drapery and the rest of the furniture, 'truly unique'.

The furniture is typical of its period, mahogany with inset ebony, with scaly bronze crocodiles on the chair backs and monopodia on the side tables. The only possible influence is the work of Thomas Hope, who was creating an Egyptian interior for his home at Duchess Street, London, which he had purchased in 1799. His Egyptianising furniture was completed by May 1802,

ABOVE The Egyptian Dining Room. The room was restored for the Earl and Countess of March in 1998, to designs by Christopher Smallwood with furnishings by Lady Victoria Waymouth.

RIGHT Detail of page from *Planches du Voyage dans la Basse at la Haute Egypte pendant les Campagnes de Bonaparte*, first printed in French in 1802 by Vivant Denon. The source of the original bronze mounts for the chimneypiece are shown: 'two birds with extended wings . . . two birds with fixed wings with monsters' heads'.

when he held a party there. Possibly James Wyatt, who was not close to Hope, somehow managed to get a look at this house and to design some furniture himself.[9] On the original chimneypiece, now copied as far as possible, birds and beasts from Denon's engravings were copied in bronze by Benjamin Vulliamy and his son.[10] The gilded pelmets boast snakes about to strike. One pair of original door plates survives, complete with escutcheons and door

handles, which provided a template for the recent restoration. The lion's head on the door handle is picked up on the edge of the dishlight.

The Duke's Egyptian Dining Room (re-created in 1998) is extraordinarily sepulchral, although the sienna scagliola prevents it from being dark. It is like a tomb in sandy-coloured rock. Illuminated at dusk or by night by candles set in the spectacular candelabra by Rundell and Bridge which were made for the room, it glitters and gleams. Dramatic orchids or huge palms are used to enhance the sense of the colourful and exotic.

ABOVE, LEFT: Gilded pelmet with snakes, Egyptian Dining Room. The cornice, derived from an engraving by Denon, was introduced in the recent restoration.

ABOVE, RIGHT Door furniture, Egyptian Dining Room, with original Regency woodgraining on the doors and on the bamboo motifs.

LEFT Candelabra made by Rundell and Bridge, the royal goldsmiths, for the Egyptian Dining Room. The stems are formed of triads of formalised Egyptian figures or telemones holding tablets bearing hieroglyphics, mounted upon bases supported by winged sphinxes. These sit on separate table bases, each bearing the Richmond coat of arms. They may have been designed by Jean-Jacques Boileau, an émigré French designer who was much influenced by one of the earliest pattern books of Egyptian images, *Diverse maniere do adornare i cammini*, published by the great Roman antiquary Giambattista Piranesi in 1769. There were four in this set; another pair was made for the Marquis Wellesley, and the Prince Regent had a set of four very similar candelabra in his Carlton House service.

FACING PAGE Dining table, the Egyptian Dining Room, with Rundell and Bridge candelabra. Beyond, the vast expanse of scagliola, with grey facings also in *scagliola*.

ABOVE   The Small Library. Originally an ante-chamber to the 2nd Duke's 'Great Room' (later the Large Library), this room was also made into a library, but in the Regency period, with the cast-iron gallery added to provide access to high shelves.

FACING PAGE   Map of the original triangular racecourse.

In the older part of the house, the Duke also fitted out a new but smaller library at this date, with a corner stairway and gallery. All the domestic offices continued to be in the basement: as at Uppark, the kitchen was still separate, linked to the house by a subterranean passage.

## RACING AT GOODWOOD

Meanwhile the Duke also had a new outdoor project. For some years the officers of the Sussex Militia had held a race meeting in the grounds of Petworth Park. Legend suggests that when George, 3rd Earl of Egremont, changed his mind about allowing them to do so, the officers turned in 1800 to their Colonel, the 3rd Duke of Richmond. He invited them to race on the Goodwood estate that spring, on the high narrow ridge called the Harroway. In conjunction with members of his own hunt, he then built a triangular course for a private meeting to be held in April 1801. The

*Sporting Magazine* reported that 'the new Racecourse on the Harroway near Goodwood' was ready.[11] John Marsh of Chichester gave a different reason for the introduction of the racecourse: 'On Monday 27th comenc'd some races at the back of the plantation at Goodwood where the Duke had to gratify Miss LeClerk (as 'twas thought) made a course & given a £50 prize with a sweepstake.'[12]

The event was very much a military affair: instead of the conventional saddling bell, a bugler announced the start of the races. Large tents were pitched to accommodate guests, in each of which 'collations, consisting of everything dainty in season, were profusely served up.'[13] Even water ices were on offer, made possible by the ice house near the main house. The weather was very hot. On the first of the three days the race was run at noon, 'by gent'n who mostly rode their own horses . . .'[14] Unfortunately the Duke was suffering from gout throughout, and had to keep to his tent. The Prince of Wales stayed at Uppark for the event but did not in the end attend. On the first evening many fashionable patrons attended the Chichester Theatre in South Street, and on the second day there was a ball in the Assembly Rooms.

This private meeting was so successful that it was decided to hold a public race meeting the following year. To this end in the summer of 1801 the Duke began to have a wooden thatched stand constructed for his guests to watch the racing the following April. The 1802 meeting, which was held over three days, was the first to which the public were admitted. A head-to-head race was the highlight of the meeting: Rebel, owned by the Prince of Wales, beat Cedar, owned by the Duke, for 100 guineas. In the Duke's stand, various local luminaries looked on, including the Earl of Chichester and Lord Egremont. The week after the event, a local newspaper ran a report of the meeting, that reflected the widespread enthusiasm: 'To the efforts of equestrian skill is to be added the princely and almost unprecedented munificence of the noble founder of the Goodwood Races, in providing the newly erected stand with a collation . . . the access was as easy as the reception was elegant and hospitable.'[15]

## MRS BENNETT

Towards the end of his life the Duke had an attractive young housekeeper. In 1797 a lifetime annuity of £50 was granted to Mrs Mary Blesard, aged twenty-nine, which was perhaps generous for her work as a housekeeper.[16] In May 1802 the Duke bought for her the smart classical house that the pioneering surgeon Dr John Hunter FRS (1728–1793) had built at Earls Court, complete with coach house and stables.[17] Hunter, brother of the Duke's physician friend Dr William Hunter, had been developing his forty-five-acre estate there since the 1760s. Around the house, the saloon of which was decorated with scenes of Cupid and Psyche, he created a menagerie that included leopards, crocodiles, ostriches and opossums, many of which he dissected for experiments. The

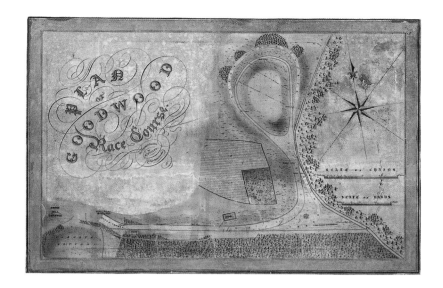

property was sold after his death, with the intention being to keep up the menagerie. It passed through two further owners until the Duke bought it for £4,000 in 1802, transferring it to Mary Blesard, who contributed £1,000 to the purchase.[18] Earls Court was a comfortable country ride of two and a half miles from Whitehall.

Mrs Bennett, as she became known, bore the Duke three daughters, Caroline (b.1804/5), Elizabeth (b.1806) and Mary (b.1807). She made the Duke's declining years very happy. In September 1806 Sarah commented that the Duke was enjoying himself like a man of twenty-one. He was in fact seventy-one. Of the three daughters, Elizabeth probably died young, while Caroline and Mary were later received into the household of Sarah's second son, George Napier, who was a widower. He was therefore secretly their elder cousin. His sister Emily also lived with them. The informal acceptance of the Duke's illegitimate offspring meant that they were received into polite society, and were also accepted by Lennoxes, Conollys and Fitzgeralds. Caroline Bennett subsequently married George Napier's youngest brother, Henry.[19]

## FINAL YEARS

The Duke still maintained his interest in politics. He was furious to hear that his heir, Charles Lennox, had voted for Pitt in 1804, complaining angrily that his nephew owed not only his seat but everything he had to him, 'an Uncle who has adopted you as his child, bred you up . . .'[20] In a diatribe against his former political ally, he revealed the continuing hurt about his own sacking eight years earlier. The Duke was particularly annoyed that no-one would take any notice of a new plan that he had devised, published in 1804 as *Thoughts on the National Defence*. His career was clearly finished in 1805, when Pitt rejected some of his new ideas for recruiting. The fear of invasion passed when Napoleon dispersed his camp at Boulogne, while Nelson defeated the French

The Egyptian Dining Room, with its vast expanse of *scagliola*, a prime example of the 3rd Duke's originality. The chimneypiece was re-made according to its original description, with bronzes derived from Denon's engravings.

and Spanish fleets at Trafalgar. Lord George died in March of that year, and Pitt himself early in 1806. Charles James Fox predeceased his uncle that September, just after succeeding in a bill to abolish slavery. Surprisingly, the Duke did not support this venture, seeing it as too idealistic.

Despite being crippled by gout, the seventy-year-old Duke was hunting into the last year of his life. That summer, now seventy-one, he was still trying to control Charles Lennox, who had turned forty: 'in you centers [*sic*] my future Pride for the Family,' he told his heir.[21] He felt that with such a large family to support, Lennox should drink and socialise less, giving an allowance to his nephew of only £1,000 a year.[22] In his last and lonely months, the irritable old Duke admitted to feeling 'low, and uncomfortable, and neglected, perhaps sowered by perpetual successes of painful disorders'.[23]

All the Duke's happiness was now derived from the women in his life, with Henrietta and Sarah caring for him at Goodwood,

and Mrs Bennett discreetly in London. His last words were to Lady Holland, the wife of his great-nephew Henry, 3rd Baron Holland: 'It don't signify, my dearest, dearest Liz.' Charles, 3rd Duke of Richmond, Lennox and Aubigny died on 27 December 1806. He was buried on Monday 5 January in Chichester Cathedral, 'in as plain a manner (by his own design) as any private gentleman'.[24]

## Setting it Right: the 3rd Duke's Will

The Duke's will was thoughtful and generous throughout. Henrietta Le Clerc received West Lavant House and Park, as well as other property and farms in neighbouring parishes. The Duke intended his own child to have authority and status. She also received a house in Parliament Street, Westminster, as well as many personal items, not least horses and dogs, and silver cutlery inscribed with her initials, ALC, for Anne Le Clerc, the name by which she had been christened.[25] She was also bequeathed all his papers. In 1808, at the age of thirty-five, Henrietta was married to Colonel John Dorrien (1758–1825) at St James's, Piccadilly, by the

Revd. John Buckner, Bishop of Chichester. The witnesses were in reality her blood cousins, from the families of Lennox, Fox and Conolly. However, the Duke of Beaufort commented of the newly-weds, 'I do not admire either of their tastes.'[26] When their son Charles was born at Lavant in 1809, the 4th Duke was his godfather. Dorrien later became a general. In the 1830s Charles Dorrien would buy from the 5th Duke Adsdean House, near Armsworth, some seven miles to the west of the estate, which the 3rd Duke had bought for £4,000 in 1800.

When he made his last will, dated 4 December 1806, the Duke allowed for the fact that Mrs Bennett was expecting a child at his death, leaving in trust pieces of land at Funtington and Westbourne for 'such first born Son as Mrs Mary Blesard now called Bennett my servant may be delivered of before my decease or within ten months after'. Mrs Bennett was given a very large additional annuity of £450. He also left her the farm at Earls Court.[27] In the event the child was a daughter. After the Duke's death, Mrs Bennett sold the farm. Later, her daughter Mary, respectably married to Colonel William Light, spent some time sailing around the Mediterranean with her husband, in a very large yacht. They subsequently parted, after which Light became the first Surveyor General of Australia.

## THE 3RD DUKE AS COLLECTOR

The 3rd Duke of Richmond was not a man who was obsessed by art, nor was he a particularly scholarly collector, but he was full of ideas. He had applied his mind in particular to sculpture and architecture and was knowledgeable enough to select only the most informed people to advise him. The prime characteristic of his patronage was a determination to have only the best and most interesting of everything. Often this meant being innovative, not for the sake of it, but because he was a true figure of the Enlightenment. Living at a time of conspicuous consumption, when so much was on offer, he instinctively saw that new discoveries in the arts could take one back to a better view of the Antique than had previously been offered, and that artists who were properly trained would provide the best results. He applauded new ideas, whether it was to have English birds on French china, small antique figures on his cupboards and ceiling, or a dining room based on Egypt; but all these innovations were executed within an existing tradition.

The 3rd Duke was certainly a man who thought for himself, but his building and collecting were never quirky, nor were they effete, nor designed to draw attention to himself. They did not particularly aim to trumpet his status, because that was already assured, and because he was by nature economical; but he naturally wanted his homes to represent who he was. Intuitively, the 3rd Duke of Richmond assembled some of the most handsome buildings, interiors, paintings, furniture, porcelain and books of his day. With his natural good taste, he did not bother to boast about them. The subjects that had impressed him on his Grand Tour remained. Military matters and public service were always uppermost in his mind.

# 13 THE EXPATRIATE

## CHARLES, 4TH DUKE OF RICHMOND, 1764–1819

LEFT *Charles Lennox, later 4th Duke of Richmond, playing cricket as a boy*, said to have been painted by his nurse, oil on panel, 25 × 20 cm / 10 × 8 in. The Duke loved cricket, playing with his regiment in Edinburgh and later in Canada. He supported the move of the MCC to Lord's.

FACING PAGE Detail of *The Duchess of Richmond's Ball*, by Robert Hillingford, 1870s, oil on canvas, 44 × 60 cm / 17½ × 23½ in.

nearest farmyard. As the nephew of the 3rd Duke, Charles Lennox grew up at his father's home at Stoke (now West Stoke), about three miles to the west of Goodwood. His mother was Lady Louisa Kerr, daughter of the 4th Marquis of Lothian. Three sisters were subsequently born, who were given the family names of Maria (or Mary), Emilia and Georgina. Charles's father, Lord George Lennox, was an active military man who at the time of his son's birth was aged twenty-seven and a colonel; he ended up as a full general. Showing the closeness of the family, in 1784 Charles Lennox was given a post as secretary to his uncle as Master of the Ordnance (1784–95). In 1785, when he was twenty-one, he followed his father into the army, joining the Coldstream Guards.

Lennox was a keen sportsman. He especially loved cricket, the game promoted by his grandfather the 2nd Duke, and in the best Goodwood tradition he played it from childhood. A capable batsman, he was a member of the White Conduit Cricket Club in the 1780s, and was a prime mover in the foundation of the Marylebone Cricket Club in 1787. When the members became dissatisfied with their current pitch, Lennox and George Finch, 9th Earl of Winchilsea, approached the publican Thomas Lord, requesting that he seek a more suitable site. Lord found a new ground on the Portman estate and the MCC began playing there in May 1787. Cricket was to prove both enjoyable and useful in Lennox's career. He was also a keen tennis player and was prominent in horse-racing circles.

Charles, 4th Duke of Richmond, was born in a barn (and spent his last hours in one). His parents, Lord and Lady George Lennox were on a fishing trip in Scotland when, on 9 September 1764, Louisa went into labour. She could be carried no further than the

## THE DUEL

Charles Lennox has always had a reputation as something of a rash young man because in 1789 he was involved in two duels. The more important and damaging one was with Prince Frederick Augustus, Duke of York, the King's second son, who, he felt, had impugned his honour. Unfortunately the Duke was the Colonel of the Coldstream Guards, Lennox's own regiment. Lennox was at the time technically a mere captain, but bearing the 'acting' rank of lieutenant colonel. The duel took place on Wimbledon Common on 26 May 1789. Lennox's bullet grazed the Duke's hair, but the Duke did not fire at all.[1]

A pamphlet about the royal duel was published by a Guards officer at the time, taking Lennox's side.[2] It stated how the original incident had happened, that the Duke of York had declared that an insulting comment had been made at a masquerade at D'Aubigny's Club, of which the masked recipient was 'believed to be' Lennox. The Duke of York had reportedly provoked a confrontation by saying that no gentleman should submit to such an insult. According to a much later version by Lennox's son, he also said that 'The Lennoxes don't fight.'[3] His comments were reported to Lennox, who felt that he had to act. At the next parade of the regiment in St James's Park he left his place to approach his commanding officer. He asked the Duke to withdraw the imputation on his character. Embarrassed, the Duke of York ordered him back to his post. Afterwards he called Lennox in and said that he would discuss the matter not as a prince but 'as a private gentleman'.[4]

This put Lennox in a great dilemma, in an age when honour and good reputation were paramount. There was an exchange of letters, with Lennox asking the Duke to name his offender, and the Duke replying that he had heard the remark, but not saying any more. Lennox then wrote a circular letter to the club members to ask if the insult had been overheard: this second course of action was even announced in the *Gentleman's Magazine*.[5] The letters of response from the members contained comments that were quizzical, uninterested, unsympathetic and downright scornful.[6] Most felt that Lennox should have left well alone. In a state of anxiety and overreaction Lennox then asked the Duke to 'clear me from any imputation against my Character', begging for an immediate reply.[7] When he had heard nothing by the next day, he decided that he had to assume that the royal Duke had himself delivered the insult. Writing that he felt he had done everything he could to avoid a personal contest, Lennox reluctantly asked the Duke of York to 'appoint the Time and Place . . .'[8]

Following the duel, officers of the Coldstream Guards met to discuss whether Lennox had behaved 'as became a Gentleman and an Officer': they concluded that he had acted 'with courage . . . but not with judgement',[9] though the officer who wrote the pamphlet challenged this view.[10] Certainly relations between the royal family and the Richmonds were not improved by the affair. Some ten days after the duel, on 4 June, the Prince of Wales deliberately snubbed Colonel Lennox at a Court Ball held for the King's birthday. The

duel was given added poignancy by the fact that Frederick, Duke of York had previously favoured Charles Lennox as a friend.[11] However, the Duke of York behaved henceforth with magnanimity. One year later he enquired about Lennox when he was ill; two years later he gave the family practical support at the time of the Richmond House fire, even protecting Lennox's own home next door. On 3 July 1789 Lennox fought another duel, this time against Theophilus Swift, who had published a pamphlet reflecting on his character. Swift was hit in the body but the wound was not fatal.

## SCOTLAND, MARRIAGE AND THE GORDONS

Lennox thought it prudent to leave London, 'exchanging' his captaincy in the Coldstream Guards to become Lieutenant Colonel of the 35th Foot. After the second duel he joined his new regiment, stationed in Edinburgh. The duels had in many ways enhanced his reputation: to welcome him, the regiment had Edinburgh Castle illuminated in his honour and he was presented with the freedom of the city. He was very popular with his regiment, and the more so when he began to play cricket with the ordinary soldiers, especially as he gave them drink money at each match.

Charles Lennox already knew Lady Charlotte Gordon from London society. After a mere seven weeks in Scotland, on 9 September, he married her, at her family home at Gordon Castle, north of Aberdeen. Contemporary cartoonists had a field day. They suggest that the Duchess of Gordon, anxious to marry her daughter to a future duke, rushed the pair to the altar. Lennox was known to be 'the heir to high dignities and a princely fortune . . .'[12] He had been in the house for five days when they were married, at no notice, in the Duchess's dressing room, with two maids as witnesses. No one in the house was told for two more days.[13] The match was typical of Jane, Duchess of Gordon: with five daughters she was eager to marry them all as well as possible. Lennox lost two wagers of 100 guineas each against his marrying before his friends, one to Lord Charles Fitzroy, son of the Duke of Grafton, and one to Frederick, Duke of York, who was diplomatic in making his prize over to Fitzroy. Sharpened by his recent dealings, the bridegroom paid up rapidly.[14]

Lady Charlotte Gordon (1768–1842) had been brought up at Gordon Castle. Life in the Highlands was remote from fashionable society, so to enhance her prospects her mother took her to Edinburgh for the winter social seasons, and thereafter to London. There the Duchess of Gordon was the leading Tory hostess, the rival to Georgiana, Duchess of Devonshire, for the Whigs. During one of Charlotte's London seasons, the Duchess even tried, with no success, to marry her to the youthful prime minister, William Pitt. Like her mother, Charlotte loved both to give and to attend parties: she was often the first to arrive and the last to leave. However, she did not always display her mother's easy style and charm. She was indicted for being bossy, unpredictable and haughty: 'Genl Lenox (now Duke of Richmond) . . . is a most

ABOVE *Charles, 4th Duke of Richmond, Lennox and Aubigny*, after John Hoppner, oil on canvas, 75 × 62 cm / 29½ × 24½ in.

LEFT *Charlotte, Duchess of Richmond*, engraved after a miniature by Richard Cosway.

friendly man, perfectly free from pride, but the Duchess is of an opposite disposition being excessively proud and disdainful of persons of inferior rank.'[15] Nevertheless, she was extremely well organised and able. At the time of their marriage Colonel Lennox can have had absolutely no inkling that he was marrying a great heiress. Charlotte's fortunes would eventually save the Lennox family, but at the time she had two younger brothers, George, Marquis of Huntly, and Lord Alexander Gordon, the elder of whom would succeed as 5th Duke of Gordon.

Lennox had many duties in Sussex. He served four times as Tory MP for the county between 1790 and 1806, and in 1807 was High Steward of Chichester. Charles Lennox took his uncle's path of supporting the King against the Prince of Wales, and was therefore on the opposite side of the House of Commons to his first cousin, Charles James Fox. He became a warm personal friend of William Pitt, after whom he named his fourth son. As he

matured, Lennox's views became more extreme: unlike his uncle, he never welcomed change. He served with his regiment in the Leeward Islands, and at St Dominica in 1794. Despite the royal duel, he obtained the rank of full colonel in 1795 and was made an ADC to the King. He was promoted to major-general in 1798 and, in 1803, was made colonel of the 35th Foot: this was an appointment of great honour, a position rather than a rank. Even as a general, he had a certain modesty: 'The Duke is a social man, & in Company will sit to the last, but if He happens to visit a man who only drinks water He will join him in that, being perfectly accomodating [sic]. While in Camp, He lay in a small tent, wrapped a Cloak round Him & made a Saddle His pillow. Since He became *Duke* no change has taken place in him.'[16]

Meanwhile Lady Charlotte was busy bearing children: all fourteen, seven boys and seven girls, survived infancy. The young family lived at Molecomb, creating a tradition for future heirs.

There had been another family wedding in 1789 when Colonel Charles Lennox's younger sister Georgina married Henry, Lord Apsley, later 3rd Earl Bathurst (1762–1834). Together they built Apsley House, on the edge of Hyde Park, known as No. 1, London, and later owned by the Duke of Wellington. Lennox moved in the right circles and was ready for his inheritance, even if his uncle felt that he drank and socialised too much.

Following the death of his uncle on December 1806, Lennox became 4th Duke of Richmond, Lennox and Aubigny. Initially he moved in to the newly extended house. Knowing how popular the 'old Duke' had been in Sussex, he tried to carry on in the same manner. However, as a result of all the building works, the new Duke found himself saddled with debts. Fortunately for his bank balance, with the death of Pitt and the formation of a new government under the elderly Duke of Portland, the 4th Duke was offered the important post of Lord Lieutenant of Ireland. His brother-in-law Henry, Earl Bathurst, was partly responsible in acquiring the position for him, seeing it as a way out of financial difficulties. It was a big change to leave his homes in London and Sussex semi-permanently, and the Duke accepted with some reluctance: but it was necessary.

## IRELAND

The family arrived in Dublin in April 1807, succeeding John, 6th Duke of Bedford, whose wife, Georgina, was Charlotte's youngest sister. The Duke of Richmond met the talented new and young Chief Secretary for Ireland, Colonel Arthur Wellesley. Recently returned from India with a high military reputation, Wellesley was the third son of an Irish peer, the 1st Earl of Mornington. Because of the demands of the military campaigns against the French, Wellesley did not spend very much time in Dublin, leaving shortly to command the expedition at Copenhagen, before being summoned to Portugal the following year. He finally resigned his Irish post in 1809 to lead the campaign in the Spanish peninsula. Nevertheless in the six months out of the two-year post that he spent in Dublin, he became very close to the Duke and his family. He used to ride out every day with their daughter, Georgiana. He subsequently wrote to the Duchess over a period of many years, often using her as a sounding board, and always sending messages to individual children.

In Ireland the Duke and Duchess lived in style at the residence in Phoenix Park. The administration took place from Dublin Castle. The political situation had recently altered, with the Act of Union in 1800 moving the Parliament from Dublin to London. The Protestant Ascendancy was well established. After a quiet start, the administration became a busy one, with confrontation between Catholics and Protestants. Nevertheless the family found time to patronise the theatre, and the Duke went hunting and racing, pursuits which endeared him to Dublin society. They travelled much around the country, mixing with the gentry: the Duke was popular for his open, easy manner. They entertained frequently at their home in Phoenix Park where their household was regarded as a court, enlivened by the many antics of a young family. Gate lodges by the architect John Nash were added, and a large silver dinner service by Benjamin Smith and Paul Storr was delivered soon after their arrival.[17] The Duchess also had a handsome silver dressing table set. Later, she spent a fortune gambling at cards, an unfortunate weakness given her husband's precarious financial situation.

The Duke was himself a hard drinker and continued to be a risk-taker. He openly showed his affection for Augusta Everitt, Lady Edward Somerset: 'The D. of Richmond makes desperate love to the latter; she rides about with him every where and he speaks to no-one else. The Dss is, as she always is, very jealous and, as all people are when jealous, very cross.' When the Duchess received a tender note which had been intended for his mistress, Augusta irreverently declared that 'The Old Puss will burst with jealousy.'[18] To the Duchess's dismay, the Duke insisted that Augusta dine with them daily. The next year, 1809, he went with the Duchess and some of their daughters to the first night of a play, *The Country Girl*, in which the celebrated London actress Mrs Dora Jordan was performing. Greatly admiring her performance, the Duke sent a message that he would like to call on her alone at 12.30 that night. This could only mean one thing. Mrs Jordan, the much-loved and well-established mistress of HRH the Duke of Clarence, was very upset by the Lord Lieutenant's misunderstanding of her position, but later managed to laugh about it.[19]

Charlotte's mother, Jane, Duchess of Gordon, visited the family in Dublin in both 1809 and 1811. At her death in a London hotel in April 1812, Charlotte was at her side. The Duke was created Knight of the Garter that year, receiving the insignia at Dublin Castle. Meanwhile, in the family's absence, the tenants and tradesmen at Goodwood celebrated the coming of age of the Earl of March on 3 August with a *fête champêtre*. Later that year the Duke and Duchess suffered the loss of their third son, Henry, a midshipman in the Royal Navy. A lock of his hair is preserved in a gold locket at Goodwood.

## VISIT OF THE ALLIED SOVEREIGNS

The whole family returned from Ireland to London in 1813. The original Richmond House was in ruins after the fire, but they lived in the adjacent house in Whitehall, in which the Duke had been born and brought up (see page 137). They also returned to Goodwood, which was in a state of disrepair. In order to raise some cash the Duke decided to sell some pictures, prints and drawings through Christie's in Pall Mall. The sale took place on Saturday, 26 March 1814, realising £559 13s 6d.[20] This was a drop in the ocean of his debts, but must have been useful in making preparations for an exciting event that was to take place at Goodwood that summer.

The Front Hall, built 1800. The Duke may have discovered the orangey-pink local Cobo granite when he commissioned the map of Guernsey in 1787. It was shipped back to Goodwood by his sloop and made into columns that decorate the back of the hall.

In the spring of 1814 Napoleon was defeated and exiled to Elba. Europe breathed a sigh of relief. A preliminary peace settlement with France was made by the four great powers of Great Britain, Russia, Austria and Prussia at the Treaty of Paris on 30 May. They still needed to arrange the new boundaries of Europe between them, so it was arranged for heads of state to meet in London, prior to more public deliberations with leaders of all the smaller states later in the year at the Congress of Vienna.

On 6 June the Allied Sovereigns arrived for their visit to England, travelling to Portsmouth for the naval review on the 22nd. On Friday 25 June the Emperor of Russia and his sister the Grand Duchess of Oldenburgh came with their suite straight to Goodwood for breakfast, which must have been served in the Egyptian Dining Room. They expressed themselves 'highly delighted with the splendid hospitality with which they were received by their noble Host and Hostess as well as with the beauties of the place.'[21] They continued to Petworth to join the rest of the party, comprising the Prince Regent and the King of Prussia and his sons. A painting at Petworth commemorates this visit. No one could have ever imagined that the peace in Europe would be interrupted by Napoleon's escape from Elba the following year.

## The Move to Brussels

The Duke had now decided that, with the burden of thirteen children, he needed to go abroad to save money. He wrote to his friend the Hon. John Capel, who already lived in Brussels, to ask him about going there with all his family for a year, 'on an Economical Plan'.[22] The Duke set out with his two eldest daughters in late August. Meanwhile the Duchess organised the extremely complicated move from England for the rest of the family. In September they took up residence in rue de la Blanchisserie, a street named after a seventeenth-century laundry that had once existed there. They had 'a delightful House & Gardens in the Lower part of the Town', the house compensating for the unfashionable area.[23] The house itself had been built only about thirty-five years earlier by a coachbuilder. It was a grand three-storey residence approached over a courtyard and flanked by two barn-like wings which had been used for a coach-building business.

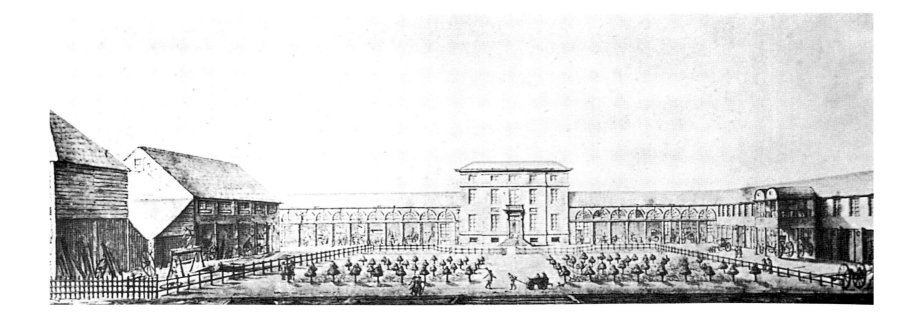

Above   The house in Brussels rented by the 4th Duke, 1778, engraving. The ball took place in the carriage house to the right. The house was entered from the far side, on the rue de la Blanchisserie, because of which name the Duke of Wellington used to refer to it as 'The Wash House'. The wings were demolished in 1827.

Below   The house in Brussels rented by the 4th Duke. The house was later encased by a hospital, all of which was demolished c.1976.

Facing Page   Marshal Prince Blücher, miniature, 7.5 cm × 6 cm / 3 × 2¼ in. The elderly and valiant Prussian General arrived with his army late in the afternoon at the Battle of Waterloo, saving the day for Wellington.

The family was growing up fast. The elder boys had been educated at Westminster and were already soldiers: Charles, Earl of March, now a captain in the 13th Light Dragoons, had served as Assistant Military Secretary and ADC to the Duke of Wellington between 1810 and 1814. He was wounded in the Peninsular War at the Battle of Orthez in February 1814, and still suffered from the effects: '[he] still has a ball in him from the effects of which he has not recovered, but faints at the least transition from heat to cold.'[24] In Brussels, he continued in light service befitting his noble rank, as an ADC to the young Hereditary Prince of Orange (son of the Sovereign Prince), who had spent most of his upbringing in England. March had his own small house within the grounds of the larger Richmond family one. The Duke's second son, Lieutenant Lord George Lennox, was in the 9th Light Dragoons and had been serving as an ADC to Wellington.

The teenage Lord William Pitt Lennox, born in 1799, their fourth (but third surviving) son, went as ADC to the Duke of Wellington for his embassy in Paris in August 1814. Paris that autumn was flooded with English visitors and he much enjoyed the privileged social life as ADC to such an eminent British ambassador as well as the hunting in the nearby countryside. In his memoirs he tells a story of how he inadvertently lamed Wellington's favourite hunter hacking back from Versailles to Paris that autumn. Lennox dreaded telling the General the bad news. To his amazement, Wellington was kind to him rather than furious.[25] The younger boys at home in Brussels were Frederick, aged thirteen, who had already been at Westminster for five years; Sussex, twelve, and Arthur, born just before his great-uncle's death in 1806, and now aged eight.

The seven daughters of the house led a more sheltered life. At the time of their arrival in Brussels in 1814, Lady Mary was aged twenty-three, Sarah was twenty-two, Georgiana twenty, Jane sixteen, Louisa eleven, Charlotte ten and Sophia five. With the

British left an army garrison in the former Austrian Netherlands, commanded by the young and inexperienced Hereditary Prince of Orange, who was a lieutenant general in the British Army. The Duke of Wellington was the Commander-in-Chief of the whole Anglo-Netherlands Army. Further arrangements had to be made at the Congress of Vienna in December 1814, under which the Sovereign Prince of Orange would become King of the Netherlands. Belgian people were therefore used to many recent changes of power and politics. The Duke of Wellington was attended in Vienna that winter by Lord William Lennox, as an ADC.

## Napoleon's Advance

On 28 February 1815 Napoleon escaped from imprisonment on the island of Elba. On his arrival in France his charisma was such that soldiers in the French army, sent out to intercept him, threw down their arms and declared for their former Emperor. On 19 March Paris fell before him. Appalled by the crisis, the four great armies of the Allies assembled on France's eastern borders, threatening to attack him, possibly in late June or early July. The Anglo-Netherlands army was in the north, with the Prussian army under Prince Blücher to its left. The Austrians were in the centre and the Russians were some distance away but advancing to join the coalition. Rumours and panic abounded in Brussels: some families fled to Antwerp. Other English expatriates moved from Paris up to Brussels. Showing courage and *sang froid*, the Richmonds stayed put.

Despite the tense political situation, the party-giving carried on. The Sovereign Prince of Orange was declared King of the Netherlands from the balcony of the Hôtel de Ville in Brussels on 17 March 1815. On 4 April the Duke of Wellington, now appointed commander of the Anglo-Netherlands army, arrived back in Brussels, accompanied by Lieutenant William Lennox. On 10 April the new King and Queen of the Netherlands entered the city in style. Wellington sent for more experienced units from London, and prepared to meet his formidable opponent. The Duke of Richmond offered his services as a military commander, hoping very much to take part, but as a full general he was deemed too senior (and probably too old) to serve in the field.[27]

During May 1815 rumours circulated wildly. Despite the feeling of impending danger, balls were still taking place: Wellington gave two, on 3 and 7 June, and the British Minister gave one on the 5th. 'Balls are going on here' wrote Lady Caroline Capel, 'as if we had had none for a year.'[28] On 12 June Napoleon left Paris, heading for the north east. On 13 June Lady Caroline wrote that 'Nobody can guess Lord Wellington's intentions.'[29]

## The Duchess of Richmond's Ball

The Duchess had planned to give a ball on 15 June but with Napoleon's army advancing, she was unsure whether it could take

exception of the youngest, every one of them bore a family name, that of a grandmother or great-aunt. Their tutor said that '[they] are the most good-humoured unaffected girls I have ever met with, exceeding highbred but without an atom of pride.'[26]

Brussels, largely a Catholic city, was at the time a garrison town, but rejoicing in its recent liberation. Belgium, comprising the Protestant United Provinces to the north and the predominantly Roman Catholic Austrian Netherlands to the south, had with the rest of the Low Countries been occupied by France under the rule of Napoleon for twenty years. The country was freed from French power by the Allies on 1 February 1814, while Napoleon retreated before the advancing Allied armies. In March the Allied Sovereigns had entered Paris. On 11 April 1814 Napoleon had abdicated and was exiled to Elba.

With peace at last, many English people began to travel again, especially to Paris and Brussels. Living was cheap: more and more upper-class families with financial problems reverted to the old eighteenth-century habit of going abroad to save money. For those with a number of daughters (the Capels already had eight), there was the added advantage of young officers from the English garrison in Brussels to provide social life. Many of these men had spent the previous six years in the Peninsula, deprived of parties and romance. By August 1814 there were about 1,500 English civilians in the city, in addition to the military. All were in an euphoric state of mind at what they believed to be the dawn of peace in Europe. The presence of the Sovereign Prince of Orange and his two sons meant that a lively social life emerged throughout 1814, with balls (often two or three a week), assemblies, dances, picnics, routs, dinners and horse races, in which the young Guards and cavalry officers took part. The Bruxellois also gave parties and joined in with those of the English.

At the Treaty of Paris that year, the whole area was formed into a new state known as the Netherlands. To maintain stability, the

ABOVE Items commemorating the Richmond presence at the Battle of Waterloo, *clockwise from top right*: the guest list for the Duchess of Richmond's ball, together with the Waterloo medal later presented to the Duchess and the Waterloo medal of the Earl of March; the silver plate, made by Biennais, Paris, *c.*1810, from which, on Sunday 18 June, Napoleon ate his last breakfast before defeat; two French hat badges collected from the battleground; and a silhouette of Charles, 4th Duke of Richmond.

FACING PAGE *The Duchess of Richmond's Ball*, by Robert Hillingford, 1870s, oil on canvas, 44 × 60 cm / 17½ × 23½ in. Hillingford was not an accurate historicising painter, but the scene shows Lieutenant Webster, the messenger, arriving at the door to give his missive (tucked in his belt) to the Duke of Wellington, who is conferring with the Duke of Brunswick and General Allava. The young Prince of Orange is seated on the ottoman with a lady.

place. Although it has since become famous as the 'Waterloo Ball', it was mere chance that the ball happened to take place on the night that Napoleon's armies invaded Belgium. This was one of a succession of glamorous events. According to Lady Georgiana Lennox, talking much later as Lady de Ros, the Duchess asked Wellington, 'Duke, I do not wish to pry into your secrets, not do I ask what your intentions may be; I wish to give a ball, and all I ask is – May I give my ball?' The Duke of Wellington is said to have replied: 'Duchess, you may give your ball with the greatest safety without fear of interruption.'[30]

On the morning of the ball, war seemed far away: the newly married Lady de Lancey, who would be widowed within the week, wrote: 'Thursday 15th June forenoon was the happiest time of my life.'[31] Wellington had reports of French movement during the morning, but carried out routine duties. In the afternoon people walked in the park which was lively, as usual:

> crowded with officers, in every variety of military uniform, with elegant women, and with lively parties and gay groups of British and Belgic people, loitering, walking, talking, and sitting under the trees! There could not be a more animated, a more holiday scene; every thing looked gay and festive, and every thing spoke of hope, confidence and busy expectation.[32]

Dinner parties were held from the usual hour of 3–5 p.m. The Prince of Orange dined with the Duke of Wellington.

Before 5 p.m. Wellington received news that Napoleon was advancing. Hearing that the French had attacked Prussian outposts and had seized Charleroi, some thirty miles south, he ordered the troops to assemble at their headquarters, ready to move. He walked to the park to give further orders. Expecting to march the following morning, he said that he would go to the ball, and hoped other officers would do the same. By late afternoon gunfire could be heard in the city.

The Duchess's ball was held in a wing to the side of their rented town house[33] (see page 162). A guest list in the Duchess's own hand is the only accurate contemporary record of who was invited to the ball.[34] Among the list of 228 people, the Duchess invited Belgian and Dutch aristocrats; British civilians, both aristocratic and not; individuals of various nationalities, some of whom were just passing through; diplomats and army officers. There was no especial formality about the guest list: she entertained whom she chose. She also invited families with daughters of a suitable age, and young army officers. Some children also attended; Lady Sophia, aged five, watched through the

banisters on the stairs.[35] The total attendance was about 200 to 210.[36]

Prominent European guests included the young Prince of Orange, wearing his scarlet jacket as a British general; his younger brother, Prince Frederick of Orange; the Duke of Brunswick, in his jet black uniform; and the Prince of Nassau (a small state in Germany).[37] Among the English were Lieutenant General the Earl of Uxbridge, who later became the Marquis of Anglesey; his sister was Lady Caroline Capel. His daughter Lady Caroline Paget would marry the Earl of March, making them the 5th Duke and Duchess: presumably they met in Brussels. The Duke's nephew, Lord Apsley, was there, as was the Hon. John Capel, with two of his many daughters.

From 10 p.m. guests began to arrive. British, Belgian and Dutch officers wore their formal evening dress, with all their different colours and varieties. The ladies were in beautiful flowing dresses of silks and satins, and younger girls and children in muslin, with silk sashes. The dancing soon began. Ladies had 'tablets', or dance cards strung together, on which they wrote their

partner's name for each dance. The new continental fashion for the waltz, in which the man actually held the woman in his arms, had been frowned on by the Duke when his family was first in Brussels, but after a while he had to give in, so that at the ball one can assume that the girls were gaily waltzing with the young officers. There was also a Scottish sword dance and Highland reel, performed as a display by four sergeants from the Gordon Highlanders.

The Duke of Wellington arrived very late at the ball. He remained outwardly cool.[38] At some time well after 11 p.m., a mud-spattered messenger arrived. Lieutenant Henry Webster, one of the ADCs to the Prince of Orange, had galloped the ten miles from the Prince's headquarters at Braine-le-Comte. The gate porter made him wait five minutes, as the company was about to rise from supper. Lieutenant Webster peeped through the door: seeing the Duchess returning to the ballroom on the Prince of Orange's arm, accompanied by Lady Charlotte Greville on that of the Duke of Wellington, he entered. He gave the despatch to the Prince, who handed it unread to the Duke. The Duke placed it in his coat pocket and walked on with his lady; but he read it shortly afterwards. He told Webster to summon the Prince's carriage, so that he could return to his headquarters. As they heard that the French were advancing, the Duke of Brunswick and other officers gradually started to slip away from the ball.

The ball was interrupted. Dancers stopped and the music halted mid-bar. Lady Jane Lennox had a full dance card and had been enjoying herself, but now the men started to depart. Many of the younger ones left cheerfully, challenged by the prospect of encounter with the enemy. Some arrived at the field of battle in the silk stockings and dancing shoes of their evening dress. Wellington asked the Duke of Richmond for a map. Richmond took him into his dressing room, and with the door closed spread a map on the bed, assisted by eleven-year-old Lady Louisa.[39] Wellington turned out not to be as well prepared as he had pretended, abruptly telling Richmond, 'Napoleon has humbugged me, by God, he has gained twenty-four hours march on me.'[40] When Richmond asked what he intended to do, Wellington said that he had told the army to concentrate at Quatre Bras, but that he would not stop Napoleon there, and if not: 'I must fight him *here*.' With these words Wellington placed his thumbnail on the position at Waterloo. He then left by a side door. By 2 a.m. he was at home getting some sleep.

The Duchess of Richmond stood at the door imploring the young men to stay just one hour more; but tender partings took place and soon mostly only the costumes of ladies could be seen.[41] Some civilian guests left just after 2 a.m., making their way home through streets alive with soldiers. Most waited to see the troops depart, for which the orders were given at 4 a.m.

## THE BATTLE OF QUATRE BRAS AND OF WATERLOO

The history of the battle of Quatre Bras, the following day, and of Waterloo on the Sunday, 18 June, is well known. The Richmonds rode out to the battlefield with Wellington.[42] The Duke insisted on watching the action, riding round with his son Lord William, who had recently been injured in a horse race.[43] After the Prince of Orange was wounded, the Earl of March was on the sidelines, as an extra ADC to Wellington. The day after the great victory, the Duke of Richmond's coachman, Peter Soar, drove him with two of his sons, Lord March and Lord George, round the battlefield, and picked up a large number of trophies and curiosities (see pages 164 and 168).[44] Lord William also reported riding round the battlefield with his father on the Tuesday; the

wounded had been removed, but he was appalled by the sight: 'there lay heaped together dead men and horses . . .'[45] Nearly seven weeks after the battle, the Duke accompanied the Capel daughters for a tour of the area. The whole battle area became a tourist attraction, with visitors hunting for scraps of armour.

After the victory at Waterloo, the English were highly popular in Brussels. Some of the glory of the Allied victory shone on the Richmonds, for their loyalty in staying in the city, and their bravery at keeping going as if nothing was happening. Fabulous trophies of war were given to them by the Duke of Wellington: Napoleon's campaign chair, which was carried on all his campaigns, and a plate from the silver service that he kept in his carriage. A couple of years later a china tea and coffee service painted with views of all the main battle sites and uniforms of the different soldiers was especially made for the Duchess and presented to her by the grateful people of Brussels. A few gilt items, also with scenes of Waterloo village and La Ferme de Houguemont, were on general sale and were acquired at the same time. A small painting of Napoleon's head-quarters on the day of Waterloo, the little farmhouse called La Belle Alliance, is also in the Goodwood collection. Wellington's portrait, by George Dawe, hangs in the house, together with a smaller painting of him on the field of battle.

## ELOPEMENT IN PARIS

In July the Allied army entered Paris. The Duke of Richmond went to join in the celebrations; to Charlotte's fury, he would not initially take her, but eventually she was permitted to go for a while. Their dramas abroad were not over. In October 1815 their second daughter, Lady Sarah, eloped in Paris with Major General Sir Peregrine Maitland. A military chaplain, the Revd G.G. Stonestreet, was summoned to attend the couple in their carriage in the street. General Maitland requested that he would marry them.[46] Mortified by the situation in which the commander of the Guards in occupied Paris wished to marry the daughter of a celebrated duke in secrecy, the chaplain told them that they must obtain a licence, either from the Duke of Wellington, or the British ambassador. The General and his sobbing bride left disconsolate, their carriage splashing away in the rain. They spent the night calling in vain upon chaplains, priests and notaries to marry them.

The next morning Maitland's ADC returned to ask the chaplain to apply on his behalf to the Duke of Wellington for consent. This he did. Wellington received him with an 'overbearing stare and abrupt questioning', but gave his permission, probably having discussed the matter with the Duke of Richmond. By now, after a night away from home, albeit in a carriage and with Sarah no doubt still *intacta*, her reputation would have been considered ruined, and there was little option. However, the Duchess was keen for her daughters to be married and the family put a good face on the situation: 'Four days after the Wedding the Bride

ABOVE   *The Duke of Wellington*, by George Dawe, oil on canvas, 236 × 152 cm / 93 × 60 in.

FACING PAGE, TOP LEFT   Campaign chair, probably by Jacob *frères*, used by Napoleon at the time of Waterloo, given as a trophy of war by the Duke of Wellington to the Duke and Duchess of Richmond.

FACING PAGE, BOTTOM LEFT   Champ de Mai banner, Lyons silk. Banners representing the different departments of France were awarded by Napoleon to his armies when they rallied before him on the Champ de Mars in Paris in May 1814. After his defeat, Louis XVIII gave most of them to the Duke of Wellington, who retained all except this one, which he gave to the Duke and Duchess of Richmond as a memento of their stalwart behaviour in Brussels. It was originally in the French national colours of red, white and blue.

FACING PAGE, TOP RIGHT   Handpainted china, depicting soldiers from the various regiments at Waterloo, made in Paris and given to the Duchess of Richmond by the grateful people of Brussels, c.1817.

FACING PAGE, BOTTOM RIGHT   Musket balls from the field of Waterloo, and a baton made from the Duke of Wellington's famous tree.

returned to the World! Made her debut at a grand family dinner, all branches delighted; . . . The Duke of Richmond, however, is in spite of all these gaieties, sensibly hurt; and he said to me . . . he had been long enough in Paris . . .'[47]

That month the Duchess took some of the children to stay with Wellington at Cambrai. They had a lively time, with dancing and theatricals in the usual Richmond manner. Following the rumbustious approach to life bequeathed by Charlotte's mother, Jane, Duchess of Gordon, the girls engaged in high jinks with the young officers, such as being dragged round the corridors of the house on carpets. Lady Charlotte Greville, fully engaged in a love affair with Wellington, also stayed at Cambrai at this time.

## Canada

After the bright lights and dark tragedies of Brussels, the family still could not afford to return to Goodwood. The diarist Joseph Farington had heard that 'By hard living, [the Duke's] person is very much altered. – He looks to be a very old man.'[48] On 6 May 1818, while still residing in Brussels, the Duke received notice of his posting as Governor-in-Chief of British North America. Some of the family went with him, including Lord William, who went with some reluctance, as an extra ADC, and several daughters, led by Lady Mary. Returning briefly to Goodwood, where he received his instructions on 22 May, they sailed from Spithead on 18 June in the frigate HMS *Iphigenia*, reaching Quebec on 29 July. At the same time Sir Peregrine Maitland was appointed Lieutenant Governor of Upper Canada. Meanwhile, the smaller house at Molecomb was used by the Earl of March. The Duchess did not go to Canada, staying behind to look after the younger children. Lord Arthur was virtually adopted by the Duchess of Wellington in his teenage years, spending all his holidays at Stratfield Saye in Hampshire with other children in her care.

The Duke was an active governor, recommending the strengthening of forts at Quebec and other locations in Lower Canada and at Kingston in Upper Canada; the opening of navigation of the Ottawa and Rideau rivers, and the construction of many canals.[49] He was also involved in the foundation of McGill University. He encouraged racing, snipe shooting, carriage-driving and theatricals, as well as the games of cricket, racquets and tennis in which he himself regularly took part. That winter the family sledged on the frozen St Lawrence river and drove horse-drawn cabriolets through the snow, jingling with bells. Balls and dinners were numerous, and the Duke's new service of gold plate and his magnificent racing cups were much admired.[50]

The appointment was a success, but it was short, ending in tragedy. During the summer of 1819 the Duke, ever active, decided to make an extensive tour of Upper Canada. In July he was mounting his horse to inspect the garrison at Fort William Henry at Sorel in Quebec, when he noticed that a soldier had with him his tame fox, which began a scuffle with his own dog. The Duke

intervened to separate the animals, whereupon the fox bit him, inflicting a nasty wound on the lower joint of his thumb.[51] His daughter Lady Louisa later described his reaction: 'my Father came into our Room with a Handkerchief over his Hand saying that the Nasty little Fox had attacked Blucher a pet spaniel always with my father and that he had saved Blucher but the Fox had bitten his hand.'[52] The dog was of course named after Marshal Blücher, commander of the victorious Prussian forces at Waterloo.

Although the wound bled, there was no cause for concern and the Duke continued with his tour of garrisons. Lord William, the third of the surviving sons, and Lady Mary, his eldest daughter, accompanied him at this stage. His other travelling companions were Lieutenant Colonel Francis Cockburn, the Inspector of Military Settlements in British North America in 1819, and Major Bowles, the Military Secretary to the Governor, as well as his Swiss valet Baptiste and another member of staff. They returned to Kingston where the Duke spent several days playing cricket with officers and men. Lord William later described these as some of the happiest days of his own life. He and his sister then left to travel directly to Montreal, while the rest of the party set off to visit settlements on the Rideau river. Although they started off from Kingston in carriages, converting to horses, much of the journey had to be made on foot owing to the lack of roads and to the landscape of lakes and marshes. The Duke particularly wanted to visit Richmond, which had recently been named in his honour.

The party stayed at the garrison at Perth between 21 and 24 August. The Duke went out for walks during the day and enjoyed dining with the officers in the evenings. At the end of the stay he began to suffer shoulder pains and insomnia, and had difficulty in swallowing. The party lodged at Beckwith on the night of the 24th, from where the Duke insisted on continuing on his journey, but as he was clearly very tired it was eventually decided to delay the arrival at Richmond until the next day. On the morning of the 26th, having slept in a cottage, he began to show early symptoms of what would turn out to be hydrophobia, refusing the daily shave of his beard by his valet, and experiencing spasms whenever he saw anyone make contact with water. He made light of his discomfort, pressing forward through the swamp and arriving in Richmond at about 10 a.m, where he made the planned visits. A surgeon, called to his inn to investigate the pain in his throat, prescribed a mild gargle. Later, the Duke called for some paper and wrote a long letter to Lady Mary. After this, his spirits were low, and he had intimations of his own demise, talking about his anxieties to Major Bowles. However he invited some officers to dine with him, and was cheerful at dinner, though he became convulsed when trying to drink a glass of wine.

On the morning of 27 August, the Duke rose at dawn and talked with Major Bowles before setting off. He was determined to head for Montreal, where he had an appointment on the 30th. As the area around Richmond was particularly swampy, and his companions were anxious about him, it was decided that it would be easiest for him to travel through the woods and marshes by canoe with Major Bowles. Initially reluctant to board, he overcame his fear, but then could not bear to stay in the boat and leapt distressed to the shore. Increasingly he could not bear the sight of the pools and lakes. Charles Lennox, 4th Duke of Richmond, Lennox and Aubigny had contracted rabies, a rare and fatal illness at that time. This was the first recorded case of rabies in Canada.

From the canoe, skirting the pools and rivulets, Richmond ran into a barn. He did not wish to be in the nearby house at Chapman's Farm, because of the sound of water very near to it. In the barn he dictated many individual messages to family and friends. The Duke then prayed, resigning himself to his fate, forgiving his enemies, and expressing full confidence in an afterlife, in which he anticipated finding his late father and uncle ready to receive him. Despite being contorted by violent spasms, he exercised extraordinary self-control, courage, and mildness of temper. During the evening he agreed to be moved by his companions into the farmhouse. The next morning, 28 August, at 8 a.m., he died there on the marshes, in the lonely cottage. He was supported to the end by Baptiste, his faithful Swiss manservant, who had not left him for a moment, and by his loyal spaniel Blucher, the unwitting cause of his death.[53]

The 4th Duke was buried in the Cathedral of the Holy Trinity in Quebec City. The shock for his family, friends and staff was unimaginable. All sorts of festivities had been arranged in Montreal, where the visit of the Governor-in-Chief was like a royal progress: triumphal arches had been set up along his route, horse races had been announced and people were turning out to greet him. Having received two letters from Major Bowles, his children were aware that he was seriously ill and were in a state of great suspense, waiting under the portico of the hotel all after-noon. The messenger sent out to greet him met a carriage bearing his coffin.

Poignant sermons in his memory were preached the following Sunday. One of the Duke's last and most endearing requests was about the dog: 'Give Blucher to Mary, it will make her cry at first, but turn him in when she is alone and shut the door.'[54] The spaniel was indeed brought back to England. A memorial cairn was erected in 1926 on the site of Chapman's Farm, near Richmond.[55] Another town of Richmond was also named after him in Quebec. The region to the north of Toronto is known as Richmond Hill and a main road in the city of Toronto is also named after him. The newly built fort on the Ile aux Noix was named Fort Lennox.

Although he made no developments to Goodwood House, the tale of the Duke who could not afford to live in his family seat is one of courage and service, and his legacies to the Goodwood collection are immensely important. The close family friendship with the Duke of Wellington was to continue for two more generations. The Duke's poignant last instructions, dictated the day before his death, show his love and consideration for his family, as well as his own personal modesty and deep Christian faith:

> Tell March that I know he will regret being Duke of Richmond but that I am satisfied I leave my titles and estates to one of the best and most honourable men in England. Tell him I know he will take care of his brothers and sisters . . . [Then messages to children and friends, including Wellington]. . . Let my funeral be moderate in the Lower Province on the Ramparts at Quebec . . . Tell Sarah that with my latest breath I forgive her and General Maitland and they and their family have my blessing . . . I die in charity with the world and in perfect confidence of mercy from the Almighty.[56]

# 14 VIRTUOUS VICTORIANS

## THE 5TH AND 6TH DUKES OF RICHMOND, 1791–1860; 1818–1903

The story of Goodwood in the nineteenth century is a quieter one. The 5th and 6th Dukes were able to capitalise on what their ancestors had created. They added little to the art collections and did only internal decorations to the house. They had large families and did good works.[1] Every Sunday a church service took place in the Long Hall.[2] This era of history at Goodwood is represented in the house by the stiff centre-parted hairstyles, prim dresses and formal frock coats seen in many early photographs and in a handful of new portraits.

As Earl of March, the future 5th Duke of Richmond (1791–1860) was educated at Westminster and, while his father was Lord Lieutenant of Ireland, at Trinity College, Dublin. He joined the Army and was immediately engaged in the Peninsular War, where he assisted in the dramatic storming of a siege at Ciudad Rodrigo. He moved to the 52nd Light Infantry, with whom at the Battle of Orthez in 1814 he was hit by a bullet. It could not be removed from his chest and was lodged dangerously in his chest. His life was saved by a young army surgeon, Dr Archibald Hair, who volunteered to take the risk of a very difficult operation. A heavy fall while hunting subsequently aggravated the wound, which always gave pain, even though Dr Hair came to Goodwood as his personal physician and secretary.[3]

In April 1817 the Earl of March married the beautiful Lady Caroline Paget (see pages 40, 166). She was the daughter of the 2nd Earl of Uxbridge, now Marquis of Anglesey, and his first wife, Lady Caroline Villiers, from whom he had parted some years earlier: both had remarried and Caroline's mother was now the Duchess of Argyll. The younger Caroline was much admired; at Ascot in 1825 the Prince of Wales, bowling along the

course in his carriage, passed her open landau and 'played off his nods and winks and kissing his hand . . .'[4] After Waterloo, March had to retire from military service, so the couple lived at Molecomb.

### GORDON GRANDSON

Following his father's premature death, Charles, 5th Duke of Richmond, inherited suddenly and unhappily in 1819. However, the biggest change for the family in the nineteenth century would come from a different direction, through his mother, Charlotte, now suddenly the Dowager Duchess of Richmond.

In 1836 Charlotte's younger brother died at his London house at 49 Belgrave Square. He was George Gordon, 5th Duke of Gordon and Marquis of Huntly, the owner of 289,000 acres of Scotland. He had no legitimate children and died without an heir, leaving his eldest sister Charlotte, Dowager Duchess of Richmond, to inherit these enormous Scottish estates in Banffshire, Aberdeenshire, Morayshire and Inverness-shire. They included Gordon Castle, the ancient home of the Marquises of Huntly, with twenty miles of fishing on the Spey; grouse moors and deer forests at Glenfiddich, where there was a rustic retreat built by their mother, Jane, with an extra lodge at Blackwater; the ancient Huntly Lodge; property at Glenlivet, Lecht, Strathavon and Inchrory; and the large Kinrara estate and grouse moor south of Aviemore, where Duchess Jane had also built the house. On Charlotte's death in 1842 all these estates were inherited by her son Charles, 5th Duke of Richmond. He also gained the welcome addition of the large London town house, then known as Gordon House.

With the inheritance came paintings, furniture, swords and armour, silver, archives and the whole panoply of Scotland's

Goodwood House in the snow, by the Earl of March.

grandest family, barons since the fifteenth century. The dukedom of Gordon was created in 1684 by Charles II for George Gordon, Marquis of Huntly, who as a Catholic proceeded to give support to James II. The family were still Jacobites at the time of the 1715 rebellion but under the influence of Lady Henrietta Mordaunt, wife to the second Duke, became Protestant, professing their loyalty to the Crown at the time of the 1745 uprising.[5] In 1836, when the dukedom became extinct, the title of Marquis of Huntly went to a cousin, so that the position of chieftain of the huge Gordon clan devolved down that line, with whose descendants, resident in Scotland, it very suitably remains. The art collection stayed at Gordon Castle.

The inheritance transformed the lives of the Dukes of Richmond at Goodwood, enabling them to finish off the Ballroom and to feel less financially pressed. In gratitude, when he inherited fully in 1842, the 5th Duke of Richmond added the name of Gordon to the family name of Lennox. The acquisition of the estates coincided with a new fashion among the English aristocracy, in particular young men, for visiting the Scottish Highlands to shoot and fish. The attraction was increased by the affection of Queen Victoria and Prince Albert for the north, and their purchase of the Balmoral estate in 1852. The family lodge at Glenfiddich was visited by Queen Victoria in 1887. The 5th and 6th Dukes and their families made regular trips north, becoming very keen on salmon fishing in the summer season, grouse shooting in August, and deer stalking in the autumn. The advent of the railways facilitated their journeys. This new Richmond family tradition would last exactly a hundred years.

The late-eighteenth-century history of the Gordon family provided a colourful legacy for Goodwood. In 1767 Alexander, 4th Duke of Gordon, a shy and retiring man, married Jane Maxwell,

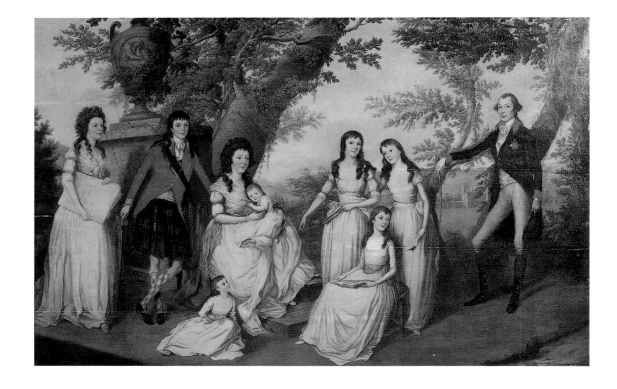

the beautiful, lively and amusing daughter of Sir William Maxwell Baronet, from Monreith in the Borders. Following her parents' separation, Jane (who as a child was called Jeannie or Jean) grew up with her mother and two sisters in Edinburgh. They lived in some poverty in a second-floor apartment in Hyndford's Close off the top of the Royal Mile, where the streets were narrow, old-fashioned and dirty. Farmers' carts would trundle through the streets, and Jane and her younger sister would play on them, leaping from cart to cart. They also liked to ride down the street on the back of a pig. The Close survives today, albeit rebuilt, and in looking over a narrow valley is still surprisingly quiet and almost rural.

Jane's childhood in Edinburgh coincided exactly with the period of the Scottish Enlightenment, when it was considered desirable for women as well as men to be well read in philosophy, religion and literature. Jane's reading was substantially developed by Henry Home, later Lord Kames, who took the bright thirteen- year-old under his wing. After a brief engagement to a young army officer who, she thought, died in battle in America, Jane met Alexander, Duke of Gordon, at a ball arranged for him by his cousin and agent, Charles Gordon, in April 1767. They were married that October.

ABOVE  *The Hunting Lodge at Glenfiddich*, by Lady Louisa Tighe, watercolour, 17.5 × 25.5 cm / 7 × 10 in.

FACING PAGE, TOP  *Gordon Castle*, faintly inscribed *J. Cassie*, 1850s, watercolour, 28 × 42.5 cm / 11 × 16¾ in.

FACING PAGE, BOTTOM  *Jane, Duchess of Gordon, Fishing*, print, from an original watercolour.

The marriage was slightly dampened from the start by the arrival of a letter from Jane's erstwhile fiancé, who, to her shock, was still alive. However, Jane produced a fine family of children for her Duke, of five daughters and two sons. They lived mostly at Gordon Castle, where some of the Duke's illegitimate children had already made their home. In the 1770s they vastly extended the castle. Here Jane created a lively family home, with educational activities such as music and reading as important as outdoor sports such as riding and sea-bathing. Jane was fabulously hospitable and famously ambitious in the matches that she made for her five daughters, helping them to land three dukes, a marquis and a baronet.[6]

## THE DOWAGER DUCHESS AND HER LEGACY

At Goodwood, Charlotte, Duchess of Richmond, continued to be a powerful matriarch. Back in 1805 the 3rd Duke had commented rather sadly to his nephew, that if only Charles himself were 'more domestic', then 'Lady Charlotte would be more pleasant'.[7] Although she was capable of showing much charm, 'pleasant' she never became. In Brussels in 1814 it was reported that 'her Temper is dreadful . . .'[8] Like her mother, Charlotte had tried to engineer good matches for her seven daughters and was especially furious whenever she was trumped.[9] In 1822 she went to Dublin to try to secure the hand of Lord Hervey for her daughter Louisa.[10] The young man was uninterested and when Louisa subsequently became engaged to William Tighe, the Duchess's fury knew no bounds. Although this caused much local merriment and mockery, it was a sad situation; during a subsequent three-month stay in Ireland, the Dowager Duchess did not speak to her son-in-law once, despite his being 'the most gentlemanlike, well-bred person possible, and evidently he and his wife the happiest with each other'.[11]

ABOVE *Charles, 5th Duke of Richmond, Lennox and Aubigny,* by Frank Wilkin, *c.*1830, oil on board, 32 × 25 cm / 12½ × 10 in. He inherited the estates of his Scottish uncle (left and facing page).

LEFT *George, 5th Duke of Gordon,* by Sir Henry Raeburn, *c.*1830, oil on canvas, 234 × 145 cm / 92 × 57 in.

FACING PAGE *George, 5th Duke of Gordon,* by George Sanders, *c.*1830, oil on canvas, 163 × 118 cm / 64 × 46½ in. The painting is always described as being of 'The Cock o' the North', a traditional appellation for the head of the Gordon clan.

From the mid-1820s the fiery Dowager Duchess was very exercised by the idea of Catholics gaining emancipation. Since becoming close to William Pitt, partly through the Gordons, the family had become Tories. Her son the 5th Duke was a hardliner on some issues, opposed both to Catholic emancipation and to Robert Peel's ideal of free trade. His speeches were said to be long-winded and he was not well read.[12] However, because he was good-looking, good-natured, sporty and sociable, the Duke was popular, and, as early as 1828, was created a Knight of the Garter by George IV. Initially spending much of his time in the country, he declined the Mastership of the Horse. He changed his political affiliation when he refused to side with Wellington against the Reform Act, and was made Postmaster General in Earl Grey's Whig government. He was very paternal both in his family and in the way he ran the estate. Two of his younger brothers were

MPs who always voted with him, and in the 1840s and 1850s all four of his surviving sons were in Parliament. Throughout the nineteenth century the Dukes of Richmond would be more conventional than at any previous period in the family history.

## DASH BEFORE CASH: THE YELLOW DRAWING ROOM

The 5th Duke acquired an incomplete Goodwood House but until he gained the Gordon inheritance he had very little money with which to achieve anything, especially as his mother had incurred gambling debts. The ground lease of the London house owned but not used by the 4th Duke (adjacent to the burnt-down Richmond House) was sold back to the Crown. The 5th Duke thereafter worked steadily at finishing off Goodwood, doing up one room per year. It was only eight years after his succession that

ABOVE   The Yellow Drawing Room (full view to apse). The furnishing was classic of the English Regency period, with French eighteenth-century cabriole chairs and Boulle clocks, set off by newly made gilded Regency settees, together with ottomans (see page 182). Portraits of the 3rd Duke by both Reynolds and Mengs hang at the far end. The room was restored in 1998, with furnishings by Lady Victoria Waymouth. French eighteenth-century chairs by Gourdin and Delanois were brought in from other rooms.

FACING PAGE, TOP   The Yellow Drawing Room (full view to main entrance hall). At the far end hang the portraits of George III and Queen Charlotte, from the studio of Allan Ramsay, ordered in August 1765 for the Duke's Paris embassy and later hung in the Richmond House Gallery. Their frames echo the earlier Kentian style of those of George II and Queen Caroline (right-hand wall). The room was clearly designed to take these large portraits, which had been saved from the Richmond House fire in 1791. Below them are French tulipwood bombé commodes, one stamped *J.P. Latz* and *I.C. Saunier*, and the other *I. Dubois JME*.

FACING PAGE, BOTTOM   Sketch of a design for filling in the panels of the Yellow Drawing Room at Goodwood with ornaments done in white and gold and painted on canvas, to be fitted in gilt frames in their places, signed with a monogram *CHT* [Charles Henry Tatham], *Queen St Mayfair, Jan 7 1827*, pencil and wash.

he was able to complete the decoration of the main drawing room to the right of the front door.

This room, which became known as the Yellow Drawing Room, had been built to take the great full-length royal portraits from Richmond House, in their gilded Kentian frames.[13] It was complete by August 1828 when the MP Thomas Creevey reported that, despite the rather irregular shape, 'The House at Goodwood is perfection. It is an immense concern and every part of it is gaiety itself . . .'[14] He felt that it was all done with 'perfect taste', and liked the front hall, which he found pleasantly uncluttered. He described 'Turning . . . on our right into the principal drawing-room, 60 feet long at least I should say, with a circular room open at the end – both rooms furnished with the brightest yellow satin . . .' It was here that they were received by the Duchess with her four sisters and friends. There were many racing visitors in the house, scattered about in the libraries, billiard room, hall and

drawing room, 'and the whole seemed as gay and cheerful a concern as one could see anywhere . . . '[15]

In 1839 William Hayley Mason similarly reported of the Yellow Drawing Room that 'The decorations and furniture are of the most elegant and costly description: the walls are hung in rich amber-coloured silk tabouret, with full draperies to the three windows, and the luxuriant sofas, ottomans, couches, and cabriole chairs, are covered in the same material.'[16] The silk was probably a very similar colour to that in the Duke of Wellington's home at Apsley House in London. The whole was muted in a subtle way by a magnificent Axminster carpet, with great scrolls of pink, green and gold. The rich style, with one colour plastered over ottomans, sofas and chairs, and an abundance of *passementerie*, tassels and braids, was very similar to that of the rooms executed for George IV at Windsor Castle at the same date.

## COMPLETING THE REGENCY INTERIORS: THE BALLROOM

At the time of the Gordon inheritance in 1836 the room that was to be the Ballroom still had neither floor nor ceiling. The 3rd

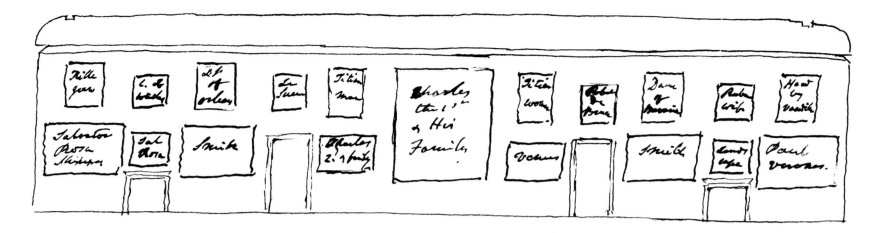

Duke had planned it as his picture gallery, sketching the way he would like the pictures laid out on the main wall. In the event it became a Ballroom. Begun in 1836, just a year before Queen Victoria came to the throne, it was completed in 1838. The architect was John Elliott of Chichester.

On 27 February 1839 a huge celebration took place for the coming of age of the Earl of March. The day began with a stag hunt, with three hundred gentlemen sitting down to dinner in the tennis court, and others with the Duke in the house. In the evening about seven hundred guests attended the ball and supper. The park was illuminated, as was the huge conservatory at the Ballroom end (in which the decorations temporarily caught fire). A bonfire was lit on St Roche's Hill. The following Friday the Duke entertained two hundred of the tenantry to dinner in the Ballroom.

ABOVE   Plan for the picture hang in the Ballroom, by Charles, 3rd Duke of Richmond, *c*.1805–6. He intended the room as a picture gallery. His newly acquired large portrait of Charles I and family by Sir Anthony Van Dyck was central to the scheme, as it is today.

FACING PAGE, TOP   The Yellow Drawing Room, mid-nineteenth-century photograph. Most of the furniture shown was lost in a fire when in store during World War II. It was replaced in the recent restoration by similar items, mostly original to the collection.

FACING PAGE, BOTTOM   The Yellow Drawing Room (curtains and mirror). The carved gilt console tables date from the 1820s, and are in the so-called 'style Louis Quatorze', or French Revival style: in fact they recall the early-eighteenth-century period of the Régence. The borders of the pier glasses surmounting them include the English rose, the Scottish thistle, and the French *fleur-de-lys*, for the different dukedoms. These reflect in two further matching glasses over the chimneypieces. The portrait of Queen Caroline is by John Vanderbank.

BELOW   Ball for the coming of age of the Earl of March, 1839, engraving.

FESTIVITIES AT GOODWOOD ON THE COMING OF AGE OF THE EARL OF MARCH: THE BALL.

The Ballroom and the Yellow Drawing Room, two wonderful examples of the French Revival style, provide a suitable setting for dukes who to this day claim the title of Aubigny in France.[17] However, the châteaux of Aubigny and La Verrerie were sold from the family in 1842, because according to the *Code Napoléon* they could not have been inherited intact by the 4th Duke, but had to be divided among numerous heirs. Unfortunately one of Emily's children had decided to raise the claim, which then meant that all other descendants of the 2nd Duke had to be included.

## THE DEVELOPMENT OF THE RACECOURSE

The 5th Duke's legacy to Goodwood was the development of the racecourse, and consequently the acquisition of a number of

ABOVE   The Round Reception Room, with chimneypiece from Richmond House. This was a sitting-out room for the Ballroom.

FACING PAGE   The Ballroom. Completed in 1836–8 in the period of the French Revival, the room is in the rococo style of Louis XV. It is executed in a typically English late-Regency way, but the romantic minstrels' gallery and the colour scheme begin to look almost Victorian. The full picture hang envisaged by the 3rd Duke was not carried out until the restoration by Alec Cobbe, in 1994.

sporting paintings for the house. His father had kept a few horses in training, but in his absence racing was at a low ebb. However, in 1812 the Goodwood Cup was founded. In 1814, the year in which the 4th Duke was back in England, the main meeting was moved from April or May to late July, thus enjoying better weather.

Of all the dukes, the 5th Duke was the most deeply interested in racing. A brave and dashing horseman until his injury, he always loved horses, bringing his favourite horse, Busaco (named after the battle), back from the Peninsular War for a long and honourable retirement at Goodwood. At his death Busaco was buried near to the ice-house, with an oak tree over his grave. The Duke's wound meant that he was no longer able to hunt, but racing was a sport which he could promote and follow.

The Duke's first success as a racehorse owner at Goodwood was in a match race in 1817. Between 1818 and 1821 his horse Roncesvalles won six races. In 1823 the Duke installed a private trainer, John Kent, who was later succeeded by his son of the same name. That year the Duke won the first running of the Goodwood Stakes with Dandizette, which, like Roncesvalles and Busaco, was painted by the artist William Webb. Four years later, he had his first classic success with Gulnare in the Oaks; this horse, held by the trainer John Kent, was immortalised in a painting by Ben

Marshall. In the same year, the Duke's horses won both the Goodwood Stakes and the Goodwood Cup, and a total of twenty-three races over various courses. He had another victory in the Goodwood Cup in 1828, and a sensational Ascot in 1829, winning all seven open races in the three days. His fortunes as an owner reached their zenith in 1845 when, with eleven horses in training, he won the Oaks with Refraction (of whom there are paintings by Abraham Cooper, Harry Hall and C. Church) as well as winning the 1000 Guineas and the Liverpool Cup with other horses.

FACING PAGE *Goodwood Grand Stand: Preparing to Start*, engraved by R.G. Reeve, from a painting by James Pollard. 'An aristocratic atmosphere pervades the whole scene. With magnificent scenery, first-rate racing and the cream of England's best society to inspirit and gratify him, a stranger would indeed be fastidious who did not consider the Goodwood racecourse the perfection and paradise of racegrounds.' (Written by a visitor, 1845.)

BELOW *Adine Winning the Goodwood Stakes*, engraving, 1853. This print was used to depict various races between 1835 and 1853, with different titles applied below and the jockeys' colours altered accordingly. Opened in 1830, the new stand was described as 'elegant and commodious'. It was capable of holding three thousand people. The ground floor contained rooms for retiring and refreshment, while on the first floor arcaded windows ran along the front of a saloon, with betting rooms adjacent.

## LORD GEORGE BENTINCK (1802–1848)

In 1824 Lord George Bentinck raced at Goodwood for the first time, entering as a rider in a light-hearted race called the Cocked Hat Stakes, in which the riders had to start and to complete each heat of the race wearing a military hat. It was Lord George's first racing win. A younger son of William Cavendish-Bentinck, 3rd Duke of Portland, he became passionate about the sport, an enthusiasm not shared by his autocratic father, who tried in vain to keep him away from the turf. Lord George managed to keep up his interests by covertly entering into racing partnerships while following a successful career as a politician. He became private secretary to his uncle, George Canning, as Foreign Secretary, and later, briefly, as Prime Minister. Bentinck entered Parliament in 1828 and in the 1840s, as a supporter of Benjamin Disraeli, he led Tory opposition to Sir Robert Peel.

Both the Duke and Bentinck were senior stewards of the Jockey Club. In 1828 they dined with George IV at a dinner given for the Jockey Club at St James's Palace, with the Dukes of Richmond and Grafton sitting each side of the King. Richmond also sat next to the gout-ridden King the following year.[18] The Duke was very active in the campaign to revise the rules of racing.

In the autumn of 1829 the course at Goodwood was relaid, with huge amounts of earth moved to level off the Downs, and the finishing straight extended to the foot of the Trundle hill. William IV had three winners at Goodwood in 1830, the year of his accession. A new stand, designed by the architect George Draper, was opened that year.

Together Bentinck and the Duke made many innovations, putting Goodwood at the leading edge of racing and forming the basis of race organisation as it is known today. Racing at the time was full of people determined to make a quick fortune, and skulduggery was rife. Throughout the dramatic racecourse developments of the 1830s, the Duke was running the meetings at a loss and it is possible that Lord George either paid for the improvements or lent the Duke the money.[19] While Bentinck placed enormous bets, and was not himself averse to some interesting dealings in this area, the Duke did not bet at all. Bentinck's main racing partner was his cousin Charles Cavendish Fulke Greville, but in 1836 they had a spectacular falling out.[20]

The Bentinck/Greville relationships with the Richmonds had a further history. Greville's father, also Charles Greville (1762–1832), was the nephew of Sir William Hamilton. The first

Charles Greville succeeded Sir Harry Fetherstonhaugh of Uppark in taking the beautiful Emma Hart as his mistress, passing her on to his uncle Hamilton in Naples when he needed to make a lucrative marriage (she became Sir William's wife and, famously, Admiral Nelson's mistress). With his heiress wife, Lady Charlotte Cavendish Bentinck, also a child of the 3rd Duke of Portland, Greville had taken a house in Brussels in 1814. The Greville family were at the heart of political life, and for forty years Charles Cavendish Fulke Greville kept a political diary, intended for publication, in which he drew on his close relationships with both Whigs and Tories.

The most telling story about the colourful Lord George is of how, owing to his commissioning of the first-ever horsebox, his horse Elis won the 1836 St Leger with very long odds. In 1841 Bentinck moved all his horses to Goodwood and turned his energies to improving the Goodwood stables. He had the Halnaker gallops laid with all-weather turf, for good exercising. With the horses of other friends also trained on the estate, the Goodwood stable became one of the most successful in the country. In 1845 the Jockey Club honoured the Duke by passing a resolution to thank him for all his hard work on behalf of racing in the House

ABOVE  *The First Horsebox*, with Elis held by the trainer John Doe, John Day up, by Abraham Cooper RA, oil on canvas, 95 × 125 cm / 37¼ × 49 in. When Lord George Bentinck's horse Elis appeared not to have left Goodwood a mere four days before the St Leger at Doncaster, it seemed that the horse could not walk the two hundred miles and then run the race successfully. Secretly Bentinck had built the first-ever horsebox. Constructed by a local coachbuilder, and padded inside, it was pulled north by carriage horses, bamboozling the betting fraternity, who gradually lengthened the odds to 12–1. Elis won the race with ease. Bentinck pocketed not only the prize, but also £12,000 from a bet.

FACING PAGE  *Lady Cecilia Lennox at Gordon Castle*, by Sir Edwin Landseer, oil on canvas, 43 × 30 cm / 17 × 12 in.

of Lords. By now the Jockey Club was following Goodwood's direction in race management.

As a result of the development of the racecourse, Goodwood week became an integral part of the aristocratic social season. From the 1830s about forty people would stay in Goodwood House for the late July race-meeting, with another dozen at Molecomb and houseparties in surrounding country houses. From the early 1840s trains brought race-goers from London, first to Fareham in Hampshire and Shoreham, and finally, from 1847,

directly to Chichester. In 1845 a visitor described it as 'the perfection and paradise of racegrounds'.[21]

The Earl of March (the future 6th Duke) was also a racing enthusiast and was the most successful race rider of the family. His principal achievement was to win four races at the Goodwood meeting in 1842. He had few horses in training, but would remain a member of the Jockey Club throughout his subsequent dukedom.

## LADY CECILIA

Caroline, the beautiful Duchess of Richmond, had borne her duke five children. However, her sixth and last child, Lady Cecilia, is said to have been the daughter of Lord George Bentinck.[22] When his cousin, the diarist Charles Greville, remonstrated with Bentinck in 1836 that he was making a fool of himself in his attentions to the Duchess, Bentinck responded that he would never do anything to put her honour at risk.[23] He lied, perhaps even to himself. It was not surprising that the Duke asked Bentinck to remove his horses from the Goodwood stables. The little girl was born the next year, the youngest of the family by nearly eight years.

When Bentinck's horses returned to Goodwood in 1841 his good relationship with the Duke appeared to revive. However, in 1846 Bentinck amazed the Goodwood houseparty by announcing at dinner that he was going to sell his string of horses for the bargain price of £10,000. A deal was done and Bentinck's racing career was over. In a final twist of fate, two years later Surplice, previously one of his horses and trained by Kent, won the Derby, the great race that had always eluded Lord George. A week later Bentinck was found dead in a field, late at night, at his home at Welbeck Abbey. An autopsy suggested that a heart condition was the cause, possibly brought on by an upset or shock. What revelations, sensations and emotions were hidden behind the outwardly stoical behaviour of the Duke, the Duchess and Lord George will never be known. The Goodwood racecourse went into a temporary decline and in 1854 the Duke of Richmond gave up his own horses.

## EDWIN LANDSEER IN SCOTLAND

A favoured youngest child, Cecilia was painted as a little girl with her skipping rope at Gordon Castle by the artist Edwin Landseer (1802–1873), whose paintings of people and animals in the Scottish Highlands were hugely popular.[24] He had shot to fame in the early 1820s, patronised by John, 6th Duke of Bedford, whose wife, Georgina Gordon, was the youngest Gordon aunt of the 5th Duke of Richmond. Landseer's love of Scotland was largely engendered by an intense relationship with Georgina, Duchess of Bedford, which would last for the rest of their lives. During the autumn of 1824 both were staying near to her brother the Marquis of Huntly's wild and romantic home at Kinrara, where the heady landscape must have been irresistible. The following autumn, of 1825, to the astonishment of her family, the still dazzling forty-four-year-old Georgina became pregnant. Her daughter, Lady Rachel Russell, is believed to have been the artist's child, conceived either at Kinrara or at Gordon Castle.[25]

By the time that Lady Cecilia was painted, Landseer had suffered a nervous collapse, but was still very much part of the family life in Scotland. Cecilia's portrait is a classic image of Victorian life: the sentimental appreciation of childhood set against the romantic medieval architecture in the Scottish Highlands. Whether or not Landseer was aware of Cecilia's true paternity, to paint another little girl from the inter-related ducal families must have been poignant.

## PEACE, POPULARITY AND THE PENINSULAR TROPHY

One of the 5th Duke's most lauded achievements was the attainment of a General Service Medal for all soldiers who had fought in the Peninsular War.[26] While Waterloo survivors were much

adorned, the veterans of the earlier conflict felt aggrieved at the lack of any recognition, and the Duke of Wellington was unmoved by their request. After managing to achieve the striking of this medal in 1848, the Duke was presented with a large table centrepiece in silver, known as 'The Trophy', with some figures in an elegantly different nacreous finish. It was executed by Hunt & Roskill, and cost 1,500 guineas, to which servicemen contributed according to their rank, with up to one pound from officers and as little as one penny from private soldiers. The piece provides a narrative history of the Peninsular War, showing four groups of soldiers and sailors, all in historical uniforms, with reliefs of the main battles, culminating in a statuette of the Duke of Richmond on the pedestal at the top.

After a dramatic early life, and the endurance of later domestic secrets, the 5th Duke's last years were unremarkable. He built many farm buildings, including the Charlton sawmill. In the 1850s he spent more time both at Goodwood and at Gordon Castle. The Goodwood tenantry memorial window at Boxgrove Priory was a final tribute to the Duke after his death in 1860.

## CHARLES, 6TH DUKE OF RICHMOND (1818–1903)

The future 6th Duke of Richmond had been born at Molecomb. He was educated at Westminster, and was the first of the family to go to Oxford, where he attended Christ Church. At the age of twenty-one he joined the Royal Regiment of Horse Guards, subsequently, in 1842, becoming an ADC to the Duke of Wellington. He retired his commission as a captain in 1844, but continued as an ADC, later also holding the post to support Wellington's successor, Lord Hill. Two years later he was elected Member of Parliament, and would develop as a serious politician.

As Earl of March, he married Bentinck's great-niece, Frances Harriet Greville (1824–1887), at St George's, Hanover Square, in November 1843. Frances Harriet's father, Algernon Greville, son of Lady Charlotte and therefore grandson of William, 3rd Duke of Portland, had been private secretary to the Duke of Wellington since 1827. It was natural that she would meet Charles, Earl of March, the dashing young ADC to the Iron Duke.

The couple began their early married life at Molecomb. Almost two years after their marriage, Frances bore her husband a son and heir: Charles Henry, Lord Settrington, the future 7th Duke of Richmond. She had a further two sons before her husband inherited. On the death of the 5th Duke in 1860, the new Duke followed the example of his father, closing up the main house for just over a year as a mark of respect. Two daughters and one more son followed. From family photographs, Frances Harriet appears to have been a model Victorian wife: highly moral and proper. Although their youngest son, Walter, became an MP, the third son was not so well behaved. Lord Francis had a reputation for sacking all his staff in the evening, when he was drunk, and then re-employing them in the morning.

The 6th Duke was an important Tory politician, becoming President of the Board of Trade, and, from 1869, Leader of the Opposition in the House of Lords. He became President of the Council in Disraeli's 1874 administration, after whose death he also worked in Opposition under Lord Salisbury. In 1876 he petitioned Queen Victoria to make him Duke of Gordon in a new creation, to which she acceded, also creating him Earl of Kinrara, the title derived from his great-grandmother's Scottish home, which was still owned by the family. The Gordon lands and titles were once again held together.

He held many public positions, taking both his Sussex and his Scottish responsibilities seriously. When the spire of Chichester Cathedral fell down in 1861, he led the procession of celebration after the rebuilding. He was Lord Lieutenant for Banffshire and Chancellor of the University of Aberdeen, as well as being created the first Secretary of State for Scotland in 1885. Lord Salisbury wrote to him, 'It really is a matter where the effulgence of two Dukedoms and the best salmon river in Scotland will go a long way.'[27] The Duke was very interested in agriculture, joining the Royal Agricultural Society within six months of its

ABOVE   Duchess Cottages, West Lavant.

RIGHT   Frances Harriet, Duchess of Richmond (wife of the 6th Duke).

FACING PAGE, TOP   Portrait of *Charles, 6th Duke of Richmond and Lennox, 1st Duke of Gordon, and Duke of Aubigny*, by Sir Francis Grant, 1875, oil on canvas, 216 × 122 cm / 85 × 48 in.

FACING PAGE, BOTTOM   The Supper Room, R&G detail. From 1876 the Dukes were known as the Dukes of Richmond and Gordon.

formation in 1838, and later serving as its president. As well as developing the livestock, he added many farm buildings to the Gordon estates in Scotland, and made technological advances at Goodwood, building a water-pumping station beside the Kennels and a private gasworks to heat and light Goodwood House.

The 6th Duke ordered over four hundred houses and cottages to be built for his estate workers. Many of these homes were named Duchess Cottages in honour of his wife, whose idea they were. Constructed to a semi-detached H-shaped design with gables, they were intended to improve the quality of life of the workers by ensuring that each family had a substantial house with a garden. A similar group of the houses built at the time are u-shaped, with the projecting wings at the rear. Some simpler rectangular shapes were also built, all with the double gables. The 6th Duke and Duchess 'restored and embellished' Goodwood House in terms of internal decorations but made no long-lasting changes.[28] They entertained some celebrated visitors at

Goodwood, including two emperors of Russia, and two German emperors.

Frances Harriet owned the Pekinese dogs which became the foundation of the breed in England. In 1860, during the occupation of Peking by Western powers, British naval officers stormed the Summer Palace. Hidden in a secluded corner of the palace were five Pekinese dogs, highly prized in China. One was presented to Queen Victoria, while two were subsequently given to the Duchess of Wellington, and two by Sir George Fitzroy to Frances Harriet. With the prefix 'Goodwood' before their names, these were the source of all future Pekinese in this country. Frances Harriet's second son and daughter-in-law, Lord and Lady Algernon Gordon-Lennox, later established the Goodwood kennels.

FACING PAGE  *The Lawn at Goodwood*, by Walter Wilson and Frank Walton, 1886, oil on canvas, 91.5 × 152.5 / 36 × 60 in. The Prince of Wales, later King Edward VII, is shown at the centre with his wife, Alexandra, and their daughters beyond to the right. The racecourse was now so fashionable that three further princes, nine dukes, sixteen earls and eighteen barons also attended, as well as Sir W.S. Gilbert and Sir Arthur Sullivan, and members of the Rothschild family. The horses for the next race are heading for the start. St Roche's Hill, known as the Trundle, is seen beyond the end of the 1830 stand.

BELOW  The Goodwood Hunt at The Kennels, 1883.

## THE GOODWOOD HUNT AND THE KENNELS

Since the disbanding of the Duke of Richmond's Hounds in 1813, Charlton Forest had been hunted by the pack of hounds belonging to Lord Leconfield at Petworth. When he decided to relinquish this in the early 1880s, the 6th Duke decided to re-create the Goodwood hunt. The announcement was greeted by locals with great delight. During the winter of 1882–3 the Duke undertook building works in the area of the existing kennels in preparation for the 1883 season. Brand-new kennels were built over the road. Constructed by a firm of builders from Belgravia, these were modelled on Lord Leconfield's own kennels at Petworth, with four draw yards in front. To their right a flinted house was built for the huntsman, with seven individual kennels adjacent for whelping. The Earl of March was the Master. The hunt at this date comprised fifty-five couple of hounds, purchased from Lord Radnor, with thirty-four hunters in the main stables.[29]

Meanwhile the original Wyatt kennels were adapted to provide accommodation in the wings for the four senior hunt servants, namely the huntsman, first whip, stud groom and kennelman. With the increased popularity of the racecourse, the long roofs over the hound lodges were raised, in order to provide attic dormitories for policemen at the races. The north wing of the old

kennels was extended for accommodation and the roofs of the two existing wings on the west side were also heightened. New chimneys were inserted. All the new chimney pots 'were Funtley Reds', from Hampshire, each with a different stripe as if on a naval or military uniform; these were also used on the Duchess Cottages.

With the agricultural depression of the later 1880s, the hunt was disbanded after only twelve years, in 1895. Owing to very low farming revenues and mortgages on all his new properties, the Duke began to feel the pinch. The Earl of March turned fifty in that year. The only member of the family to hunt after this date was his son, the 8th Duke, as Earl of March, until he contracted polio in World War I. The 1880s kennels were in turn rebuilt in the mid-twentieth century into Hound Lodge, with the adjacent huntsman's house retained as Greenkeeper's Cottage. The garden area was redesigned for the restoration of The Kennels in 2006.

In the last years of the nineteenth century it was the well-established racecourse that most symbolised Goodwood. Its popularity was partly due to the patronage of the Prince of Wales, later Edward VII, who first visited in the early 1880s, at the height of his three-year affair with Lillie Langtry. The 'most beautiful girl in Jersey' was a violet-eyed vicar's daughter, and at the time a young married woman. Lillie's appearance at the Goodwood races, openly paraded by the Prince of Wales, added to their lustre. Meanwhile, if the Danish-born Princess Alexandra should decide to accompany her husband to Goodwood, she

could luckily find a companion in the 6th Duke's sister Lady Augusta, who through her marriage was the Princess of Saxe-Meininghen.

As the Prince's attentions began to turn elsewhere, Lillie bore a child by another lover and separated from her husband. Her subsequent acting career brought her fame and wealth, enabling her to buy racehorses and to return to Goodwood, where, ownership by a woman being deemed incorrect, her horses were run under the name of 'Mr Jersey'. She met her second husband at the racecourse, becoming Lady de Bathe. Lillie subsequently developed an affectionate friendship with the Prince, who would always visit her during race week at her lodging at Singleton, taking tea in the garden. At his coronation in 1901 she sat with his other mistresses Lady Warwick and Mrs Keppel in what the tabloid press dubbed 'the King's loose box'. When the King was on his deathbed in 1910, Lillie was the only one of his former mistresses to be sent for by Queen Alexandra.

Mrs Keppel also visited Goodwood. Married to a younger son of William Keppel, 7th Earl of Albemarle (who was a distant Richmond relation), Alice Keppel was the popular and amusing daughter of a baronet. Like Lillie, she met the Prince when she was a young married woman, having already had several affairs with glamorous and aristocratic men. Behaviour in young aristocratic society in the late nineteenth century was very free, in decided contrast to the strict discipline and rigid moral values set earlier by Queen Victoria. The contrast could be felt at Goodwood,

FACING PAGE, TOP    Shooting at Gordon Castle, *c*.1875, with the Earl of March, later 7th Duke of Richmond and Gordon, Lord Settrington (future 8th Duke), Lords Bernard and Esmé, and keepers.

FACING PAGE, BOTTOM    The Earl of March, shooting at Gordon Castle, *c*.1875.

where the Prince usually stayed in Goodwood House. One year the 6th Duke declined to have one of the King's lady friends staying in the house. Instead, and initially rather huffily, he went to West Dean, where Evie James was prepared to entertain his *petites amies*. Her own son, Edward James, was born in 1907 at a time when her husband Willie had been ill for a year. He looked extraordinarily like the King, who was his godfather. When questioned late in life, Edward James replied that he was not the King's son, but that his mother was the King's daughter; but this may have been one of his famous teases.[30]

This was the beginning of a new era in the history of both Goodwood House and Racecourse; and the Prince of Wales was certainly no Virtuous Victorian. The 6th Duke died at Gordon Castle in September 1903, a wise, respected, kind old man and an important national politician. He had already enjoyed his Scottish summer season. The tradition of long family summers in Scotland for fishing, shooting and stalking continued for his son and grandson, but would eventually die out in the next century.

# 15  MODERN GOODWOOD

## EDWARDIAN TO ELIZABETHAN

'After Goodwood is over, I always feel rather restless,' complained Bertie Wooster, the idle young master of P.G. Wodehouse's famous novels. The prevalent image of Goodwood in the early twentieth century came from the racecourse, with its royal visitors, great houseparties, sleek horses and glamorous entertainment. It is paradoxical that it should be during the tenure of Charles, 7th Duke of Richmond (1845–1928), that Goodwood should attain its social apotheosis. A gruff, formal figure, of military bearing and impeccable correctness, the 7th Duke of Richmond was for forty years a widower. Owing to the popularity of the racecourse with Edward VII, the Goodwood four-day meeting at the end of July became the climax of the aristocratic social season, providing an end-of-term euphoria before the yachting set moved over to Cowes and the rest gathered their tweeds for Scotland.

The racecourse became known as 'Glorious Goodwood' and was described as 'a garden party with racing attached'.[1] While the aristocracy paraded in their own enclosure, local employers gave a mid-week half-holiday so that shopworkers and labourers could also attend the Goodwood Cup. 'There is an atmosphere of gaiety and irresponsibility which one does not associate with any other meeting,' wrote a journalist in 1903.[2]

### THE WIDOWER DUKE

As Earl of March, the 7th Duke had the usual happy Goodwood childhood. In 1868 he married the beautiful auburn-haired Amy Ricardo. The Ricardos were an intellectual family, descended from the famous economist David Ricardo, originally Jewish but having converted to Christianity. They were in no way connected with the English aristocracy. Amy was bookish and artistic, a surprising consort for a young man who spent so much time shooting, fishing and stalking. It was a very happy marriage. Amy simply took her books

ABOVE  *Amy Ricardo, Countess of March*, 1875

FACING PAGE  The main portico, by James Wyatt. The capitals are marked Coade and Sealy, Lambeth, 1802. The magnolias on the house are traditional: some of the first magnolias in England were planted at Goodwood.

out on the fishing trips, and whiled away the hours at Gordon Castle by composing her album with poems and dried flowers or putting together, in 1877, the first catalogue of the paintings there, with carefully researched entries on the biographies of all the portrait sitters. She completed the same for Goodwood in 1879.

Amy bore the Earl of March five children in quick succession, but in 1879, as a result of complications after the birth of their son Bernard, she died. A plait of her long, lustrous hair was kept by her grieving husband. Three years later he married again, perhaps too quickly. Isabel Craven bore him two daughters, Muriel and Helen, but, unable to stand the northern gloom along with the constant discussions about dead game, she departed suddenly one autumn from Gordon Castle, with no plans to return.[3]

Two years later she too was dead, of typhoid. The Earl of March was at her bedside in London. He brought up his younger children at 49 Belgrave Square, the former Gordon House, where his sister Caroline, known as 'Aunt Lina', took charge of them all, especially becoming a substitute mother to the two youngest girls. The family also had the use of Molecomb. Ever scarred by the loss of Amy and traumatised by what had happened with Isabel, March avoided any subsequent remarriage. In 1903, aged fifty-seven, and twice a widower, he succeeded his father as the 7th Duke.

## ROYAL VISITORS

The King no longer lent the racecourse a slightly raffish air, but, surrounded by impeccable courtiers in black top hats and morning dress, a courtly and glamorous one. A meeting of the Privy Council would always be held in the Tapestry Drawing Room during Raceweek at the end of July. The new Duke responded rapidly to the change, by replacing the racecourse stand in the winter of 1903. The new building had a high and open seating area like the earlier stand, at the back of which was a sheltered, though unglazed, arcade. The design was by Arthur Henderson of Esher.

For the benefit of the new King, a royal pavilion was attached at the paddock end of the stand. A ladies' box at the other end, overlooking both the course and the woods, was developed into the Queen's box. Here Queen Alexandra enjoyed watching the picnics under the trees, with the flounced costumes, frilled parasols and luxurious table settings. An underground passage ran from that end of the stand to the royal box. The Queen, who was deaf and did not like being surrounded by chattering people, could sweep away down the subway when necessary, taking care to avoid her husband's various mistresses. No expense was spared for either box: the King's lavatory was made of monogrammed marble.

From the racecourse the royal and other guests would return to Goodwood House for tennis and croquet, cocktails and dinner. Despite having no duchess, the Duke had his house run as he believed it should be, to the highest and most hospitable standards. In the early years Lady Caroline, Aunt Lina, was in charge of the domestic details. She had her own little sitting room in one of the turrets, leaving the main run of the rooms to her brother. Later, provided with a Greville inheritance, she decamped to a London home in Wilton Terrace, handing over the running of Raceweek to the Duke's youngest daughter, the tall and beautiful Lady Helen, who in 1911 married Earl Percy, the future 8th Duke of Northumberland. After the death of Edward VII in 1910, George V continued to visit the races. The Duke added a smoking room to the back of the house for the gentlemen. A regular visitor for the Raceweek houseparty in the time of George V was 'The Yellow Earl', Hugh Lowther, 5th Earl of Lonsdale, who as a young man was also a lover of Lillie Langtry. He was enormously

extravagant and exhibitionist, always wearing a yellow tie in a variety of designs, and travelling from the house up to the races in his canary-yellow carriage, with postillions dressed in yellow livery. He was a close companion of the King, riding out with him every morning during Raceweek.

For royal guests, the 1770s State Apartments on the ground floor in the north wing were put to good use. Although the Tapestry Bedroom had the grandest bed, with its George III royal emblems, and was sometimes referred to as the King's Room, Queen Alexandra occupied this main bedchamber while Edward VII used the more modestly furnished adjacent dressing room, with an iron bedstead.[4] Under the influence of the Arts and Crafts movement, a large Jacobean chimneypiece adorned the room, which by 1905 was known as the 'Oak Bedroom', a Jacobean four-

TOP, LEFT   The royal box, with Edward VII in the centre and Queen Alexandra next to him. In 1904 the King changed the dress code unexpectedly, appearing in a white silk top hat instead of a black one.

TOP, RIGHT   Raceweek houseparty, 1904.

BOTTOM, LEFT   The racecourse, c.1930.

BOTTOM, RIGHT  Raceweek houseparty, 1906. The King had completed the sartorial downgrade, switching to an ordinary suit, with the choice of a white bowler or derby.

FACING PAGE   *Charles, Earl of March and Kinrara, shortly afterwards 7th Duke of Richmond, Lennox, Gordon and Aubigny, by Sir Arthur Stockdale Cope RA, 1903, oil on canvas, 226 × 119 cm/ 89 × 47 in.* A widower for forty years, the 7th Duke was a gruff, authoritarian figure, but he was a kind and generous father, allowing great freedom to his children, who especially loved their summers in Scotland. Later, however, his grandson, the 9th Duke, felt that an 'iron curtain' existed between his elderly grandfather in Goodwood House and his own parents with their four children at Molecomb.

poster now replacing the older bed.[5] It was subsequently also used by George V, who when he was there without Queen Mary would be called in the morning with a glass of whisky.[6] By the 1930s the Tapestry Bedroom was categorically named the Queen's Room.[7]

By 1906 all the original details of the Egyptian Dining Room scheme had been removed, reportedly because Edward VII did not like it.[8] The Duke had the room modified into an elegant, Georgian-style interior, as it indeed was, with its apse at one end echoed by a blank arch at the other. The statuary marble chimneypiece was removed, never to be seen again, as was the mirror above and the large looking-glass at the end of the room, together with four huge decorations, probably trophies in gilt-bronze, from the walls. Some items were retained in the house, but all except one of the crocodiles were removed from the backs of the dining chairs. A handsome Georgian-style cornice was placed around the top of the room and painted white. Bamboo decoration and door furniture was removed from the doors.

In the manner of many Edwardians, the 7th Duke had a great feel for the Georgian history of the house. Some of the rather fussy details that appear in Victorian photographs of the interiors were removed. In photographs of his houseparties the house seems Georgian indeed, only the less formal furniture arrangements and the adornment by huge palms giving a hint to the date. In the grounds he created a garden below Carné's Seat, with a pair of steps climbing up the ha-ha to the folly itself. Shooting was well organised on the estate, with about twelve days of sport between early November and the end of January. The guests, mostly members of the aristocracy, would stay in the house for several days, enjoying their day out under the auspices of the gamekeeper, assisted by three further keepers clad in brown coats with velvet collars. Lunch would be brought in a hamper and was usually delivered to one of the keepers' cottages.

Every summer, the day after Raceweek ended, the family would depart for Gordon Castle, travelling up from Euston Station in their own railway carriage, filled with trunks, bicycles, food baskets and servants. As well as the major preoccupation with salmon fishing on the Spey, there would be excursions to the grouse moor, and extra houseparties at Glenfiddich and Blackwater Lodge for the deer-stalking. Edwardian hospitality was lavish. Scottish traditions prevailed: everyone was expected to dance reels, and the ladies knitted shooting socks for their men.

## Golf at Goodwood

Partly because the future 7th Duke needed to entertain such a large family of teenagers and young adults, another new sport came to Goodwood. Golf had become fashionable in England in the 1880s, owing to its popularity with the Prince of Wales. Locally, it became organised when six gentlemen founded the Chichester Golf Club in 1892, playing on rented land at North Mundham. Golf became popular throughout the Gordon Lennox family in the later 1890s. Lady Helen was playing by the age of fourteen.

In the autumn of 1900 it was decided to close the course at North Mundham. By invitation of the elderly 6th Duke of Richmond, the club was moved the following year to Goodwood, where a short 18-hole course was laid out and maintained by estate employees. The full membership was to be sixty, with just fifteen ladies, who had their own sub-committee. A smart but optional club costume was introduced, of a red coat with a dark blue collar. Sunday golfing was not allowed. The 7th Duke continued to encourage the sport, becoming president of the club. He let the members use the former kennels as a clubhouse without charge, but asked if they could take on the upkeep of the greens. In 1911 the club became the Goodwood Golf Club. Lord Bernard Gordon Lennox, the Duke's charming and handsome youngest son, took charge of improvements, writing to champion

golfer James Braid to ask him to lay out a new course. Work was completed in the spring of 1914, when Lord Bernard was captain for a second year. For the opening day on 30 May 1914 he arranged for the Open champions, James Braid and Ted Ray, to play an exhibition match, teeing off in front of hundreds of spectators. Lord Bernard also presented a cup for competition.

Tragically, that autumn Lord Bernard was killed at Ypres. The Duke received a letter of sympathy from the club, which he politely acknowledged from Gordon Castle. His widowed daughter-in-law, Evelyn, wrote more fully:

> I know what a real pleasure it was to Bernard to do anything for the Golf Course and to help in any way the Committee and Club and I hope we shall see in the future the good results and steady growth of the Club and the improvements in the Course which he was so proud of and in which he took a such a real interest.
>
> For ourselves the loss is terrible and life can never be the same again.'[9]

Lord Bernard's death is shown sadly in the Members Register simply in red ink as 'Roll of Honour'. Lord Bernard's brother Lord Esmé Gordon Lennox took on his mantle as captain of the Golf Club in 1915. The Duke installed the little family of Evelyn and her

ABOVE    Lord Settrington (1899–1919)

FACING PAGE TOP    Park Lodge, with the gatepost bearing the memorial to Lord Settrington.

FACING PAGE, BOTTOM    After dinner at Molecomb (photograph courtesy of Lady Penn). Winter at Molecomb in 1918–19 included a visit from the amusing Lady Elizabeth Bowes-Lyon, shown fifth from left, as a guest of Lady Doris. To the left can be seen the Earl and Countess of March, later 8th Duke and Duchess, with the Hon. Frederick Gordon Lennox, later 9th Duke. Shortly after this photograph was taken, Lady Elizabeth played the bagpipes.

two sons at Halnaker, from where with Georgie [George] and Sandy [Alexander] she would join the old Duke at Gordon Castle every summer, the boys fulfilling his dreams by enjoying the fishing and shooting and becoming respectively a general and an admiral. Lady Bernard Gordon Lennox was herself killed when the Guards Chapel in London was bombed in the Second World War.

## CHARLES, 8TH DUKE OF RICHMOND (1870–1935)

The long arm of the First World War would affect Goodwood for generations. In 1915 the Earl of March, future 8th Duke, contracted polio while with his Territorial Army regiment, of which he was colonel, near Canterbury, the virus having struck a nearby camp of Canadian soldiers. The fever struck while he was alone with his wife for the weekend in the home of the Dean of Canterbury in the Cathedral Close, which had been lent to them. Distraught and initially unable to find a doctor, his Countess had a terrifying weekend with a very sick man. March's life was saved but he lost the use of both legs. He was able to walk with crutches, but to go anywhere beyond the precincts of his home, he had to use a Bath chair.

In the spring of 1918 the Earl of March's son, Lord Settrington, was sent to fight in France. He was twenty years old, with classic good looks and irresistible charm. Settrington was captured by the Germans, spending some months as a prisoner of war. His return home after Armistice in time for Christmas in 1918 was greeted with much rejoicing, with the Molecomb servants lined up to welcome him back. However, he felt that he needed further adventure; after showing aptitude on a Wireless Telegraph course, he applied to go as brigade signals officer with the Royal Fusiliers to the remote Russian town of Archangel to fight against the Bolsheviks. Here he was wounded in the chest by gunshot, and died of gangrene on a hospital ship. He was given a military funeral in Archangel. The news was received by the family at Gordon Castle, his grandfather carrying on as if nothing had happened. Although group photographs reflect houseparties as usual for Raceweek at Goodwood in the 1920s, this was a sad period. The deaths of the Duke's son and grandson hung over the estate; both were commemorated in the piers of gates at Park Lodge.

Inheriting in 1928, Charles, 8th Duke of Richmond (1870–1935), was a sensitive man who might have been a stronger leader had it not been for the dominating personalities of those closest to him. As a young man he loved both the army and sport, but his authoritarian father allowed him neither to have any kind of career, nor to share the running of the estate. This caused much ill feeling between the 7th Duke and his son's wife, Hilda Brassey. Hilda came from a family that had acquired wealth recently, through trade: her grandfather, Thomas Brassey, was a great railway pioneer. As a result her father and her uncles had all instantly become gentlemen, living in large houses and hunting to hounds; and Hilda had a very strong sense of what upper-class behaviour should be. Hilda met Lord Settrington (as he then was) when he was up at Christ Church, Oxford, with her brother, Leonard Brassey, in a set of hunting-mad young men who did very little academic work; 'Sett', as he was always known, did not complete his degree. In 1893 he married Hilda, honeymooning in his father's country home at Molecomb, while Leonard married his sister, Lady Violet. Hilda gave birth to two daughters, Amy (1894) and Doris (1896).

Keen that her husband should not just while away his time as the heir to a great estate, Hilda persuaded him, as an officer in the militia battalion of the Royal Sussex Regiment, to go in 1895 as ADC to General Roberts in Dublin. The move infuriated her father-in-law, and she later claimed that it was due to the ensuing row that she gave birth prematurely to a son, who died. March also went as ADC to Field Marshal Lord Roberts, as he now was, in South Africa, and was gazetted in 1900 to the Irish Guards, serving in the Boer War. Hilda accompanied him on both postings.

In 1906 March retired from his professional army career and the couple came to live at Molecomb, with their daughters and the two younger boys, a move that Hilda later admitted was a great mistake. Despite formal visits to the big house on Sundays, the two households remained very separate, and the Marches were not involved in the golfing activities. It was irksome to Hilda that Aunt Lina and Helen had such authority. Lord March tried to avoid the problems of his family situation by writing a history of the Charlton Hunt and going through bundles of old letters,

which he published.[10] A romantic, artistic man with a great love of nature, he made many friendships with women to whom he wrote conversational letters that reflected a quiet life, with not enough to do.[11] At the start of the Great War he commanded the Sussex Yeomanry, training them for active service. Later, he spent much time in London, staying at the Hyde Park Hotel, meeting friends in the Park, and enjoying music and theatre.

The tragedy of the 8th Duke was not only that he should be restricted both by his father and his health, dying before his time, but also that the talents of Hilda, who was extremely able and energetic, were not entirely fulfilled. During their brief tenure of Goodwood and Gordon Castle between 1928 and 1935 the couple paid off practically all their death duties of £180,000 and formed estate companies for both Goodwood and the Scottish property. Hilda also reorganised the furnishing of both houses. Her son Frederick gave her much credit for her achievements. She also did many charitable works, being one of the founding members of The Soldiers', Sailors' and Air Force Association, an enthusiastic member of the West Sussex County Council, and the first chairman of Chichester High School for Girls. She was a JP both in Sussex and in Scotland, where she continued to run Gordon Castle after the death of her husband. For her charitable works she was awarded the DBE in 1946. She also played cricket.

## 'FREDDIE MARCH': FREDERICK, 9TH DUKE OF RICHMOND (1904–1989)

The second-longest holder of the Richmond dukedom was not born to be a duke. The Hon. Frederick Gordon Lennox had a natural talent for carpentry and mechanics and as a child was given his own workshop at Molecomb to make model cars and aeroplanes. His passion for cars developed from an early admiration for his Aunt Lina's dark green Daimler, an enthusiasm that was shared by his brother Charles, Lord Settrington, at a time when motoring was new and exciting. Again like his brother, Freddie was also very keen on motor bikes, owning one in his last year at Eton; but his principal passion was for aeroplanes. In 1917 the Royal Flying Corps took over Tangmere, hitherto a let farm on the Goodwood estate. Freddie spent all his school holidays there, and by the end of the war felt that he knew as much about the planes as the pilots did. During their last spring together, that of 1919, Charles Settrington drove his fifteen-year-old brother around in his Morgan, both of them intent on all things mechanical, even visiting Sir Henry Royce at West Wittering to investigate the possibility of a job at Rolls-Royce for Charles. Freddie's life was shattered by the death of his brother in August that year. Quite unexpectedly he became, after his father, the heir to all the family titles.

RIGHT Goodwood Revival Meeting, 2002. The circuit was reopened for historic motor racing in 1998, by the Earl of March, fifty years to the day after its original opening by his grandfather.

BELOW Goodwood Motor Circuit, 1950s. The circuit was opened in 1948; it closed in 1966.

FACING PAGE Freddie March (the Earl of March, later Frederick, 9th Duke of Richmond, Lennox, Gordon and Aubigny) winning the Brooklands Double 12, 1931, with his co-driver Chris Staniland.

Now Lord Settrington, a name which initially caused him great distress, Freddie's life took a second unexpected turn. He left Eton in the summer of 1920, and was sent to cram for the Oxford exams with the Revd Thomas Hudson at Great Shefford, near Oxford. Here he loved the freedom and rumbustiousness of their family life, so different from his own upbringing under the tense insistence on correct behaviour at all times, and the dominant interest in country sports. He became completely absorbed by the vicar's vivacious red-headed daughter, Elizabeth. After he went up to Oxford, where he half-heartedly read Agriculture at Christ Church, he used to drive out to visit her at home. In the spring of 1924, just before taking his finals, to his parents' consternation he decided to give up his studies in order to see more of Elizabeth and to take up an apprenticeship with the new

LEFT *Elizabeth, Duchess of Richmond*, by Olive Snell, oil on canvas, 60 × 49 cm / 23½ × 19¼ in. A vicar's daughter, the Duchess loved Goodwood, filling the rooms with flowers and investing every gathering with her gaiety.

BELOW, LEFT *The 10th Duke of Richmond, Lennox, Gordon and Aubigny*, by Paul Brason, PPRP, 1998, oil on canvas, 180 × 122 cm / 72 × 48 in.

BELOW, RIGHT *The Duchess of Richmond*, by Paul Brason PPRP, 2002, oil on canvas, 180 × 122 cm / 72 × 48 in.

FACING PAGE The Earl of March and Kinrara, driving a Porsche 804.

Bentley motor company. He rode back to Goodwood on his motor bike to break the news to the family. When he announced that he was going to work for a motor company, his grandfather was furious. His parents were resigned about this particular decision, but less happy about Elizabeth. In 1926 there was a formal meeting in London in which, in the presence of the family lawyer, he was asked to give her up. Anticipating what might occur, he took his own lawyer to the meeting, and refused. There followed a serious family rift.

Over the three years at Bentley between 1924 and 1927, Frederick became a trained mechanic, moving to London for a brief period as salesman, and then back to Bentley on an increased salary. This meant that, in December 1927, at the age of twenty-three, he could afford to marry Elizabeth Hudson, who was now twenty-seven. His parents finally gave in, led by his father, who greeted him with warmth. The old Duke died less than two months later, the last to be buried in the family vault in Chichester Cathedral. Now that he was married, and his parents were preoccupied with the dukedom, Frederick at last felt happy and free, working in London at Bentley in Cork Street, living in the large house bought for them at 12 Norfolk Crescent and at Molecomb, learning to fly and beginning to take part in motor races. In May 1931 he was invited to drive in a Brooklands twenty-four-hour race known as the Brooklands Double 12, which he won. His parents had known nothing about it and were shocked and amazed to hear the news. His professional motoring name of Freddie March survived as a legend for considerably longer than the brief seven years for which he was Earl

of March; he inherited the dukedom on the early death of his invalid father in 1935.

Frederick's first task as 9th Duke of Richmond was to sort out the problems of two sets of enormous death duties at a time when estates were still suffering the economic effects of the Great War and were not profitable. This he did by selling all the Scottish estates, as well as many of the Gordon paintings, silver and arms and armour. The new Duke and Duchess had two young sons, Charles, the present Duke, born in 1929, followed by Nicholas (1931–2004). They lived much of the time in London and, with the outbreak of the Second World War in 1939, Goodwood House was once again given over to be a hospital, this time for Canadian servicemen, while a field on the Westhampnett part of the estate was made into an airfield. After the war, further economies had to be made, with the estate office moved into the Ballroom and the house seeming empty, the Yellow Drawing Room furniture having been destroyed by fire while in store. The Duke and Duchess built a modern house next to the banqueting house at Carné's Seat and lived there at weekends, while continuing to spend much time in

Above, Left   The Earl and Countess of March and Kinrara, with Lady Alexandra Gordon Lennox, Raceweek, 2006.

Above, Right   Lord Settrington (b.1994), by Etienne Milner, 1999, bronze.

Right   The Kennels, following the restoration, with *Tapster*, 1733, by John Wootton.

Facing Page   Walking to The Kennels for Sunday lunch, 2006; the Earl and Countess of March.

London. The Duke's passion for cars persisted, and he opened a perimeter road round the Westhampnett airfield as his new motor racing circuit in 1948.

The racecourse regained its former momentum, with the young Queen Elizabeth visiting from early in her reign. There would be a Raceweek ball in the main house every two years in aid of the Red Cross (the ball was held at Arundel Castle in alternate years). However, in these post-war years entertaining at Goodwood was much more sparse than it had been in earlier times; when the present Duke took over the running of the estate as Earl of March in 1969, it was unclear whether he and his wife, formerly Susan Grenville-Grey, would be able to afford to keep the house going. However, Lady March, who had started coming to Goodwood as a young teenager, when the Earl of March was her brother's schoolfriend, loved the house and they decided to risk the attempt. They redecorated the rooms on a tight budget, and Goodwood House became once more a lively family home.

This is not the story of the present generations. The 9th Duke's legacy was to bring something of the modern world to the estate. Even if he had wished to, he could not have run the house in the traditional way. The 10th Duke similarly undertook a professional training, in his case as an accountant, and worked to place the estate back on a firmer financial footing. His son the Earl of March is a photographer and a racing driver, and he has used these skills to restore the house and associated buildings, and to create a new momentum. All the sports that have developed quite naturally over the centuries at Goodwood continue to be played on the estate. A sculpture park, under separate ownership, has also been established, within the flint walls at Hat Hill. Goodwood is still characterised by style and good humour, following in the tradition set by its Georgian masters, the 2nd and 3rd Dukes of Richmond.

# THE
# FAMILY TREE

*The Lineage of the Dukes of Richmond, Lennox, Gordon and Aubigny
Earls of March, Darnley and Kinrara, Barons Settrington and Torbolton
from the reign of His Majesty King Charles II*

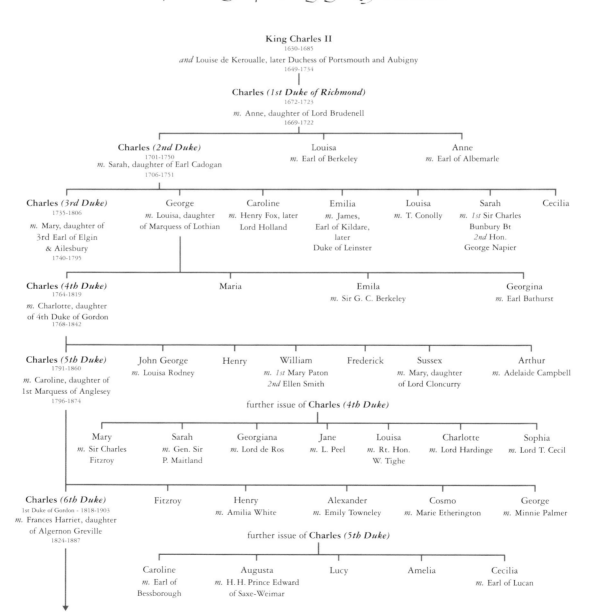

**King Charles II**
1630-1685

*and* Louise de Keroualle, later Duchess of Portsmouth and Aubigny
1649-1734

**Charles** *(1st Duke of Richmond)*
1672-1723

*m.* Anne, daughter of Lord Brudenell
1669-1722

**Charles** *(2nd Duke)*
1701-1750
*m.* Sarah, daughter of Earl Cadogan
1706-1751

Louisa
*m.* Earl of Berkeley

Anne
*m.* Earl of Albemarle

**Charles** *(3rd Duke)*
1735-1806
*m.* Mary, daughter of
3rd Earl of Elgin
& Ailesbury
1740-1795

George
*m.* Louisa, daughter
of Marquess of Lothian

Caroline
*m.* Henry Fox, later
Lord Holland

Emilia
*m.* James,
Earl of Kildare,
later
Duke of Leinster

Louisa
*m.* T. Conolly

Sarah
*m. 1st* Sir Charles
Bunbury Bt
*2nd* Hon.
George Napier

Cecilia

**Charles** *(4th Duke)*
1764-1819
*m.* Charlotte, daughter
of 4th Duke of Gordon
1768-1842

Maria

Emila
*m.* Sir G. C. Berkeley

Georgina
*m.* Earl Bathurst

**Charles** *(5th Duke)*
1791-1860
*m.* Caroline, daughter of
1st Marquess of Anglesey
1796-1874

John George
*m.* Louisa Rodney

Henry

William
*m. 1st* Mary Paton
*2nd* Ellen Smith

Frederick

Sussex
*m.* Mary, daughter
of Lord Cloncurry

Arthur
*m.* Adelaide Campbell

further issue of **Charles** *(4th Duke)*

Mary
*m.* Sir Charles
Fitzroy

Sarah
*m.* Gen. Sir
P. Maitland

Georgiana
*m.* Lord de Ros

Jane
*m.* L. Peel

Louisa
*m.* Rt. Hon.
W. Tighe

Charlotte
*m.* Lord Hardinge

Sophia
*m.* Lord T. Cecil

**Charles** *(6th Duke)*
1st Duke of Gordon - 1818-1903
*m.* Frances Harriet, daughter
of Algernon Greville
1824-1887

Fitzroy

Henry
*m.* Amilia White

Alexander
*m.* Emily Towneley

Cosmo
*m.* Marie Etherington

George
*m.* Minnie Palmer

further issue of **Charles** *(5th Duke)*

Caroline
*m.* Earl of
Bessborough

Augusta
*m.* H. H. Prince Edward
of Saxe-Weimar

Lucy

Amelia

Cecilia
*m.* Earl of Lucan

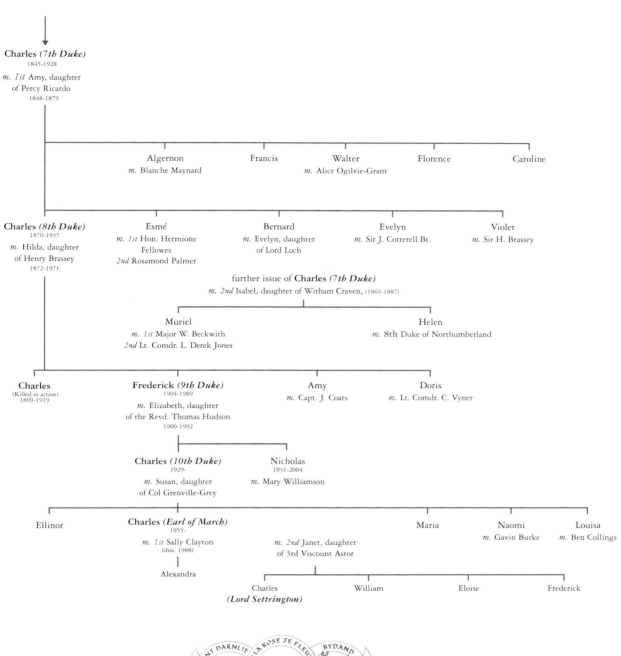

**Charles** *(7th Duke)*
1845-1928

*m. 1st* Amy, daughter
of Percy Ricardo
1848-1879

| | Algernon | Francis | Walter | Florence | Caroline |
|---|---|---|---|---|---|
| | *m.* Blanche Maynard | | *m.* Alice Ogilvie-Grant | | |

**Charles** *(8th Duke)*
1870-1935

*m.* Hilda, daughter
of Henry Brassey
1872-1971

Esmé
*m. 1st* Hon. Hermione
Fellowes
*2nd* Rosamond Palmer

Bernard
*m.* Evelyn, daughter
of Lord Loch

Evelyn
*m.* Sir J. Cotterell Bt.

Violet
*m.* Sir H. Brassey

further issue of **Charles** *(7th Duke)*
*m. 2nd* Isabel, daughter of Witham Craven, (1863-1887)

Muriel
*m. 1st* Major W. Beckwith
*2nd* Lt. Comdr. L. Derek Jones

Helen
*m.* 8th Duke of Northumberland

**Charles**
(Killed in action)
1899-1919

**Frederick** *(9th Duke)*
1904-1989

*m.* Elizabeth, daughter
of the Revd. Thomas Hudson
1900-1992

Amy
*m.* Capt. J. Coats

Doris
*m.* Lt. Comdr. C. Vyner

**Charles** *(10th Duke)*
1929-

*m.* Susan, daughter
of Col Grenville-Grey

Nicholas
1931-2004
*m.* Mary Williamson

Ellinor

**Charles** *(Earl of March)*
1955-

*m. 1st* Sally Clayton
(diss. 1988)

*m. 2nd* Janet, daughter
of 3rd Viscount Astor

Maria

Naomi
*m.* Gavin Burke

Louisa
*m.* Ben Collings

Alexandra

Charles
*(Lord Settrington)*

William

Eloise

Frederick

OPPOSITE TOP: ARMS OF CHARLES, 2ND DUKE OF RICHMOND   ABOVE: ARMS OF CHARLES, 7TH DUKE OF RICHMOND AND HIS SUCCESSORS, AS USED BY THE PRESENT DUKE

# NOTES

Abbreviations

DR        Duke of Richmond

BL        British Library
HMC       Historical Manuscripts Commission
NLI       National Library of Ireland
PRONI     Public Record Office of Northern Ireland
RIBA      Royal Institute of British Architects Drawings Collection
WSRO      West Sussex Record Office, Chichester

Where no location is given for a manuscript, it is in the Goodwood Archive
at the WSRO.

Introduction

1   WSRO, Goodwood MS 1436, f.390, Henrietta Le Clerc to 5th Duke of
    Richmond, 20 November 1832

Chapter 1

1   Portrait of Marie de Medici, after Rubens, Goodwood
2   WSRO, Goodwood, MS 1427, n.15, reproduced in *Goodwood Royal
    Letters*, ed. Timothy J. McCann, Trustees of the Goodwood Collection,
    1977, p. 4
3   The senior ducal title and that of the seigneurie did not always coincide:
    the seigneur had to pay homage to the French king and live at least
    partly in France, so was sometimes a younger son. The French count
    twelve seigneurs, where English books count only eleven, excluding
    Alain, briefly 2nd Seigneur.
4   He was the son of Elizabeth Blount, a maid of honour to Catherine of
    Aragon.
5   Settrington is near Richmond, in Yorkshire.
6   The earldom of March was an old Scottish one, first given to Robert
    Stuart in 1579/80. It was re-created for Esmé Stuart, 3rd Duke of
    Lennox and 8th Seigneur of Aubigny, in 1619.
7   The portrait of Barbara, by Sir Peter Lely, is at Goodwood. That of
    Nell, also by Lely, was sold. There is also a portrait at Goodwood of
    Mrs Middleton, studio of Lely.
8   Document at Arundel Castle
9   A contemporary painting of it is in a private collection in West Sussex.
    A modern, imaginary image of the ship has also been painted, based
    on extensive research.
10  HMC, *Report on the Manuscripts of the Earl of Egmont*, vol. ii, HMSO,
    Dublin, 1909, p. 150, James Fraser to unknown, 10 Feb 1685
11  The story of Louise de Keroualle's art collecting is told in the author's
    earlier book, *Mistress of the House: Great Ladies and Grand Houses
    1670–1830*, Weidenfeld and Nicolson, London, 2003.
12  According to a local historian, not the present house: it was between
    the quai and the rue de Lille.
13  'Before 10 January': *DNB*
14  Records of the Corporation of St Pancras, Chichester, 4 November
    1689
15  In 1737 the 2nd DR asked the Duke of Somerset at Petworth House to
    send him the deeds. In a letter dated 20 January 1737, the Duke of
    Somerset quoted Mr (John) Caryll from Harting and the Earl of
    Middleton as being the owners, saying the 1st DR bought it from the
    latter. He may well have left some owners out. John Caryll from
    Harting was attainted for treason in 1696. Another source suggests that
    the Duke purchased it from the Compton family.
16  Adsdean Book, collection of Mr Tom Wilmot of Pimlico, a collateral
    descendant of the family of Henrietta Le Clerc, the 3rd Duke's natural
    daughter, having inherited it from his grandmother, from the family
    papers at Adsdean House, Lavant. The statement was made by Harry
    Budd of Charlton, a member of the farming family who were great
    supporters of the hunt. He is listed, Register of Servants, MS 229, as the
    gamekeeper, having started work for the 2nd DR in 1734. He died in
    1806 aged about ninety-four. The book paper is watermarked Golding
    and Snelgrove 1809. The book contains a copy of the famous hunt
    poem (the Goodwood original is MS 151), two pages of notes, and a
    copy of the record of the 'remarkable Chace', an especially long hunt
    on 26 January 1738/9. It was written by an anonymous but diligent
    hunt enthusiast who knew Harry Budd.
17  MS 23, f. 117
18  Luttrell, p. 431, 27 Sept. 1698
19  All from MS 23: the cradle is f. 3, Mr Wright the Upholsterers Bill, Sept.
    1701
20  MS 23, f. 85, Mr King's Bill for East India Goods

21  It at least had a pair: see Lucy Wood, *Catalogue of Upholstered Furniture in the Lady Lever Art Gallery*, Yale University Press, forthcoming 2007.

22  All from MS 23

23  MS 12

24  MS 23, f. 110

25  MS 29, Bills of Samuel Philips, Mercer, 1713–21

26  All portraits at Goodwood

27  MS 20, July 1713, Whitehall; and MS 24, f. 9

28  *A Duke and his Friends* (henceforth *DF*), p. 142, Lord Cardigan to 2nd DR, Deene Park, 28 May 1727

29  *DF*, pp. 20–21, 1st DR to Louise, Duchess of Portsmouth and Aubigny, London, 5 August 1712 (translated from the French)

30  ibid.

31  ibid.

32  *The Complete Peerage*, vol. 4, pp. 406–7, note (e)

33  *DF*, p. 15, Anne, Duchess of Richmond, to Louise, Duchess of Portsmouth and Aubigny, 31 January, *c*.1710–11

34  ibid.

35  ibid.

36  Toby Barnard and Jane Clark (ed.), *Lord Burlington: Architecture and Life*, The Hambledon Press, London, 1995

37  MS 151. The 2nd DR wrote in the flyleaf that this poem was 'Brought to me by a porter in the beginning of February 1737/8' (i.e. 1738).

38  The full process of deduction, with details of the location, is published in Rosemary Baird, *Sussex Archaeological Collections*, The Sussex Archaeological Society, Lewes, 2005, vol. 143, pp. 215–38.

39  There is no surviving complete list of all the original subscribers, only of those who belonged when it was later made into a more formal Hunt Club in 1738.

40  Adsdean Book, also from the pages of notes

41  ibid.

42  *DF*, p. 57, Anne, Duchess of Richmond, to Charles, Earl of March, 31 January 1721

43  *DF*, p. 73, Duchess of Portsmouth to 2nd DR, Aubigny, 26 June 1723

44  Francis Steer, 'The Funeral Account of the 1st Duke of Richmond and Lennox', (Goodwood MS 120, f. 32), *Sussex Archaeological Collections*, vol. XCVIII, 1960, pp. 156–64, with special reprint

## CHAPTER 2

1  Quoted by David Hunn, *Goodwood*, Davis-Poynter Ltd, London, 1975 (henceforth Hunn), pp. 45–6. MS 6, f. 5, Goodwood, 24 July [1713/14]

2  *DF*, p. 35, Earl of March to his mother, 17 July 1720

3  BL 51424, f. 178, 3rd DR to Henry Fox, Milan, 29 June 1755, referring to his father's having spent a year there

4  *DF*, pp. 38–9, Johnny Breval to the Earl of March, Augsburg, 3 Aug 1721. Also conversation about Angeletta with Tim Llewellyn, 2005, to whom I am grateful for information about McSwiny; he is especially working on the Venice connection.

5  They were supposedly being sent in 1727: MS 105, f. 33 Owen McSwiny to 2nd DR, Venice, 7 March 1726/7 NS. A 'fate' happened to one of them, perhaps Angeletta's, f. 42. The one of the Earl of March, a very glamorous young image, must have been given to Louisa and is now at her home at Castletown, near Dublin. Various spellings are given of the agent's name: all his letters in the Goodwood archive are signed McSwiny.

6  MS 103, ff. 138–44, 26 July to 6 September 1721, and then again f.145, 28 February 1722

7  John Ingamells, *A Dictionary of British and Irish Travellers in Italy 1701–1800*, Yale University Press, New Haven and London, 1997, p. 640, this reference from the *Daily Journal*, 21 April 1721. For departure to Naples, see Bodleian Library, Oxford, Rawl. MS D 1180, p. 339.

8  MS 139: f. 2, H.F. van Lindt, 23 June 1721; f. 3, van Vittel, 23 June 1721; f. 4, Sebastiano Conca, 9 Sept 1721, and again f. 6, 8 October 1723

9  *DF*, p. 255, 2nd DR to Martin Folkes, Hampton Court, 12 August 1733

10  MS 110, f. 65, G. Cholmondeley at Brussels to Charles, Earl of March, at Florence, 25 November 1721

11  *DF*, p. 51, Cadogan to the Earl of March, The Hague, 17 July 1720

12  *DF*, p. 48, Anne, Duchess of Richmond, to Charles, Earl of March, 29 Nov 1721 (EoMp48)

13  Colen Campbell, *Vitruvicus Britannicus*, vol. III, 1725, p. 9

14  A powerful portrait of Anne, Countess of Albemarle, as a mature lady, by Reynolds, hangs in the National Portrait Gallery in London.

15  MS 9, f. 2, Duchess of Portsmouth to the Earl of March, Aubigny, 24 April 1723

16  *DF*, p. 78, Duchess of Portsmouth to 2nd DR, Aubigny, 25 December 1723

17  Michael Broughton to 2nd DR, Dublin Castle, 12 March [1724], of the daughters of Lord Carteret

18  *The Complete Works of Voltaire*, Oxford 1996, p.126, this section ed. by David Williams; letters D456 and D499

19  *DF*, p. 182, 2nd DR to Labbé, 4 May 1729

20  The burial is mentioned in the funeral accounts of the 1st DR (Goodwood MS 23) published by Francis W. Steer, 'The Funeral Account of the 1st. Duke of Richmond and Lennox', in *Sussex Archaeological Collections*, vol. XCVIII, 1960, 156–64.

21  The published engravings are: plates 51–2, aerial plan of the house within the park; 53 is the east elevation of 9 bays and a ground plan; 54 is the west front, of 7 bays. The three published plates can be seen at MS E5067. A small volume of seven original drawings, once catalogued in the Small Library, I1, is in the WSRO, MS 2227. These are attributed to Morris, working for Campbell. The one of the west façade was probably the basis for the engraving, but the east façades differ. There are further loose drawings for Goodwood, some inscribed by Campbell, in Royal Institute of British Architects Drawings Collection, Colen Campbell Catalogue (3), nos. 1–13.

22  MS 104, P. de Carné's letters, 22 Aug 1724, no. 343

23  ibid., 28 Aug 1724, no. 344

24  ibid, 8 September 1724, no. 345

25  Daniel Defoe, *A Tour Thro' the Whole Island of Great Britain . . .*, London, 1738, p. 205

26  BL, Add. MS 15776, Travel Journal of Jeremiah Miller DD, 'An Account of a Tour in Hampshire and Sussex . . . to Midhurst, Petworth, Arundel, Chichester . . . Begun on Thursday the 15th of September finished on Tuesday the 20th of September 1743'

27  MS 135, February–May 1725

28  *DF*, p. 202, Sir Thomas Dereham to 2nd DR, 25 August 1731

29  Small Library, Shelf D4

30  Jeremy Howard, 'Owen McSwiny and the Tombs of the British Worthies', *The European Fine Art Fair Handbook*, Basel, 1995, pp. 17–22, quoting Zanotti

31  W.G. Constable and J.G. Links, *Canaletto: Giovanni Antonio Canal, 1697–1768*, Oxford University Press, 1976, pp. 470–71, nos. 516 (Somers) and 517 (Tillotson), Owen McSwiny to the Earl of March, 8 March 1722

32  Edward Croft-Murray, *Decorative Painting in England*, Country Life, London, 1970, lists them all, pp 239–42. The present locations of nine out of ten of the paintings are known.

33  Quoted by Sotheby's, London, from *Arte Veneta*, 1985, in the cataloguing of *An Allegorical Monument to King George I*, sold December 1998

34  MS 105, f. 13, Owen McSwiny to 2nd DR, Venice, 8 March 1726

35  Goodwood purchased a set from the Christopher Gibbs sale, Christie's, Clifton Hampden, 25 September 2000.

36  'Vertue Note Books, volume V', *Walpole Society Journal*, vol. 26, 1938. The sketch suggests twelve pictures, allowing for the eight verticals and two horizontals identified, but leaving one at the end of the room unidentified (possibly a mirror) and one horizontal on the side. Scholars (Links, Croft-Murray) have always said that there were only ten tomb paintings at Goodwood.

37 Christie's, 26 March 1814. A landscape (described as Riley) was probably one of the Wootton overdoors.

38 MS 139 and 103. The bill must have been re-sent as all items on the first appear on the second, longer bill. The Van Vitelli is not the one of the Forum, still in the collection, which was bought as a 'Vanvitelli'.

39 At Goodwood

40 Wearing the Order of the Bath. He was also painted by Highmore as a Knight of the Bath.

41 I am grateful to Tim Llewellyn for this information.

42 MS 120, f. 89

43 MS 110, f. 143, Martin Folkes to 2nd DR, 23 July 1737

44 MS 121, f. 181, all from the bill of Alexander Reid

45 ibid., f. 105, bill of Thomas Tremaine, January 1732

46 MS 120, f. 256, bill of William Morton, 1727

47 MS 139, bill of James Reith, 1724

48 MS 121, f. 105, bill of Thomas Tremaine, 12 September 1731

49 MS 1884. Mr Alan Brodrick (1702–55), later Viscount Midleton (sic), was one of the Comptrollers of the Accounts of the Army, and thus a neighbour to the Duke in London, living in the old Richmond House.

50 MS 127, Housekeeping Book, 1731–43, f. 14: £19 in c.1730 and £21 on 23 and £10 10s on 30 August 1731. See also MS 120, ff. 150, 154, 157, 167

51 MS 110, J. Fuller to 2nd DR, 18 August 1746

52 MS 111, f. 198, Earl of Home to 2nd DR, Holyrood House, 27 August 1745

53 DF, p. 155, 2nd DR to Martin Folkes, 3 October 1728

54 BL, Sloane MS 4050, f. 129, 2nd DR to Sir Hans Sloane, Paris, 8 June, 1729

55 DF, p. 184, Thomas Hill to Labbé, 3 August 1729

56 ibid.

57 MS 117. A first payment to Thomas Micklam for bricks was dated July.

58 DF, p.191, 2nd DR to Labbé, Charlton, 18 February 1730

59 Haslam says 1729 (March 1729/30) but S. Rees correctly transcribes it 1730.

60 BL, Add. MS 28228, The Caryll Correspondence, f. 449 (previously 456), 2nd DR to John Caryll, Whitehall 30 October 1731; and f. 451 (previously 458) 2nd DR to John Caryll, 10 November 1731

61 108, f. 734, Charles Seymour, 6th Duke of Somerset to 2nd DR, 20 January 1739

62 Simon Rees, The Charlton Hunt, Phillimore & Co. Ltd, Chichester, 1998, pp. 111–26

63 MS 110, f. 70, Philip Stanhope, 4th Earl of Chesterfield, The Hague, 17 August 1728, to 2nd DR in Paris. He wanted a 'Maître Cuisinier d'un Génie Supérieur'.

64 MS 112, f. 293, William Pulteney to 2nd DR, 10 September 1730

65 DF, p. 195, Duchess of Portsmouth to her grandson, 2nd DR

66 MS 111, f. 183, Duke of Hamilton and Brandon to 2nd DR, 10 October 1730

67 MS 121, f. 205, 12 September 1731

# CHAPTER 3

1 MS 120, f. 54, bill of John Pine, April 1726

2 DF, p. 173, 2nd DR to Labbé, 25 January 1729, Lisbon: 'There is a debt which I contracted, a long time ago, of a hundred pieces, to Highmore, the artist, in Lincoln's Inn Fields, so . . . I pray you to pay this artist.' MS 121, f. 22, bill of Jos. Highmore 'for a picture of himself . . . in the Bath Habit', paid by Labbé, 30 December 1729, £100. This is not the one still in the collection, which is by Seeman.

3 DF, p. 132, Tom Hill to 2nd DR, 17 September 1725

4 MS 120, f. 211, bill from William Clarke for 10 guineas

5 MS 121, f. 137, in a bill for picture frames done by William Chisholm, 1730

6 DF, p. 192, reference in 2nd DR to Labbé, 15 August 1730, Tunbridge Wells

7 MS 56 is the Warrant of 1727 for her to be a Lady of the Queen's Bedchamber

8 The first version of the Goodwood (seated) portrait is at the National Portrait Gallery, with another at Syon House, Middlesex (Duke of Northumberland). The equestrian portrait was sold at Sotheby's, 15 July 1987, lot 49.

9 DF, p. 259, 2nd DR to Martin Folkes, Hampton Court, 11 October 1733

10 MS 112, f. 335, Paris, 9 January 1730, written by one of them; see also f. 336, written by them both, with much emphasis on 'je vous aime'.

11 MS 112, f. 387, Voltaire to 2nd DR, Paris, 27 June (crossed out) 8 July 1732; published as D 499 in The Complete Works of Voltaire, Oxford, 1996

12 Bernard E. Jones, Freemason's Guide and Compendium, Harrap, London, 1956, pp. 188–9, 528. I am grateful to Hugh McNeill for looking at my first draft on Freemasonry and for the references. His book Chichester Freemasonry: the first 300 Years is forthcoming. Also to Ricky Pounds of Chiswick House for Jacobite–Masonic history. Modern Masonic interpretation says that discussion of religion or politics is never allowed at lodges, but this is believed to have been different in the early days.

13 Minutes of the Grand Lodge, 2 March 1732, for the latter; see also London Evening Post, 7–9 April 1730. D. Jacques, Librarian of Goodwood, A Visit to Goodwood . . . the seat of His Grace the Duke of Richmond, 1822 (henceforth Jacques, 1822), pp. 92–5 for the former, giving 1698; John Kent's Records and Reminiscences of Goodwood and the Dukes of Richmond, Sampston Low, Marston & Company, London, 1896 (henceforth Kent), pp. 3–4, gives 1693, using a better source.

14 The Weekly Journal or British Gazeteer, 11 April 1730

15 DF, p. 110, London, June 1725

16 DF, p. 163, A. Albemarle to 2nd DR, 11 November 1728

17 MS 110, f. 78, Colley Cibber to 2nd DR, 7 February 1732, also DF, pp. 210–11

18 The handbill for this performance (illustrated) is MS 141.

19 The spelling is as given in the parish register of St Margaret's, Westminster. She was baptised there on 31 October by the Bishop of Chichester.

20 Warrant to Lord Lynn, Master of the Jewel Office, ref. Sotheby's sale. The item was sold by Emily's descendant the Duke of Leinster.

21 MS 126, f. 16

22 National Archive, Ind. 4623, p. 196, quoted by The Survey of London, vol. 13, p. 241

23 Earl of Ilchester, Lord Hervey and his Friends, 1952, p. 142

24 Lord Burlington's designs, once on loan to RIBA, are now in WSRO, Goodwood MS 2226, ten drawings. Four are published in John Harris, The Palladians, RIBA Drawings Series, Trefoil Books, 1981.

25 DF, p. 241, Earl of Pembroke to 2nd DR, Privy Garden, 13 February 1733

26 MS 126, 12 May 1733: one Captain Hall was paid to attend the site for three weeks.

27 MS 126, 15 June 1733, 'the Consideration mony agreed to be paid upon exchanging the contract'.

28 ibid., 2 July 1733, Captain Hall

29 The Loudoun and Mar house, but not Richmond House, can be seen in a print of the Privy Garden looking back, from the north end, with the Banqueting House on the right. See Sheila O'Connell, London 1753, The British Museum Press 2003 (exhibition catalogue), p. 195, ill. 4.16, John Boydell, A View of the Privy Garden. Also see fuller article on Richmond House by the author in the British Art Journal, September 2007.

30 Edward Croft-Murray, Decorative Painting in England, vol. ii, p. 226

31 These long buildings shown in Rocque's map were probably a reduction from those shown by Lediard and were replaced by the 3rd DR's Sculpture Gallery. In the time of the 3rd DR, redecorations were carried out by Sir William Chambers in 1757 and by James Wyatt in 1782 and 1787.

32 Croft-Murray, Decorative Painting in England, vol ii, p. 234. The ceiling is in Richmond Terrace, which was rebuilt on the site of Richmond House in 1818, and was believed by Croft-Murray to be from Richmond House and 'stylistically near to Kent'.

33 MS 102, f. 46

34  Richard Hewlings, *Chiswick House and Gardens*, Guidebook, 1989. He says that Kent does however seem to have designed at least the Summer Parlour at Chiswick and to have done the ceiling paintings.

35  This was pointed out by John Kenworthy Browne, visit to Goodwood, 1996.

36  Christine Hiskie, *The Building of Holkham Hall: Newly Discovered Letters*, Architectural History, XL, 1997

37  MS 230, f. 96, Matthew Brettingham to 3rd DR, 25 April 1757

38  Three survive, one in the Victoria and Albert Museum. The Goodwood pair were given to Chichester City Council by 1785 and were bought back by private treaty in 1996, having been catalogued by Sotheby's in their sale for 15 November 1996, lot 17.

39  They are identical to two sets in other collections. See Gervase Jackson-Stops (ed.), *The Treasure Houses of Britain*, National Gallery of Art, Washington, Yale University Press, New Haven and London, 1985, no. 145 at Temple Newsam House, Leeds; and private collection, Dublin.

40  MS 139, D14 for a list of the subjects. One surviving tapestry is in a private collection. It was given to Georgina, Countess Bathurst, by her uncle the 3rd DR after the Richmond House fire. The others had presumably been burnt.

41  ibid.

42  WSRO Goodwood MS 99, ff. 16–36, *Inventory of the Goods of his Grace the Duke of Richmond taken at His House at Whitehall*

43  MS 99, f. 12

44  *DF* 242, Earl of Pembroke to 2nd DR, Privy Garden, 13 February 1733

45  Marble Hill, Twickenham. The library was designed by William Kent.

46  Goodwood House, West Wing

47  W.S. Lewis *et al.*, *Horace Walpole's Correspondence*, Yale University Press, New Haven, 1937–83 (henceforth Lewis, *Walpole's Correspondence*), vol. 17, p. 184, Horace Walpole (henceforth HW) to Horace Mann, 2 November 1741

48  ibid., vol. 18, p. 442, HW to Sir Horace Mann, 8 May 1744

49  ibid., vol. 18, p. 450, HW to Mann, 29 May 1744. The emotive correspondence surrounding the Duke's refusal of Fox as a suitor is in the BL, Add. MS 51424, from f.1.

50  Croft-Murray, *Decorative Painting in England*, vol ii, p. 226. The paintings must have perished in the Richmond House fire; possibly they were inset into panelling.

51  MS 731: a list dated 1814 giving earlier RH locations

52  MS 105, f. 41, Owen McSwiny to 2nd DR, Venice, 5 December 1727

53  Now in the Royal Collection. See Martin Clayton, *Canaletto in Venice*, Royal Collection Enterprises Ltd, 2005.

54  See Francis Russell, 'Patterns of Patronage', in *Canaletto in England: A Venetian Artist Abroad 1746–1755*, Yale Center for British Art, Dulwich Picture Gallery, and Yale University Press, New Haven and London, 2006.

55  See Katharine Baetjer and J.G. Links, *Canaletto*, The Metropolitan Museum of Art, New York, 1989, pp. 5–15, 58. The offer of more paintings is in MS 105, f. 41, letter of 5 December 1727, McSwiny to the Duke.

56  Timothy J. McCann, *The Correspondence of the Dukes of Richmond and Newcastle*, Sussex Record Society, 1984, pp. 35–6, Richmond to Newcastle, Whitehall, 16 July 1740

57  See Francis Russell, 'Patterns of Patronage', in *Canaletto in England*. I am grateful to Francis and to John Somerville for their help in my findings on Prince Lobkowicz (see below).

58  MS 103, f. 244, Tom Hill to 2nd DR, Plantation Office, 20 May 1746

59  See Rosemary Baird, 'Letters of Introduction: The Duke of Richmond, Prince Lobkowicz and Canaletto', *Burlington Magazine*, March 2007.

60  Duke of Buccleuch

61  Both sketches are in W.G. Constable and J.G. Links, *Canaletto: Giovanni Antonio Canal, 1697–1768*, 1976; no. 754, *Whitehall and the Privy Garden looking North*, probably summer 1746 (private collection, location now unknown); and no. 744, *The Thames and the City from Richmond House*, (Birmingham Museums and Art Gallery); also for the latter see Charles Beddington, *Canaletto in England*, Yale Center for British Art and Dulwich Picture Gallery, 2006, p. 96, no. 21. See also no. 22 of this catalogue for another view of the terrace. Also see Constable and Links, no. 439, a much broader view, from a different viewpoint, of *Whitehall and the Privy Garden looking North* (Duke of Buccleuch, Bowhill).

62  William Hayley Mason, *Goodwood, its House, Park and Grounds with a Catalogue Raisonné of the Pictures in the Gallery of His Grace the Duke of Richmond KG*, Smith, Elder & Co., Cornhill, London, 1839 (henceforth Mason), 1839, p. 130, 'let into the panels'; confirmed by one being shown in the *Sussex County Magazine*, July 1929, facing p. 434, in the Yellow Drawing Room, in a very plain frame. In 1932 they were shown in new frames, Christopher Hussey, 'Goodwood', I, *Country Life*, 9 July 1932, p. 7: either the 8th DR (inherited 1928) and his duchess found these frames in the attic, and they were the original ones, or they bought them specially.

63  Published in *Miscellanies by Henry Fielding, Esq.*, April 1743

64  Martin Folkes, Goodwood, 1747, quoted in old *DNB* from Nicolls, *Lit. Anec.*, iv, p. 636. Martin Folkes was close enough to the Duke to be painted with him: see Alison Shepherd Lewis, 'Joseph Highmore: 1692–1780', Harvard University Ph.D., 1975, vol. ii, Catalogue no. 148, *The Duke of Richmond and his Three Esquires*. The others were Thomas Hill and Matthew Snow (picture believed destroyed).

## CHAPTER 4

1  Henry Herbert inherited in January 1733. Although he was called Lord Herbert in the 1720s, he is referred to here as Pembroke because this is the name by which he is generally known as an architect.

2  Howard Colvin, *Dictionary of British Architects*, 3rd ed., 1995

3  G.L.M. Goodfellow, 'Colen Campbell's Last Years', *Burlington Magazine*, CXI, 1969, pp. 189–90

4  WSRO Goodwood MS 121, f. 107. Dated 6 March 1729/30, the bill is from John Hughes.

5  I am grateful to Richard Hewlings for this suggestion. The cornice in the Long Hall itself is simpler.

6  See MS 126 for payment of premium in April 1732 and 1733.

7  MS 98. It is well summarised in Hunn, p. 57.

8  See also Rosemary Baird, 'Foxed by Fox Hall', *Sussex Archaeological Collections*, May 2006.

9  MS 99, f. 9

10  For an exposition of the attribution to Roger Morris see Rosemary Baird, 'Fox Hall', *Country Life*, January 2002; Charlotte Haslam, unpublished notes on Fox Hall for the Landmark Trust, 1994.

11  WSRO, Goodwood MS 117, f. 64 for the bricklayer, William Elmes; f. 104 for the sawyer, William Vallantine

12  WSRO, Goodwood MS 102, f. 110, written from Greenwich; and f. 113, 2nd DR at Goodwood to Labbé: 'so that now there is nothing more due to him (to Mr Shales, his banker), excepting for this new building at Charleton, and not much for that, for I have had most of the bricks from Roil, & others . . .'

13  WSRO, Goodwood MS 121, f. 105. The bill is dated 12 September 1731, but he has added in the 1732 date.

14  Adsdean document, in the possession of Mr T. Wilmot of Pimlico: copy in WSRO, MP 3701 (earlier than the Adsdean Book)

15  MS 126, f. 61, 16 August 1732, for 2 gns. The second payment was on 17 October 1732.

16  MS E4992

17  MS 151, *The Historical Account of the Rise, and Progress, of the Charlton Congress*; the Duke wrote in the flyleaf that this was 'Brought to me by a porter in the beginning of February 1737/8'.

18  MS 99, f. 9

19  MS 3766

20  MS E100, f. 11

21 J.J. Cartwright (ed.), Dr Richard Pococke, *Travels*, Camden Society, 1889. Pococke also observed 'the cover'd place in which they sometime used to dine', presumably the 'small dark cell' mentioned near the end of Chapter 1 of the anonymous poem, which was replaced by the Dome.

22 His name is marked on the 1732 map of Charlton.

23 Chatsworth MSS 201:0 Duke of R. to Ld Burlington, 29 June 1730

24 RIBA, G3/2/2, inscribed by the 2nd Duke: *a draught of the Earl of Burlington's, for the front, of the Council House, for the corporation of Chichester*

25 Walpole Society, *Vertue Notebooks*, V, p. 144

26 *DF*, vol. I, p 251, Martin Folkes to 2nd DR, 1733

27 Martin Folkes, ibid.

28 Chatsworth MS 201.5, undated letter *c.*1734 or 1735

29 MS 137

30 Richard Hewlings. The letter is dated 1744.

31 BL, Add. 28726, f. 122, 2nd DR to Peter Collinson, Goodwood, 5 December 1742

32 They were removed from Chiswick after 1753; displayed on the gate of Devonshire House from 1897, and moved with it in 1921. I am grateful to Simon Bradley for confirmation.

33 One of the group of Arundel marbles given by the Countess of Pomfret to the Ashmolean Museum, Oxford, the sphinx was for a time in the Oxford Botanic Gardens, where it became damaged.

34 Walpole Society, *Vertue Notebooks*,V, p. 145

35 Jacques (1822), pp. 88–9, talks of this 'once elegant room', mentioning the 'beautiful chimneypiece, together with the remnant of painting and gilding on the ceiling and walls'. Mason (1839) is more elaborate. He says it was 'originally fitted up in a very costly and magnificent manner, most elaborately painted and gilt, and with statuary marble chimneypieces.' By 1839 it was 'finished more plainly and substantially'.

36 MS 60, a charming little vellum notebook, principally listing 'Officers and Servants of His Majesty's Stables' in August 1745. In the back 2nd DR has jotted several notes, including these details.

37 Small Library, W6

38 Brian Fitzgerald, *Correspondence of Emily, Duchess of Leinster (1731–1814)*, Dublin 1953, vol. i, p. 164, Marchioness of Kildare to Marquis of Kildare, Kildare House [Dublin], Christmas Day [1762]

39 Marquis of Kildare, *The Earls of Kildare and their Ancestors from 1057 to 1773*, 4th edition, 1864, p. 144, quoting from one of many letters in the Earl of Roden's library from Emily to the Hon. Anne Hamilton, later Countess of Roden, 10 May 1747

40 MS 112, f. 328, extract or copy of a letter from Sir Thomas Robinson, Governor of Barbados, to 2nd DR, dated by WSRO *c.*1744 but probably a little later

41 MS 102, f. 74, Emily, Countess of Kildare, to Sarah, Duchess of Richmond, 6 August 1748

42 *DF*, p. 721, Charles Knowles to John Russell, Jamaica, 4 April 1739

43 MS 110, f. 171, T. Gibberd to 2nd DR, Westminster, 24 September 1748

44 BL, Add. 28727, f. 12, 2nd DR to Peter Collinson, undated but *c.*1748

45 MS 102, f. 70, Emily, Countess of Kildare to 2nd DR, Carton, 8 October [1748] (sometimes given as 1747 but is in a run of letters, internal references making it 1748)

46 BL, 2nd DR to his duchess, 1750

47 MS 60

48 It was found when a cellar was dug under the house on the corner of St Martin's Lane and North Street. M. Hills, 'Remarks on a Stone bearing a Roman Inscription. Found at Chichester in 1723, and now at Goodwood', *Sussex Archaeological Collections* (1854), pp. 61–3; Roger Gale, *An Account of a Roman Inscription, found at Chichester*, in Philosophical Transactions, 32, no. 379, (1723), 391–400.

49 The temple was later taken down and the tablet is now back in Chichester, appropriately set into the wall of the Council House, near to where it was originally found. The statues were sold, but were bought back for Goodwood in 2004.

50 BL, Add. MS 15776, Travel Journal of the Revd Jeremiah Miller

CHAPTER 5

1 BL, Add. 28726, f. 156, 2nd DR to Peter Collinson, Goodwood, 27 June 1746. These letters are in the Sloane collection.

2 The map was dated February 1731 and is therefore actually 1732 in modern style.

3 MS E30, 'A Terrier of the Manors of Boxgrove and Halnaker', by Yeakell and Gardner, 1781, Map 1; see also MS E31, f.. 78, *c.*1790.

4 George Edwards, *Gleanings of Natural History*, The Royal College of Physicians, vol. I, 1758

5 *DF*, p. 97, Earl Cadogan to 2nd DR, 1 August 1724

6 MS 112, f. 333, Sir Hans Sloane to 2nd DR, 20 March 1728

7 As a result of Elizabeth Sloane's marriage to Charles Cadogan (who was the heir to his brother's barony but not to his earldom) the Cadogan descendants acquired vast estates in Chelsea, adjacent to Sloane Square, which they still own today. After Sloane's death his huge scientific collections were acquired by the nation, in what became in 1754 the British Museum.

8 Francis Steer, *The Memoirs of James Spershott*, Chichester City Council, Chichester Papers 30, 1962

9 See John Strype, *A Survey of the Cities of London and Westminster*, 1720

10 MS 120, f. 82

11 British Library, Sloane MS 4078, f. 66, 2nd DR to Sir Hans Sloane, n.d.

12 MS 112, f. 319, Sir Thomas Robinson to 2nd DR, Pilgrim House, Barbados, 31 August 1742

13 MS 108, f. 815, Henry Foster to 2nd DR, April 1730

14 Details from Timothy J. McCann, 'The Duke of Richmond's Menagerie at Goodwood', *Sussex Archaeological Collections*, vol. 132, 1994, pp. 143–9

15 *A Catalogue of the Egyptian and other Antiquities . . . Belonging to the Museum of his Grace the late Duke of Richmond*, 24–27 May 1751, day 2, pp. 7–8

16 MS 102, f. 31, Lady Emily Lennox to 2nd DR, London, Thursday 14th [?] 1746

17 Jacques (1822), p. 77

18 MS 102, f. 67, Emily, Countess of Kildare, to 2nd DR, 18 August (currently dated 1747 but may be 1748)

19 Walpole Society, *Vertue Notebooks* V (1939), p. 143

20 BL, Add. MS 15776, f. 221, Travel Journal of the Revd Jeremiah Miller

21 MS 102, f. 67, Cartown [*sic*], 18 August [1748: sometimes given as 1747 but ff. 68, 69, 70, 71, 72, 73 are all 1748, themes within them recurring, so f. 67 is probably also 1748]

22 MS 102, f. 70, Emily, Countess of Kildare to 2nd DR, Dublin, 8 October [1748]

23 Jacques (1822), p. 70, *DF*, p. 194. The dog died on 26 Sept 1741. According to Emily's letter, MS 102, f. 67, 18 August [1748] all the epitaphs were written by Chandler.

24 MS 112, f. 294, J. Pelham to 2nd DR, Charles St, 4 September 1736

25 MS 134: see below; bill of December 1733

26 It is labelled as the Pheasantry on map E 31, *c.*1785. A servant, Eliza Marley, is first recorded up there in 1766, MS 229, f. 25. The Stewards' Accounts for 1770s mention a keeper, Elizabeth Stout.

27 BL, Sloane 4056, f. 126, 2nd DR to Sir Hans Sloane, Goodwood, 7 October 1739

28 Paul Foster (ed.), *Marsh of Chichester: Gentleman, Composer, Musician, Writer 1752–1828*, University College, Chichester, Otter Memorial Paper no. 19, Chapter IV by Timothy J. McCann, p. 106, from Marsh's diary for June 1787

29 Viscount Palmerston, *Tour of Sussex*, section of his unpublished travel diary, 1788, Hampshire Record Office, 27M60/1924

30 I am grateful to Jon O'Donoghue for sending me this extract. Other original journals (19 volumes) are in the Senate House Library, University of London.

31 These further include a few stones and tiles denoting the very top pitch of the folly at the back, where it was set into the steep side of the

quarry; a brick cell built into the wall beside it (which could either be a coal bunker or a cell for an animal); and a large number of old bricks and cut stones nearby, denoting other built areas.

32 MS 229, Register of Servants, Mary Quin, at Carné's Seat from 20 October 1746

33 MS 1593, f. 275, Harry Elms to 5th DR, 9 April 1838

34 BL, Add. MSS 51424, 2nd DR to Henry Fox, Goodwood, 5 January 1750

35 At least one tulip tree was planted to the north of the house, near where the orangery was later built (Jacques, 1822, p. 76).

36 MS 112, f. 407, Francis Yonge to 2nd DR, Westminster, 4 December 1747; BL, Add. MS 51424, f. 76, quoted above

37 BL, op. cit, f. 131, 2nd DR to Peter Collinson, Charlton, 15 February 1743

38 Philip Miller, *The Gardener's Dictionary, containing the means of cultivating . . . the garden . . . conservatory and vineyard*, London, 1732, 3rd ed., 1737

39 BL, Add. 28726, f. 121, 2nd DR to Peter Collinson, Goodwood, 12 November 1742; also f. 122, 2nd DR to Peter Collinson, Goodwood, 5 December 1742. The complete BL Collinson correspondence, November 1741–December 1767, is transcribed WSRO MS 2074.

40 About seven years later the Duke just could not resist some more, from another source: 'the small magnolias are confounded dear, but I must have them.' BL, Add. 28727, f. 8, 2nd DR to Peter Collinson, undated (1747)

41 MS 112, f. 297, Robert 8th Baron Petre to 2nd DR, Thorndon, 23 March 1739/40

42 BL, Add. 28726, f. 127, 2nd DR to Peter Collinson, Goodwood, 5 December 1742

43 Ibid., f. 124, 2nd DR to Peter Collinson, Goodwood, 17 December 1742. He was quite happy to have the other items 'for love or mony'.

44 Ibid., f. 127, 2nd DR to Peter Collinson, Goodwood, 28 December 1742

45 Hunn, p. 41

46 BL, Add. 28726, f. 129, 2nd DR to Peter Collinson, Whitehall, 29 January 1743

47 ibid., 2nd DR to Peter Collinson, Charlton, 21 February 1745

48 BL, Add. 28727, f. 6, 2nd DR to Peter Collinson, Charlton, 6 March 1748

49 MS 111, f. 212, Earl of Hopetoun to 2nd DR, Hopetoun House, 7 March 1749

50 ibid., f. 213, Earl of Hopetoun to 2nd DR, Hopetoun House, 20 April 1749

51 MS 102, f. 82, Emily, Countess of Kildare to 2nd DR, Carton, 8 October 1749

52 MS 112, f. 389, Voltaire to 2nd DR. My own idea, but I am grateful to Anthea Gentry for clarification about Linnaeus and for information about the agouti.

53 Many of these are now in the British Museum. The earliest dated one is 1732; most are 1740–42.

54 Letter quoted by Edwards, *A Natural History of Birds*, vol. IV, p. 228

55 This and other information on George Edwards is from A. Stuart Mason, *George Edwards, The Bedell and his Birds*, Royal College of Physicians, 1992, p. 29

56 Joanna Selborne, 'Dedicated to a Duke: Goodwood's Uncommon Birds', *Country Life*, 12 March 1998, pp. 87–9

57 Information from the Catalogue of the Hunterian Museum, Glasgow, where the portrait now is. An anonymous painting of Leather-coat Jack was also in the collection of Dr John Hunter and is now in the Hunterian Museum, Royal College of Surgeons, London: engravings were also made after works by Hubert Gravelot, published in 1742, and after B. Smith. The Glasgow Museum houses the collection of Dr William Hunter, the London one that of his brother Dr John Hunter.

58 Both items were in the sale that took place after the Duke's death, on 24–7 May 1751: lot 31 was 'The curious skeleton of a famous Dwarf, called Leather coat Jack . . .', and lot 32 was 'A painting in oil of the same Dwarf by Highmore'. (In fact the style of this small work does not look very like Highmore.) The two lots were unsold and must have returned to the Duke of Richmond's family. They were presumably,

at a later date, given to Dr William Hunter for his museum, as the picture is now in the Hunterian Art Gallery, Glasgow, and the remnant of the skeleton (only a foot) is in the associated Hunterian Museum.

59 Lot 19 of 'Artificial Curiosities' in the sale after his death; and Day 3, lot 30.

60 One of these mummies was at Goodwood well into the twentieth century and is now in the Brighton Museum. There is also a mummy case lid that belonged to the Duke in the Sir John Soane Museum. See also Tim Knox, 'The Vyne Ramesses: "Egyptian Monstrosities" in British Country House Collections', *Apollo: National Trust Historic Houses and Collections Annual*, Col. CLVII, no. 494 (New Series), April 2003, pp. 32–6.

61 Royal Society, *Philosophical Transactions*, 42, p. 510, letter of 2nd DR, June 1744

62 Baker, p. 134, British Library, Bentinck papers, *Correspondence of Count Bentinck with his son Antoine, and his tutors*, f. 98

CHAPTER 6

1 The first quote is from Colley Cibber (see below). The second is MS 60, on the inside cover of a little notebook which gives a list of all the royal stables staff for the Duke, as Master of the Horse. This note is added in the Duke's hand: August 1745.

2 WSRO, Archives of the City of Chichester, C1, p. 400

3 *DF*, p. 304, John Collis to 'another Sussex worthy'

4 *DF*, p. 313, Colonel J. Pelham of Crowhurst, MP for Hastings, to 2nd DR, 14 September 1736

5 MS 111, ff. 237–40, Mohammed Ben Ali Abgali (Moroccan Ambassador) to 2nd DR. The Duke also owned a portrait of him by Enoch Seeman. He was Ambassador from 14 August 1725 to February 1727.

6 MS 100, f. 108, M. de Cambis to 2nd DR

7 Sybil Rosenfeld, *Temples of Thespis: Some Private Theatres and Theatricals in England and Wales, 1700–1820*, Society for Theatre Research, London, 1978, p. 35, sourced from a Burney Collection clipping, 4 June 1788; the Richmond House Theatre is discussed between pp. 34 and 52.

8 MS 110, f. 165, Colley Cibber to 2nd DR, n.d. There is another lively letter from Cibber at f. 78.

9 MS 99

10 Still at Goodwood, with two other similar small classical reliefs

11 Mr Cock, Piazza, Covent Garden, 8 March 1741/2 and the 5 next days; marked-up catalogue in the private library of Charles Sebag-Montefiore, Putney

12 All from MS 127, Housekeeping Book 1731–43

13 By Arthur Pond

14 Letters about the Jacobite advance are in Timothy J. McCann, *The Correspondence of the Dukes of Richmond and Newcastle*, Sussex Record Society, vol. 73, 1984, nos. 186–7, 192, 196, 199–200; one about the siege is BL, Add. MS 32705, f. 468.

15 Lewis, *Walpole's Correspondence*, vol. 19, p. 176, HW to Horace Mann, 29 November 1745, Arlington Street

16 Now in the Music Room and West Lobby. No receipt exists, so the date of acquisition is speculative.

17 MS 112, f. 395, John Wootton to 2nd DR, Cavendish Square, 11 August 1733 (*DF*, p. 262)

18 Private collection, by descent from his daughter to the Dukes of Wellington

19 Sold Christie's 8 June 2006, lot 18

20 The hunting scene is now in another private collection.

21 This suggestion was made by Sir Howard Colvin.

22 First suggested by Dr Timothy Connor, 'Architecture and Planting at Goodwood', 1723–1750, *Sussex Archaeological Collections*, 1970

23 MS 109, f. 862, 23 July 1745, Duchess of Richmond to M. Brettingham. This was about the paying of bills for the work by different trades at Richmond House in London.

24 It clearly has nothing to do with the distinctive hand of Chambers, a deattribution now agreed by John Harris.

25 MS 102, f. 72, Emily, Countess of Kildare to 2nd DR, 3 August [1748]

26 ibid., f. 74, Emily, Countess of Kildare to Sarah, Duchess of Richmond, 6 August [1748]

27 ibid., f. 76, Emily, Countess of Kildare to 2nd DR, 6 September [1748]

28 WSRO, Goodwood MS 109, f. 847, 13 February 1749/50, Matthew Brettingham, presumably at Sheffield Place, Sussex, to Duchess of Richmond

29 ibid., f. 863, 18 Feb 1749/50, Duchess of Richmond to Matthew Brettingham

30 Portraits of both at Goodwood, by Jan Wandelaar and Joshua Reynolds respectively

31 Jacques (1822), p. 73. See also MS 136, 'Abstract of the Expence of building the new kitchen & Servants' hall, begun in Michmas Quar 1748': this suggests that a new kitchen was also included in the basement, while the separate one, linked by a tunnel, stayed in use.

32 BL, Holland House papers, Add. MS 51424, f. 33, 2nd DR to Lady Caroline Fox, 26 March 1748; this is the main reconciliation letter.

33 Walpole Society, *Vertue Notebooks*, V, p. 142

34 Lewis, *Walpole's Correspondence*, vol. 9, p. 57, HW to George Montagu, 26 May 1748

35 MS 61

36 MS 111, f. 210, the Constable of Navarre to 2nd DR, 1 January 1749

37 R.D.E. Eagles, 'Francophobia and Francophilia in English Society, 1748–1783', Oxford University PhD thesis, 1996

38 Lewis, *Walpole's Correspondence*, vol. 20, p. 28, HW to Horace Mann, 8 March 1749

39 There is now a copy in place, with the original, by Hubert le Sueur, at Pallant House Gallery.

40 Lewis, *Walpole's Correspondence*, vol. 30, HW to Lord Lincoln, 1743/4

41 *Walpole's Correspondence*, Henry Colburn, London, 1837, vol. ii, p. 114, Walpole to Mann, 25 February 1750

42 MS 10, f. 86, Emily, Countess of Kildare to Sarah, Duchess of Richmond, Dublin, 6 March 1750

43 MS 102, f. 82, Emily, Countess of Kildare to 2nd DR, Carton, 8 October 1749

44 BL, Holland House Papers, Add. MS 51424, f. 93, 2nd DR to Henry Fox, 8 June 1750, describing his discomfort. The surgeon, Francis Robert Tomkins (c.1720–94), had previously assisted the Duke of Cumberland at Dettingen, where he probably met the Duke of Richmond. He was the author's four-greats-grandfather. See also ff. 95, 97, 99 for the illness.

45 John R. Baker, *Abraham Trembley of Geneva, Scientist and Philosopher, 1710–1784*, Edward Arnold & Co., London, 1952, p. 137, quoting Abraham Trembley, 1775, *Instruction d'un père a ses enfans, sur la nature et la religion*

46 BL, Holland House Papers, Add. MS 51424, f. 105: notes on the Duke's will, dated 26 February 1749

CHAPTER 7

1 MS 102, f. 73, Emily, Countess of Kildare, to Sarah, Duchess of Richmond, 9 August [1748]

2 BL, Add. MS 51424, Holland House Papers, Earl of March to Henry Fox, Whitehall, 2 June 1750

3 John R. Baker, *Abraham Trembley of Geneva*, p. 138, quoting BL, Egerton Papers, Add. MS 1726, f. 154

4 BL, Add. MS 51424, f.157, 3rd DR to Henry Fox, 12 April 1755

5 The Duke gave the prime version to his sister Caroline for the picture gallery that she began to create at Holland House from 1760; now in a private collection. He retained the replica, also by the artist himself, still at Goodwood. The portrait of Lord George is at Goodwood.

6 Add. MS 51424, f. 179, 3rd DR to Henry Fox, 29 June 1755

7 HMC, *The Bathurst Papers*, pp. 676–7, 3rd DR to Lord George Lennox, 25 January 1757

8 MS 224, f. 1, n.d., 3rd DR to Major-General the Hon. Henry Seymour Conway

9 MS 110, f 105. Major-General the Hon. Henry Seymour Conway to 3rd DR, presumably 1756. This undated letter, written at Little Warwick Street (London) appears in the 2nd DR's papers, but must have been written to the 3rd Duke. There are also two other undated letters from Conway to the Duke.

10 It was through the descendants of this marriage that the titles of Ailesbury and Cardigan became conjoined.

11 Lewis, *Walpole's Correspondence*, vol. 21, p. 67, HW to Mann, Arlington Street, 17 March 1751

12 Fitzgerald, *Correspondence of Emily*, vol. i, p. 178, Caroline to Emily, 26 August [1758]

13 The Countess of Ilchester and Lord Stavordale (ed.), *The Life and Letters of Lady Sarah Lennox, 1745–1806*, John Murray, London, 1904, p. 261, Lady Sarah Lennox to Lady Susan O'Brien, Stoke, 19 September 1776: 'Was not you surprised at poor Mr Damer's death? I had no idea he was *maddish* even, & in my mind he has proved he was *quite mad*, for I cannot account for his death & the manner of it any other way.' Sarah seems to have reverted from using her married name of Bunbury to that of Lennox in 1776.

14 Lewis, *Walpole's Correspondence*, vol. 25, p. 576, HW to Sir Horace Mann, 7 May 1785

15 See David Mannings, *Sir Joshua Reynolds: a Complete Catalogue of his Paintings*, published for the Paul Mellon Centre for Studies in British Art by Yale University Press, New Haven and London, 2000, nos. 1117 and 1118. The profile portrait of the Duchess is in a private collection in Texas, the three-quarter-length portrait in a private collection in England. The third portrait, c.1764–7, no. 1119, is at Goodwood.

16 Not recorded since: possibly lost in the Richmond House fire.

17 Quoted by Larry Ward, unpublished manuscript in the Goodwood archives. Not found in Lewis.

18 Henry B. Wheatley (ed.), *The Historical and Posthumous Memoirs of Sir Nathaniel William Wraxall 1772–1784*, London, Bickers & Son, 1884, vol. ii, p. 59

19 Lewis, *Walpole's Correspondence*, vol. 37, p. 483, Conway to HW, Goodwood, 29 May 1757

20 Fitzgerald, *Correspondence of Emily*, vol. i, p. 221, Caroline to Emily, May 1759

21 Lewis, *Walpole's Correspondence*, vol. 9, p. 234, HW to George Montagu, Arlington St, 1 May 1759

22 Hon. J.A. Home (ed.), *The Letters and Journals of Lady Mary Coke*, privately printed by David Douglas, Edinburgh, 1889–96, vol. i, p. 83, quoting Walpole

23 Fitzgerald, *Correspondence of Emily*, vol. i, p. 174, Caroline to Emily, 8 August [1758]

24 ibid., vol. i, p. 178, Caroline to Emily, 26 August [1758]

25 Lewis, *Walpole's Correspondence*, vol. 9, p. 237, HW to George Montagu, 2 June 1759

26 ibid., vol. 38, p. 117, HW to Conway, Arlington St, 9 September 1761

27 Fitzgerald, *Correspondence of Emily*, vol. i, p. 179, Caroline to Emily, 26 August [1758]

28 Lewis, *Walpole's Correspondence*, vol. 22, p. 115, HW to Mann, Arlington Street, 11 August 1763

29 The King wrote to his mentor, the Marquis of Bute, about her: ed. Romney Sedgewick, *Letters from George III to Lord Bute 1756–1766*, Macmillan, London, 1939, pp. 37ff., in one of which, written in the winter of 1759–60 he describes Sarah as 'the dear object of my love'.

30 BL, Add. MS 1862, f. 86, 3rd DR to William, Count Bentinck, 21 December 1760

31 Henry Reeve (ed.), *The Greville Memoirs*, Longmans, Green & Co., London, 1875, p. 129, conversation at Holland House with the 3rd Lord Holland (grandson of Henry Fox, 1st Baron Holland)

32  Fitzgerald, *Correspondence of Emily*, vol. i, p. 271, Caroline to Emily, 31 January [1760]

33  BL, Add. MS 51424, f. 235, 3rd DR to Henry Fox, 5 March 1762; and f. 241, Whitehall, 23 October 1764

34  Lewis, *Walpole's Correspondence*, HW to Horace Mann, vol. 40, p. 284n, quoting vol. 22, pp. 148–9

35  ibid., vol. 22, pp. 148–9, HW to Horace Mann, 7 June 1763

36  Her journals provide useful comments and insights into fashionable London life: Home (ed.), *The Letters and Journals of Lady Mary Coke*. John, 2nd Duke of Argyll (1680–1743) was succeeded as 3rd Duke by his brother Archibald (1682–1761) and then as 4th Duke by their cousin, John (1693–1770). Lady Mary was the daughter of the 2nd Duke, Lady Ailesbury of the 4th.

37  Having inherited his own family titles in 1732, Brudenell was created duke in 1766 because his wife, Mary, was the daughter of John, 2nd Duke of Montagu, who died without heir in 1749. Mary's mother was Lady Mary Churchill, youngest daughter of John, 1st Duke of Marlborough. Brudenell tends to be described by his descendants as the 3rd Duke of Montagu.

38  A bundle of charming teenage letters written by George to his mother from Eton and from Richmond House was kept by her: now at PRONI, with copies in microfilm at University of Maynooth,

39  BL, Add. MS 28234, f. 15, 3rd DR to John Caryll, Goodwood, 15 July (1760). The house was 'full of company'.

40  H.B. Wheatley (ed.), *Historical and Posthumous Memoirs of Sir Nathaniel Wraxall*, London 1884, vol. iv, p. 104

41  *The Times*, 27 March 1789: 'Yesterday the Duke of Richmond gave a sumptuous entertainment at his house in Privy Garden.' In 1801 and 1802 the racecourse hospitality was also superb.

42  Linnean Society, PC Letterbooks, 52–53, MS 591001–2, Peter Collinson to Henry Fox, Goodwood, 1 October 1759

43  A.R. Horwood, 'Goodwood in the Thirties' (i.e., the 1830s), *The Sussex Country Magazine*, July 1929, p. 442

44  For land acquisitions see Introduction to Francis W. Steer and J.E. Amanda Venables (ed.), *The Goodwood Estate Archives*, vol. i, West Sussex County Council, 1970, pp. x–xii

CHAPTER 8

1  *Daily Advertiser*, 28 February 1758

2  Edward Edwards, *Anecdotes of Painting*, 1770, published posthumously, 1808, Walpole Society, vol. XXXVIII, 1960–62, pp. xvi–xix

3  ibid.

4  See Joan Coutu, ' "A very grand and seigneurial design": the Duke of Richmond's Academy in Whitehall', *British Art Journal*, vol. I, No. 2, Spring 2000, pp. 47–54, to whom I am indebted for much of this material. I am also grateful to John Kenworthy Browne, who has lectured on the gallery and knows a good deal about the casts. See Coutu, p. 50, for some interesting comments on the origins of the idea. John Kenworthy Browne also believes that the notion germinated in Florence. The only pictorial representation of the gallery, recorded by Edward Edwards, has not survived.

5  Drawing for therm in the Metropolitan Museum, New York; for gateway in his *Treatise on Civil Architecture*. See John Harris, *Sir William Chambers*, A. Zwemmer Ltd, London 1970, p. 62.

6  Celina Fox, 'Art and Trade – From the Society of Arts to the Royal Academy of Arts', in Sheila O'Connell (ed.), *London 1753*, The British Museum Press, London, 2003, pp. 24–5

7  W.S. Lewis (ed.), *Horace Walpole's Correspondence*, vol. 21, p. 173, Walpole to Mann, 9 Feb 1758

8  There were roughly similar lists by Edward Edwards, *Anecdotes of Painting*, written in 1770, and by Robert Dossie, *Memoirs of Agriculture*, published in 1782. See references to some in Francis

Haskell and Nicholas Penny's seminal work, *Taste and the Antique: the Lure of Classical Sculpture, 1500–1900*, Yale University Press, New Haven and London, 1981

9  BL, Add. MS 51424, f. 161, 3rd DR to Henry Fox, Florence, 3 May 1755, as a postscript

10  MS 230, f. 139, £100 on account for Apollo, 13 November 1758. A larger-than-life Apollo is at Goodwood, presumably damaged in the Richmond House fire as the head and shoulders are lopped off at a strange angle; the other, at Sledmere, Yorkshire, is more likely to have been by Wilton, though according to John Kenworthy Browne it does not have the quality of his *Dancing Faun*.

11  Information from John Kenworthy Browne. There are six bills from Wilton to the Duke in the archive, MS 230, 1756–9.

12  Edwards, *Anecdotes of Painting*

13  'Memoirs of Thomas Jones', *Walpole Society*, vol. 32, 1951

14  Syon Park, Dining Room. Account for £50 in the Duke of Northumberland's archive, dated 10 July 1761

15  National Portrait Gallery, No. 987

16  John Kenworthy Browne points to thirteen in early drawings that may have come from the Duke's gallery.

17  Rosemary Baird, 'Foxed by Fox Hall', *Sussex Archaeological Collections*, May 2006

18  MS 230, f. 263, starting in 1757. The bill was paid on 19 May 1759, signed off by Chambers.

19  MS 2010, Money Matters, f. 72

20  MS 230, f. 263

21  RIBA J4/20. It is not known if it was executed.

22  Anthony Mould, Ozias Humphry and Joseph Mayer (ed.), *A Memoir of George Stubbs*, Pallas Athene, London, 2005, p. 57. (Henceforth Humphry.) Humphry probably knew Stubbs from early on, before he even departed for Rome. His manuscript notes were made following conversations with the ageing painter in 1797, and were then written up by his relative the manuscript collector William Upton, who was himself well informed about Stubbs. From this Joseph Mayer wrote up a memoir which was published in 1876. In fact the expedition to Havannah left in March 1762, so either the painter or one of the memorialists must have misremembered.

23  ibid.

24  'Tis said that nought so much the temper rubs/Of that ingenious artist, Mister Stubbs,/As calling him a horse-painter – how strange,/That Stubbs the title should desire to change!' 'Peter Pindar', 1782, quoted in Robin Blake and Matthew Warner, *Stubbs and the Horse*, Yale University Press, New Haven and London, 2005, p. xiii

25  Robin Blake, *George Stubbs and the Wide Creation*, Chatto & Windus, London, 2005, p. 129

26  Henry Angelo, *Reminiscences of Henry Angelo with memoirs of his late father and friends*, Colburn and Bentley, London, 1830, quoted also by Constance-Anne Parker, *Mr Stubbs the Horse Painter*, J.A. Allen & Co., Ltd, London, 1971, p. 32

27  Jacques (1822), p. 40. He was describing the Billiard Room, 'In which we find three large paintings, by Stubbs, one with the third Duke of Richmond, his Brother Lord George Lennox, and General Jones on horseback, with servants and dogs . . .'

28  Eadweard Muybridge first showed the actions of a horse's legs at the gallop by publishing a series of sequential photographs. See Malcolm Warner and Robin Blake, *Stubbs and the Horse*, Yale University Press, New Haven and London, 2004, catalogue of the exhibition organised by the Kimbell Art Museum, Fort Worth, in association with the Walters Art Museum, Baltimore and the National Gallery London, 2004–5, p. 57, fig. 58, *Gallop: Thoroughbred Bay Mare (Annie G.)*, plate 626 from Eadweard Muybridge, *Animal Locomotion: An Electro-Photographic Investigation of the Phases of Animal Movements*, 1887, from the Harry Ransom Humanities Research Centre, University of Texas at Austin.

29 Identified by Judy Egerton, *George Stubbs 1724–1806*, Tate Gallery 1984, p. 53, drawing on Goodwood MS 229, Register of Servants at London and Goodwood, *c.*1727–80

30 All hunt details are from Simon Rees, *The Charlton Hunt*, Phillimore, West Sussex, 1998.

31 He is said by Humphry to have visited the Vatican and would no doubt have seen instances of continuous narration on the side walls of the Sistine Chapel.

32 Private collection, by descent from Lord George

33 In both Jacques (1822) and Mason (1839), she is referred to in the context of this picture as Lady Louisa. Since the publication of Stella Tillyard's *Aristocrats* she is more often called Lady George in order to avoid confusion with her sister-in-law Lady Louisa Conolly, *née* Lennox.

34 Judy Egerton, *George Stubbs,* p. 57, deduced from the Register of Servants

35 MS 244; e.g., 27 November 1775: 800 partridge eggs

36 Judy Egerton, *George Stubbs*

37 Jacques (1822), p. 63, clearly describes it as 'In the third, Lord Holland, the Earl of Albemarle and others shooting . . .'

38 Both Henry and William were registered as gamekeepers, but if William appeared in the earlier racing painting, this is likely to be Henry.

39 Peg Woffington, a famous and beautiful young actress, was at that time having an affair with the old reprobate Owen McSwiny, which caused much mirth in the Richmond family, before moving on to be the mistress of Charles Hanbury Williams.

40 Private collection

41 Christie's 26 March 1814, lot 28

42 MS with a copy at Goodwood House

43 Lord Herbert (ed.), *Letters and Diaries of Henry, Tenth Earl of Pembroke and his Circle*, Jonathan Cape, 1950, p.69, Lord Pembroke to Lord Camarthen, December 1780: 'The Duke of Richmond, I believe, feels himself equally free, though his personal, private friendship for Ld Rockingham is, I make no doubt, as great as ever.'

44 Egyptian Dining Room, where it has been since the room was created

45 BL, Add. MS 28727, f. 117, 3rd DR to Peter Collinson, 31 December 1767

46 Gilbert White, *The Natural History and Antiquities of Selborne*, various editions, Letter XXVIII, to Thomas Pennant, Selborne, March 1770. White visited on Michaelmas Day, 1768: the moose had died the previous day.

47 As shown by W.D. Ian Rolfe in a conference paper entitled 'William and John Hunter; breaking the Great Chain of Being', in W.F. Bynum and Roy Porter (ed.), *William Hunter and the Eighteenth-century Medical World*, Cambridge University Press, 1985. See also Roy Porter, 'William Hunter: a surgeon and a Gentleman' in the same volume, for his life story, as well as the catalogue of the exhibition at the Hunterian Art Gallery Glasgow, 2007. The moose's antlers are in the Hunterian Museum. I am grateful to Ann Dulau of the Hunterian Art Gallery for all this information, and to Dr Caroline Grigson for checking my text.

48 All four works are in the Hunterian Art Gallery, University of Glasgow. See W.D. Ian Rolfe, 'A Stubbs drawing recognised', *Burlington Magazine*, vol. 125, no. 969 (December 1983), pp. 738, 740-41

49 Intended for the *Philosophical Transactions* of the Royal Society, it was eventually published by W.D.I. Rolfe, 'William Hunter (1718–83) on Irish 'elk' and Stubbs' Moose', *Archives of Natural History*, 11, 1983, pp. 263–90. Hunter did deliver a paper on the *nilghau*.

50 See Chapter 5, n. 58.

51 Jacques (1822), p. 84

52 Joanna Selborne, 'Life of Ryley', *Goodwood Magazine*, 2006. I am grateful to Joanna Selborne for explaining the origin of this group of drawings recently purchased for Goodwood from Sotheby's.

53 *Goodwood's Oak*, p. 250, contemporary local newspaper report, unsourced

54 W.S. Lewis, vol. 11, p. 118, H.W. to Mary Berry, 16 October 1790. The accident was also reported in the *London Chronicle*, 19–21 October, and

*St. James Chronicle*, 19–21 October, with his recovery reported on 23–26 and 4–6 November 1790.

55 Humphry, p. 68

56 Jacques (1822), p. 63

57 Now in the Long Hall

## CHAPTER 9

1 M.M. Reese, *Goodwood's Oak*, p. 109n, letter from 3rd DR to H. Fox. He presented credentials on 24 October.

2 Lewis, *Walpole's Correspondence*, vol. 10, p. 172, HW to Montagu, Strawberry Hill, 31 August 1765. Details of the Richmonds' residence are in Harlan W. Hamilton, 'Sterne's Sermon in Paris and its Background', *Proceedings of the American Philosophical Society*, 1984, vol. 128, no. 4, pp. 318–21.

3 James, so-called 3rd Duke of Berwick and Liria y Xerica (1718–1785), was the son of James, 2nd Duke of Berwick and Liria y Xerica (1696–1738).

4 Fitzgerald, *Correspondence of Emily*, vol. i, p. 461, Caroline to Emily, Kingsgate, 9 August [1766]

5 Roland E. Protheroe, *Private Letters of Edward Gibbon (1753–1794)*, John Murray, London, 1896, vol. I, p. 30, EG to his stepmother, Paris, 12 February 1765

6 Lewis, *Walpole's Correspondence*, vol. 7, quoting Revd William Cole, *Journal of my Journey to Paris*, p. 34. In fact, according to Rosalind Savill, Director of the Wallace Collection and England's leading Sèvres expert, it cost even more.

7 The service is now at Alnwick Castle, Northumberland.

8 Manufacture Nationale de Sèvres Archives, F8 (1765–6): I am grateful to Rosalind Savill for this reference, and for many of the following points about the porcelain.

9 David Peters, *Identification of plates and services in the Sèvres sales registers*, The French Porcelain Society, I, 1985

10 Rosalind Savill, *The Wallace Collection: Catalogue of Sèvres Porcelain*, The Trustees of the Wallace Collection, London, 1988, p. 207, n20: the pieces were worth up to 600 livres.

11 Hon. J.A. Home (ed.), *The Letters and Journals of Lady Mary Coke*, privately printed by David Douglas, Edinburgh, 1889–96, vol. i, p. 201, 6 April 1767

12 BL, Add. MS 51424, 3rd DR to Henry Fox, thinking of paying homage in 1752

13 This reference in: The Duke of Argyll KT, *Intimate Society Letters of the Eighteenth Century*, Stanley Paul & Co., London, 1910, Mr Andrew Stuart commenting on it to the Duchess of Argyll, 1 July 1776. Madame du Deffand mentioned the process many times to HW in 1770 and 1776. See Chapter 14.

14 Armand Louis de Gontaut, Duc de Lauzun, transl. C.K. Scott Moncrieff, *Memoirs of the Duc de Lauzun*, Routledge, London, 1928, pp. 26–41. Lauzun's memoirs were first published in 1822 but were suppressed as being scandalous. No Christian name identification was given for Madame de Cambis.

15 Hon. J.A. Home (ed.), *The Letters and Journals of Lady Mary Coke*, vol. ii, pp. 26–31

16 ibid., vol ii, p. 45, 17 March 1769: Lady Charlotte Finch reported this rumour to Lady Mary Coke.

17 Fitzgerald, *Correspondence of Emily*, vol. i, p. 237, Caroline to Emily, 22 June 1759

18 Ilchester and Stavordale (ed.), *The Life and Letters of Lady Sarah Lennox*, p. 260, Sarah to Susan O'Brien, 20 November 1777

19 Fitzgerald, *Correspondence of Emily*, vol. iii, p. 216, Louisa to Emily, Black Rock 23 August [1776] Madame du Deffand also commented on how upset the Duke was at the little girl's death; *Walpole's Correspondence*, vol. 6, p. 352 , Mme du Deffand (henceforth D) to HW, Mon 26th [1776].

20  This view of the identity of Henriette's mother is found in a letter written by the widow of Henriette's grandson Frederick. Mrs Frederick Dorrien's letter is in the possession of Tom Wilmot. The Dorrien Smith and Wilmot families are Henriette's descendants.

21  The register of deaths for Richmond, Surrey, February 1809, lists her as Louise Françoise Gabrielle d'Alsace de Chimay, Vicomtesse de Cambis. However, Mrs Paget Toynbee, *Lettres de la Marquise du Deffand à Horace Walpole (1766–80)*, Methuen, 1912, identified her as Gabrielle Charlotte Françoise d'Alsace-Hénin-Liétard, Princesse de Chimai (1729–1809). It is not known what was her source, but she did make occasional errors. C.K. Scott Moncrieff in his translation of the *Memoirs of the Duc de Lauzun*, gives her the same names as Mrs Toynbee, but with the later dates of 1739–1809: her death certificate states that she was seventy-one, so at least this date is correct. Brian Fitzgerald also followed the earlier authors. In fact it seems likely that the names on her death certificate were correct.

22  MS 110, f. 86, M. de Cambis to 2nd DR, London, 20 May 1738, thanking him for the 'billet' for Epsom; and f. 87, the Comtesse de Cambis thanking him for marks of friendship

23  See also MS 110, ff. 101, 102, two notes to the 2nd Duke, nd, hereby identified as signed *de Chimay*, suggesting that the 2nd Duke had also known either Madame's brother Thomas or her father, Alexandre.

24  Lewis, *Walpole's Correspondence*, vol. 3, p. 18, D to HW, 23 April 1766

25  Mrs Paget Toynbee, *Lettres de la Marquise du Deffand à Horace Walpole (1766–1780)*, vol. i, p. 211, 10 October 1769. The affair is most easily followed in her edition, it being much shorter than Lewis, *Walpole's Correspondence*, and especially in her vol. iii. However, Lewis also gives the return letters from Horace Walpole, so is more complete. This ref. Lewis, vol. 4, p. 277.

26  Lewis, *Walpole's Correspondence*, vol. 4, p. 277, D to HW, 10 October 1769

27  ibid., vol. 5, p. 434, D to HW, dated 20 but actually 19 December 1773

28  ibid., vol. 39, p. 218, Lady Ailesbury to HW, Paris, 23 November 1774

29  ibid., vol. 6, p. 338, D to HW, 14 July 1776

30  Fitzgerald, *Correspondence of Emily*, vol. ii, p. 173, Sarah to Emily, Goodwood, 21 April [1776]

31  ibid., vol. 3, p. 216, Louisa to Emily, Black Rock, 23 August [1776]

32  ibid.

33  Lewis, *Walpole's Correspondence*, vol. 6, p. 331, D to HW, Paris 18 June 1776

34  ibid., vol. 6, p. 338, D to HW, 14 July 1776

35  ibid., vol. 6, p. 356, D to HW, 15 September 1776

36  ibid., vol. 6, p. 430, D to HW, 5 April 1777: '*Elle a commencé à apprendre l'anglais dans le mois de novembre, elle le sait fort bien . . .*'

37  Fitzgerald, *Correspondence of Emily*, vol. ii, p. 213, Sarah to Emily, Stoke, 22 January 1777

38  Lewis, *Walpole's Correspondence*, vol. 6, p. 431, D to HW, 5 April 1777, '*elle est naturellement sèche, silencieuse, et toute concentré à un seul objet . . .*' The *Portraits* are about to be translated in this letter, apparently for Madame du Deffand, and, p. 353, on 27 July, had been done.

39  ibid., p. 441, D to HW, Sunday 11 May 1777

40  ibid., p. 444, D to HW, Sunday 18 May 1777, '*Parlons de M. Richmond. Je le vois souvent, il ne se porte bien, il est extremement occupé.*'

41  Roland E. Protheroe (ed.), *Private Letters of Edward Gibbon*, p. 312, Paris, 16 June 1777

42  ibid., p. 316, Gibbon to his stepmother, Paris, 24 July 1777

43  Lewis, *Walpole's Correspondence*, vol. 6, p. 431, D to HW, p. 444, Sunday 25 May 1777

44  Ilchester and Stavordale, *The Life and Letters of Lady Sarah Lennox*, vol. i, p. 260, Lady Sarah Lennox to Lady Susan O'Brien, 20 November 1777

45  Lewis, *Walpole's Correspondence*, vol. 6, p. 496, D to HW, 1 December 1777

46  *Mémoires inédits de Madame la Comtesse de Genlis*, vol. 2, Paris, and Colburn, London, 1825, 1827

47  Brian Fitzgerald, *Emily, Duchess of Leinster: A Study of her Life and Times,* 1949, pp. 155–6, Emily, Duchess of Leinster, to Lady Sarah Bunbury, Paris, 4 February 1778

48  Fitzgerald, *Correspondence of Emily,* vol. iii, p. 265, Louisa to Emily, Dieppe, 'the 6th' [April 1778]

49  ibid., vol. iii, p. 268, Louisa to Emily, London, 9 April 1778: and p. 271, 17 April 1778

50  ibid., vol. iii, p. 271, Louisa to Emily, London, 17 April 1778

51  ibid., vol. iii, p. 274, Louisa to Emily, London, 21 April 1778

52  ibid., vol. iii, p. 275, Louisa to Emily, London, 24 April 1778

53  ibid., vol. iii, p. 284, Louisa to Emily, London, 19 May 1778

54  Lewis, *Walpole's Correspondence,* vol. 6, p. 431, D to HW; vol. 7, p. 16, 8 February 1778, '*J'ai une amie qui aura plus de joie que moi de son arrivée . . .*'

55  MS 241, f. 42 reverse; from the travel movements of his footman.

56  Lewis, *Walpole's Correspondence,* vol. 5, D to HW, dated 20 but actually 19 December 1773

57  Fitzgerald, *Correspondence of Emily*, vol. ii, p. 316, Sarah to Emily, Goodwood 28 April [1780]

58  ibid., vol. 3, p. 284, Louisa to Emily, London, 19 May 1778

59  ibid., vol. 3, p 309, Louisa to Emily, Castletown, 30 August 1778

60  Lewis, *Walpole's Correspondence,* vol. 7, D to HW, p. 96, 28 December 1778; and p. 97, 30 December 1778, referring to a long Christmas letter by her to him. Also p. 234, 30 June 1780, of his letters to her: 'I have a friend who gets more news than me.'

61  Toynbee, *Lettres de la Marquise du Deffand à Horace Walpole*, vol. 3, p. 502, D to HW, 5 March 1779. Not in Lewis.

62  Lewis, *Walpole's Correspondence,* vol. 39, HW to Conway, Strawberry Hill, 16 June 1779

63  ibid., vol. 7, p. 222, D to HW, 20 April 1780

64  Fitzgerald, *Correspondence of Emily,* vol. ii, Lord Edward Fitzgerald to William Ogilvie, Portsmouth, 1 August 1786

65  ibid., vol. ii, pp. 231–2, Louisa Bunbury to Emily, 36 April 1778

66  ibid., vol. ii, p. 234, Sarah to Emily, Goodwood, 13 July 1778. Sarah's letters give a very good account of Goodwood at this period.

67  ibid., vol. ii, p. 292, Sarah to Emily, Spring Gardens, 15 October 1779 (Henrietta remained in Sussex with Louisa Bunbury)

68  ibid., vol. ii, pp. 316–17, Sarah to Emily, Goodwood, 28 April [1780]

69  ibid., vol. ii, p. 317, Sarah to Emily, Goodwood, 28 April [1780]

70  Yellow Drawing Room, Goodwood

71  Sold in 1995

## CHAPTER 10

1   Dr John Martin Robinson, 'The Glories of Goodwood', *Country Life*, 25 September 1997, pp. 78–85

2   The table was repaired for it in 1778: MS 241, f. 39 (reverse), Lady Day.

3   MS 244, p. 2

4   See Viccy Coltman, *Fabricating the Antique: Neo-Classicism in Britain 1760–1800*, University of Chicago Press, 2006

5   BL, Add. MS 41197, f. 73, copy (or draft) in his own hand of W. Hamilton's letter to Charles, 3rd DR, Naples, 9 December 1765. There are further letters in the BL.

6   Fitzgerald, *Correspondence of Emily*, vol. iii, 1957, p. 459

7   ibid., p. 67, 21 January 1773, Louisa to Emily

8   Jacques (1822), p. 41

9   For the way in which Hamilton's designs were used, see Viccy Coltman, 'Sir William Hamilton's Vase Publications (1766–1776)', *Journal of Design History*, vol. 14, no. 1, The Design History Society, 2001 (or Chapter 3 in her book *Fabricating the Antique*).

10  Christie's, 26 March 1814, lots 10 and 13 were drawings by him, but lot 46 'CR Riley . . . A grand allegorical composition' was probably a mistake for a Wootton from the Old Dining Room. The Ingram collection

of little sketches of animals, of which an album was recently acquired for The Kennels, includes some on envelopes addressed to Riley at Goodwood. These were mostly copies by Riley of prints in *Recueil des Lions,* by Bernard Picart after Rembrandt.

11  Fitzgerald, *Correspondence of Emily,* vol. ii, pp. 214–15, Sarah to Emily, Goodwood, 5 March 1777

12  See Eagles, *Francophobia and Francophilia in English Society, 1748–1783,* for a recent exposition of the aristocratic influences in both countries.

13  Quoted by Eagles, ibid., chapter 1

14  Jacques (1822), pp. 68–9

15  MS 241, f. 18, October 1776 for the curtain; Jacques (1822), p. 69, for the ambassadorial canopy

16  Miguel de Cervantes Saavedra, *Don Quijote de la Mancha,* published 1604–14. The Don Quixote tapestry, *La Dorothée,* is now in the Bathurst collection at Cirencester Park, part of a group of items from Richmond House given by the 3rd DR to his niece Georgina, then Lady Apsley, later Countess Bathurst, a few years after the fire.

17  Archives Nationales Paris, O'2789, 15,483 livres paid to Neilson of the Gobelins, 24 August 1766, signed or agreed by the Marquis de Marigny, 24 August 1766. All details from the late George Hughes-Hartman of Sotheby's, using Maurice Fenaille, *Etat général des Tapisseries de la Manufacture des Gobelins,* Paris, 1904, vol. III: IX: 'Histoire de Don Quichotte. D'après Charles Coypel. Cinquième Tenture. Du Château de Marly. – Quatrième alentour (1749–1763)', pp. 206–19; also Thierry Lefrancois, *Charles Coypel, Peintre du roi (1694–1752),* Paris, Arthena, 1994, which illustrates the original paintings and records the known locations of the various tapestries.

18  The eighth series comprised fifty-eight, which were used as gifts to foreign royals, most famously the Grand Duke and Grand Duchess of Russia, travelling as the Comte and Comtesse du Nord: two of these are now at Pavlovsk, looking very similar to the Goodwood tapestries, apart from the colour. The pair in the Getty Museum are believed to be from the set given to the Duke and Duchess of Saxe-Teschen.

19  Eileen Harris, *The Genius of Robert Adam: his Interiors,* Paul Mellon Centre for Studies in British Art, Yale University Press, New Haven and London, 2001, p. 173, n. 89 . Only Croome and Osterley are likely to have been known by the 3rd Duke, and it is not known if he actually visited either. There is no record of his having banked with Child's Bank.

20  MS 241, f. 33, John Parvin was paid £6 6s at Michaelmas 1777 and, f. 36, just 9s for working on the tapestry at Christmas, presumably finishing off.

21  MS 244, f. 11, paid 23 August 1775, to a draft of the Duke of 18 June

22  See photo *The Antique Collector,* December 1939, p. 265.

23  Jacques (1822), p. 71. The whole was said, Mason (1839), p. 141, to have cost £500, but payments in MS 244, Steward's Accounts, totalled only £276 16s: f. 12, the Duke made a first draft for £100 to pay for 'statuary in part for the chimney for the new Drawing Room' on 14 April 1775; f. 18, a second draft for £100 on 10 November 1775; and f. 23, a third draft on 20 February 1776 for £76 16s.

24  Jacques (1822), p. 72

25  *The Diary of Joseph Farington,* Yale University Press, New Haven and London, 1978–84, vol. 1, p. 146, 19 January 1794

26  ibid., vol. 6, p. 2214, 8 January 1804

27  See Viscountess Wolseley, 'Historic Houses of Sussex No. 21 – Goodwood', *The Sussex County Magazine,* July 1929, p. 440 for layout; Jacques (1822), p. 69 for details.

28  MS 244, Steward's Accounts, Lady Day Quarter, 1777

29  MS 241, f. 25, Sept 30 1775; and f. 95 reverse: her 'woman', Mrs Hochstetter, was there in the autumn of 1772, presumably with her.

30  Ilchester and Stavordale (ed.), *The Life and Letters of Lady Sarah Lennox,* p. 261, Lady Sarah Lennox to Lady Susan O'Brien, 20 November 1777

31  Fitzgerald, *Correspondence of Emily,* p. 174, Sarah to Emily, Goodwood, 21 April [1776]. However, she would stroll daily down the garden 'to gather her roses' (ibid., p. 280, Sarah to Emily, 24 June 1779).

32  MS 244, p. 60, Michaelmas 1777

33  Fitzgerald, *Correspondence of Emily,* vol. ii, p. 227, Sarah to Emily, Itchenor, 12 August 1777

34  Basil Cozens-Hardy (ed.), *The Diary of Silas Neville 1767–1788,* Oxford University Press, 1950, p. 287

35  Brian Robins (ed.), *The John Marsh Journals: The Life and Times of a Gentleman Composer (1752–1828),* Sociology of Music no. 9, Pendragon Press, Stuyvesant, New York, 1998, p. 403, 21 July 1787. Marsh walked up to Goodwood for the first time in May that year.

36  Paul Foster (ed.), *Marsh of Chichester,* Chapter IV by Timothy J. McCann, p. 94, quoting from Marsh's diary, Monday 21 March 1789

37  Robins (ed.), *The John Marsh Journals,* 28 August 1787

38  Hon. J.A. Home (ed.), *The Letters and Journals of Lady Mary Coke,* vol. ii, p. 260, 1768: 'she was certainly born to be a Soldier's wife, for I think she has always gone where ever he had been sent, which, in a few years, has been to many different Countrys.'

39  MS 241, f. 25 (reverse): payment to Revd J. Buckner, executor to late Mr Richard Buckner, Lady Day Quarter, 1777

40  *Memoirs of the Duc de Lauzun,* p. 67

41  Fitzgerald, *Correspondence of Emily,* p. 218, Sarah to Emily, Goodwood, 1 April 1777

42  NLI, Leinster Papers, MS 41, p. 552, Sarah to Emily, Itchenor, 20 November 1777

43  Ilchester and Stavordale (ed.), *The Life and Letters of Lady Sarah Lennox,* p. 259, Lady Sarah Lennox to Lady Susan O'Brien, 20 November 1777

44  Fitzgerald, *Correspondence of Emily,* p. 311, Sarah to William Ogilvie, Goodwood, 18 February 1780; and p. 313 to Emily, 26 February 1780

45  Fitzgerald, *Correspondence of Emily,* vol. iii, p. 77, Louisa to Emily, Goodwood, 7 March [1773]

46  MS 244, p. 35, with deeds at E2664–2679, and farm buildings at E2652–2662

47  ibid., pp. 222, 230, 1784

48  ibid., p. 300, 1786

49  This is the view of Alex Kidson of the Walker Art Gallery.

50  At Goodwood in the nineteenth century, and praised by John Kent, 1896, p. 198; Humphry Ward and W. Roberts, *Romney, Catalogue Raisonné,* vol. ii, p. 132

51  Both at Goodwood

52  Ward and Roberts, *Romney,* vol. ii, p. 132

53  At Goodwood

54  Formerly at Goodwood, now Beaverbrook Foundation, Fredericton, Canada

55  Both the first version and one copy are at Goodwood.

56  Jacques (1822), p. 36; in a dressing room near the main portico

57  ibid., pp. 81–2

58  Kent, p. 37. As Kent lived in the house after the wings ceased to be used for hounds, he is a reliable witness for the existence of the heated plates.

59  We can only guess at how this arrangement worked. The print shows two chimneys each side, but not central to the wings. The heat was therefore presumably conducted from these end points. Chimneys no longer survive in these locations. There are now five chimney pots in each wing, in what were the 'lodge' sections, suggesting that there were three fireplaces on the long side and two on the shorter side, offset back to back against each other. These were a later modification, extra flues being inserted when the Kennels were made into staff houses in the 1880s.

60  Accounts in MS 247, from 1795–1804

61  Viscount Palmerston, from the *Tour of Sussex* section of his unpublished Travel Diary (Hampshire Record Office, 27M60/1924), copy at WSRO (MP 854)

62  Jacques (1822). All contemporary reports and comments are fully recorded by the author in her booklet *The Kennels,* to be published by the Goodwood Estate Company, 2007/8.

63 Peregrine Project and Timothy Type (actually John Marsh, writing under this pseudonym), *A Tour through some of the Southern Counties of England*, London, Vernon and Hood, 1804, p. 183

64 MS 244, p. 363, Michaelmas 1787

65 Lord William Pitt Lennox, *Fifty Years Biographical Reminiscences*, Hurst and Blackett, London, 1863, vol. I, p. 20

66 Francis W. Steer, The Chichester Theatre, Chichester Papers no. 9, 1957

67 Lewis, *Walpole's Correspondence* , vol. 33, p. 564n

68 MS 244, p. 338–9, Midsummer 1787

69 Sybil Rosenfeld, *Temples of Thespis, some private theatres and theatricals in England and Wales 1700–1820*, The Society for Theatre Research, London, 1978, from which much of this information comes; this reference is from the Burney clippings. See also HMC, Report XV, Appendix 8, p. 281, Diary of Thomas, Earl of Ailesbury, 17 May 1787.

CHAPTER 11

1 *The Letters and Journals of Lady Mary Coke*, vol. iv, p. 181, Brussels, Saturday 3 July 1772

2 Henry Reeve (ed.), Charles Greville, *Journal*, London,1874, p. 129

3 Private collection

4 Lord Herbert (ed.), *Letters and Diaries of Henry, Tenth Earl of Pembroke and his Circle*, p. 108, Lord Pembroke to the Revd W. Coxe, London, 7 April 1778

5 Painted 1779. Tate Gallery. There used to be a version at Goodwood, sold Christie's 26 March 1814, lot 12.

6 Priscilla Napier, *My Brother Richmond: the Third Duke of Richmond Reflected in his Sisters' Correspondence*, privately printed by the Duke of Richmond, 1994, p. 372, Sarah to Susan, February 1783

7 M.M. Reese, *Goodwood's Oak*, quoting Russell (ed.), *Memorials and Correspondence of Charles James Fox*, London 1853, vol. 1, p. 455

8 A drawing is reproduced in *Goodwood's Oak*, p. 205.

9 BL, Add. MS 34902, f. 11, from the papers of Admiral Horatio Nelson; and Add. MS 34933, Nelson Papers, mainly official correspondence, December 1788–June 1789

10 Published *c.*1755 by the Royal Geographer Emmanuel Bowen with a richly embellished dedicatory cartouche to the Duke of Richmond

11 Known as the Duke of Cumberland's Map of Scotland, 1747–55. The watercolour artist Paul Sandby worked with Roy at this time, as a result of which connection there is a rare oil painting by him of Richmond Castle in the collection.

12 MS 242, p. 188, Lady Day 1790. Believed by Anthony Mould to be the one now in the Burrell Collection, Glasgow.

13 Gaston Maugras (translated), *The Duc de Lauzun and the Court of Marie Antoinette*, Osgood, McIlvaine & Co., London 1896, p. 368, Chevalier de Boufflers to Mme de Sabran. See also p. 440.

14 MS 2010, Money Matters, ff. 26–8, and f. 42: the debt was annulled on 19 April 1805.

15 BL Add. MS 58937, Grenville correspondence, Lord Robert to 3rd DR, Paris, 1 July 1791

16 *Public Advertiser*, 22 and 23 December 1791; *The Times*, 22 December 1791; *Annual Register*, 1791, pp. 46–7; *Gentleman's Magazine lxi*, 1791, p. 1155. The two last reports appear to draw on the *Public Advertiser*, to which the *Annual Register* adds the information about the unknown helper.

17 *Public Advertiser*, 23 December 1791 (second report)

18 NLI, Richmond Papers, vol. 60, f. 253, Charles, 3rd DR, to Colonel Charles Lennox, 5 June 1792, explaining the attack; also HMC, Bathurst Papers, p. 704, 6 June 1792, the Duke to Lord George Lennox

19 It became called the Chestnut Troop in the nineteenth century. Reputedly Wellington said 'Where are my chestnuts?' The Troop was in fact not under his charge, but under that of the Ordnance.

20 NLI, Richmond Papers, vol. 69. The correspondence is published in the Bathurst Papers, HMC, 1928, pp. 706–12, from copies sent to Lord George by Henrietta Le Clerc.

21 *The Times*, Wednesday 14 July 1796 (rehearsal) and Saturday 6 August 1796 (review)

22 *The Diary of Joseph Farington*, vol. 3, p. 939, 8 December 1797, reportedly said to the sculptor Nollekens

23 Quoted by Brian Fitzgerald, *Lady Louisa Conolly*, Staples Press, London and New York, 1950, p. 131, from the letters in the NLI

24 MS 244, p. 344, Midsummer 1787

25 *Public Advertiser*, 22 and 23 December 1791

26 3rd DR to Duchess, 1795

27 *The Diary of Joseph Farington*, vol. 2, p. 480, 22 January 1796

28 ibid., vol. 3, p. 938, 8 December 1797

29 Lord William Pitt Lennox, *Fifty Years Biographical Reminiscences*, Hurst and Blackett, London, 1863, vol. 1, p. 101

30 Lord William Pitt Lennox, *My Recollections, from 1806 to 1873*, Hurst and Blackett, London, 1874, pp. 28–9

31 Some were sold at Christie's, 26 March 1814, lots 47–51.

32 Project and Type (John Marsh), *A Tour through some of the Southern Counties of England*, pp. 179–80

33 Lewis, *Walpole's Correspondence*, vol. 34, pp. 221–2, HW to Lady Ossory, Strawberry Hill, 13 November 1796

34 *Gentleman's Magazine*, 1796, lxvi part 2, p. 970

35 Project and Type (John Marsh), *A Tour through some of the Southern Counties of England*, p. 180

36 William S. Child-Pemberton, *The Earl Bishop, the Life of Frederick Hervey, Bishop of Derry, Earl of Bristol*, Hurst and Blackett, 1925, vol. 2, p. 496, Naples, 6 March 1796. He was referring to Ickworth.

37 Castalia, Countess Granville (ed.), *Lord Granville Leveson Gower, Private Correspondence 1781–1821*, John Murray, London, 1916, vol. 1, p. 195, Lady Bessborough to Granville Leveson Gower, Thursday 18 [probably Feb] [1798].

38 Jacques (1822), p. 72. In 1822 this was still located in the main Tapestry Drawing Room.

39 NLI, MS 41, 552, f. 48, Lord Cornwallis to 3rd DR, Dublin Castle, 11 August 1798. Fascinating documents about his imprisonment and burial are in the PRONI papers, copied at Maynooth, under D3078/3/8, on reel 16, as well as letters in the Leinster papers at the NLI.

40 *The Diary of Joseph Farington*, vol. 4, p. 1241. He also mentioned income: 'Duke of Richmond told Wyatt that when he came of age He had only £2500 *landed estate*. He has now £12,000 a year in Sussex [*then the part about his character*] . . . In London he has accustomed his servants to be on board and wages & to keep for himself a very private table, – at Goodwood He lives in a very suitable style.'

CHAPTER 12

1 Paul Foster (ed.), *Marsh of Chichester*, chapter IV, 'Marsh at Goodwood' by Timothy J. McCann, pp. 89–112

2 Jacques (1822), p. 18

3 Project and Type (John Marsh), *A Tour through some of the Southern Counties of England*, pp. 179–80. I am grateful to Timothy J. McCann for finding this important contemporary comment.

4 Jacques (1822), p. 65

5 MS 244, Steward's Accounts, p. 12, October 1775, 'a ballance for the Octagon barn – £16'

6 MS 2010, Money Matters, Small Library E3, Goodwood. For the Duke's finances see M.M. Reese, *Goodwood's Oak*, chapter 22. His bankers were Messrs Boldero, Adey & Co, 30 Cornhill, London.

7 Jacques (1822), pp. 21–2

8 MS 241, f. 75, Lady Day Quarter, 1781, £41 13s 9d. They are simple half-moon tops on pedestals. The instinct not to return them to the restored Egyptian Dining Room seems to have been correct.

9 I am grateful to Philip Hewat-Jaboor for his suggestions about Wyatt furniture: see his essay on Fonthill in Derek E. Ostergard (ed.),

*William Beckford, 1760–1844: An Eye for the Magnificent*, Yale University Press, New Haven and London, 2002.

10 National Archive, Vulliamy Papers, Ornament Book 1 and Invoice Book 31. I am grateful to Sir Geoffrey de Bellaigue for this information. See his article 'The Vulliamy Chimneypieces', *Furniture History*, vol. xxiii, 1997, p. 190.

11 *Sporting Magazine*, April 1801

12 Brian Robins (ed.), *The John Marsh Journals*, p. 733

13 *Sporting Magazine*, April 1801, quoted by Larry Ward

14 Robins (ed.), *The John Marsh Journals*, p. 733

15 *Sussex Chronicle and Chichester Advertiser*, no. 18, 5 May 1802

16 MS 2010, Money Matters, f. 1

17 Engraving, belonging to the Wellcome Trust, at Hunterian Museum, Royal College of Surgeons, London

18 MS 2010, Money Matters, f. 22

19 Henry Napier (1789–1853) became a captain in the Royal Navy and the historian of Florence, where Caroline and her mother were buried in the Protestant cemetery. Marriages within the family abounded: Emily Napier married (as his second wife) Sir Henry Bunbury, 7th Baronet, the nephew of Sarah's husband.

20 NLI, vol. 70, f. 1274, 3rd DR to Charles Lennox, Whitehall, 6 June 1804; and again at f. 1273, 12 June 1804

21 MS 224, f. 8, 3rd DR to General Charles Lennox, 5 June 1806

22 *The Diary of Joseph Farington*, vol. 15, p. 5261, 8 September 1818. Farington's companion on a visit to Goodwood was a Clergyman who 'informed me that the later Duke of Richmond, Uncle of the present Duke, allowed Him only one thousand pounds per annum, though He had then a large family now increased to 14 children.'

23 MS 224, f. 8

24 Foster (ed.), *Marsh of Chichester*, p. 98, from the diary of John Marsh

25 She is the first named beneficiary and is introduced: 'Miss Henriette Anne le Clerc (who resides with me and though christened by the name of Anne only is called Henriette and whom I have educated from her childhood.)' It is worth noting that Anne was a family name of Madame de Cambis.

26 Foster (ed.), *Marsh of Chichester*, p. 99

27 If the report in the *Annual Register* was true, that Mrs Bennett and her three daughters had each received fifty thousand pounds under the will, it was not surprising that the estate was further bankrupted: it is more likely that this referred to the value of the Earls Court property, which was all that the *Gentleman's Magazine* ascribed as inheritance.

## Chapter 13

1 The duel is described by the seconds, Lord Rawdon (for the Duke of York) and the Earl of Winchilsea (for Lieutenant Colonel Lennox) in the *Gentleman's Magazine*, LIX, 26 May 1789. Some later reports say that the Duke of York fired in the air, but this clearly says that he did not fire at all, a fact confirmed by the pamphlet (see below).

2 Pamphlet, 'By the Captain of a Company in one of the Regiments of Guards', *A Short Review of the Recent Affair of Honor between His Royal Highness the Duke of York and Lieutenant Colonel Lenox with free and impartial strictures and comments upon the circumstances attending it*, J. Bell, British Library, 1789

3 Lord William Pitt Lennox, *Fifty Years Biographical Reminiscences*, Hurst and Blackett, London, 1863, vol. i, pp. 7–8. Like the pamphleteer, he puts emphasis on the political background as being the reason the Duke of York wanted to discredit Lennox. Brigadier General E.A. Cruickshank, LLD, FRSC, FRHist.S, published this version in 'Charles Lennox, the Fourth Duke of Richmond', *Papers and Records of the Ontario Historical Society*, vol. 24, 1928, pp. 323–51, but did not use the other contemporary sources.

4 The 'private gentleman' notion is also reported in the officer's account. The parade incident is entirely from Lord William Lennox's memoirs.

5 *Gentleman's Magazine*, LIX, Monday 25 May 1789, saying that he had written the letters at Richmond House on 18 May

6 They make fascinating reading: NLI, Richmond Papers, vol. 70, most documents between ff. 678 and 690 (which is a scornful riposte from his cousin Charles James Fox); also f. 695. These papers were not fully sorted before being put into the albums and often appear out of order and out of subject group.

7 Many drafts of a subsequent letter from Lennox to the Duke of York on that day are in the NLI, Richmond Papers, vol. 70, ff. 658, 659, 660, 661, 673, 696. The last two appear to be full and final versions, maybe the draft and the copy.

8 A full copy of the challenge is in the NLI, Richmond Papers, vol. 70, f. 669. It is dated as 26 May, but the duel took place that day.

9 NLI, Richmond Papers, vol. 70, ff. 668 and 697. In f. 675 the meeting is given as being at 11 a.m. on Friday 28 May. See also *Gentleman's Magazine*, 30 May 1789.

10 Pamphlet, 'By the Captain of a Company in one of the Regiments of Guards', 1789: he felt that it was the Duke of York who behaved dishonourably. He saw the affair as a political plot arising out of the argument over a possible regency at the time of the King's illness, in which the Duke of Richmond had felt the Prince of Wales's powers should be limited. The officer saw the aim as being to alienate the newly recovered King against the Duke.

11 Only three years earlier Frederick had been writing him light-hearted letters about the joys of hunting and cricket: NLI, Richmond Papers, vol. 70, ff. 1275–8.

12 Pamphlet, 'By the Captain of a Company in one of the Regiments of Guards', 1789, p. 14. In the conclusion on p. 42, it further mentions 'Colonel Lenox's own personal merit, added to his certain prospect of one day enjoying a large fortune, and a splendid title'.

13 According to Lady Muriel Beckwith (daughter of the 7th DR), in *When I Remember*, Ivor Nicholson and Watson, London, 1936, no one knew anything about it until her husband was called on to propose her health at a large dinner party, and gave it as Lady Charlotte Lennox.

14 NLI, Richmond Papers, vol. 70, f. 1281, Charles Fitzroy to Charles Lennox, Tower (presumably on Guard Duty), 22 March 1790, claiming the debt; and again, f. 1283, Half Moon Street, 3 April, thanking him for 'the handsome manner in which you sent me the Draught'.

15 *The Diary of Joseph Farington*, vol. 13, p. 3027, 20 April 1807. Farington was told all this by an army wife. It continues: 'They have 13 children. She is very jealous of him.'

16 ibid., following on from above

17 Twenty-four silver dishes by Paul Storr are in the Fundação Madeiros e Almeida, Lisbon, with many entrée dishes and salts by Benjamin Smith and Paul Storr surviving at Goodwood. They also subsequently acquired a magnificent gilt service (see n. 50).

18 Castalia Countess Granville (ed.), *Lord Granville Leveson Gower, Private Correspondence 1781–1821*, John Murray, London, 1916, vol. ii, pp. 333–4, Harriet, Lady Bessborough to Granville Leveson Gower, Dublin 1 Oct [1808]

19 The story is recounted in a letter by her, published in Claire Tomalin, *Mrs Jordan's Profession*, Viking 1994 and Penguin 1995, pp. 221–2

20 I am grateful to Burton B. Fredericksen of the Getty Information Institute for providing me with a copy of the sale. Only four copies are known to have survived, of which two are in England. Although the sale was anonymous, the copy at Christie's, and one in Amsterdam, are annotated with the name of the owner.

21 Jacques (1822), pp. 22–3

22 The Marquis of Anglesey FSA (ed.), *The Capel Letters, Being the Correspondence of Lady Caroline Capel and her daughters with the Dowager Countess of Uxbridge, from Brussels and Switzerland, 1814–1817*, Jonathan Cape, London, 1955, p. 57, Lady Caroline Capel to her mother, Lady Uxbridge, Brussels, July 1814

23 ibid., p. 71

24 ibid., p. 69, Lady Maria Capel to her grandmother, Lady Uxbridge, Brussels, 19 August 1814

25 Lord William Pitt Lennox, *Fifty Years Biographical Reminiscences*, vol. I, pp. 173–4

26 Beatrice Madan (ed.), *Spencer and Waterloo: The Letters of Spencer Madan, 1814–1816*, LS&P, London, 1970, p. 53, Spencer Madan to Dr Madan, Brussels, 11 November 1814

27 Bathurst Papers, 4th DR to his brother-in-law Henry, 3rd Earl Bathurst, 10 April 1815. See also Nick Foulkes, *Dancing into Battle*, Weidenfeld & Nicolson, London, 2006, pp. 73–4.

28 The Marquis of Anglesey FSA (ed.), *The Capel Letters*, p. 102, Lady Caroline Capel to her mother, Lady Uxbridge, early June 1815

29 ibid., p. 107, Lady Caroline Capel to her mother, 13 June 1815

30 The Hon. Blanche Swinton (ed.), *A Sketch of the Life of Lady de Ros, with some reminiscences of her family and friends, including the Duke of Wellington*, John Murray, London, 1893, p.122

31 Miller, *The Duchess of Richmond's Ball*, p. 133, and *Lady de Lancey at Waterloo*, Spellmount, Staplehurst, 2000, p. 106

32 Miller, *The Duchess of Richmond's Ball*, p. 134, quoting Miss Charlotte Waldie, a new arrival in Brussels. Her comments were edited by Hannibal Lloyd and published as being by 'A Near Observer', in *The Battle of Waterloo*, mentioned in the *Gentleman's Magazine*, vol. XXVIII, 1847, pp. 324–6.

33 Beatrice Brocklebank, 'Home of the Waterloo Ball', *Country Life*, 11 December 1975, says it was to the right in the print of the house, but Lady de Ros said it was to the left of the entrance, *Murray's Magazine*, p. 40: she was referring to the entrance from the other side, which was on to the street. See Miller, *The Duchess of Richmond's Ball*, plan, p. 129.

34 See Miller, *The Duchess of Richmond's Ball*, in which this list is published, pp. 149–53, as well as two others, pp. 155–64, both later in date and deriving from that of the Duchess via her daughter, Georgiana, who became Lady de Ros.

35 Conversation with Mrs Jane Leefe, 2006. Her late husband, b.1874, was the grandson of Lady Sarah Maitland. He was close to his great-aunt Sophia (d.1902).

36 Some people on the list did not attend (sometimes marked with an O); others were present who were not on the list. See Miller, *The Duchess of Richmond's Ball*.

37 Prince Maurice of Nassau had been a member of the Charlton Hunt in the 1730s, and there was a portrait of an ancestor of his at Goodwood, so there must have been some kind of family friendship.

38 See Sir Herbert Maxwell (ed.), *The Creevey Papers, A Selection from the correspondence and diaries of the late Thomas Creevey MP (1768–1838)*, John Murray, London, 1904, vol. I, p. 223, from his journal, 16 June: 'The girls just returned from a ball at the Duke of Richmond's . . . Our troops are all moving from this place at present. Lord Wellington was at the ball to-night as composed as ever.'

39 Conversation with Mrs Jane Leefe, 2006

40 See Miller, *The Duchess of Richmond's Ball*, p. 143, n. 31. The surprise element is confirmed in John Gore (ed.), *Creevey's Life and Times; a further selection from the correspondence of Thomas Creevey, born 1768–died 1838*, John Murray, London, 1934, p. 91, Mrs Creevey to [her son] William Ord [at Florence] (part of her daughter's letter), Brussels, 9 July 1815.

41 Sir Herbert Maxwell (ed.), *The Creevey Papers*, vol. I, p. 229. Creevey's stepdaughters and stepson, the Misses and Mr Ord, returned from the ball at about 2.30 a.m: 'There had been plenty of officers at the ball, and some tender scenes had taken place upon the ladies parting with them.'

42 In a large painting at the former United Services Club, Pall Mall, by George Jones RA, the Duke is shown at the centre of all the battle formations, close to Wellington but dismounted. This is characteristic of how his role was seen.

43 Lord William Pitt Lennox, *Fifty Years Biographical Reminiscences*, Hurst and Blackett, London, 1863, vol. ii, pp. 240–46. Lord William loyally refuted the imputation that Wellington had been unready, p. 233.

44 Kent, p. 50

45 Lord William Pitt Lennox, *Fifty Years Biographical Reminiscences*, p. 265

46 Letter of Revd G.G. Stonestreet to George Trower Esq., dated 16 October 1815. This and a second letter were discovered by David Miller and published by him in full in *The Duchess of Richmond's Ball*, pp. 187–91.

47 Miller, *The Duchess of Richmond's Ball*, p. 190, letter of 23 November

48 *The Diary of Joseph Farington*, vol. 15, p. 5210, 26 May 1818; Mrs Girdlestone's report of the Bishop of Quebec's description

49 A full account of his administration in Canada can be found in Brigadier General E.A. Cruikshank, 'Charles Lennox, the Fourth Duke of Richmond', *Papers and Records of the Ontario Historical Society*, vol. 24, 1928, pp. 323–51, in which much use is made of the Bathurst letters.

50 Lord William Pitt Lennox, *Fifty Years Biographical Reminiscences*, vol. ii, p. 113

51 There are several versions of the story of how he was bitten by an animal, but one of the most reliable ones would seem to be from the memoirs of his son, Lord William Pitt Lennox, *Fifty Years Biographical Reminiscences*, vol. ii, pp. 113–18.

52 Parliamentary Library, Ottawa, Canada, Lady Louisa Tighe to James C. Stuart, Woodstock, Ireland, 10 May 1898. Lady Louisa was ninety-five when she wrote the letter, but hers and Lord William's reports seem deliberately to have aimed to put right errors made in other early reports, some of which had said that it was the dog that bit him and went mad. Copies of these, and a summary, are on file at Goodwood.

53 The two principal sources for the Duke's last illness (which do not mention how he contracted it) are on-the-spot reports from the journals of Colonel Francis Cockburn and Major George Bowles, his companions on the tour. These manuscripts are in the Thomas Fisher Rare Book Library of the University of Toronto, 4th Duke of Richmond Papers, 1839, ref. HEB R5326. Photocopies (believed to be the only ones) are at Goodwood, with a copy of the transcript of Colonel Cockburn's report, from the Library ref. MG 24, A 14. Major Bowles' report was published, slightly edited, in *The Edinburgh Evening Courant*, 8 October 1819. These statements by the two men appear to have been written separately but agree remarkably well on all essential aspects of the last days of the Duke's life.

54 Bowles, Toronto. This was not published in the newspaper account.

55 The memorial plaque on this cairn was renewed in 2003 to give greater detail.

56 Bowles, ibid.

## CHAPTER 14

1 Jacques (1822), p. 64: 'If required a hundred Beds can be made ready at short notice.'

2 ibid., p. 62

3 Kent, pp. 76–7. See also The Marquis of Anglesey FSA (ed.), *The Capel Letters, being the Correspondence of Lady Caroline Capel and her daughters with the Dowager Countess of Uxbridge from Brussels and Switzerland*, Jonathan Cape, London, 1955, p. 73, Lady Caroline Capel to her mother, Lady Uxbridge, Brussels, 7 October 1814: 'Poor Lord March has been confined to his House & Bed ever since I last wrote to you – I am afraid he is in a very precarious state . . .'

4 Sir Herbert Maxwell (ed.), *The Creevey Papers, A Selection from the correspondence and diaries of the late Thomas Creevey MP (1768–1838)*, John Murray, 1904, vol. ii, p. 88, Thomas Creevey to [his step-daughter] Miss Ord, 6th [June 1825].

5 A charming portrait of Henrietta as a child, by Sir Peter Lely, is in the Goodwood Collection.

6 Jane Maxwell's story is more fully told in the author's earlier book, *Mistress of the House: Great Ladies and Grand Houses 1670–1830*, Weidenfeld and Nicolson, London, 2003

7 The Duke's 'great remonstrance' to his heir, 5 June 1806, Goodwood MS 224, f. 8

8 The Marquis of Anglesey FSA (ed.), *The Capel Letters*, p. 73, Lady Caroline Capel to her mother, Lady Uxbridge, Brussels, 7 October 1814. On 1 November (p. 75) she commented further on her anger and unpredictability.

9 ibid., p 78, Georgina Capel to her grandmother, Lady Uxbridge, Brussels, 21 November 1814: describes how the Dowager Duchess failed in her negotiations for Mary with Lord O'Neil, and with Sarah for her husband's nephew Lord Apsley.

10 Hampshire Record Office, Winchester, MS 26.M62/F/C17, Frederick Calthorpe to his brother Lord Calthorpe, 18 August 1824: 'I hear the Duchess of Richmond's flight to Dublin is for the purpose of catching him for one of her daughters. She had been endeavouring to entrap him during the last season, & though Hervey showed no penchant for the daughter, the Duchess the true daughter of her mother continues to persevere. I hope she will not succeed.'

11 According to Thomas Creevey, MP: Sir Herbert Maxwell (ed.), *The Creevey Papers, A Selection from the correspondence and diaries of the late Thomas Creevey MP (1768–1838)*, John Murray, London, 1904, vol. ii, p. 185, Thomas Creevey to Miss Ord, Woodstock, Kilkenny [Mr Tighe's home], 3 Nov [1828]

12 According to the acerbic diarist Charles Greville, in Philip Whitwell Wilson (ed.), *The Greville Diary*, William Heinemann Ltd, London, 1927, p. 196, entry for 10 July 1829: 'He lives in the country, is well versed in rural affairs, and the business of the quarter sessions, has a certain calibre of understanding, is prejudiced, narrow-minded, illiterate, and ignorant, good-looking, good-humoured, and unaffected, tedious, prolix, unassuming, and a duke.'

13 Jacques (1822), pp. 49–51: in 1822 these were still hanging in the new Billiard Room (now the Red Hall). In 1814 the Ramsays had been at the new Richmond House.

14 Sir Herbert Maxwell (ed.), *The Creevey Papers*, vol. ii, p. 162, 15th [August 1828]. See also, for comments on the front hall and park, and on the racing guests, John Gore (ed.), *Creevey's Life and Times; a further selection from the correspondence of Thomas Creevey, born 1768–died 1838*, John Murray, London, 1934, pp. 268–70.

15 John Gore (ed.), *Creevey's Life and Times*, p. 270

16 Mason (1839), p. 39

17 The question of the validity of the Aubigny dukedom is occasionally raised. The 3rd DR had ensured that he held it legally by paying homage to Louis XV in 1777. All titles were abolished in 1790. In 1814 a charter by Louis XVIII restored in full all legal titles of old nobility. The claim of the 4th DR was uncertain, as he was not the son of the 3rd DR. The *Complete Peerage*, Vol. X, p. 841, note (b) says that Dukedom of Aubigny was conferred on the 4th DR by Louis XVIII on 18 March 1818. There is no trace of this in French records, but according to the Hon. Mrs J.R. Swinton, *A Sketch of the Life of Georgiana, Lady de Ros*, John Murray, London, 1893, p. 9, the Duke was indeed at Aubigny shortly before going to Canada in 1818. However, an enquiry to the Office de la Noblesse in Paris made in 1991 was told that the last investiture for this title was 1814 (in which year the 4th DR was also in Paris). The Office said that recognition by the Republic is purely formal. It acknowledges if you are the best placed person to inherit the title bestowed on a deceased ancestor, but since 1859 no title has been granted to a pretender of another nationality.

18 Described in the diary of Charles Greville, who as a steward also attended; see Christopher Hibbert, *Greville's England*, The Folio Society, London, 1981, pp. 38–9 and p. 54.

19 Hunn, p. 117, for details

20 There is a portrait of Charles C.F. Greville at Goodwood, by Edwin Long RA; as well as an oil sketch of his mother, Lady Charlotte, by Lawrence; and a portrait of her as an old lady, by H.P. Danloux; and of his brother, the father of the (6th) Duchess, Algernon Greville, by O. Manara.

21 Quoted by Kent, pp. 99–100

22 Conversation with a Seymour descendant, 2004, whose grandmother, Rosalind Bingham, Duchess of Abercorn, was devastated to be told after church one Sunday that her mother, Lady Cecilia, was not the daughter of the Duke of Richmond. The rumour of an affair had always persisted, through Greville, but this was the first proof.

23 Greville reported in his diary that Bentinck 'confessed his sentiments without disguise', Hunn, pp. 119–20.

24 At Goodwood

25 Rachel Trethewey, *Mistress of the Arts*, Review (Hodder), London, 2002, p. 203, Landseer to William Ross, Blair Atholl, September 1825. The whole affair is documented by Trethewey, pp. 193–220. There is a painting by Landseer of Georgina with her brother George, 5th Duke of Gordon, and her son, Lord Alexander Russell (on loan from a private collection to the National Gallery of Scotland, Edinburgh).

26 See Kent, pp. 114–25 for a description of the process.

27 MS 871

28 Kent, p. 194

29 Simon Rees, *The Charlton Hunt*, Phillimore, 1998, p. 219

30 Anecdote recorded by West Dean College. On another occasion he declared that his father was George V, which was most unlikely: conversation with Mrs Antonia Leaf, *née* Farquhar, 2006. Amusing, hand-coloured letters from the elderly Edward James to the present Earl of March as a child are MS 2315.

## CHAPTER 15

1 The 'Glorious' epithet is first documented by H. Avray Tipping, 'Goodwood House, Sussex', caption from *English Homes; The internal character, furniture and adornments of some of the most notable houses of England . . .* (photographs), Offices of *Country Life* and George Newnes, London, 1904–1909

2 Edward Moorhouse, *The Racing Year*, 1903

3 Related in the diaries of his grandson, Frederick, 9th DR

4 Indicated by the modest interior described on an early postcard as 'King Edward VII's bedchamber' and, in the case of George V, described in the diary of a royal courtier

5 *Country Life*, 12 August 1905, p. 204

6 Described in the private diary of a royal courtier: see Camilla Cecil, *Glorious Goodwood*, Kenneth Mason Publications and Goodwood Racecourse, 2002, p. 125

7 Christopher Hussey, 'Goodwood I', *Country Life*, 9 July 1932, for naming of the King's Room; and *The Antique Collector*, December 1939, for the naming of the Tapestry Bedroom as the Queen's Room.

8 MS E5494, George Trollope & Sons, work in April to July, paid 15 June 1906

9 The Duke wrote from Gordon Castle on 27 November. Lady Bernard wrote on 30 November.

10 The Earl of March, *Records of the Old Charlton Hunt*, Elkin Matthews, 1910; The Earl of March, *A Duke and His Friends: The Life and Letters of the Second Duke of Richmond*, Hutchinson, 1911

11 The 8th DR's letters to Kathleen Caroll are MS 2192; to Barbara Nancy Millington [Babette] MS 2193 and to Mary de Crispigny, a young girl confined to a wheelchair following an accident, MS 2274. He had a long affair with a very beautiful actress called Isabel Jeans.

# BIBLIOGRAPHY

## General

The Marquess of Anglesey FSA (ed.), *The Capel Letters, Being the Correspondence of Lady Caroline Capel and her daughters with the Dowager Countess of Uxbridge, from Brussels and Switzerland, 1814–1817*, Jonathan Cape, London, 1955

Katharine Baetjer and J.G. Links, *Canaletto*, The Metropolitan Museum of Art, New York, 1989

John R. Baker, *Abraham Trembley of Geneva, Scientist and Philosopher, 1710–1784*, Edward Arnold & Co., London, 1952

Toby Barnard and Jane Clark (ed.), *Lord Burlington: Architecture and Life*, The Hambledon Press, London, 1995

*Beautiful Britain: the Scenery and the Splendours of the United Kingdom*, The Werner Company, London, 1898

Charles Beddington, with essays by Brian Allen and Francis Russell, *Canaletto in England: A Venetian Artist Abroad 1746–1755*, Yale Center for British Art, Dulwich Picture Gallery, and Yale University Press, New Haven and London, 2006

Geoffrey de Bellaigue, 'The Vulliamy Chimneypieces', *Furniture History*, vol. xxiii, 1997, p. 190

Robin Blake and Matthew Warner, *Stubbs and the Horse*, Yale University Press, New Haven and London, 2005

Robin Blake, *George Stubbs and the Wide Creation*, Chatto & Windus, London, 2005

Priscilla Boniface (ed.), *In Search of English Gardens: the travels of John Claudius Loudon and his wife Jane*, Lennard, Wheathampstead, 1987. Visit of 1829.

Georges A. Bonnard (ed.), *Edward Gibbon, Memoirs of my Life*, Nelson, 1966

Edward Brynn, *Crown and Castle: British Rule in Ireland 1800–1830*, O'Brien, Dublin, 1978

Kirsty Carpenter and Philip Mansel (ed.), *The French Emigrés in Europe and the Struggle against Revolution, 1789–1814*, Macmillan, London, 1999, Harper Collins, London, 1997

Eileen Cassavetti, *The Lion and the Lilies: the Stuarts and France*, Macdonald and Jane's, London, 1977

Martin Clayton, *Canaletto in Venice*, Royal Collection Enterprises, London, 2005

Viccy Coltman, 'Sir William Hamilton's Vase Publications (1766–1776): A Case Study in the Reproduction and Dissemination of Antiquity', *Journal of Design History*, Vol. 14, no. 1, 2001, pp. 1–16

Viccy Coltman, *Fabricating the Antique*, University of Chicago, 2006

W.G. Constable and J.G. Links, *Canaletto: Giovanni Antonio Canal, 1697–c.1768*, Clarendon Press, Oxford, 1976

John Cornforth, 'Surprises of the Silver Age', *Country Life*, 9 March 1989. Tapestries.

Edward Corp and contributors, *A Court in Exile: The Stuarts in France 1689–1718*, Cambridge University Press, 2004

Basil Cozens-Hardy (ed.), *The Diary of Silas Neville 1767–1788*, Oxford University Press, 1950

James Dallaway, *A History of the Western Division of the County of Sussex*, J.B. Nichols & Son, London, 1832 (reprinted from 1815)

Daniel Defoe, *A Tour Thro' the Whole Island of Great Britain . . .*, London, 1738

R.D.E. Eagles, *Francophobia and Francophilia in English Society 1748–1783*, Oxford University Ph.D, 1996

Edward Edwards, *Anecdotes of Painting*, 1770, published posthumously, 1808, *Journal of the Walpole Society*, vol. XXXVIII, 1960–62

Judy Egerton, *George Stubbs, 1724–1806*, Tate Gallery, London, 1984

Judy Egerton, *George Stubbs, Painter, Catalogue Raisonné*, Yale University Press, New Haven and London, 2007

*Excursions in the County of Sussex*, Longman, Hurst, etc., London, 1822

Sally Festing, 'Animal Crackers', *Country Life*, 11 June 1987. Menageries.

Ian Gow, *Scotland's Lost Houses*, National Trust of Scotland, Aurum, London, 2006

Nick Foulkes, *Dancing into Battle*, Harper Collins, London, 2006

Kenneth Garlick and Joseph Macintyre (ed.), and later Kathryn Cave (ed.), *The Diary of Joseph Farington*, Yale University Press, New Haven and London, 1978–84

William Gilpin, Prebendary of Salisbury, *Observations on the Coasts of Hampshire, Sussex and Kent relative chiefly to picturesque beauty, made in the summer of the year 1774*, T. Cadell and W. Davies, London, 1804

John Gore (ed.), *Creevey's Life and Times; a further selection from the correspondence of Thomas Creevey, born 1768–died 1838*, John Murray, London, 1934

Castalia Countess Granville (ed.), *Lord Granville Leveson Gower, Private Correspondence 1781–1821*, John Murray, London, 1916

David J. Griffin and Caroline Pegum, *Leinster House*, The Irish Architectural Archive in conjunction with the Office of Public Works, Dublin, 2000

*Handbook for Travellers in Kent and Sussex*, John Murray, London, 1868

John Harris, *The Palladians*, RIBA Drawings Series, Trefoil, London, 1981

Christopher Hibbert, *Greville's England, Selections from the diaries of Charles Greville 1818–1860*, The Folio Society, London, 1981

Carola Hicks, *Improper Pursuits: the Scandalous Life of Lady Di Beauclerk*, Macmillan, London, 2001

Historical Monuments Commission, *Reports* (Bathurst, Charlemont & Egmont Papers)

Hon. J.A. Home (ed.), *The Letters and Journals of Lady Mary Coke*, privately printed by David Douglas, Edinburgh, 1889–96 (reprinted 1970)

Jeremy Howard, 'Owen McSwinny and the Tombs of the British Worthies', *The European Fine Art Fair Handbook*, Basel, 1995. A good overview

*Illustrated London News*, from many different years, for the Racecourse

Hazelle Jackson, *Shell Houses and Grottoes*, Shire Publications, Princes Risborough, 2001

Gervase Jackson-Stops (ed.), *The Treasure Houses of Britain*, National Gallery of Art, Washington, Yale University Press, New Haven and London, 1985; nos 157, 158 (Canaletto), 225 (marble dogs), 396 (snuff box) and 409 (three Sèvres vases)

Ian Jenkins and Kim Sloane (ed.), *Vases and Volcanoes: Sir William Hamilton and his Collection*, Trustees of the British Museum, Lodnon, 1996

Alex Kidson, *George Romney, 1734–1802*, National Portrait Gallery, London

Pamela D. Kingsbury, *Lord Burlington's Town Architecture*, RIBA Heinz Gallery, London, 1995

George Knox, '*The Tombs of Famous Englishmen* as described in the letters of Owen McSwiny to the Duke of Richmond', Magazine *Arte Veneta*, vol. 37, 1983

Tim Knox, 'The Vyne Ramesses: "Egyptian Monstrosities" in British Country House Collections', *Apollo: National Trust Historic Houses and Collections Annual*, col. CLVII, no. 494 (New Series) April 2003, pp. 32-36

Thierry Lefrancois, *Charles Coypel, Peintre du roi (1694–1752)*, Paris, Arthena, 1994

London County Council, *The Survey of London*, vol. 13, 1930

W.S. Lewis et al. (ed.), *Horace Walpole's Correspondence*, Yale University Press, New Haven and London, 1937–83

Michael Liversidge and Jane Farrington (ed.), *Canaletto & England*, for Birmingham Museums and Art Gallery, Merrell Holberton, London, 1993

David Mannings, *Sir Joshua Reynolds, A Complete Catalogue of his Paintings*, Yale University Press, New Haven and London, 2000

Stuart Mason, *George Edwards: the Bedell and his Birds*, Royal College of Physicians, London, 1992

Sir Herbert Maxwell (ed.), *The Creevey Papers, A Selection from the correspondence and diaries of the late Thomas Creevey MP (1768–1838)*, John Murray, London, 1904

Timothy J. McCann, *Sussex Cricket in the Eighteenth Century*, Sussex Record Society, vol. 88, 2004

David Miller, *The Duchess of Richmond's Ball*, Spellmount, Staplehurst, 2005

Leslie Mitchell, *The Whig World*, Hambledon and London, London and New York, 2005

Anthony Mould, Ozias Humphry and Joseph Mayer (ed.), *A Memoir of George Stubbs*, Pallas Athene, London, 2005

(J.P. Neale), *Views of the seats of noblemen and gentlemen in England, Wales, Scotland and Ireland*, from drawings by J.P. Neale, 1818–23, published London 1824–29

Richard Ormond, *The Monarch of the Glen: Landseer in the Highlands*, National Galleries of Scotland, Edinburgh, 2005

Tim Owen and Elaine Pilbeam, *Ordnance Survey: Map Makers to Britain since 1791*, Ordnance Survey, Southampton: London, HMSO, 1991

David Peters, 'Identification of plates and services in the Sèvres sales registers', *The French Porcelain Society*, I, 1985

Peregrine Project and Timothy Type (actually John Marsh), *A Tour through some of the Southern Counties of England*, Vernor and Hood, London, 1804, pp. 179–83

Roy Porter, 'William Hunter: a surgeon and a Gentleman', in W.F. Bynum and Roy Porter (ed.), *William Hunter and the Eighteenth-century medical world*, Cambridge University Press, 1985

Rowland E. Prothero (ed.), *Private Letters of Edward Gibbon (1753–1794)*, J. Murray, 1896

Henry Reeve (ed.), *The Greville Memoirs, A Journal of the reigns of King George IV and King William IV by the late Charles C.F. Greville Esq.*, Longmans, Green and Co., London 1875

Simon Rees, *The Charlton Hunt*, Phillimore, Chichester, 1998

Brian Robins (ed.), *The John Marsh Journals: the life and times of a gentleman composer (1752–1828)*, Stuyvesant, New York: Pendragon Press, 1998

W.D. Ian Rolfe, 'William Hunter (1718–83) on Irish "elk" and Stubbs' Moose', *Archives of Natural History*, 11, 1983, pp. 263–90

W.D. Ian Rolfe, 'A Stubbs Drawing Recognised', *The Burlington Magazine*, Vol. 125, No. 969, December 1983, pp. 738–41

W.D. Ian Rolfe, 'William and John Hunter; breaking the Great Chain of Being', conference paper in W.F. Bynum and Roy Porter (ed.), *William Hunter and the Eighteenth-century medical world*, Cambridge University Press, 1985

Sybil Rosenfeld, *Temples of Thespis, some private theatres and theatricals in England and Wales 1700–1820*, The Society for Theatre Research, London, 1978, pp. 34–52 for the Richmond House Theatre

Michael Seth-Smith, *Lord Paramount of the Turf: Lord George Bentinck, 1802–1848*, Faber and Faber, London, 1971

Ann Somerset, *Ladies in Waiting, from the Tudors to the Present Day*, Weidenfeld and Nicolson, 1984

Francis Steer, *The Memoirs of James Spershott*, Chichester City Council, 1962

David Torrance, *The Scottish Secretaries*, Birlinn, Edinburgh, 2006

Jenny Uglow, *Hogarth: A Life and a World*, Faber & Faber, London, 1997

Anon. (ed.), 'Vertue's Notebooks V', *Journal of the Walpole Society*, 1939, pp. 142–5 (BL Add Ms 23089)

Maureen Waller, *Ungrateful Daughters: the Stuart Princesses who Stole their Father's Crown*, Hodder & Stoughton, London, 2002

Humphry Ward and W. Roberts, *Romney: a biographical and critical essay with a catalogue raisonné of his works*, Agnew, London, 1904

David Watkin, 'The Lure of Egypt' in Christopher Hartop (ed.), *Royal Goldsmiths: the Art of Rundell & Bridge, 1797–1843*, John Adamson, Cambridge for Koopman Rare Art, pp. 55–60

F.J.B. Watson, 'An Allegorical Painting by Canaletto, Piazzetta, and Cimaroli', *The Burlington Magazine*, 1953, pp. 362–5

J.N.P. Watson, *Marlborough's Shadow: the Life of the First Earl Cadogan*, Leo Cooper, Pen & Sword, 2003

Henry B. Wheatley (ed.), *The Historical and Posthumous Memoirs of Sir Nathaniel William Wraxall 1772–1784*, London, Bickers & Son, 1884

Arthur Young, *A Six Weeks' Tour Through the Southern Counties of England and Wales . . .*, W. Nicoll, London, 1768

## Publications on the Dukes of Richmond, on their Families and on Goodwood

Major A. McK Annand, 'Charles, 5th Duke of Richmond and his Charger "Busaco"', *Journal of the Society for Army Historical Research*, Vol. XLVI 46/188 (Winter 1968), pp. 213–16

Rosemary Baird, 'The Refurbishment of the State Rooms at Goodwood House', *Apollo* Magazine, January 1997

Rosemary Baird, 'Goodwood House, Sussex', *Country Life*, 24 July 1997

Rosemary Baird, 'Crocodiles and Cobras Return to Goodwood', *Country Life*, 23 April 1998

Rosemary Baird, 'Fox Hall, West Sussex', *Country Life*, 17 January 2002

Rosemary Baird, 'Foxed by Fox Hall', *Sussex Archaeological Collections*, The Sussex Archaeological Society, Lewes, vol. 143, 2005, pp. 215–38

Rosemary Baird, 'Letters of Introduction', *Burlington Magazine*, March 2007. Canaletto

Rosemary Baird, 'Richmond House, Whitehall', *British Art Journal*, September 2007

Earl Bathurst, *Letters from the Three Duchesses of Richmond 1726–1761*, privately printed, 1925

Lady Muriel Beckwith, *When I Remember*, Ivor Nicholson and Watson, London, 1936. Excellent history of late-Victorian childhood in Scotland and of Edwardian Goodwood.

Marcus Binney, 'From Kennel to Sporting Palace', *Country Life*, 19 October 2006

T.P. Connor, 'Architecture and Planting at Goodwood, 1723–1750', *Sussex Archaeological Collections*, 1970

B. Brocklebank, 'Home of the Waterloo Ball', *Country Life*, 11 December 1975

Joan Coutu, 'A very grand and seigneurial design: the Duke of Richmond's Academy in Whitehall', *British Art Journal*, Vol. I, no. 2, Spring 2000

Edith Roelker Curtis, *Lady Sarah Lennox: An Irrepressible Stuart, 1745–1826*, W.H. Allen, London, 1947

Brian Fitzgerald, *Emily, Duchess of Leinster, 1731–1814, A Study of her Life and Times*, Staples Press, London and New York, 1949

Brian Fitzgerald, *Lady Louisa Conolly*, Staples Press, London and New York, 1950

Brian Fitzgerald, *Correspondence of Emily Duchess of Leinster (1731–1814)*, Stationery Office, Dublin, 1949–57: vol. i (1949), has letters to Kildare/Leinster and from Caroline; vol. ii (1953), from Lord Edward Fitzgerald and from Sarah; and vol. iii (1957), from Louisa, as well as from other correspondents

Paul Foster (ed.), *Marsh of Chichester: Gentleman, Composer, Musician, Writer 1752–1828*, University College, Chichester, Otter Memorial Paper no. 19, chapter IV by Timothy J. McCann, pp. 89–112, 'Marsh at Goodwood'

'Goodwood House, West Sussex', *In English Homes*, 1932

'Goodwood House: The Sussex Seat of The Duke of Richmond & Gordon', *Antique Collector*, September and December 1939

David J. Green and Caroline Pegum, *Leinster House: 1744–2000, an architectural history*, Irish Architectural Archive, Dublin, 2000

A.R. Horwood, 'Goodwood in the ' Thirties [i.e. 1830s]', *The Sussex Country Magazine*, July 1929, pp. 441–3

David Hunn, *Goodwood*, Davis-Poynter Ltd, 1975. Best on the nineteenth-century racing history; useful on the history of the estate, with good synopses of documents in the archive, but inaccurate on the architectural history of the house and on the 2nd Duke.

Christopher Hussey, 'Goodwood I', *Country Life*, 9 July 1932

Christopher Hussey, 'Goodwood II', *Country Life*, 16 July 1932

Christopher Hussey, 'Goodwood III: The Charlton Hunt Pictures at Goodwood', *Country Life*, 23 July 1932

The Countess of Ilchester and Lord Stavordale (ed.), *The Life and Letters of Lady Sarah Lennox*, John Murray, 1901. Lady Sarah Lennox's letters to Lady Susan Fox Strangways, later O'Brien, eldest daughter of Lord and Lady Ilchester

D. Jacques, Librarian of Goodwood, *Visit to Goodwood, the Seat of His Grace the Duke of Richmond near Chichester*, published by the author, Dennett Jacques, North Street, Chichester, 1822. Begun after taking some foreign royals round the house in 1818, completed 1821.

John Kent, *Records and Reminiscences of Goodwood and the Dukes of Richmond*, Sampston Low, Marston & Company, London, 1896. Military, political and racing life of the 5th Duke

Marquis of Kildare, *The Earls of Kildare and their Ancestors from 1057 to 1773*, 4th edition, 1864

William Hayley Mason, *Goodwood, Its House Park and Grounds with a Catalogue Raisonné of the Pictures in the Gallery of His Grace the Duke of Richmond KG*, Smith, Elder & Co., Cornhill, London, 1839. A revision

of Jacques' guidebook, of which his father was the printer, with long lists of paintings added.

Lord William Pitt Lennox, *Story of my Life*, London, 1857

Lord William Pitt Lennox, *Memoir of C.G. Lennox, 5th Duke of Richmond, with a portrait*, London, 1862

Lord William Pitt Lennox, *Fifty Years Biographical Reminiscences*, Hurst and Blackett, London, 1863

Lord William Pitt Lennox, *My Recollections from 1806 to 1873*, London, 1874

Lord William Pitt Lennox, *Drafts on my Memory, being men I have known, things I have seen, places I have visited*, London, 1866, Chapman and Hall, London, 1886

The Earl of March, *Records of the Old Charlton Hunt*, Elkin Matthews, 1910

The Earl of March, *A Duke and His Friends: The Life and Letters of the Second Duke of Richmond*, Hutchinson, 1911. Useful if subjective publication by the future 8th Duke of selected letters, sometimes undated or misdated: always worth going back to originals in the archive. Some letters quoted do not survive, making this a vital source.

Timothy J. McCann (ed.), *The Correspondence of the Dukes of Richmond and Newcastle*, Sussex Record Society, Vol. 73, Lewes, 1984

Timothy J. McCann (ed.), *Royal Letters: Mary Queen of Scots to Elizabeth II*, Trustees of the Goodwood Collection, 1977

John Marshall, *The Duke who was Cricket*, Frederick Muller Ltd, London, 1961

David Morris, *The Honour of Richmond: A History of the Lords, Earls and Dukes of Richmond*, William Sessions Ltd, York, 2000. Useful early material on other dynasties bearing Richmond titles

Jeremy Musson, 'Her Grace's Grotto Comes out of its Shell', *Country Life*, 25 September 1997

Priscilla Napier, *The Sword Dance: Lady Sarah Lennox and the Napiers*, Michael Joseph, London, 1971

Priscilla Napier, *My Brother Richmond: The Third Duke of Richmond Reflected in his Sisters' Correspondence*, privately printed by the Duke of Richmond, 1994. Thorough trawl of the letters published by Fitzgerald

Brenda Niall, *Georgiana: a Biography of Georgiana McCrae, painter, diarist, pioneer*, Melbourne University Press, 1994. Natural daughter of George, 5th Duke of Gordon

Alison Olson, *The Radical Duke, Career and correspondence of Charles Lennox, Third Duke of Richmond*, Oxford University Press, London, 1961

'Pheasantry and Racing', *Country Life*, 1897. Photographs of Molecomb

M.M. Reese, *Goodwood's Oak: The Life and Times of the Third Duke of Richmond, Lennox and Aubigny*, Threshold Books Ltd, 1987. Useful basic story, but, owing to the lack of documents, padded out with wider political history; good for the Duke's military career and character.

Tim Richardson, 'The Good Wood of Goodwood', *Country Life*, 25 September 1997

John Martin Robinson, 'The Glories of Goodwood', *Country Life*, 25 September 1997

Joanna Selborne, 'Dedicated to a Duke: Goodwood's Uncommon Birds', *Country Life*, 12 March 1998

Robin Simon, 'Dynasty: The Lennox Family of Cricketers', *The Cricket Quarterly*, vol. 14, no. 1, 1986, pp. 2–5

Robin Simon, 'Three Centuries of Country House Cricket', *Country Life*, 9 May 2002

The Hon. Blanche Swinton (ed.), *A Sketch of the Life of Lady de Ros, with some reminiscences of her family and friends, including the Duke of Wellington*, John Murray, London, 1893, p. 122

Stella Tillyard, *Aristocrats*, Chatto & Windus, 1994; and republished, Folio Society, 2007. Excellent history of the lives of the daughters of the 2nd Duke

H. Avray Tipping, 'Goodwood House, Sussex', in *In English Homes; The internal character, furniture and adornments of some of the most notable houses of England historically depicted from photographs specially taken by C. Latham*, offices of *Country Life* and George Newnes, London, vol. I, 1904, p. 413

H. Avray Tipping, 'Goodwood House, Sussex: The Seat of the Duke of Richmond', *Country Life*, 12 August 1905. Text as above article, with same nine photographs in different order

Rachel Trethewey, *Mistress of the Arts*, Review (Hodder), London, 2002. Biography of Georgina, Duchess of Bedford, sister of Charlotte, Duchess of Richmond

Larry Ward, *The Third Duke of Richmond: the public and private man and his descendants*, unpublished manuscript, 1980s, Goodwood archive. Useful background on non-artistic points. Good archival research but contemporary quotations not sourced

Richard Wells, Vicar of Boxgrove, *Goodwood: Being some account of its Owners, their Park, House and a few of its contents*, Chichester, 1924

Roger White, 'Historical Present', *House and Garden*, April 1998. The restoration

Viscountess Wolseley, 'Historic Houses of Sussex No. 21 – Goodwood', *The Sussex County Magazine*, July 1929, pp. 430–40

Giles Worsley, 'The Stables, Goodwood', *Country Life*, 25 September 1997

John Worman, *Under the Trundle: Goodwood Golf Club 1892-1992*, privately printed 1992

Ghenete Zelleke, *From Chantilly to Sèvres: French Porcelain for the Dukes of Richmond*, The French Porcelain Society, vii, 1991

In recent years scholars and journalists have been commissioned, often at the recommendation of the author, to write pieces for the annual *Goodwood Magazine*. These articles are primarily good overviews for Racecourse members, but some contain interesting new research:

| | | |
|---|---|---|
| Anon. | *Restoration Drama* (ballroom restoration) | 1995 |
| Robin Simon | *Goodwood House* (the restoration) | 1998 |
| David Lee | *Fine Art?* (Stubbs) | 2000 |
| Ann Somerset Miles | *Good Wood* (trees) | 2001 |
| Mike Cable | *300 Not Out* (cricket) | 2002 |
| Thomas Woodcock | *Up in Arms* (armorial history) | 2003 |
| Rosemary Baird | *Master Strokes* (Canaletto) | 2003 |
| Ann Somerset Miles | *Where the Wild Things Were* (menagerie) | 2003 |
| Camilla Cecil | *Perfect Beauty* (Lillie Langtry) | 2004 |
| Ann Somerset Miles | *The Mapping Pioneer* (3rd Duke) | 2005 |
| Ann Somerset Miles | *French Connection* (Aubigny) | 2005 |
| Susan Foister | *Stubbs and the Horse* | 2005 |
| Tim Knox | *Egyptomania* | 2005 |
| Tim Knox | *Egyptian Illumination* | 2006 |
| Joanna Selborne | *Life of Ryley* (animal drawings) | 2006 |

## MANUSCRIPTS

### West Sussex Record Office, Chichester

The entire Goodwood archive is settled here.

Francis Steer, *Catalogue of the Goodwood Estate Archives*, West Sussex County Council, 1970, three volumes, the third by Timothy J. McCann, with a fourth, unpublished, volume by Timothy J. McCann, 2005

Gordon Castle, watercolour, by J. Cassie PD/7 (p. 176)

Card Indexes to the accounts of the 1st, 2nd and 3rd Dukes

### British Library

More than 200 documents relating to various Dukes of Richmond. Of these the most important are in the Sloane, Holland House and Bathurst papers.

### Hampshire Record Office, Winchester

Viscount Palmerston, *Tour of Sussex* section of his unpublished travel diary, 1788 (27M60/1924)

### National Library of Ireland, Dublin

Nearly 2,000 letters of the 4th Duke of Richmond's correspondence, covering his time in Ireland, catalogued as *Papers of the 4th Duke of Richmond 1794–1818* (in fact some are earlier), in red volumes numbered 58–75a, the last volume being the index of correspondence by name. These papers were not fully sorted before being put into the albums and often appear out of order and out of subject group There is also a useful small subject index, in which the contents of packets of letters from important correspondents are described, not least those from Arthur Wellesley, later Duke of Wellington.

There are also extensive Leinster papers. The correspondence of Emily, Duchess of Leinster, comprising 1,770 letters, was purchased by the Library in 1933, through Sotheby's. Of these 897 were published by Brian Fitzgerald, *Correspondence of Emily Duchess of Leinster (1731–1814)*, Stationery Office, Dublin, 1949–57.

### Public Record Office, Kew

Papers relating to Richmond House ground leases.

### Public Record Office of Northern Ireland, Belfast, and University of Maynooth, near Dublin

Shortly before Partition, the Public Record Office of Northern Ireland took the wise precaution of writing to landed estates to ask if their owners would like to deposit papers with them. Many Leinster papers were deposited, at no charge. There are copies on microfilm at the University of Maynooth, near Dublin, the core of which is housed in wonderful eighteenth-century buildings and a magnificent Jesuit seminary by Pugin.

### Register House, Princes Street, Edinburgh

Eight tons of Gordon documents from the muniments room at Gordon Castle, some kept off-site. Some Gordon documents, mostly relating to Jane, Duchess of Gordon, were sent to Goodwood.

## ARCHITECTURAL DRAWINGS

*(apart from any in the Collection at Goodwood House)*

### West Sussex Record Office, Goodwood Archive

Drawing of Goodwood House with new kitchen, 1724–45, (Ms 2054, album) (p. 22)

Drawings for 'The Duke of Richmond's House at Whitehall' (Ms 2226) (pp. 34–5)

Drawings for Colen Campbell by Roger Morris for the proposed house, as published in *Vitruvius Britannicus*, vol. iii, 1725: these were for a while on loan to RIBA, catalogued as SC8/4, but are now back in WSRO (Ms 2227) (pp. 20–21)

Sketch of the 3rd Duke hunting (GPD 7) (p. 98)

Other drawings and old photographs

### British Library

Four watercolours of scenes at Goodwood by S.H. Grimm (Add. Ms 5675, f. 67–70) (two only, pp. 66, 121)

### Metropolitan Museum, New York

Design for a therm at Richmond House, c.1759, William Chambers (34.78.2 (17))

Design for a ceiling, identified by John Harris as for a bedroom at Goodwood, James Wyatt, 1770s (58.511: 21) (p. 128)

## Royal Institute of British Architects Drawings Collection, Victoria & Albert Museum

John Harris, *Catalogue of the Drawings Collection of the Royal Institute of British Architects*, Gregg International Publishing Ltd, 1973

SC8/3: Nos 1 and 2 (p. 20), Colen Campbell survey drawings of Goodwood House; the rest, his proposals, of which 3–7 were for a first project, with 8 and 9 preparatory drawings for the versions that were published in *Vitruvius Britannicus*, vol. iii, 1725; 10, garden survey, later used for engraving; 11, drawing of long low elevation with central pedimented arch, inscribed 'A Design for some distant offices at Goodwood, 1724 C:C' ; also 13, similar, more worked up. Side elevations of stables by Chambers similar to this. (See also a related drawing for the stables, V&A Print Room, no. 3352.)

SC68/4: William Chambers, Design for an entrance Gateway, inscribed 'the Principal Entrance to Goodwood Park, s. & d. W, Chambers Invent ao 1760'. Possibly executed but later demolished.

SB89/251: Drawing for a house in Sussex, unexecuted; believed by John Martin Robinson to be for Goodwood, (see *Country Life*, 25 September, 1997)

## Sir John Soane Museum

Design for a ceiling for the Sculpture Gallery, Richmond House, Whitehall, by William Chambers (Drawer 43, set 6) (p. 96)

# INDEX

# AUTHOR'S NOTE

In 1991 I was working at Sotheby's as a freelance consultant in the Department of British Paintings. I was handed whatever research came the way of the Directors: the biography of an interesting portrait sitter, the identification of an unknown house, the authentification by comparison from photographs of an artist's style.

One day a project came in from Goodwood. The Duke of Richmond, who had inherited his father's title only two years previously, was to exhibit some of his collection in Paris in March 1992. He wanted help with the catalogue. While the experts would pronounce on individual paintings, I was asked to unravel the early history of the family, of how the Knights of Darnley and the Earls of Lennox were ancestors through King Charles II of the Dukes of Richmond and Lennox. This I did with absorption. I did not believe that any family history could be so interesting, revolving as it did around the three countries that I loved most, England, Scotland and France. Sadly, I did not ever attend the exhibition organised by the British Ambassador – whose residence I knew well from the time when I had been its official guide while living in Paris some ten years earlier – because of the lingering death from cancer of my first husband, Andrew Baird, in April 1992.

When, through the good offices of Sotheby's, I was invited for interview at Goodwood in 1995, I was surprised to find myself reading my own words in an exhibition guide that I had never seen. After my appointment as Curator of the Goodwood Collection, I thought that perhaps I would stay three years, or five, that I would get to know the collection and then move on. However, the story of the Dukes of Richmond, Lennox, Gordon and Aubigny proved so fascinating, the art collection and buildings so alluring, and the modern-day projects so challenging, that after twelve years I find myself still with tasks to undertake.

After as England, Scotland and France, I am passionate about Italy. To my surprise, and that of my art-historical colleagues, the story of Goodwood also comprises that hugely important Palladian movement in architecture, in which early-eighteenth-century patrons and architects copied the work of the Italian sixteenth-century architect Andrea Palladio. The 2nd and 3rd Dukes made fascinating Grand Tours and brought back Italian paintings. For me, perhaps parochially, it is enough to travel little further than these four countries, with their wealth of history expressed in art and architecture. It is a joy and a privilege to be able to work every day surrounded by the visual evidence of a family story that draws on them all.

# ACKNOWLEDGEMENTS

I owe a large retrospective debt to my postgraduate tutor at Oxford, the late Professor Francis Haskell FBA. While discovering the eighteenth century in a blinding light on Oxford High Street (it was not the subject that I was studying), I learnt his methodology, which was that one must look back to how people thought at the time. As one of the first historians of taste, Francis Haskell was considerably ahead of his peers in introducing an approach that is now widely accepted. A collection is not just what still survives from it, but also what else was once in it, and what its owners sought to acquire at the time. It has been my policy in compiling this book also to consider, albeit briefly, what else was once at Goodwood.

I am very grateful to Timothy McCann, for forty years Assistant County Archivist in charge of the Goodwood archive at the West Sussex Record Office in Chichester, for his consistent help, and for reading the manuscript; and to the rest of the staff in the West Sussex Record Office in Chichester; and to David Moore-Gwyn of Sotheby's for his support over many years. Many other scholars have generously given information or presented new findings; in particular, Dr John Martin Robinson, Dr Rosalind Savill, Sir Geoffrey de Bellaigue, Ann Dulau, Joe Friedman, John Kenworthy Browne, Alex Kidson, David Miller, Martin Snape and Richard Pailthorpe. Others are mentioned for their specific findings in the footnotes, or in the bibliography. In France, Comte Béraud de Vogüé, at the Château de la Verrerie at Aubigny-sur-Nère, has always been hospitable, as have the *mairies* of both Aubigny and of Brest (for the Château de Keroual); also, in Scotland, Major-General and Mrs Bernard Gordon Lennox at Gordon Castle and Major and Mrs Robin McLaren at Kinrara; and, in Ireland, Colette Jordan of the University of Maynooth, near Dublin. I am grateful to Tom Wilmot for access to family material; to the staff at the London Library and British Library; to photographer Clive Boursnell, working with whom was a constant source of hilarity; to my agent, Teresa Chris; to Douglas Matthews, the King of Indexers; and at Frances Lincoln to my publisher, John Nicoll, and to my Somervillian editor, Jo Christian, and her team.

My thanks also to all my wonderful colleagues at Goodwood, not least for being so patient with my departures for library and archive, in particular to my assistant at the time, Natasha Wakefield, and to Ann Dommett; and to Ellen Westbrook and Paul Melbert in the photolibrary, as well as to the Goodwood Guides for their enthusiasm and boundless curiosity. I am especially grateful to the Duke and Duchess of Richmond and the Earl and Countess of March and Kinrara, for enabling me to undertake this research on their history and home, as well as to the wider family. Finally, my thanks as always to my husband, Peter Andreae, who luckily also likes to while away the hours in his study.

## Photograph Credits